Life, Love, and Sex

A Search for Answers to Today's Moral Issues

By

Joseph H. Casey, S.J.

1663 LIBERTY DRIVE, SUITE 200
BLOOMINGTON, INDIANA 47403
(800) 839-8640
www.authorhouse.com

© 2004 Joseph H. Casey, S.J.
All Rights Reserved.

No part of this book may be reproduced, stored in a retrieval system, or transmitted by any means without the written permission of the author.

First published by AuthorHouse 03/29/04

ISBN: 1-4184-0677-5 (e)
ISBN: 1-4184-0678-3 (sc)

Printed in the United States of America
Bloomington, Indiana

This book is printed on acid-free paper.

CONTENTS

PART ONE ETHICAL THEORY 1

    CHAPTER 1 THE MORAL DIMENSION 2
        When Do Problems Arise? 3
        The Moral Dimension... 4
        Conscience... 5
            Development of Conscience 6
            Conscience Defined and Its Sacredness............................ 8
        Forming One's Conscience 10
        Conclusion.. 11

    CHAPTER 2 FREEDOM AND ITS ABUSE 12
        Hope Within Confusion.. 12
        Are We Really Free? 15
            Three Main Errors 15
                (1) Not Seeing Dependence of Freedom on Truth 15
                (2) Distorted Subjectivism.. 15
                (3) "Missing Forest for Trees" 16
        Intrinsically Good, Intrinsically Evil Acts............................. 17
        Restatement 18
            Revelation 18
        Freedom Of Self-Determination... 20
        Determinism 20
        Arguing for Freedom of Self-Determination......................... 21
            Choices Do Last—Creating the Self................................. 23
        Abuse Of Freedom (1) 24
            Church Teaching On This Abuse...................................... 24
                Fact One 24
                Fact Two... 24
                Fact Three 25
        Abuse of Freedom (2)... 26
            Germain Grisez 26
        Conclusion.. 27

CHAPTER 3 HUMAN GOODS AND HUMAN FULFILLMENT: "WHERE IS MORALITY?" 28
Fulfillment 29
Two False Ideas Of Fulfillment 30
    What Happiness Is For Catholic Believers 30
What Happiness Is For All Human Beings 31
    Basic Human Goods 31
    Commitments 34
        Impact of Truth and Faith in Providence 35
Fulfillment And Morality 35
    Moral Good And Fulfillment 37
Conclusion 38

CHAPTER 4 WHY IS THE IMMORAL IMMORAL? 39
Catechism 40
    The Splendor Of Truth 42
        The Moral Act 44
Consequentialism And Proportionalism Rejected 45
"Object OF THE ACT" 47
Germain Grisez 48
Basic Human Goods And First Principle Of Morality 48
    First Approach: Criterion Of Morality 49
    Second Approach: Practical Reason 50
Modes Of Responsibility 53
Conclusion 54
How To Approach Moral Issues 54
    First Step 54
    Second Step 55
Example: Sean And Richard 55

PART TWO CONTEMPORARY PROBLEMS: LIFE 57

CHAPTER 5 SUICIDE, ASSISTED SUICIDE: THE PROBLEM 58
Assisted Suicide, Prelude To The Supreme Court Decision 59
Kind Of Legal Thinking In The Lower Courts 60
    "Due Process Clause" Or "Equal Protection Clause" 60
Reaction Of Medical Profession 62
Congressional Reactions 64

The United States Supreme Court 65
    Concurring Opinions: Grounds for Assisted Suicide 67
    Rehnquist v. Stevens 69
Conclusion 72

CHAPTER 6 SUICIDE, ASSISTED SUICIDE—REASONED AND CATHOLIC RESPONSE 74

Kierkegaard, Suicide And Neo-Paganism 74
Morality Of Suicide And Assisted Suicide 76
    Catechism Of The Catholic Church 76
Grisez On Suicide 77
    Application To A Difficult Case 79
Omissions, Killing And Letting Die 80
    Refusing or Omitting Treatment 81
Application Of The Two Step Approach 83
    Should a wife consent to removing her husband's respirator "to get it over with"? 83
The Ambiguous Case 85
What Is Action From A Moral Point Of View? 86
    More Refined Explanation Of The Ambiguous Case 89
Application Of The Two-Step Approach To Moral Issues
Assisting Suicide Is Immoral 90
    Transition 91
Care For The Dying: Hospice 91
Conclusion 96

CHAPTER 7 CAPITAL PUNISHMENT—PART I 97

    Recent History—A Puzzling Picture 98
A Sweeping View Of Capital Punishment In The West 99
Change 101
The American Scene 104
How The Bishops Turned Around 106
Official Teaching Of The Church 109
Conclusion 109

CHAPTER 8 CAPITAL PUNISHMENT—PART II 111

Catechism Of The Catholic Church 112
The Gospel Of Life 113
Legitimate Defense, Capital Punishment, Its Limitations 114
Germain Grisez 115
    Punishment 115

Retribution 116
Retribution And The Death Penalty 118
Conclusion 119
Application Of The Two-Step Approach To Moral Issues 121
    Capital Punishment Is Not Immoral In Itself. 121
    Capital Punishment In The U. S. Today Is Immoral 121

CHAPTER 9 QUESTIONS NOT ASKED ABOUT ABORTION 123
    Question One: 126
        Pro-Life And Pro-Choice Conversations 126
            Civilized Discourse 127
            Two World Views 128
            The Mind Is Made for Truth 131
            Subtleties, Emotional Factors, and Truth 132
    Question Two: 133
    Question Three: 134
    Question Four: 135
    Question Five: 135
    Question Six: 137
        Person? Bodily Person? Consciousness With A Body? 140
    Were You Ever A Zygote? 141
            Twins And Hydatidiform Mole 142
        To Our Question 143
    Question Seven: 143
        Does The End Justify The Means? 144
    Question Eight: 146
    Question Nine: 149
        Accepting Death As a Side Effect 149
        Priority of Baby's Life 150
    Epilogue 151
    Application Of Two-Step Approach To Moral Issues   Abortion Is Immoral. 155

CHAPTER 10 CONTRACEPTION - PART I THE PRESENT SITUATION 156
    Signs Of Change? 157
    Two Roads To Rejection Of Church Teaching 160
        Road One: Five Years Of Ambiguity 160
        Road Two: Theologians Become Dissenters/Revisionists 162

Changing Methodology 164
Changing Ecclesiology 165
John Paul Ii On Methodology 167
John Paul Ii On Ecclesiology 168
The Gospel Of Life 168
Conclusion 170

CHAPTER 11 CONTRACEPTION - PART II THE TEACHING AND REASONING ABOUT CONTRACEPTION 172

Humanae Vitae And The *Catechism* 173
    "Section Iii - The Love Of Husband And Wife" 174
    "Conjugal Fidelity" 174
    "The Fecundity of Marriage" 175
Grisez Becomes Involved 175
    Contraception Contra-Life In *Living A Christian Life* 177
    Contraception And Conjugal Love *Living A Christian Life* .. 180
Natural Family Planning 182
    Nfp: Brief History 182
    Benefits Of Nfp 184
Nfp And Morality 184
    Nfp And End Of Life Issues 186
    Conclusion: At Last — A Solution: Nfp 188
Appplication Of Two-Step Approach To Moral Issues 190
    Contraception Is Contra-Life. 190
    Contraception Is Contra-Married Love. 191
    Natural Family Planning With Contraceptive Intent Is Immoral. 192
    Natural Family Planning Without Contraceptive Intent Is Morally Justifiable. 193

PART THREE MORALITY OF SEXUAL CONDUCT 195

CHAPTER 12 REFLECTIONS ON LOVE 196

Love, Sex, Morality, Happiness 196
Natural Purposes Of Sexual Intercourse 198
    Sensuality, Sentimentality, Love 199
        Sentimentality and Love 200
        Integrating Love 201
        Betrothed Love 203

Conclusion..205

CHAPTER 13 INTRODUCING THE MORALITY OF SEXUAL CONDUCT 206
"The Trouble With Premarital Sex" 207
Not All Is Lost..209
"True Love Waits"..212
Spectrum Of Moral Positions.......................................213
Traditional Natural Law Morality Vs. Secular Humanist Morality..214
Where Is The Truth?..215
The Stakes Are High 217
The Christian Dimension 219
Summary And Conclusion 220

CHAPTER 14 THE MARRIED 222
Marriage Is A Basic Human Good 223
Thomas Aquinas and Basic Human Goods 223
Grisez Establishes Marriage As Basic Human Good 224
Proof Marriage Is A Basic Human Good................227
Sexual Acts Expressive Of Marital Communion 228
Marital Chastity..229
Adultery..231
Conclusion..232
Application Of Two-Step Approach To Moral Issues Sexual Intercourse In Marriage Is Morally Good. 233
Non-Loving Intercourse In Marriage.....................234
Contraceptive Intercourse In Marriage 235
Adultery 236

CHAPTER 15 THE UNMARRIED 237
The *Catechism*...239
Masturbation 239
Fornication..241
Grisez: *Living A Christian Life* 241
Masturbation 242
Fornication..243
"Trial Marriage" and "Living Together"................245
Conclusion..247
Application Of Two-Step Approach To Moral Issues 249
Masturbation 249

    Fornication (Without Affection) 250
    Fornication (Between Engaged) 251
        Fornication "Trial Marriage" 252
        Fornication (Living Together) 253

CHAPTER 16 HOMOSEXUALITY—PART I UNDERSTANDING, RESPECT, TRUTH 254
    Homosexuality And The Law 255
    Churches And Gays 256
    Gay Lifestyle And The Theater 261
    Genetics 263
        Reaction: American Public Philosophy Institute 267
    Conclusion Struggling To Be Open-Minded, Open-Hearted 269

CHAPTER 17 HOMOSEXUALITY—PART II MORAL REFLECTION: FAITH AND REASON 271
    Catechism Of The Catholic Church 272
        Church Teaching And Fulfillment 275
    L'Osservatore Romano 278
        Conflict of Lifestyles 280
        Intellectual Examination of the Question 281
        Subjective Morality of Homosexual Acts 282
        "Rights" of Homosexual Persons 282
    Paradoxes In The Church's Teaching 283
    Homosexual Acts And Reason 284
        Homosexual "Marriage"? 285
        "Monogamous" Long-Term Relationship 285
    Catholics And Catholic Teaching On Homosexuality 287
    Conclusion 288
    Application Of Two Step Approach To Moral Issues 290
        Homosexual Acts (Without Love Or In Exchange) 290
    Homosexual Acts Are Immoral. (With Genuine Love And Commitment) 291
    Epilogue 292

APPENDIXES 293
    Appendix For Chapter One – Conscience 294
        Conscience, Personal But Not Arbitrary 294
            Erroneous Conscience 295
        Deeper Understanding Of The Moral Dimension 296

Appendix For Chapter Two Exaltation Of Freedom Over Truth: Additional Errors 299
    Other Common Errors 299
    Grisez On Fundamental Option 301
Appendix For Chapter Three 302
Appendix For Chapter Four Intermediate Modes And The Beatitudes 303
Appendix For Chapter Six Grisez On Legalizing Assisted Suicide 304
    Laws Against Suicide 304
    Assisted Suicide From The Legal Perspective 306
        Recommendations for a Law on Assisted Suicide 308
    Reflections On Present State 309
Appendix For Chapter 11 Development Of Grisez's Position 310
    Contraception And The Natural Law 310
    Tenth Anniversary Of *Humanae Vitae* - And Ten Years Later 310
    Contraception In "'Every Marital Act Ought To Be Open To New Life': Toward A Clearer Understanding" 312
    Further Explanation 314
    Subsumption: Contraception and Natural Family Planning ... 316
Appendix For Chapter 13 Traditional Natural Law Morality Vs. Secular Humanist Morality 317
Appendix For Chapter 14 Challenge To Claim—Marriage Is A Basic Human Good 322
    Virginity, Celibacy, Gays? 322

Dedicated
to
Chad
my godchild
with a prayer
he live
up
to
his potential
as
Christian
and
intellectual

ACKNOWLEDGEMENTS

My thanks go out to my many students whose bright young minds demanded clear explanations and cogent justification on all these issues.

To my fellow Jesuits at Boston College I say thank you sincerely for your financial support.

PART ONE

ETHICAL THEORY

CHAPTER 1

THE MORAL DIMENSION

There is much good in our culture as well as much evil. There is general consensus on many wonderful moral attitudes and yet keen difference of opinion on significant moral issues.

Clerical sexual abuse of minors is roiling the Church and the nation. But no one raises a question about the immorality of this sexual abuse. It is seen as despicable, criminal. But immoral? Not at issue. Risking one's life to save others is praised as morally good, indeed noble behavior. People rush to help those suffering disaster and money is poured out to aid them. It is judged morally good to do this. On these and many other issues there is moral agreement. Two of the issues which generate keen difference of opinion about the morality involved, however, are assisted suicide and abortion. Many people, moreover, are disconcerted by the current teaching of the Catholic Church that capital punishment is immoral. And living together seems to be more and more acceptable to young people but disconcerts older people. People have become confused about the morality of sex in general. It is politically correct to approve gay lifestyle, although many, especially older people, cannot understand it; they still may avoid discussing it. The abortion division goes on; few discuss it, for positions seem hardened and unbreachable. Contraception no longer seems a moral issue for the large percentage of people, including Catholics. So raising the question of its being immoral startles some.

Because I believe many intelligent educated Catholics experience confusion and anguish as they find themselves confronted with these moral issues, I offer this book, treating each of those contemporary issues. I do not attempt to propose an original approach to moral thinking or a scholarly treatment. I do clarify each issue, let the reader know what the Church teaches (using the *Catechism of the Catholic Church* and Pope John Paul II's encyclicals). And I show how reasonable the Church's position is (utilizing the writings of Professor Germain Grisez, a distinguished lay moral theologian and philosopher). Catholics need to be equipped to offer reasoned arguments to justify their own choices and to discuss these issues with non-Catholics.

When Do Problems Arise?

Normally people simply follow their habitual ways of living. They incorporate moral principles within a lifestyle and have no reason to re-examine that lifestyle or its moral principles. The cashier returns $10 dollars too much to a customer and without hesitation that customer calls her attention to it. People habitually live honestly. If an elderly person looks confused, a person offers to help. Most people have incorporated the Golden Rule into their lifestyle.

Only when we experience challenge do we re-examine our lifestyle and its underlying intellectual presuppositions. Challenge occurs when we foresee unhappiness will result from habitual response or when there is a conflict of lifestyles or when the intellectual presuppositions are denied.

Today people are challenged by conflicting lifestyles. It was just taken for granted that couples would be married before they lived together. Now one's own children are doing just that. Which lifestyle is right?

For a long time it has been taken for granted that we do not kill the old, but as medical advances provide for longer life, is it truly loving to prolong lives that seem miserable? Is it not kinder to help people die when they choose to end it all? Or for those unable to make a choice, is it not the loving thing to put them out of their misery? So the practice of assisted suicide and euthanasia is being proposed.

In conflicting lifestyles people "feel" what they habitually do is right. Young couples may brush off any challenge to their living together by benignly treating parents and others as behind the times. Older people more likely experience the challenge as demanding resolution. They must, then, disengage the critical intellectual presuppositions which generate the conflict. In this case these presuppositions are: Sexual intercourse ought to be (or need not be) restricted to marriage. If the former is true, the increasingly acceptable lifestyle is based on error. If sexual intercourse need not be restricted to marriage, living together may well be justifiable.

We shall not only consider this precise proposition but explain how to assess any moral proposition, judge whether it is true or not. Needless to say, supposing the older lifestyle is based on truth, this may merely provide parents with confidence in their position. Their children may not even be concerned about looking at the issue.

The procedure is the same for the emerging demand to practice assisted suicide and euthanasia. People convinced that we may not, must not, kill the old or the sick feel challenged by the thrust to euthanasia. The critical presupposition is: It is always wrong (or not always wrong) to choose to kill a human person.

This issue we shall also address and show why it is always wrong to choose to kill a person. For the moment, however, it is enough to see how we separate the critical presupposition and decide whether it is true or false.

The Moral Dimension

The two examples below make clear that human action and human living do have a moral dimension. Most contemporary moral issues are precisely about that moral dimension in actions affecting life and love and sex.

We have been talking about general moral propositions, not individual actions. Strangely, people become aware of this moral dimension as they experience moral questions about particular actions. General moral principles are involved, of course, to resolve such questions — which principles, moreover, are normally taken for granted.

To illustrate, consider that people usually don't find themselves discussing whether lying is wrong, but whether, for example, it is all right to phone in that one is sick so that he/she can go to the beach. Or is it all right not to declare cash received for small jobs when making tax returns?

As will be made evident it is conscience which makes us aware of the moral dimension. And so we turn to the human response of conscience.

Let us create two plausible scenarios for our purpose.

Sean suffers as he watches his wife Helen near death and in pain. He wants to move her into a hospice setting. Richard, their son, wants to ask Dr. Kevorkian's help. What is the right thing for them to do?

Jean and Lionel are in love, but financial and family problems compel an extended engagement. Is it all right for them to sleep together?

Such questions highlight a distinctive dimension of human conduct. Everybody recognizes the medical dimension in the conduct under discussion: what medications are available to relieve her pain? What medical procedures can be utilized? The financial dimension is clear: how much will the alternative procedures cost? A legal dimension immediately comes to mind. Sean and Richard may agree with regard to these aspects of possible conduct. But is it all right to have Helen killed – even though love prompts such consideration?

This last question manifests a distinctive dimension, the moral dimension. But does everyone recognize the dimension? Every normally developed person asks not only technical, financial, and legal questions about their projects, but also moral questions.

Most actions, of course, do not provoke moral questions . Daily routine actions like eating breakfast, dressing, driving to work, and buying groceries seldom evoke moral questions. But people normally recognize the moral dimension if it is raised and address such questions before acting. For example, a woman is told the dress she plans to wear is immodest or you are asked if the watch you are about to buy was stolen.

The moral dimension is, I submit, raised and recognized by "conscience." Everyone experiences choices and conflict of choices and at times a question like, "Is it morally right to arrange that Helen be put out of her misery by death or should I transfer her to hospice care?" If you read an account of a man who engaged in an affair while going to a marriage counselor to work out marriage problems with his wife and claims he experienced no qualms about doing so, would you not ask, "Has he no conscience?"

Every normally developed person experiences conscience questions in facing decisions and in reflecting on past decisions. Yet a little probing uncovers serious conflicts of opinion. What _is_ conscience and whose conscience is _right_? So let us continue our journey together by reflecting on "conscience."

CONSCIENCE

Sean, in the opening example, declares he simply cannot "kill" his wife – anguished as he is watching her suffer. His conscience is clear on this. Richard argues, "Dad, God cannot possibly want Mom to suffer like this. I have no doubt in my conscience. It will be hard to live with, but I know I can."

Jean and Lionel are equally divided. Jean says, "It's wrong. We have to wait until we are married." Lionel acknowledges that ordinarily sexual intercourse should be restricted to marriage but "We are already committed to one another for life. A ceremony and a piece of paper won't change that. In our case it is different. God sees nothing wrong with our sleeping together."

What is going on here? In both cases, two sincere, loving, principled people judge differently about particular actions. Each appeals to conscience to justify doing what is proposed.

Just what is this "conscience"?

Some people think conscience is the way they "feel" about performing a certain action. Certainly conscience is the final response of one's entire person. A person puts himself on the line in conscience decisions.

"Feeling" in this context refers to one's lifestyle or holistic response, which involves "knowing" and "feeling". But critical and essential is the knowing response. We can "feel" what we are doing is right when we ought not. Slave owners "felt" justified in selling their slaves. Many raised in a cultural environment in which cheating on tax returns is taken for granted "feel" right in doing so.

At times people "feel" guilty about actions when they ought not. A parent can "feel" guilty about disciplining a child when he ought to discipline him/her. I have "felt" guilty for injuring an automobile mechanic accidentally.

On the other hand, "feeling" can alert one that she/he is rationalizing. A spouse tempted to flirt with a fellow employee may tell himself there is nothing wrong, but "feels" he doesn't want the spouse to know. Reflection on such feeling reveals the rationalizing one is doing.

When Richard speaks of being able to live with the decision to stop his mother's suffering by having her killed, he reminds me of a field officer in a panel discussion professing that it would be all right to kill one of his prisoners in order to get information from the others – provided one could live with it. Such a position certainly implies that it is morally justifiable to do what is immoral, provided your conscience won't persist in accusing you.

Development of Conscience

In order to clarify just what conscience is examination of its development should help. Initially, the "moral" dimension is simply superego response. To behave in a way which results in a negative reaction from persons with whom a child is significantly bonded means experiencing not being loved, insecurity, being cut off, and so "being bad." To avoid such dire consequences the child interiorizes the demands of parents and others on whom she depends. The "moral" dimension is an emotional response. No insight. "Bad" simply means parents don't want me to do this. I'll be punished. They won't love me.

Although this superego response is proper to a child, most of us retain such responses in certain areas of our lives. The superego's dictates tend to be rigid and non-rational, oppressive at times, certainly irrelevant often to what is truly humanly good or bad.

As children advance in age the peer group becomes very important. Rules approved by the group are adopted as the norm. Thus begins the attitude of thinking that the moral dimension consists of "social conventions." It seems many, many people identify what is right and what is wrong with what the culture declares to be such. Some research suggests that the majority of adults live on this level.

Needless to say, most social requirements have some basis at least in moral truth. But there is a significant flaw or deficiency in the response based on social convention. If a person identifies with the group, he makes its demands his own. If one is not wholly identified with the group, its demands seem to be impositions. People responding on this level do not have insight into reasons for the group's evaluations. Catholics with limited maturity of conscience perceive the moral teachings of the Church as something they must accept in order to enjoy the benefits of being a Catholic. Not infrequently such persons experience compulsive and guilt feelings at the level of superego as well.

Nonetheless, people responding on the conventional level can still relate to what their conscience so structured proposes as seriously, even sacredly obliging.

Normal development leads people to recognize the goods at stake in moral choices as related to their development as human persons. They see (understand) what one will require of themselves in order to act reasonably. They recognize the moral dimension as a matter of real human goodness and reasonableness. To do wrong thus is a kind of self mutilation. The mature person does not ask, "What is the minimum I have to do?" Rather one asks "What must I do to be good at being a person? What is the good and holy thing to do? What does God want me to do?"

Understanding, insight is achieved because the mature person judges particular actions in the light of moral principles he embraces by reason or faith. One freely and intelligently accepts these principles.

> "Good is to be done and promoted,
> harm to any good is to be avoided."

St. Thomas Aquinas's explanation of the natural law may shed light on this process.

The two distinctively human responses are knowing and willing. Human knowing is not only sense knowing (seeing, hearing, touching, etc.) but intellectual knowing. We see and touch water, but we intellectually understand that it is water. We understand 2+2=4. We understand that whatever begins to be has a cause. (We know a man and a woman caused each of us to be.)

We not only understand things by intelligence, we act intelligently. If the car won't start and the fuel registers empty, we "think" about the need for gas. The moral dimension always concerns actions—something we do. The first, the fundamental principle guiding everything we do is, "Good is to be done and promoted, harm to any good is to be avoided." Whatever our intelligence grasps as good it understands as something to be done and promoted and harm to it is to be avoided. And the objects of our natural inclinations our intelligence grasps as good. Thus, for example, we have a natural inclination to stay alive—and we naturally grasp that life is good and is to be promoted and harm to life is to be avoided.

Again, we have a natural inclination to sexual indulgence and we grasp that sexual indulgence is good and to be done and promoted. But we also know that this indulgence is to be reasonable and thus must be indulged in freely and, since it is the normal way to communicate life, indulgence must be properly related to the communication of life and the consequent nurturing of offspring.

Later we shall expand on these natural inclinations and the goods to be promoted. But it should be clear how we come to "see," to understand these moral principles. Often extensive human experience and close reasoning have been necessary to establish moral principles. For example, it must have taken a long time to recognize the need of free choice for sexual indulgence to be reasonable. And probably centuries to relate sexual intercourse and offspring.

The mature conscience, then, applies accepted moral principles to particular actions and dictates what we ought to do. Free will allows us to follow our conscience or not.

Conscience Defined and Its Sacredness

At this point we can define conscience. This may help people recognize whether or not they have achieved maturity in conscience. Conscience strictly speaking is one's last and best judgment concerning what one should choose to do. Sean, for example, anguishes over the possible choices to relieve his wife's suffering. He heard his son's urging for assisted killing. In the depths of his being he embraces God's command, "Thou shalt not kill" and knows he simply cannot agree to have her killed.

Now, how does one form that last best judgment? "Conscience" can also be used to refer to awareness of moral principles as well as to the process of reasoning from principles to conclusions – those last best judgments about what I ought to do. One reaches that last best judgment by reasoning from the pertinent moral principles to the practical conclusion. Sean: "I must not resort to killing even to stop my beloved wife's suffering. I'll search for other ways." He does and decides hospice is the way he must go.

Vatican II called attention to the richness and sacredness of serious conscience judgments. "Deep within his conscience man discovers a law which he has not laid upon himself but which he must obey. Its voice ever calling him to love and to do what is good and to avoid evil sounds in his heart at the right moment . . . For man has in his heart a law inscribed by God. His conscience is man's most secret core and his sanctuary." (GS 16)

The Catechism quotes that section of *The Pastoral Constitution of the Church in the Modern World* and observes "when he listens to his conscience, the prudent man can hear God speaking."

GOD AND CONSCIENCE

This intimate, sacred encounter between a person and God is an experience everyone to some extent shares. (To the extent one is religious one knows the experience as an encounter with God. The irreligious person does not call it an encounter with God, but knows it as an experience both profound and serious.)

What made Thomas More's decision sacred – and what gave him the strength to persevere in his stand was his judgment in the depths of his being before God.

This conscience is the result of dialogue with oneself and witness to himself of the sincerity of his decision. But it is also a dialogue with God and a witness of God's will. Conscience is a herald of God, letting the person know God's will and command. It is the witness of God himself, whose voice penetrates to the very heart of the person calling him or her to obey. Conscience judgments bind not because the person so judges but because God tells him or her what is the truth, what is the true good she/he is called by God to do.

Conscience does not create the truth but discovers the truth by listening to what God says through the moral principles deep within one's heart.

It may clarify the issue if we keep in mind that conscience is <u>not</u> the decision to act. It is the last best judgment that one ought to so act. After the judgment is reached one remains free to act accordingly or not.

Shrewdly, the Catechism calls attention to what is needed for a person to "hear God speaking." "It is important for every person to be sufficiently present to himself in order to hear and follow the voice of his conscience. This requirement of <u>interiority</u> is all the more necessary as life distracts us from any reflection, self-examination or introspection."

For many of us, when erroneous decisions are made, seemingly in sincerity, underneath genuine conscience gnaws at our hearts. Keeping busy and distracted provides the buzzing that muffles the voice of conscience. As reported in a recent article, Edward who sought counseling to salvage his marriage at the same time was having an affair. He claims he did not recognize the contradiction in his behavior. Mustn't he have experienced *some* gnawing?

Almost everywhere freedom of conscience and the right to follow one's conscience are held sacred. Intuitively, people recognize conscience is where we live – where we are who we are – the source of personal dignity. When a mother urged me to change her son's mark so he could graduate ("We know all it takes is a stroke of the pen.") I was deeply conscious that the basis of my dignity as a professor was my integrity – abiding by my conscience. And this mother asked me to abandon my integrity.

FORMING ONE'S CONSCIENCE

If we all have a conscience and all have intelligence, why do people differ so profoundly on issues like assisted suicide and abortion—as well as the other contemporary moral issues bitterly debated? Chapter Two will uncover the source of these differences,—related to how the formation of conscience is affected. A brief explanation of how we form our conscience, then, is in order.

We have seen that every normally developed person recognizes the moral dimension in our actions. And that conscience it is which makes us aware of that dimension.

To grasp how ideally conscience directs a person, imagine a person who is 1) good, 2) mature, and 3) integrated, a man like Thomas More. 1) The good person seeks to live by the truth; he has no reason to evade the truth, to hide from the light. 2) Because he is mature he does not approach action guided by superego or social convention. He has embraced moral principles and judges moral cases by them. 3) As well integrated he is not excessively distracted by disorganized thought and the clamor of external inclinations from the various parts of the self. He is present to himself – wanting to find the truth and to do the good and loving thing.

Sean, as mentioned earlier, does not allow feelings of compassion to blind him from the evil of killing.

Being good, mature, and integrated, living a virtuous life involves a solid formation of conscience. The indispensable foundation of an upright conscience is commitment to live a morally good life. On the level of knowledge, three things are required for sound judgments of conscience. First, clear awareness of the norms which distinguish right from wrong. Second, sufficient knowledge of practical possibilities at hand, including something at least morally acceptable. Third, one must attend to the relationship between the norms and the practical possibilities.

Those three elements identify how to form one's conscience. A person has to learn what the true norms of morality are. We all first learn norms from the persons and groups significant in our lives – from parents, religious community, today from television, etc. We accept them unquestioningly. But at some point, teenage perhaps, we experience challenge to our norms and we face the necessity of embracing them, rejecting or modifying them. Unfortunately, we may reaffirm them from a superego response or reject them from peer or media pressure. Hopefully, we examine them reflectively and with the help of good teaching establish the norms we acknowledge as genuine.

THE MORAL DIMENSION

Few have the opportunity to process all this in an ethics class. Since we are born with an inclination to do what is humanly fulfilling and an inclination to doing that as obligatory (I refer to the natural law), then experience and religious instruction clarify these principles. Christians find the Gospel message clarifies. Catholics are assisted by the teaching of the Church.

Indeed, only if Catholics have embraced the moral directives of Christ as articulated by the Church, can they consider that they have a Catholic conscience. The Jewish, the Lutheran, the Moslem, the Hindu conscience demands acceptance of the teaching of the respective religious communities.

Experience, religious instruction, and cultural influences, likewise contribute to the habit of recognizing practical possibilities in different areas of conduct. For example, a man may feel he has no choice between following an immoral directive from his boss or losing his job. Yet what about appealing to a higher official?

Learning to ask moral questions is essential if one is to form one's conscience. Children tend to act spontaneously without reflection or not much beyond the object of their present desire. Most of us build up habits of response and often these may be fashioned by superego and promptings of social convention.

Basic in the formation of conscience, then, is encouragement to ask moral questions – to ask whether superego demands and those of social convention are reasonable or not. A physician at an abortion clinic was asked whether he thought abortion was immoral. "I avoid those questions," he replied, "and it _is_ legal." Only if moral questions are raised will one acquire the habit of relating one's moral principles to the practical possibilities.

CONCLUSION

We may not be in a position to address Sean and Richard's problem about Helen's suffering or whether Jean and Lionel may sleep together, but we do have grounds for our claim that there exists a moral dimension in choices and actions.

There is a moral dimension to human decisions and all normally developed persons acknowledge it. Conscience evokes awareness of this dimension and, invoking moral principles, dictates, not what we will do, but what we ought to do: our last best judgment about what we ought to do. Our actions affect external reality and choices of those actions determine our very selves. Always involved is freedom—our next concern, as we lay the groundwork for dealing with the contemporary issues which agitate people's minds, issues about life, love, and sex.

Further, more sophisticated aspects of conscience may be pursued in the appendices located at the end of this book.

CHAPTER 2

FREEDOM AND ITS ABUSE

HOPE WITHIN CONFUSION

Admittedly, then, people acknowledge the moral dimension in their lives. Their consciences kick in on numerous choices – and people possess a stock of moral principles to guide their conscience judgments. But, as is too painfully evident, there are vast differences of opinion on many issues.

Those with no religion give advice to Sean and Richard quite different from the advice believers give. A few years ago at a performance of Shakespeare's *Measure for Measure* the audience burst out laughing when Isabella, the young sister, explains that she could not sleep with Angelo in order to save her brother's life. Virginity once treasured has been trivialized. Eternal damnation is deemed a nothing compared to a man's life. And not only do Protestants differ from Catholics on significant issues but for thirty years Catholics themselves have been hearing contradictory voices in their own Church.

If we are to discuss the contemporary moral issues of assisted suicide, abortion, living together and the like, it is essential we understand this diversity of opinions and approaches—as well as causes of such diversity.

With all due respect for people's right to form their own judgment, tolerance of such plurality of moral positions must not succumb to the chaos of relativism. While we must call no person wicked we simply cannot call falsehood truth. At the same time understanding why others see things differently allows for respect and patience with persistent disagreement.

Still, hope gleams on the horizon. I really believe God has blessed us richly with three timeless works to work through the confusion: *Catechism of the Catholic Church* and a pair of Pope John Paul II's encyclicals, *The Splendor of Truth* and *The Gospel of Life*.

Those who enjoy the leisure to be intellectually concerned about what is happening in today's world will want those three documents. A fourth deserves a place on their bookshelves, *Living a Christian Life* by Germain Grisez. He is an outstanding theologian who "thinks with the church" in a creative and principled way. Grisez, an American of Alsatian descent, holds the Flynn Chair of Christian Ethics at Mt. St. Mary's College (and Seminary) in Emmitsburg, Maryland. Unlike most professors at Catholic seminaries, he is not a priest but a married Catholic layman. He and his wife Jeannette, who works very closely with him, have four grown sons, one of whom died in an accident some years ago.

Perceptive of what is needed, and clearly ahead of his times, he wrote a book on contraception in 1964. It was published before Pope John XXIII set up his commission on population and family planning that climaxed in Paul IV's encyclical, *Humanae Vitae*, 1968. Three years before Roe v. Wade, Grisez published a thorough study of abortion (*Abortion: the Myths, the Realities and the Arguments*). Foreseeing as early as 1979 that abortion would open the door to euthanasia, he produced a solid, thoroughly researched and profound volume on euthanasia and related issues (*Life and Death with Liberty and Justice*). In the midst of the cold war he challenged the nuclear deterrence policy of the United States in a collaborative effort, *Nuclear Deterrence and the Natural Law*, 1987. This work was an important contribution to the international debate on nuclear deterrence as well as an example, writ large, of the meaninglessness of proportionalism, a moral methodology criticized by John Paul II, one which will be treated later.

As far back as the Second Vatican Council Grisez accepted the Council's reading of the signs of the times that a revision of moral theological thinking was demanded – a revision which maintained union with Church teaching. Grisez's efforts bore fruit in 1983 with the first of four volumes on Christian moral living, *The Way of the Lord Jesus*, Volume One – *Christian Moral Principles*. The challenges from dissenting theologians as well as from Catholic thinkers reluctant to change perspective needed the scholarly, even recondite treatment of this first volume. With the help of Russell Shaw, Director of Publications for the Knights of Columbus, this learned work was revised in summary form and published in 1991 as

Fulfillment in Christ. It was designed to be read rather than for reference and study.

Living a Christian Life, Volume two, came to us in 1993 followed by Volume Three, *Difficult Moral Questions* in 1997. Grisez is working on the final volume devoted to the Christian moral perspective on religious and priestly life as well as on Church structures. The four volumes, each 900 to 1000 pages, will constitute an invaluable legacy for Catholic thinking and living.

How significant is Grisez's work? One admirer, Professor Robert P. George, dares to claim, "Grisez's work in fundamental moral theory represents the most important advance in this field at least since the Christian humanist movement and scholastic revival of the sixteenth century." Time alone will prove or disprove that claim. That Grisez is a challenge to dissenting theologians is evident by the, at least apparently, calculated silent treatment by opponents on the left. At the same time his originality evokes serious criticism by some conservative Catholic thinkers who fault him for deviating from Thomist thought. We agree with Professor George and embrace the view of the late John Connery, S.J. who judges Grisez's *Way of the Lord Jesus*, Vol. 1, *Christian Moral Principles*, "a monumental work" and with Benedict M. Ashley, O.P., who goes on record that Grisez's project "proves to be the most important work in the field . . . since Vatican II."

With the guidance of the *Catechism*, Pope John Paul II's encyclicals and the theological writings of Grisez, we shall attempt to clarify today's confusion in moral thinking and provide a clearly reasoned position on presently agitated moral issues.

Alan Wolfe reports in his *Moral Freedom* that the dominant mindset of people today about moral matters is freedom. He does not find people licentious but determined to make up their own minds about issues, refusing to let others (any others—culture, family, religion) tell them what is right or wrong. Professor Wolfe cautions that this attitude should be faced as a challenge, not as something that must be corrected.

Personally, I agree: people, especially young people, are not denying that there is truth on the moral dimension of, for example, sexual indulgence. They consider they have it. Assuming this interpretation of today's mindset then the challenge is to respect their judgment, appreciate the possibilities it holds, but attempt to explain and justify what we think is the truth.

Pope John Paul II is keenly aware of the current emphasis on freedom, seeing its development as one of the great contemporary achievements. To guide us in appropriating this sense of freedom he identifies three main errors related to current understanding of freedom.

ARE WE REALLY FREE?

Three Main Errors

(1) Not Seeing Dependence of Freedom on Truth

As mentioned above, John Paul II fully appreciates the reality and the dignity of human freedom. On the other hand, he points out, failure to recognize and live in accord with the dependence of freedom on truth endangers freedom and human fulfillment. *The Splendor of Truth* makes clear that this challenge is central: "The human issues most frequently debated and differently resolved in contemporary moral reflection are all closely related, albeit in various ways, to a crucial issue: human freedom." (31)

He confronts abuse of freedom. "Certain currents of modern thought have gone so far as to exalt freedom to such an extent that it becomes an absolute, which would then be the source of values." The result of such thinking is to make conscience "the supreme tribunal of moral judgment which hands down categorical and infallible decisions about good and evil." (32)

(2) Distorted Subjectivism

While recognizing the duty to follow one's conscience, this erroneous position claims that a person's moral judgment is true merely because one's conscience says so. Truth has no bearing, rather the criterion of morality is sincerity, authenticity and "being at peace with oneself." Richard's justification of the decision to summon Dr. Kevorkian for his mother echoes such voices.

The Pope identifies four interrelated errors which generate this distorted subjectivism. The idea that there is universal truth about the good which human reason can know has been lost. Conscience then is no longer understood as fundamentally an act of intelligence whose function is to apply universal principles to specific situations thus determining what one ought to do here and now. But that is the function of conscience—as we have explained. For example, the police-woman who crawled on hands and knees in the smoke-filled corridors knocking on doors knew she ought to help the people in the burning building because she knew one ought to help others in need. Again, Sean knows he cannot have his wife Helen killed in order to stop her suffering because he knows it is wrong to kill.

Replacing this true understanding of conscience is the tendency to grant to each person's conscience the right to determine the criteria of moral good and evil and to act accordingly. This is individual subjectivism and the road to chaos. Finally, "Taken to its extreme consequences, this individualism leads to a denial of the very idea of human nature." (Ibid.`)

John Paul II identifies the tendencies in contemporary moral theology to novel interpretations of traditional issues and makes clear that what is at stake is the fundamental dependence of freedom on truth.

It is essential to keep in mind that ethics always presupposes much: an epistemology, a metaphysics, a psychology. John Paul II takes as true and established that God exists and has created us and this universe. Sartre, for example, denies there are any natures of things because that presupposes a creator of the natures. Each of the Pope's philosophical and theological presuppositions is, of course, subject to challenge and in principle requires justification . On the other hand, every other ethician likewise is working with parallel, often different, intellectual presuppositions. As a matter of fact disputes about ethical issues often are radically disputes about metaphysics. And certainly believers more easily accept the natural law than non believers, even though natural law can be established without reference to God.

That freedom depends upon truth in other contexts is obvious; one is not free to pay one's $1,000 bill with $100. One is not free to have his or her love returned. In earthquake areas one is not free to build survivable structures using cement without iron or steel rods.

(3) "Missing Forest for Trees"

or

Blind to Life-Plan

Is a person free to make deliberate killing of the innocent a morally good act? *The Splendor of Truth* grounds conduct in the nature of the person as creature, destined to perfect happiness in the possession of God. God willed people to be and to be so destined. As developing beings people achieve that end by acting to perfect themselves. Acts which contribute to their fulfillment are good; acts which impede fulfillment are bad.

In creating people God willed they perform the good acts and avoid bad acts. This plan of God imperating those fulfilling acts is eternal law—which as naturally known by people is the natural law.

"Law," for many connotes extrinsic control. But the idea of natural law is communicated by "Innate life-plan for human liberation and fulfillment." Everyone is born with an inclination to what is good—humanly fulfilling—as well as an inclination to know he or she ought to perform those acts. Needless to say everyone has an innate inclination to avoid what is contrary to human fulfillment and to know this is to be avoided.

Clearly, then, only those acts which do contribute to human fulfillment, to the perfection of the nature of the human person as created by God, only those acts are good. Acts which rather than contributing to human fulfillment according to God's plan, actually violate that plan are evil.

To illustrate, God made our bodies in such a way that proper diet nurtures us. Some things in the diet we instinctively know are good, others so bad they will make us sick. Centuries of medical development have taught us what constitutes a good diet.

We may become convinced that a certain diet will be beneficial. If we have made a mistake our conviction and sincerity will not make this bad diet good. It simply will not benefit us.

The relation of diet to health is a necessary relation, i.e. the laws are outside our free control. Eating properly necessarily benefits us. Eating according to an erroneous diet necessarily will not benefit us, may harm us.

Since God created us free, the innate inclinations to do good must leave us free. God's infinite love created men and women structured according to God's infinite wisdom—inclined to what will fulfill and lead to our ultimate perfection—possession of God for eternity. This was/is referred to as the eternal (and/or divine law). But since essential to law is promulgation, people's natural knowledge of God's plan for human fulfillment, the eternal law, is the natural law. Thus God equipped us to know what God wants us to do but empowered us to do it or not, freely.

Questions arise about how much of that plan is known naturally and whether that knowledge can be blotted out by unsound customs and education for example.

But the point being emphasized is that there is a divine plan for human fulfillment, knowledge of which provides true moral directives. This explains why there is objective morality. People are no more free to change this objective morality than they are to change a bad diet into a good one by choosing to do it. We discover truth; we do not make things true. We discover the diet that actually nourishes (or we don't). We discover what is truly humanly fulfilling or we don't.

We may sincerely be convinced diet or moral choice is good, but conviction does not make error truth. Sincerely believed good, but actually bad, diet hurts us. Sincere, but bad conduct does not bring fulfillment. John Paul II insists it is simply not acceptable "to make the moral value of an act performed with a true and correct conscience equivalent to the moral value of an act performed by following the judgment of an erroneous judgment." When a person sincerely judges erroneously, the evil of the act is not imputable to that person, "but even in this case it does not cease to be an evil, a disorder in relation to the truth about the good." (63)

INTRINSICALLY GOOD, INTRINSICALLY EVIL ACTS

Certain acts are in their very nature able to be ordered to human fulfillment and ordered to God. Others are "incapable of being ordered to

God." These are "intrinsically evil" acts. These are always immoral. No good intention can make such acts morally good. "The Second Vatican Council. . .in discussing the respect due to the human person, gives a number of examples of such acts: 'Whatever is hostile to life itself, such as. . . homicide, genocide, abortion, euthanasia, and voluntary suicide; whatever violates the integrity of the human person, such as mutilation, physical and mental torture. . .; whatever is offensive to human dignity, such as subhuman living conditions, arbitrary imprisonment,. . .slavery, trafficking in women and children. . .' " A good intention cannot remove the intrinsic evil of such acts, even though a good intention or particular circumstances may diminish it.

RESTATEMENT

Let me try all that again. God's love motivated the communication of God's goodness, the creation of the universe. The universe is a developing universe, not something complete and perfect as it begins. To ensure the universe developed in a perfecting way God imprinted in things inclinations to proper development.

All things apart from human beings are moved with necessity to do whatever they do. God wanted human beings to be free and to image God as free collaborators with God's plan. Understanding what was required for human beings to be fulfilled God imprinted in us inclinations to fulfillment as well as an inclination to form judgments that we <u>should</u> (ought to) follow those inclinations. These judgments are what is referred to as "natural law" (or, as I suggest, "Innate life-plan for human liberation and fulfillment.").

Love of what is humanly good and sincerity in seeking the truth allows us to discover what God's plan is and how particular situations and decisions fit into that plan.

We are free to choose to act in accord with such knowledge—or to prefer some other, more immediate good. Sean knows he ought not have his wife killed, but pity for her in her suffering may lead him to reject the truth. He is free and able to do what he knows is wrong. He is not free or able to make killing his wife right.

John Paul II emphasizes that freedom depends on truth. Truth does not depend on freedom.

Revelation

God, our Creator, is likewise our Father. Recognizing human weakness and the effect of original sin on human reason our Father enlightens us by divine Revelation. The Ten Commandments given on Mt. Sinai, taught also by Jesus Christ, express key elements of the natural law, now known by the gift of faith. In addition, the Church received and communicates the New

Law, the fulfillment of God's law in Jesus Christ and in His Spirit. The Holy Spirit dwells within the baptized and not only teaches what "to do by enlightening the intellect on the things to be done but also inclines the affections to act with uprightness." God has given us the Church to teach us these truths. Rather than imposition of directives from outside, Church teaching is the presentation of truth. Cardinal Ratzinger uses the idea of anamnesis to explain natural knowledge of what is right: "The pope does not impose from without. Rather he elucidates the Christian memory and defends it." He defends it against the destruction of memory by "a subjectivity forgetful of its foundation as well as by the presence of social and cultural conformity."

Thus equipped by the natural law and faith we are able to know what is truly humanly fulfilling and by accepting God's moral directives we pursue our fulfillment. Truth makes freedom genuine.

Yes, many today tend to separate freedom from its dependence on truth, abusing this precious gift. But our freedom and expansion of the exercise of freedom must be appreciated and encouraged. And, paradoxically, many who exalt freedom beyond truth deny we possess genuine, fundamental freedom.

It is traditional thought, especially Christian tradition, which intellectually grounds human freedom, esteems human freedom, and protects it from abuse.

Freedom: both glory and problem. Anyone who belongs to the 21st century takes freedom for granted. The *Catechism* puts it this way: "By free will one shapes one's own life. Human freedom is a force for growth and maturity in truth and goodness; it attains its perfection when directed toward God, our beatitude." (#1731)

Pope John Paul II builds his encyclical, *The Splendor of Truth*, around the issue of freedom. "Certainly people today have a particularly strong sense of freedom . . . 'the dignity of the human person is a concern of which people of our time are becoming increasingly aware.' Hence the insistent demand that people be permitted to 'enjoy use of their own responsible judgment and freedom' . . . This heightened sense of the dignity of the human person . . . and of the respect due to the journey of conscience, certainly represents one of the positive achievements of modern culture." (31)

On the other hand, as we have seen, the Pope identifies the exaltation of freedom over truth as the source of most of our problems today. What concerns us now is that he also calls attention to the paradox of denying freedom while at the same time most stridently claiming to defend it. "Side by side with its exaltation of freedom, yet oddly in contrast with it, modern culture radically questions the very existence of this freedom." (33)

Life, Love, and Sex

FREEDOM OF SELF-DETERMINATION

A distinction and a little history by theologian Germain Grisez can help to clarify the paradox. Freedom-to-do-as-one-pleases is not freedom of self-determination. The former is what slaves are denied and what adolescents clamor for. To the extent that a person's choices are determined by laws, rules, or customs one is not free to do as one pleases. For example, a person is not free to drive through a red light nor to attend a presidential inaugural ball wearing a bikini. However, one retains freedom of self-determination to defy authority and run a red light or to disregard the norms of proper dress and go to the ball bikini-clad. We do enjoy wide areas of freedom-to-do-as-one-pleases. Our sense of duty limits those areas of freedom, as do the arbitrary impositions of others.

Free choice or freedom of self-determination on the other hand consists in "making up one's mind to do this rather than that, or to do this rather than not doing it, when both alternatives are real possibilities for the one making the choice." (*Fulfillment in Christ*, p.19) When we choose freely, our actions are our own, our lives are our own; our moral identity is our own. We are what we choose to do.

This is the freedom which grounds human dignity – and which is, in intellectual circles, generally denied. Within the theistic perspective, common until the 18th century, freedom of self-determination was taken for granted. Although freedom-to-do-as-one-pleases was markedly circumscribed, Christians had a keen sense of freedom of self-determination. They knew well that their eternity was in their hands. Enter modern philosophers like Hobbes and Spinoza, who proposed to replace traditional theism with a naturalistic conception of the world and its people. Naturalism gradually became the world view framing science; the success of modern science made naturalism plausible. Within the naturalistic perspective, "It seems evident that whenever anything happens, however contingent it might be, what does happen is the only possible outcome of conditions given prior to the event." Soon this view was applied to human choice. "Philosophers like Hobbes squarely faced this issue (the incompatibility between the traditional and the modern view) and argued for the position – one unpopular at the time – that human choices are no exception to the determinacy of nature. The heretical thesis of Hobbes is the orthodox position today." (Grisez, *Free Choice*, 1)

DETERMINISM

A theological position on free will condemned by the Church in the 16th century identifies the issue. The proposition condemned was "What comes about voluntarily, even if it comes about necessarily, still comes about freely." In this view moral responsibility requires physical freedom for acts to be human, but grace (or some other cause) determines precisely what one will do. Grisez notes, "This teaching is important today because most contemporary social scientists, psychologists, and non-believing philosophers admit freedom in human choice only in this sense, which the Church teaches is insufficient for moral responsibility." (*Christian Moral Principles*, 47, #5) Not grace, but genetic or psychological or social conditioning is judged to control our choices so that whatever we choose to do we could not have done otherwise.

Thus the principal opposition to the reality of free choice today is not theological; it is conventional educated opinion. " . . . Except for believing Christians and Jews, this is the view of virtually all those associated with modern scholarship and science. A formidable intellectual array against freedom." *(Fulfillment in Christ*, 13)

How many recent media and real-life dramas propose mental disorder or conditioning influence to explain and excuse criminal behavior! Contrast them with plays like Arthur Miller's' *All of My Sons*. Joe Turner is portrayed as responsible for the death of 21 pilots – and indirectly for his son's suicide once he learned of his father's evil decision to sell defective engines to the Air Force.

Freedom, all the world wants it. The Church recognizes its genuine worth and defends its existence by reason and by faith. Conventional educated opinion, called Secular Humanism these days, holds that people ultimately are conditioned, pre-determined in all they do. But common sense indicates plainly that society is, and has to be, built on the conviction that people freely obey laws, freely commit themselves in marriage, freely sacrifice their lives for others in emergencies and for their country in time of war. Society declares that those charged with crimes are not to be held responsible if the evidence shows that they acted under compulsion.

We have, then, a paradox: People lay claim to freedom while denying that freedom exists. In other words, the proclamation of freedom and thirst for more and more freedom is contradicted by ideology, by world view interpretation of experience.

Arguing for Freedom of Self-Determination

Are we, then, really free? Proof is needed today for a "Yes" to that question. We begin our proof by appeal to experience. Readers may be put off by the way this issue is argued. We simply have to argue philosophically. Psychology attempts to explain how and why we act. Sociology helps us understand the way we become conditioned to act in certain ways. Neither can address the question whether we human persons have the capacity to make any free choices. So the proof will not offer statistics or analysis of the process of decision-making. In one sense philosophy is reflectively grasped common sense. In another it is very abstract. We ask patience and openness as you follow the arguments.

Consider that everyone experiences free choice. Who has not had the experience of being inclined to do something for a good reason, even while recognizing that they are also disinclined to go forward, also for a good reason? They experience a conflict of wantings. For example, Mary and John have been going together for two years. Mary feels they should break up; she is convinced genuine love is absent from the relationship. She wants to tell John her decision to break up, but fear of hurting him causes her to hesitate. What results is a conflict of wantings, so choice must be made. After agonizing over the decision and consulting a spiritual advisor, she makes up her mind and tells John their romance is over. She made the decision and took action. It didn't just happen to her. As Grisez puts it, "Choice one does not encounter, but makes." (*Fulfillment*, 19)

Everyone can tell of similar experiences. Women face grave decisions about abortion. Men and women make decisions – to follow their principles by "blowing the whistle" on corrupt practices in business – or to keep silent rather than jeopardize their jobs.

Experience certainly points to the reality of free choices. Determinist, then, have no recourse but to offer arguments to convince us that "choices" only seem to be free, that actually our choices are all predetermined.

Arguments can be grounded very differently. We shall avoid developing any of these arguments. Some can point to sociological and/or psychological conditioning. Others can be based on universal determinism (inspired by modern science) or on philosophical fatalism (deducing the proposition, "no one can make a free choice," from logical truths).

Since no argument for or against free choice is truly compelling, whatever the argument, determinists must always appeal to loyalty to the pursuit of truth. "In view of this/that argument, since it is more reasonable to judge that people do not make free choices than to judge that they do, you <u>ought</u> to accept determinism." But this "ought," this appeal to be loyal to the pursuit of truth, is impossible if there are no free choices. A person can only do as she/he "ought" to do in this process of reasoning if one is able to make and keep the commitment (choice) to pursue the truth and be reasonable. It is, then, impossible to make an argument for determinism which does not implicitly make an appeal that either falsifies the claim of determinism or would be pointless if determinism were true.

For example, self-referential falsification: "No one can formulate a grammatically correct sentence." Just as the sentence just quoted falsifies itself, so determinists are falsifying their claim by exercising, and requiring their readers to exercise, free choice.

Self-referential, self-defeating (pointless): if determinism were true, determinists would be requiring readers to do what they cannot do – make a free choice.

Granted we all experience free choice (as determinists acknowledge) and granted every argument for determinism is self-defeating, it is utterly reasonable to affirm that we possess freedom of self-determination.

Needless to say, we have become aware that people are more conditioned and predetermined than we had previously thought to be the case. Determinists are correct in calling attention to this fact and to the fact that some people literally cannot choose to do what others judge desirable for them. People simply cannot choose what they do not see any way of doing. The ghetto drug addict may have tried to give up drugs, failed and become convinced – reasonably – that his history and background make it impossible to "make something of himself."

Still, that does not prove this person has no freedom of choice. Within the situation one can make many free choices: to be faithful to one's spouse, to look for work, and so forth.

The self-referential philosophical argument developed by Grisez and his colleagues is, I submit, definitive. (*Free Choice*) But for believers, constantly searching for and trying to follow the will of God, it is much easier to recognize the truth that we are free. "In sum, only those who accept the Judeo-Christian account of creation are likely to admit the reality of free choice . . . Only in the case of the Creator and his pro-creators can novelties emerge from and in harmony with an antecedent, real principle, emerge shaped by wisdom and expressed by love: emerge through *Logos* and *Agape*."

"In making free choices, human persons display the image of God in which they are made." (*Christian Moral Principles*, 69)

Choices Do Last—Creating the Self

Before we move to the abuse of freedom an important point must be brought out: a thread of relationship connects these three—the reality of free choice, freedom of self-determination, and human dignity. People create the selves they are to be. They intuitively know that in choices they create their own selves. Choices last. Once I make a decision I am the kind of person who makes such a decision: I remain a loving, sacrificing self or a lying, thieving self – until or unless I determine my self by another contrary choice. And in serious choices I face the creation of my "self" before God. I know what God's love is inviting me to do, and I embrace God's will or defy God and turn away.

"One who thinks of choices as transient cannot expect to understand sin, the redemptive life of Jesus, the act of faith, personal vocation, or the sacraments. Moreover, the intrinsic relationship between our present lives

Life, Love, and Sex

and heavenly fulfillment in Jesus is intelligent only if we grasp the connection between what we make ourselves now by our choices and what we will be forever by the persistence of these same spiritual acts." (*Christian Moral Principles*, 52, #7)

The Church jubilantly proclaims the dignity we possess as free agents made in the image of God. Only after such grateful acknowledgment does the Church sound an alert about the abuse of freedom.

ABUSE OF FREEDOM (1)

CHURCH TEACHING ON THIS ABUSE

Central to all morality is the issue of freedom. Only actions freely chosen are morally good or bad. Both the *Catechism* and John Paul II's *The Splendor of Truth* fully acknowledge the role of freedom in each person's dignity, but these documents also alert us to the dangers of abusing freedom. John Paul II clearly states that making freedom an absolute in itself is the precise evil of our day. Consider some cultural facts that <u>illustrate the problem</u>:

Fact One

"Kids," a controversial film of the 90's, portrays destructive New York City teenagers who see nothing they do as wrong or outrageous. Whether they are shop-lifting, pot-smoking, trespassing, seducing virgins, or engaged in assault, rape, or possibly murder, the youngsters come through not as screaming wild animals but as dull and mindless individuals, unaffected by ideals or fear of consequences. Is unlicensed freedom the route to happiness?

Three men were accused of picking up a teenage girl, raping her and then beating her. Two of the three took turns trying to break her neck. Finally, they tossed the girl's dead body into a quarry. Were these criminals acting freely or were they the slaves of sinful impulses?

Fact Two

A chaplain at a Catholic college deplored what he called "ritual Catholics" – people who are attracted to the trappings of Catholicism, attend Mass in large numbers, but ignore the Church's teachings. "They like the Church's liturgy but they consider themselves free to pick and choose what they believe and practice," said the chaplain. Are we becoming a society interested only in form – without substance?

His term, "ritual Catholics," applies elsewhere, too. The Church teaches that contraception in immoral. Yet, a large percentage of Catholics reject that teaching. The Church teaches that premarital sex is immoral. Yet, large numbers of Catholics live together before marriage. Hard to believe but a Catholic woman stated she would not support her parish building plans so long as the cardinal kept talking against abortion. The bishops and the Pope have taught: "In the case of an intrinsically unjust law, such as a law permitting abortion or euthanasia, it is . . . never licit . . . to take part in a propaganda campaign in favor of such a law or vote for it." Yet, numerous Catholics support "pro-choice" legislation and nominally-Catholic politicians vote for it.

Perhaps the acme of "picking and choosing," of freedom to make true what we want, is the reasoning of the Supreme Court in Casey. "At the heart of liberty is the right to defend one's own concept of existence, of meaning, of the universe, and of the mystery of human life." Implicitly, the Supreme Court is ready to abandon all moral principles, all claims to the understanding of truth, replacing them with individual choice. Can you imagine the Court accepting as justification of murder that the accused had chosen to define the meaning of his life as achieving goals by any means, theft and murder included? Talk about confusion.

Fact Three

A similar phenomenon exists among some moral theologians. Carefully orchestrated protests and polemics carried on in the media are opposed to ecclesial communion and to a correct understanding of the hierarchical constitution of the People of God. The Pope clearly condemns such dissent and links it to abuse of freedom: "a new situation has come about *within the Christian community itself* . . . It is no longer a matter of limited and occasional dissent, but of an overall and systematic calling into question of traditional moral doctrine . . . At the root (of these presuppositions) is the more or less obvious influence of currents of thought which end by detaching human freedom from its essential and constitutive relationship to truth." (*Splendor of Truth*, 4)

In summary, in the popular culture, even among professed Catholics and some moral theologians, freedom is exalted at the expense of truth and is often preferred to truth.

Pope John Paul notes the tendency to "exalt freedom to such an extent that it becomes an absolute, which would then be the source of values." (*Splendor of Truth*, 32) Freedom, rather, is not an absolute. Freedom is not an end in itself, but is ordered to the being or fulfillment of the person – and is to be guided by truth.

As the *Catechism* states (under the heading, "Threats to Freedom"), "the exercise of freedom does not imply a right to say or do anything. It is false to maintain that man, 'the subject of this freedom,' is 'an individual who is fully self-sufficient and whose finality is the satisfaction of his own interests in the enjoyment of earthly goods.'" (#1740)

Abuse of Freedom (2)

Germain Grisez

Germain Grisez's first volume of *The Way of the Lord Jesus, Christian Moral Principles*, examines, issue by issue, the Church's stance on the abuse of freedom. He was one of the first to recognize the radical transformation of traditional Catholic moral theology that consequentialists/proportionalists were attempting. Cogently and relentlessly he argued that their theory is meaningless. It is simply impossible to measure diverse basic human goods by the same criterion, the essential requirement of their methodology. Although not a strictly moral example, how can a young woman deliberating about her career weigh the good she would achieve as a physician and the good a lawyer achieves? In an admittedly moral issue, how can one weigh the benefit of three months extension of life against the pain and/or cost of chemotherapy? Chided for what some call a "nervous fear" of consequences, Grisez answered his critics by saying, "My attitude is not one of fear . . . [but] of reasonable terror. For, as I see it, consequentialism is not merely a meaningless theory, it also is a pernicious method of rationalization." ("Against Consequentialism," p.67) More on proportionalism later.

As we saw in Chapter 1, Grisez sheds light even more directly on the issue of freedom and truth within the context of conscience and moral subjectivism. Conscience, he points out, is often confused with what is arbitrary. "My conscience tells me it is all right to do X – and so it is all right for me, and nobody else can tell me I'm wrong." (*Christian Moral Principles*, 86, #1) Reducing conscience to moral subjectivism is to some extent rationalizing a refusal to submit to moral norms.

Excess of freedom especially impacts conscience judgments. Hence it is essential to recognize that conscience is primarily an intellectual judgment, one's final, best judgment about what one ought to do. And, in knowing, in judging, one is open to the real, to truth, one does not choose what is to be true.

Chapter 1 develops the insight but Grisez's neat summary is worth memorizing; it defines objective morality in the face of moral subjectivism.
1. "We are free to choose what we will do.
2. But we are not free to make whatever we choose right.
3. We must follow our best judgment concerning what we ought to do.
4. But our best judgment can be mistaken."

(Beyond the New Morality, 66)

As John Paul II insists, freedom is not an end in itself, is not an absolute. Grisez heartily agrees and, like the Pope, tries to identify and correct the abuse of freedom.

CONCLUSION

Commitment to "moral freedom" certainly affects the diversity of opinions on significant issues like assisted suicide, capital punishment, and homosexuality. This "fact" should be dealt with as a challenge rather than something to be corrected. John Paul II shows keen awareness of this insistence on freedom. If, as we suggest, people today far from rejecting moral truth, feel confident they possess the truth, then they should be open to hear the reasons that the Catholic Church thinks it has something worthwhile to contribute on these issues.

Fortunately we have the recent *Catechism of the Catholic Church*, John Paul II's writings, and the work of Germain Grisez to learn just what those reasons are. And it must be noted that the Church proclaims, justifies and argues for personal freedom of self-determinism. Moreover, to protect this freedom, the Church alerts us to the <u>fact</u> that freedom depends on truth, not truth on freedom.

The long tradition of "natural law," especially understood as "Innate Life-plan for Liberation and Fulfillment," identifies the way God provides for our fulfillment. We create, we are "parents" of the self be become.

But appeal to natural law under any phrasing fails to provide sufficient insight. What is needed for contemporary minds is an ethical (moral) theory which rings valid. We may not succeed in convincing people of this ethics, but at least they should recognize that it makes sense.

Our efforts to articulate such an ethics consists in answering two questions. What is happiness or fulfillment? And what makes any act morally good or bad? Chapter Three addresses the first.

CHAPTER 3

HUMAN GOODS AND HUMAN FULFILLMENT: "WHERE IS MORALITY?"

As explained, we simply are not free to judge $100 compensates for a $1000 debt. We may desperately want our love to be returned, but we are not free to have it so. Similarly, we are not free to make assisted suicide or abortion or the like morally good or morally bad. Freedom is dependent upon truth.

Jean thinks premarital sex is wrong. Lionel thinks, since he and she are engaged, it is all right for them to sleep together. How can they decide who has the truth? They cannot make it right or wrong by choice. It is simply impossible without an understanding of what makes any act morally good or morally bad.

It may seem strange but preliminary to addressing and related to that problem is the question of the relation of morally good or bad actions to happiness. Recall that morality directly and immediately affects the person choosing to perform that action.

To illustrate: why do we have no doubt that if Harry accidentally breaks Gwendolyn's nose it is very different from Jason's deliberately breaking it? The effect is the same: her nose is broken. So Jason's action is immoral because he freely chose to hurt her. Jason makes himself a hateful person.

Since choices last, that is how Jason _is_ until/unless he makes another choice to repent hurting her.

A person's fulfillment clearly involves his interior choices. Traditionally thinkers asked about happiness, but perhaps today it is appropriate to focus on "fulfillment," the most authentic and satisfying happiness people are capable of. So we ask what constitutes fulfillment or happiness?

FULFILLMENT

Do you know anyone who does not want to be happy or fulfilled? As St. Augustine claims, "We all want to live happily; in the whole human race there is no one who does not assent to this proposition, even before it is fully articulated."

However, people differ profoundly as to what constitutes happiness and the way to become happy. Everyone wants to be healthy, to have enough money, to be united in love, to enjoy a steady state of contentment punctuated with moments (some long, some short) of intense pleasure and some moments of rich joy. Is this what happiness is?

Yet most people set limits on what they will do to be healthy or to get money or to be united in love. Normally they are willing in certain circumstances to sacrifice contentment and moments of pleasure and joy. They may even give up their lives. What do people want that makes such limits worthwhile? They want to maintain personal integrity, to be a good person, and some want to reach eternal happiness.

Assuming people are free, one approach to the question of happiness is to ask, "What do I want to do with the rest of my life?"

Most people do not bother with questions like this. Either they are too busy "living," doing what has to be done, or they more or less assume doing what their religion tells them to do will bring happiness or they accept from their culture "what they want to do with the rest of their lives." Surely "they" (whoever influences them) know the way to be happy, to be fulfilled. Traveling that road, however, may force them to challenge the decision when they experience dissatisfaction or unhappiness. Socrates centuries ago challenged his fellow Athenians—"The unexamined life is not worth living." It is our hope that our readers may be in the mood to accept Socrates's challenge and confront that question. Religion can satisfy many—and richly. But for control of one's life, for an understanding of morality, it really helps to spend some time trying to put order into one's life by crystallizing just what the person wants to do with his life.

Many young people set their hearts on wealth or fame. Often pursuit of wealth or fame results in loss of friendship or inner peace. Once dissatisfaction or even unhappiness is experienced, the question rises sharply to mind, "Have I set my heart and bet my life on the wrong goal?"

TWO FALSE IDEAS OF FULFILLMENT

Grisez calls attention to two experiences that can mislead many about happiness. The experience of intense pleasure can lead some to devote their lives to pursuit of as much intense pleasure as possible. This won't work. Nausea and loss of meaning normally results; the reason being that pleasure satisfies only part of the self, one's consciousness. To be fulfilling, choices must relate to the whole person. An extreme example can make the point: a person could intensely enjoy food that has been poisoned — and die. Hardly what one means by fulfillment. C. S. Lewis learned that we have to be surprised by joy. We do things that bring pleasure. It is choice of such things that matters.

On the other hand, some people deliberately structure their lives by setting goals and striving to achieve them. Without doubt this can keep lives meaningful. And setting goals, (as well as providing for pleasure) is a necessary part of life, but as with wealth and fame, achieving goals is not enough.

Living to achieve goals is living mainly for the future and robs the present of meaning and value in itself. The counterculture of the '60's and '70's taught us the error of postponed living: living only for the future. Indeed since achievement of one's goal immediately sets a person off in pursuit of another goal, fulfillment in this view must consist in the frustrating experience of never being really satisfied. There is only one "now" and searching for fulfillment in setting and achieving goals in the future continually robs a person of living—which is always "now"!

Clearly, then, whatever fulfillment consists of, it must be something <u>continuous</u> (not fleeting momentary pleasure) and <u>present</u> in each unique moment of our lives (not always postponed for the future).

WHAT HAPPINESS IS FOR CATHOLIC BELIEVERS

Catholic believers know God created them to praise, reverence, and serve God and so to save their souls. What they want to do with the rest of their lives is get to Heaven. Isn't this pursuing a future goal? Let's see.

Many Catholics say this and making decisions in terms of Heaven can help to keep one honest. A better approach is to ask what God's plan is in creating the world and how we fit into that plan.

God loved the world into existence to communicate God's goodness and *all* things are to be fulfilled in Christ. "When all things are subjected to him, then the Son himself will also be subjected to him who put all things under him, that God may be everything to everyone."

Each person is unique and has a personal vocation to join Jesus Christ, working with him to bring the universe—materially, socially, economically, politically—to fulfillment in Him. Personal fulfillment, then, consists in allowing God to live and love through him or her, as God through Jesus works out God's plan for creation, the fulfillment of creation in Christ.

This over-all plan acknowledged, each person then asks, "How do I discover my very own personal vocation?" By learning to look upon one's talents as signs of vocation and matching opportunities providentially supplied. Sometimes, when talents match opportunities in more than one morally good option, prayerful discernment is required.

What do people want to do with the rest of their lives? Believers want to discover and fulfill their personal vocations, collaborating with Jesus spreading the Kingdom to the benefit of humankind in this world and eternity, culminating in eternal union with God. This is Christian humanism within the framework of the eternal.

Fulfillment for believers is continuous and here and now. So much so that this living simply flowers into eternal union with God; it is not simply the means to a future goal.

WHAT HAPPINESS IS FOR ALL HUMAN BEINGS

After five centuries of living without God and religion, now many reflective people — artists like Norman Mailer, politicians like Vaclav Havel, physicists and physicians — find the religious question arising insistently. Just when they experience success in whatever they once thought would make them happy, they "bump into their finitude—and their infinite hunger."

Nonbelievers discovering the respectability of the religious question, yet without an answer to it, still always experience the desire for happiness. The following nonreligious explanation of happiness or fulfillment may allow believers and nonbelievers to agree on what one ought to do with the rest of one's life. This lays the foundation for the meaning of morality.

BASIC HUMAN GOODS

People steeped in science are not taught to think of persons having "intellects" and "wills." Aristotle, on the other hand, has a rich analytic interpretation of human experience. Focusing upon actions he reasons that if a thing performs an action it has the power to do so. Since we "see" things, we must have the power to see things. Since we imagine things (like being in London) we must have the power of imagination. Since we not only see and touch water, but also understand that certain things are water, in fact understand what water is, we must have power of understanding.

Aristotle thus helps us to recognize that we human beings are sentient (seeing, touching), understanding beings. So we have sense powers and intellectual powers (intellect).

Life, Love, and Sex

But we also characteristically "want" things. I can see the chocolate cake, understand it is really a chocolate cake—and I can <u>want</u> to eat it. I have sense appetite (wanting) and intellectual wanting. For example, I "want" to eat that cake, (sight of it stimulates sense appetite) but I remember it is bad for my diabetes and so I "want" not to eat it; I want my health.

Aristotle starts with actions and reasons to powers. He also reasons to the kind of actions by attending to the object of the power to act. The object of all acts of seeing is color (and shape). The object of intellect is being, whatever is. The object of wanting is what is perceived as "good," as "desirable," as worthwhile.

This sketchy treatment of philosophical psychology is essential to understand fulfillment and morality.

To address the question of fulfillment the starting point is free choice or the exercise of the power to want. And free choice is pivotal—explaining what it is I do—explaining who I am by so doing. Always choice is about action and it is by actions that we are fulfilled.

What are the things I can choose? Whatever I choose I choose because it presents itself to me as worthwhile pursuing or as good. Often things are good as means to something else, but always there is ultimately something understood as worthwhile in itself—as a basic human good.

It is difficult to imagine anyone quarreling with the experienced need and desire for harmony in one's life. Grisez summarily describes four basic human goods desired for their own sake as forms of harmony: "We experience inner tension and the need to struggle for inner harmony; the good is *self-integration*. Our practical insight, will, and behavior are not in perfect agreement; the good is *authenticity*. We have strained relationships and conflicts with others; the goods are *justice and friendship*. We experience sin and alienation from God; the goods are *peace and friendship with God* which are the concerns of all true religion."

Positively, everyone is inclined to want self-integration as a good in itself. Everyone sees authenticity, being true to oneself, as worthwhile. Friendship, harmony with others, intimacy is treasured by all. Not everyone has God prominently in their lives, atheists and agnostics specifically. Yet everyone does have some more-than-human ultimate source of meaning, (found in some general world-view) in his or her life as desirable. Religious people give "religion," harmony with God, an absolutely essential place in life.

To be fulfilled everyone needs those four "reflexive goods". "Reflexive" because choice is included in their very definition. For example, part of the meaning of the first good, integrity, is choice, which brings aspects of oneself into harmony; choice (and performance) consistent with one's insight and values is part of the meaning of authenticity. They also are "existential goods" because they fulfill persons insofar as persons can make free choices and are capable of moral good and evil.

Reference to "existential goods" prompts a definition of the human person—in terms of 4 orders of reality. We experience <u>physical</u> things like stones, mountains, river, people. We experience ideas, feelings, propositions, reasoning—clearly different from physical things. These constitute the <u>intentional</u> or knowing order of reality. *Free choices* we experience as different from both the physical and the intentional and we call this the <u>existential</u> order. Finally we experience <u>cultural</u> things like cooking utensils, houses, banks, institutions.

The human person belongs to all four orders of reality. To be a person is to be a physical body, a propositional knower, a chooser and a culture maker. Goods correspond to each aspect of the person. Fulfillment requires choices of goods which fulfill each of these aspects.

Beyond the four existential goods, moreover, there are three other goods, objects which can be chosen for their own sake and which fulfill dimensions of persons other than the existential dimension just treated. Life and health as an aspect of life obviously fulfill persons inasmuch as they are bodily beings; fulfilling persons inasmuch as they are intellectual beings are knowledge of truth and appreciation of beauty; inasmuch as persons are culture-makers, play and skillful performance fulfill them. These can be called substantive goods.

Clearly these seven goods can be valued for their own sake. The gas station attendant works to get money in order to live (and provide for his family). He will be genuinely puzzled, if not insulted, if you ask why he wants to live (or to provide for his family). A child takes a clock apart just to see how it works. A young couple sit gazing at the sunset enjoying the beauty. No further good in either case need be sought. Games of tennis and golf can be indulged in simply for fun. Many, fortunately, go to work in business or education not only for the paycheck but because they enjoy the work for itself. Basic human goods are those goods capable of being chosen for themselves, as worthwhile in themselves.

One can verify them as basic human goods by asking why people act. Explicitly or implicitly, one or other of these goods is the basis for a person's actions.

An eighth basic human good is marriage, the permanent union of a man and a woman, which normally unfolds into parenthood and family life. It is, however, different from the preceding seven inasmuch as it is both substantive and reflexive. Since it fulfills the natural capacities of man and woman to become co-principles of new life and to raise the children it is substantive; it is reflexive because it includes the free choice by which a man and woman mutually give themselves and take each other as spouses, committing themselves to fulfill the responsibilities of marriage and family life.

How do we establish these eight motives or objectives for action? By pushing questions to ultimate reasons for acting. Confirmation can be obtained by observing human inclinations as well as by attending to results of studies in psychology and anthropology.

It is not without significance that there are several categories of goods or objects which a person can choose for their own sake. These goods are irreducible, none can be reduced to another or to some more fundamental good or purpose. Life is simply different from friendship. They express the intrinsic complexity of human nature. They correspond to different aspects of being human, they are part of the full-being, the fulfillment of human persons.

At issue is what each of us chooses to do with his or her life; what choices each makes among the possible choices open to them. At the minimum each person must be open to these goods in order to provide for the different aspects of being human.

Certainly I want to remain true to myself, to live a balanced life, to have friends and to be at peace with God. To the extent it is in my control I provide for my life and health, I seek to know as much as I can and to provide recreation as well as to engage in activities I enjoy. I esteem the good of marriage, help others to preserve and nurture their marriages as the opportunity arises. Later we shall address marriage as a basic human good at length.

COMMITMENTS

Openness to all these basic human goods is essential but inadequate. Commitments are necessary. Friendship in its various forms, for example, so crucial for happiness, in certain forms requires commitment. Unless commitments to life, personal growth, and religion structure my life I shall be chasing immediate pleasures and never experience fulfillment. These commitments, of course, must be harmonious and respectful of all aspects of being a person. Needless to say, to be fulfilled one must live out one's long-term choices or commitments.

To be fulfilled, then, is to be complete as a person and to be complete as a person involves five factors.
1) Openness to all the basic human goods, thus providing for all aspects of oneself
2) Making some commitments
3) Which are harmonious
4) And respectful of all aspects of being a person
5) Finally, living out one's commitment

This definition of fulfillment is abstract, but everyone, I believe, can fit his or her ideas of happiness or fulfillment within this framework. The uniqueness of each person is presumed. My commitments may very well differ from yours and you may be able to harmonize commitments which I could not. How each person lives out commitments can differ widely.

But unless a person provides for or at least is open to providing for all aspects of oneself, and lives with harmonious and morally good commitments, he or she simply will not be fulfilled.

What do you want to do with the rest of your life? Whatever be the concrete circumstances of your life, we are suggesting that you—implicitly at least—are wanting to be complete as a person—to be fulfilled as a person.

Impact of Truth and Faith in Providence

The atheist can pursue fulfillment in accord with these five elements. It matters, of course, whether all five are in accord with objective truth or not. Life can be meaningful whether the person is in truth or error; happiness and genuine fulfillment depend on truth. The Catholic transforms the entire project by commitment to Jesus Christ and by pursuing his or her personal vocation collaborating in God's plan to restore all things in Jesus Christ. But fulfillment of Catholics always is human fulfillment even when transformed—involving the five factors above.

Later we shall establish the first principle of morality as "One ought to choose in a way compatible with integral human fulfillment." "Integral" refers to all people. One ought to pursue human goods wherever they are found, recognizing that goods are not "my goods" but goods found in any person. Thus one is opened out to the entire human community.

There is no evidence or guarantee that integral human fulfillment is possible except in faith that all things are to be restored in Christ Jesus. Catholics, then, can live fulfilled lives, confident that fulfillment in Jesus Christ and in eternity remains truly possible and the most sublime of all possible purposes. For nonbelievers integral human fulfillment functions as an ideal.

FULFILLMENT AND MORALITY

The careful reader will wonder just how the moral dimension of human actions is related to fulfillment. Well, what do we mean when we call an action morally good or morally bad?

A number of steps lead to the answer. We begin with the very common use of the terms "good" and "bad" as evaluative terms. We claim a car is "good" when it does what a car "ought" to do. You and I may differ in what a car ought to do. For you, have sleek looks and quick pick-up; for me, need few repairs and have low gas mileage. But we agree with the correlation of "good" and "ought."

So action is morally good when it is as it ought to be.

This doesn't really get us very far. Next consider that we *are*, but are not yet everything we *can* be. The child is capable of becoming an adult. What we are potentially, we can become actually. Still we have possibilities for bad results as well. So making actual what we are potentially can be morally good or bad. Still we are on the right path.

Take health and disease. Why do we judge health is good and disease bad? Health is good for an organism; it allows it to live more fully than it would otherwise. Disease is bad for an organism; it impedes its living and eventually will kill it.

A similar pattern can be detected in the area of thought and inquiry. A good argument, for example, is clear, certain, has explanatory power and is consistent. When these characteristics are present knowledge can continue to grow and expand. When they are absent, further growth in understanding becomes impossible. So in this area of thought what is good is what makes possible further growth in knowledge. Bad is what frustrates and renders impossible further growth in knowledge.

We find a similar pattern in creativity in art and technology. And to generalize from these uses of "good" and "bad", good is that which leads to being and being more; we judge "bad" that which cuts off further possibilities and tends toward restriction of being.

Applying this understanding of "good" and "bad" to freely chosen actions, to human conduct, we conclude, moral good is that which fosters human being and being more; moral bad or evil is that which limits human being and contracts human life.

How often we distinguish being good as a physician and as a person. She is an excellent surgeon, but I would not like her as a friend. I do not respect her as a person. If you are in trouble, I would highly recommend this man as a lawyer. But do not get involved with him. I do not look on him as a good person.

Moral good and bad refer to the person as a whole. A morally good action contributes to him or her as a person. So moral good is that about a chosen action which contributes to the person as a whole, thus to his or her fulfillment. Moral evil is that about an action which damages the person as a whole. Moral evil is a sort of existential self-mutilation.

Every normally developed person takes into account the moral dimension of actions. A friend of mine recently had a dizzy spell and collapsed at the door of a hospital. Three different people rushed to him. "I work at the hospital. Don't move. I'll get help." In moments, medical personnel surrounded him and carried him into the emergency room. Why would people act that way? They just knew they ought to help a person in need.

Repeatedly people act heroically—sacrificing time and risking their lives to assist others. Some garage attendants pass up occasions to sell products when they judge there really is no need of replacing parts.

I am not so naïve as to think everyone can be trusted. But cheating, lying make sense in terms of immediate benefit to oneself. Deliberate refusal to take advantage of such situations is what I call attention to. Only acknowledgment of the moral dimension explains the latter actions.

MORAL GOOD AND FULFILLMENT

A person knows what he/she is depends on living according to conscience. We respect the person of integrity—no matter the social status. We keep our guard up with the skilled professional whose moral integrity we are skeptical about.

What are we claiming? Be good and you'll be happy? No. One critical factor in fulfillment is indeed morally good living. Material and professional success certainly bring benefits, but if that success is accompanied by, and especially if it depends upon, immoral choices, I do not think fulfillment will be experienced. One surely will be aware of inauthentic being and without harmony of heart, there can be no full happiness. This, of course, is where stifling of conscience comes in.

On the other hand, a truly moral person can be chronically ill or lose a dearly beloved by death or abandonment. To call that person happy strains language. He or she probably will bear the sickness or loss better because of his or her moral character, but will hardly be happy.

In other words, morally good living is necessary, but not sufficient for happiness. And, of course, morally good persons of limited intelligence will not have "quality of life" usually associated with happiness.

Such qualifications reveal the profound difference between those who assess fulfillment and morality within the frame of life to death and those who incorporate eternity.

The readership we address directly is Catholic but the moral issues are human, challenging everybody in today's society. Since moral good/bad is related to human fulfillment, the discussion of our issues (sex, life etc.) will for the most part be based upon human reason shared by all. Certainly in our pluralistic society recourse must be to what can be shared by all if issues are to be settled by discussion.

Catholics will be thinking within the framework of eternity and will have the support of Scripture and Church teaching. But Catholics also know full well that they must always distinguish faith and reason, keeping aware whether they ground their assent to conclusions about these sensitive issues on faith or reason. And in public discussion they may report what their faith proposes, but they must rely on the reasonableness of their positions—respecting the fact their faith is not shared by all.

Jason immediately hurts himself by deliberately striking Gwendolyn. Morality is in the heart, in one's free choices. He may feel relief from pent-up anger by his action, but most people acknowledge he is not being good at being a human person. Choices last and until Jason changes his heart by repenting he remains a hating sort of self.

Catholics and nonbelievers are likely to agree with what Jason must do to be fulfilled. But it is still not clear what makes his action immoral. Deliberately hurting Gwendolyn is wrong most would agree, but what *makes* it — or any action — morally bad?

CONCLUSION

We have been laying the foundation for a moral theory which we can employ to assess whether acts like assisted suicide, abortion, and fornication are morally good or bad. The moral dimension revealed in conscience led us to the issue of freedom and responsibility.

We then discovered that fulfillment, which we all desire, consisted in providing for all aspects of the person, making harmonious and proper commitments as well as living out those commitments. What opened the way to make this discovery was the recognition that there are basic human goods motivating all choices. And these goods are related to specific aspects of the human person.

As a pivotal step to determining what makes any act morally good or bad we asked just what we mean by "moral good" and "moral bad." An act is morally good, we saw, if it fosters human being as a whole, morally bad if it limits human being and contracts human life.

We all want to be fulfilled and so we should choose those acts which foster human being and avoid those that limit human being.

The critical point has been reached. What is it about an act which empowers it to foster human being—or to contract human life? In other words, what makes an immoral act immoral?

CHAPTER 4

WHY IS THE IMMORAL IMMORAL?

Sean feels he cannot bring an end to his wife's suffering by having her killed. It is immoral. Jean refuses to sleep with her fiancé, Lionel. It is immoral.

Everyone gets much more interested in morality when faced with a concrete choice: how can I, Sean, stop my wife Helen's suffering? May we, Jean and Lionel, sleep together before our marriage? But to answer concrete questions we have to invoke moral principles. Sean knows direct killing of an innocent person is immoral, so he cannot agree to have Helen killed. Jean knows sexual intercourse is supposed to be restricted to marriage. She wants so much to make love with Lionel and to please him, but feels she just cannot.

Most people carry a list of moral principles in their hearts – learned from family or religious community or from friends and media. Normally people don't question these guiding norms unless they experience challenge to them by unhappiness resulting from following those norms or by conflict of lifestyles based on different morals or by hearing arguments against one's morals.

Oliver, for example, always believed adultery was wrong. Unaware that Sally was married he has fallen in love with her. Can expressing that love by sleeping together be so bad? Walter grew up in a family in which drugs were taboo. Finding that his college roommate Joe regularly indulges, he is torn. To him smoking pot is evil, but he is expected to join Joe and his friends daily. To Joe drugs are good. Whose lifestyle is right? Winifred has her house for sale and has promised to keep any of "those people" from spoiling the neighborhood and lowering the value of her friends' properties. But she listens to a panel discussion on TV about discrimination. "Am I wrong?" she now asks herself.

Once one's moral principles are challenged, one is implicitly forced to examine the foundations of morality. Since most people feel unequipped to probe those foundations, they settle for "commonsense" or cultural relativism—or, especially today, their own "moral freedom," individual subjectivism. Our intention is to equip readers so they can establish fundamental principles.

For centuries, for example, euthanasia, abortion, and active homosexuality have been unquestionably assumed to be immoral. Not so today. It is important to know the terms ethos, ethics, and meta-ethics and to know just how they differ from one another.

Ethos refers to what is customarily done. Ethics refers to the specific moral principle involved in the customary practice. Metaethics distinguishes what makes any act morally good or morally bad. Discovering the answer to that question empowers one to assess the truth of the specific principles involved in the customs. And customs are good or bad depending on the morality of such principles.

Previous to 1973 and *Roe v. Wade* the ethos or custom was that generally only therapeutic abortions were done. The basis for the custom was the conviction that direct, deliberate abortion was immoral. Once the Supreme Court struck down state laws restricting abortions, clinics sprang up everywhere and abortions became common. Presumably people judged that abortion in certain circumstances was morally justifiable.

The issues we plan to address are currently debated so heatedly as to eliminate the need for spelling out their ethos and ethics. Clearly, we must simply establish what it is that makes <u>any</u> action morally good or morally bad before we can assess the moral principles supporting the opposed stances on each issue.

CATECHISM

When the specific moral principles of one's lifestyle are challenged, probing for a solution may not lead the individual to the logically ultimate question, "What makes an action morally good or bad?" But that is where reason drives one and there we shall go. First we shall look at official Catholic teaching as found in the *Catechism* and John Paul II's writing. Then we shall study Grisez's ethics.

One hundred pages are devoted in the *Catechism* to the foundations of Christian morality *before* it addresses the specific norms of the ten commandments. Framing the treatment within the Christians' call to sanctity and to letting Christ live in and through them, "Section One, Man's Vocation, Life in the Spirit" addresses our concern.

And the introduction to Chapter One shows how sweeping the treatment is:
The dignity of the human person is rooted in his creation in the image and likeness of God (article 1); it is fulfilled in his vocation to divine beatitude (article 2). It is essential to a human being freely to direct himself to this fulfillment (article 3). By his deliberate action (article 4), the human person does, or does not, conform to the good promised by God and attested by moral conscience (article 5). Human beings make their own contributions to their interior growth; they make their whole sentient and spiritual lives into means of this growth (article 6). With the help of grace they grow in virtue (article 7), avoid sin, and if they sin they entrust themselves as did the prodigal son to the mercy of our Father in heaven (article 8). In this way they attain to the perfection of charity. (#1700)

Article 4, "The Morality of Human Acts" focuses on our present concern. Building on its treatment of freedom the Catechism begins the section by observing that "freedom makes man a moral subject" for "when he acts deliberately, man is, so to speak, *the father of his acts.*" (#1749)

It is by their moral acts that people create the kind of selves they are to be and pursue fulfillment or not. How, then, do we evaluate these human, free acts? We look to three aspects of every chosen act: the object chosen, the intention, and the action's circumstances. These are the constitutive elements of the morality of human acts, what makes them morally good or bad acts.

Take a concrete example. Philip is determined to finance his daughter's college education. That is the "intention," the "end in view." He considers the possibilities: he can mortgage the home (the object of his act aimed at or with the intention of financing Ingrid's college education). He could, he reflects, take advantage of his position in the bank and get the money by discreet, undetectable withdrawals. Note that his intention, loving as it is, does not change "what he is doing," the object of his act. The fact he has this position is due to his father-in-law's trust in him and concern for his daughter, Philip's wife.

The Catechism speaks of the object chosen as morally good "insofar as reason recognizes and judges it to be in conformity with the true good." And it states "the objective norms of morality express the rational order of good and evil, attested to by conscience." Unfortunately, the *Catechism* does not explain just what this "true good" is nor what the criterion of conformity to it is. John Paul II and Grisez are more specific.

Essential to the teaching is the insistence that "a good intention . . .does not make behavior that is intrinsically disordered. . . good or just. The end does not justify the means."

As for the circumstances, they are secondary elements of the moral act. Circumstances can increase or lessen the moral goodness or evil. At times they diminish or increase the person's responsibility. But they cannot of themselves change the morality of acts themselves; and action in itself evil cannot be made good by the circumstances.

In our example, Philip's intention is a loving choice and can be pursued by the morally good or indifferent means of taking out a mortgage. But his noble intention cannot change his surreptitious withdrawing of bank funds from being immoral stealing. Betraying his father-in-law's trust, I submit, would increase the evil of the act.

In summary, then, to determine the morality of a deliberately chosen act, one reflects on the object of the act, the intention in choosing it, and the circumstances including the consequences. All three aspects must be morally good. While an intention cannot change an evil act into something good, an evil intention can violate an otherwise morally good act. Prayer or fasting, obviously good acts, can be made immoral by the intention "to be seen by men."

In light of the method of moral reasoning currently proposed by dissident theologians, called consequentialism or proportionalism, which denies there are any moral absolutes, the most important teaching is the unequivocal statement, "There are some concrete acts – such as fornication – that it is always wrong to choose, because choosing them entails a disorder of the will, that is, a moral evil." (#1755)

THE SPLENDOR OF TRUTH

Ever since Pope Paul VI's encyclical, *Humanae Vitae*, on the morality of contraception, a profound division has developed between authentic teaching of the Church and dissident theologians. There has emerged not only a denial of specific moral teachings but a radical rejection of traditional moral or ethical method.

Until about 1965 there was pretty much monolithic unanimity with Church teaching among theologians on the immorality of contraception. With the advent of the contraceptive pill (coupled with the long standing compassion and puzzlement over couples with serious problems in this matter) some few theologians insisted that while contraception certainly was immoral, use of the pill is not contraception. Not many joined that story and no one for long. Whether one prevents conception by chemical or by mechanical means is of no moral significance.

Soon, however, ranks were broken as the distinction was proposed between an overall openness to life and individual contraceptive acts. The married couple intending to have children could have recourse to contraception in planning their family; their will need not be anti-life.

Since contraception had long been declared immoral, indeed intrinsically evil, something had to be thought up to allow for the above distinction. Shortly a learned article argued there are no intrinsically evil acts, no absolute moral norms.

This, of course, could not stand with the traditional understanding of the natural law and the method of forming moral judgments. Consequentialism emerged, the theory that when more good or less evil could be achieved by an action, the choice was centered on the greater good or lesser evil – not on any direct harm to a human good. Moral evil consists in the permission or causing of physical evil without proportionate reason.

Consequentialism and proportionalism spread rapidly. As a result many of the moral absolutes traditionally taught by the Church were denied. Since the Church was currently repeating those teachings, theologians introduced a new ecclesiology: the Church possessed no authority to teach authoritatively on specific moral principles. According to this understanding of the Church, the magisterium could teach authoritatively only the broadest moral principles – to love God and neighbor. For all other, specific moral principles the Church could only exhort people to follow them.

This was the state of moral theology which prompted Pope John Paul II in 1993 to write *The Splendor of Truth*. He articulated clearly the purpose of the encyclical. Reminding all that the Church had for centuries been teaching what morality demanded in the areas of human sexuality, the family, and social, economic and political life, he declares: "Today. . . it seems *necessary to reflect on the whole of the Church's moral teaching*, with the precise goal of recalling certain fundamental truths of Catholic doctrine which, in the present circumstances, risk being distorted or denied." *Splendor of Truth*, (4)

The Pope characterizes things as "a new situation" within the Church: spread of doubts and objections to the Church's moral teachings. "It is no longer a matter of limited and occasional dissent, but of an overall and systematic calling into question of traditional moral doctrine." At the root of the new ethical presupposition, he declares, is the current detaching of human freedom from its relationship with truth. As a result the Church's traditional teaching of the natural law with the universal, permanent validity of its precepts is rejected. These dissenters find certain moral teachings simply unacceptable. "And the Magisterium itself is considered capable of intervening in matters of morality only in order to 'exhort conscience' and to 'propose values' in the light of which each individual will independently make his or her decisions and life choices." (Ibid.)

Two years later without reference to this denial of Church authority to teach specific moral principles or to this limiting of the Church's capability to exhortation, the Pope in *The Gospel of Life* proceeds to declare in language barely short of solemn definition that abortion and euthanasia are immoral, two specific kinds of acts.

Note the solemnity of these three condemnations. First, direct killing in general: "Therefore, by the authority which Christ conferred upon Peter and his Successors, and in communion with the bishops of the Catholic Church, I confirm that the direct and voluntary killing of an innocent human being is always gravely immoral." And the Pope bases the teaching on the natural law, the unwritten law people find in their hearts, on Scripture and tradition and "through the authority of the Magisterium." (*The Gospel of Life*, 57) This last source cited is one of the ways designated by Vatican II in which the Church teaches infallibly.

After stating unequivocally that direct killing is immoral John Paul II, using almost identical, solemn language, applies the principle to abortion. "Therefore, by the authority which Christ conferred upon Peter and his Successors, in communion with the bishops – who on various occasions have condemned abortion and who in the aforementioned consultation, albeit dispersed throughout the world, have shown unanimous agreement concerning this doctrine, declare that direct abortion, that is, abortion willed as an end or as a means, always constitutes a grave moral disorder, since it is the deliberate killing of an innocent human being." Again he states this teaching is based on the natural law, scripture, and "is transmitted by the Church's tradition, and taught by the ordinary and universal Magisterium." (*The Gospel of Life*, 62)

The condemnation of euthanasia is expressed in almost identical language and the basis of the teaching is identified as in the previous.

Is it not significant that the successor of St. Peter, in the present context and climate of theological dissent and denial that the Church is capable of teaching authoritatively specific moral principles, that the Pope teaches as infallible that abortion and euthanasia are gravely immoral because they both are the killing of innocent human life?

The Moral Act

To return to *The Splendor of Truth*, John Paul II proceeds to analyze the moral act in order to show why consequentialism is wrong and to insist that there are intrinsically evil acts, absolute moral principles. (*The Splendor of Truth*, IV The Moral Act, 71 sq.)

Earlier we warned that when the moral principles undergirding one's position on euthanasia, abortion, etc. are challenged, reason drives us back to the ultimate question, "What makes any act morally good or bad?"

Committed parents, even committed professional people and scientists may feel they do not have time to investigate such an abstract issue. Either they must take on "faith" (natural or supernatural) the answer to the question or they must make time to engage in it. Catholics have the blessing of our learned pope under the inspiration of the Holy Spirit directly addressing our ultimate question. His explanation is based on human reason and should be accessible and acceptable to all. The concepts, of course, are technical and an effort is required to follow the explanations. We shall try to keep it as simple as possible.

Just how freedom and God's law are related is manifest in "human" acts, acts freely and deliberately chosen. By human acts the person perfects him or herself and attains perfection or beatitude by seeking and cleaving to God.

It is essential to focus on the fact that what human deliberate acts immediately and directly affect is the person acting – not the state of affairs outside the agent, important as this indeed is.

Pope John Paul II is working within the framework of the "natural law." Natural law is natural knowledge of God's plan, "Eternal Law," for human fulfillment. The heart of natural law has also been revealed by God, as we find in the Old and New Testaments. But, since it is "natural law," every normally developed human person knows or at least can know it.

Acts, then, are morally good when the good chosen is authentic good. What is authentically good is established by Divine Wisdom, the "Eternal Law," which orders all things toward their proper end or fulfillment. So morally good acts are those which are ordered to the person's ultimate end, the possession of God.

It follows that human acts cannot be evaluated morally by attending to their effectiveness in achieving goals. We have already developed this idea of the moral dimension. Effective as bombing civilians or dishonest business practices may be, the actions are not in accord with the person's genuine good.

John Paul II asks, using traditional sources of morality, *"What is it that ensures this ordering of human acts to God? Is it the intention of the acting subject, the circumstances – and in particular the consequences – of his action, or the object itself of his act?"* (*The Splendor of Truth*, 74)

CONSEQUENTIALISM AND PROPORTIONALISM REJECTED

In context of this problem, he reports, new theological developments require discernment by the Magisterium. Certain "teleological" ethical theories propose that the criteria of moral rightness of actions derive from "weighing of the non-moral or pre-moral goods to be gained and the corresponding non/pre-moral values to be respected." Morally good acts "maximize" goods and "minimize" evils. (74)

Errors in such efforts to specify the criterion of morality are linked with "an inadequate understanding of the object of moral action." "Consequentialism" is defined and distinguished from "proportionalism." The former claims to draw the criteria of the rightness of a given way of acting solely from a calculation of foreseeable consequences derived from a given choice. The latter, by weighing the various values and goods being sought, focuses rather on the proportion acknowledged between the good and bad effects of that choice, with a view to the "greater good" or "lesser evil" actually possible in a particular situation.

Proponents of these theories deny the possibility of formulating "an absolute prohibition of particular kinds of behavior which could be in conflict, in every circumstance and in every culture, with those values." They see persons responsible for attaining the values pursued but in two ways: "the values or goods involved in a human act would be from one viewpoint, of the moral order (in relation to properly moral values, such as love of God and neighbor, justice, etc.) and, from another viewpoint, of the pre-moral order. . .(in relation to the advantages and disadvantages accruing both to the agent and to all other persons possibly involved, such as, for example, health or its endangerment, physical integrity, life, death, loss of material goods, etc.)" (*The Splendor of Truth*, 75)

Thus two judgments are in order: the moral goodness of acts "would be judged on the basis of the subject's intention in reference to moral goods and its 'rightness' on the basis of a consideration of its foreseeable effects or consequences and of their proportion." (Ibid.)

The significance of this distinction stands out brilliantly when it is claimed individual acts may directly violate pre-moral goods by contradiction of a universal negative norm and yet be morally acceptable "if the intention of the subject is focused, in accordance with a 'responsible' assessment of the goods involved in the concrete action, on the moral value judged to be decisive in the situation." (Ibid.)

In other words, "The evaluation of the consequences of the action, based on the proportion between the act and its effects and between the effects themselves, would regard only the pre-moral order. The moral specificity of acts . . . would be determined exclusively by the faithfulness of the person to the highest values of charity and prudence" – even when the choice is contrary to particular moral principles. Exceptions to traditionally absolute moral principles are then introduced. (Ibid.)

As Richard A. McCormick, S.J. states this position, "common to all so-called proportionalists is the insistence that causing certain disvalues (ontic, nonmoral, premoral evils) in our conduct does not ipso facto make the action morally wrong, as certain traditional formulations supposed. The action becomes morally wrong when. . . there is not proportionate reason. Thus, just as not every killing is murder, not every falsehood a lie, so not every artificial contraception is necessarily an unchaste act. Not every termination of a pregnancy is necessarily an abortion in the moral sense." (*Theological Studies* 50: 1989. "Moral Theology 1940-89: An Overview")

Acknowledging the good intention of proponents of these theories, the Pope firmly denies they can be grounded in Catholic moral tradition, attempting as they do, to "justify, as morally good, deliberate choices of kinds of behavior contrary to the commandments of the divine and natural law." (76) Furthermore, the encyclical insists that the weighing of the goods and evils "is not an adequate method for determining whether the choice of that concrete kind of behavior is 'according to its species,' or 'in itself,' morally good or bad, licit or illicit." (77)

"OBJECT OF THE ACT"

Perhaps the critical section of the encyclical for rejecting consequentialism and proportionalism and for identifying what makes acts morally good or bad is Number 78 where the "object of the act" is treated. It is the object of the act on which the morality "depends primarily and fundamentally."

To understand this insight, one must "place oneself in the perspective of the acting person." What is the person willing? The object being willed is a "freely chosen kind of behavior." (above: Philip considers choosing discreet, undetectable withdrawals from the bank where he works—or mortgaging his home.) If the kind of behavior (mortgaging the home/undetectable withdrawals) is in conformity with the order of reason, it causes the will to be good. Such an act perfects the person morally, disposing the person to our ultimate purpose, possession of God.

It should be evident that the object of a moral act is not some process or event of the physical order, assessable by its effectiveness in achieving a desired state of affairs outside the person acting. Rather, the object of the act is "the proximate end of a deliberate decision which determines the act of willing on the part of the acting person."

The Catechism is quoted with agreement—"specific kinds of behavior are always wrong to choose, because choosing them involves a disorder of the will, that is, moral evil."

A good intention is not sufficient. Any human act depends on its object, "whether that object is capable or not of being ordered to God . . . and thus brings about the perfection of the person." (78)

The encyclical proceeds to insist that there are intrinsically evil acts. "Reason attests that there are objects of the human act which are by their nature 'incapable of being ordered' to God, because they radically contradict the good of the person made in his image." These "intrinsically evil" acts the church teaches are always seriously wrong by reason of their object. And Pope John Paul II quotes the Second Vatican Council's examples: homicide, genocide, abortion, euthanasia, suicide, physical and mental torture, arbitrary imprisonment, slavery, prostitution, treating laborers as mere instruments of profit and numerous others. He likewise refers to Paul VI's condemnation of contraception and his general teaching of intrinsically evil acts: " . . . it is never lawful, . . . to do evil that good may come of it." (80) The same teaching is found in Scripture and in St. Augustine. (81)

Finally the Pope links the rejection of the erroneous moral theories with the protection of objective morality. "This would be to the detriment of the human fraternity and the truth about the good, and would be injurious to ecclesial communion as well." (82)

GERMAIN GRISEZ

The Pope insists on objective morality—an aspect of freely chosen acts which are ordered to God's plan for human fulfillment. Certain acts are so definitely not so ordered that they are intrinsically evil, always immoral. The natural law identifies which acts are morally good or bad.

Germain Grisez succeeds in making even clearer just what makes an act morally good or bad. He must have found *The Splendor of Truth* most reassuring. He had challenged consequentialism and proportionalism from its very inception. As early as 1970, writes Richard McCormick, "Germain Grisez says of Knauer (at the beginning of consequentialism) that he is carrying through a revolution in principle while pretending only a clarification of traditional ideas." (op cit.) Repeatedly, Grisez has written critically of the movement, insisting that consequentialism/proportionalism is not false but meaningless, requiring what simply cannot be done, weighing of the human goods. He declares it is a sophisticated form of rationalization.

More importantly, Grisez strongly supports traditional church teaching that there are intrinsically evil acts, and so absolute moral principles. He appreciated especially the encyclical's emphasis on the object of the moral act.

His approach, however, differs from the traditional "sources of morality," object of the act, intention and circumstances. Actually, these three are involved, but he does not focus on them in his creative approach.

BASIC HUMAN GOODS AND FIRST PRINCIPLE OF MORALITY

"What do you want to do with the rest of your life?" became our practical starting point for the meaning of happiness. Presupposed was freedom of choice and we asked, "What can we choose?" Eight basic human goods were identified—and as related to eight aspects of being a person. Fulfillment obviously involved all the aspects of being a person and the corresponding goods, possession of which would fulfill these aspects.

Moral good and moral bad we discovered related to human fulfillment. Moral good is that which "fosters human being and being more." Moral evil is that which puts limits on human being and contracts human life As "ought'" in other applications points toward full, fuller and fullest being, moral ought points to full, fuller, fullest freedom of self-determination—toward an ideal of the fullest possible personhood and the richest possible community.

We have learned what we mean by moral good and moral bad. But we have not identified what makes some acts morally good (fostering human being and being more); what makes some acts morally bad (limiting and contracting human being).

FIRST APPROACH: CRITERION OF MORALITY

Earlier we noted that as color is the object of sight and sound the object of hearing, so "good" is the object of the will. Choice is an act of willing and we simply cannot will anything other than something perceived as good, as worthwhile. But choice only occurs when one experiences a conflict of wantings. One can, then, choose to pursue a good in a way which respects the other (and all) goods, choosing inclusivistically. Or one can choose to pursue a good in a way that excludes, that damages, destroys or impedes the (another) good. This is choosing exclusivistically.

Sean anguishing over his wife's painful suffering deliberates between moving her into a hospice setting or, as Richard, his son, urges, euthanasia. He chooses hospice, pursuing a way to ease Helen's suffering, without damaging any basic human good. His choice is morally good because it is inclusivistic choosing.

Richard's proposal would relieve his mother's suffering but by destroying the basic human good of life. Such an act would be immoral because it is exclusivistic choosing.

Philip, determined to finance his daughter's education in choosing to mortgage his home, chooses to pursue the good of parental friendship in a way that respects all other goods. Inclusivistic choosing. If he had taken the money by discreet, undetectable withdrawals from the bank, he would have been going against the good of friendship (all depositors, etc.) and the good of trusting friendship of his father-in-law. Exclusivistic and immoral choosing.

For Grisez, then the criterion of morality, that standard by which actions are constituted morally good or bad, and by which we can judge whether they are good or bad, is inclusivistic or exclusivistic choosing. Such reflections on the morality of choices opens into the first principle of morality. Granted each of the basic human goods is grasped as something which is to be pursued, how do we know how to choose among competing goods? Grisez formulates the first principle of morality; ("In voluntarily acting for human goods and avoiding what is opposed to them, a person should choose and otherwise will those possibilities, and only those, which it is compatible with integral human fulfillment to will.")

This sounds ponderous and complicated; he is keeping in mind multiple ways the human will acts. A simpler, user-friendly formulation is: "One ought always to choose in a way compatible with integral human fulfillment."

To explain: it seems obvious free choices should be made consistently in the light of all the basic human goods. If choices were so made, the result would be fulfillment of all persons in all basic human goods. So "integral" refers to all people, all communities.

Limited to what reason can know, fulfillment of all people (integral human fulfillment, IHF) is not something concrete, not an objective attainable by some giant master plan. It functions as a guiding ideal and remains constantly open-ended. IHF, again, is not a supreme sort of good. The reasons for all choosing remain the basic human goods; IHF functions to guide the interplay between and among these reasons. It is to ensure that one's choices respect all the goods, are inclusivistic so there is no unreasonable preference for some persons or some goods over others.

The Christian in faith knows that "integral human fulfillment is more than an ideal, for it will be realized in the fulfillment of all things in Jesus." Thus the Christian life transforms the entire realm of the moral.

This formulation of the first principle of morality can, then, be acceptable to non-believers as well as believers, the latter deepening its meaning.

Grisez has, I submit, made clear "what makes any act morally good or bad." This will equip us to assess the conflicting moral principles undergirding assisted suicide, capital punishment and the other contemporary issues.

Because insight into thie criterion or standard by which we know whether an act is morally goood or bad is so critical, some readers may find the second approach clearer, others will, I hope, feel confirmed by it.

SECOND APPROACH: PRACTICAL REASON

Since many readers may not be familiar with traditional distinctions within philosophical psychology, I call attention to their own experiences which undergird those distinctions. Two characteristically human responses are knowing and wanting. You walk through a kitchen with steaks sizzling on the stove—hours since you've eaten. You <u>know</u> steaks are sizzling and instinctively <u>wanting</u> some arises. You walk through the same kitchen with steaks sizzling after a sumptuous dinner. You <u>know</u> steaks are sizzling, but there is <u>no wanting</u>.

Knowing is two-fold, sense knowing and intellectual knowing. You <u>see</u> Trixie, your neighbor's dog, and you know, you understand it is a dog. Millions of things you can <u>know</u>, understand to be dogs. You do not <u>see</u> "dog." You see color, shape, movements, etc. which you have become accustomed to know as "dog."

Intellectual knowing is both "is knowing" and "ought knowing." Whenever you know facts or theories you are affirming that something <u>is</u> or <u>is not</u>. "The United States landed men on the moon 30 years ago." "Orange juice is frequently a breakfast drink." "Today is the 22nd of July." This is "is thinking" the intelligence functioning as "speculative reason" (seeking insight into what is).

It is important to attend to the fact that you are also thinking intellectually when you are acting intelligently. "I don't feel right. I must/ought/should see my doctor." This is "ought thinking" and is the intelligence functioning as "practical" (doing).

Whenever you do "is thinking," exercising "speculative reason," you are in the order of being. And the first, ultimate principle of speculative reason is the principle of non-contradiction. "A thing cannot be and not be at one and the same time"—or "The same thing cannot be affirmed and denied of the same subject." It is impossible that you be sitting down and not sitting down. I simply cannot think, "Mary is my sister and is not my sister."

Obviously we do not explicitly invoke or attend to the principle of non-contradiction in our acts of knowledge. But we do so implicitly. For if we did not subscribe to that principle we could know nothing. If I did not implicitly invoke it, when I affirm, "The lights are on," it is possible they not be.

Whenever you do "ought-thinking" you are in the order of the "good," the order of what makes acting or doing worthwhile. "I don't feel right. I must/ought/should see my doctor." Seeing my doctor I understand as good, as worthwhile, as means to get well. I understand getting the plunger as "good," as worthwhile, as means to clear the sink.

As the principle of non-contradiction is the first principle of speculative reason, implicitly grounding every act of "is-thinking," so there is a first principle of practical reason, practical thinking. The very way we come to know things, actions, as good is in the light of this principle, "Good is to be done and pursued; evil is to be avoided." In the light of feeling strange I think of seeing my doctor as something "good," as what will take care of the way I feel. It is in the light of the same principle I think of the plunger as "good."

I simply cannot act intelligently without observing this first principle. The primary human goods are discovered by attending to basic human inclinations. Everyone has a natural inclination to preserve her or his life and everyone naturally forms the practical judgment, "Life is good and is to be preserved, indeed is to be pursued." Being in harmony with others everyone recognizes as good and everyone is naturally inclined to form the practical judgment, "Friendship is good and ought to be pursued." Of course, everyone likewise forms the opposite judgments, "Harm to life, harm to friendship, is to be avoided."

Thus the basic goods we have listed give content to the first principle of practical reason. These goods tell us what is-to-be-pursued and what is-to-be-avoided.

Before we even attempt the moral dimension in undertakings we are being directed by practical reason in terms of what can be done. Sean, concerned about his wife's suffering, considers that getting medical advice is good and to be pursued. He recalls that hospice care controls pain and attempts to make one's final days as worth living as possible and so is good. Richard's proposal of euthanasia is not proposed as bad but as a good means to relieve his mother's suffering.

The moral dimension leaps to mind: if always good is chosen, what constitutes immoral choosing? Sometimes we follow emotional goods rather than attending to real, intelligible goods. Hopefully they blend together, emotional and intelligible goods. The mother cuddling her child experiences the emotional desire to comfort and please her child, and knows doing so is really good, intelligibly good for child and herself. But if she allows the baby's insistence she be held by mother to keep her from surrendering the child to the nurse or doctor for needed care, she is allowing emotional good to prevent genuine, intelligible good.

In other situations we can choose one good, as Richard does, relief to his mother, at the expense of another good, her life. Or we can choose one's own or one's family's good, at the expense of somebody else's good. Wilfred cooperates with his boss's deceitful action to get rid of the foreman with the promise to have the foreman's job. "Nothing personal, you know. I'm just looking out for my family."

Whether I choose one or another of these actions I am acting in accord with the first principle of practical reason. Both Sean and his son, Richard, are acting intelligently and so in accord with "Good is to be done and pursued, evil is to be avoided." How, then, can we know which choices are morally good or bad?

Corresponding to the entire set of basic human goods is the entire set of principles of practical reasoning. Life is to be pursued, harm to life is to be avoided. Friendship is to be pursued, harm to friendship is to be avoided. And so of all the other basic human goods. Even immoral acts respond to some of these principles.

Clearly, then, no one of the principles of practical reason is a moral norm in itself. But all together they provide a moral norm. Some proposed actions are consistent with all these principles—as is Sean's decision to move his wife into hospice care. Others are consistent with one or some of these principles, but inconsistent with at least one—as is Richard's proposal of euthanasia in pursuit of the good of relieving his mother's pain.

What is needed is a first principle which bears precisely on choices among the basic human goods which provides standards for practical judgment. And in this way Grisez arrives at the same earlier formulation of the first principle of morality. As I rephrased it, "One ought always to choose in a way compatible with integral human fulfillment."

Notice the positive thrust to what is good—what is fulfilling not only to self, but to all people. Being morally good is not a matter primarily of avoiding evil, but of creating good.

MODES OF RESPONSIBILITY

The criterion of morality (inclusivistic or exclusivistic choosing) and the first principle of morality apply to absolutely every moral choice and action. A clear understanding of these two insights empowers one to assess specific moral principles, especially culturally assumed principles.

Why, for instance, is stealing wrong? Because it violates the good of friendship. Philip, tempted to finance his daughter's education by discreet undetectable withdrawals from the bank is pursuing something good: having money for his daughter is good. But he cannot have this money without hurting its owners—the bank and its depositors.

Again, owning and selling slaves was culturally acceptable. Only after centuries of such practices did we come to perceive the evil in slavery—of hurting other human persons, of violating the good of friendship.

However, the criterion and the first principle are so broad it can be very difficult to see how they apply to certain situations. Grisez has developed principles intermediate between the first principle of morality and specific principles such as "stealing, murder, perjury are wrong." He calls them Modes of Responsibility, so called because they shape and control moral responsibilities.

Two very distinctive features of Grisez's ethics are his careful identification of basic human goods and these Modes of Responsibility. Not distinctive but central to his position is the insight that nonintegrated emotional factors are what lead people to choose immorally, to choose in a way different from that in which they would choose if their reason were not affected by these feelings.

Each mode picks out a certain emotion or feeling and directs us not to allow it to lead us to make the wrong choice. Hence the modes are expressed negatively. But it is an attempt to exclude ways of choosing which are incompatible with integral human fulfillment, freeing the person to pursue IHF.

Grisez in *Christian Moral Principles* proceeds as a theologian to treat the Christian as committed in faith to Jesus Christ and called to transform morally good living into Christian living. As an aid Grisez studies the Beatitudes as Christ's directives for his followers and derives eight "Modes of Christian Response." Related to and derived from the Beatitudes, they transform (by no means negating) the eight Modes of Responsibility.

A student in an introductory course (a Daughter of St. Paul) paralleled the two sets of modes together with the Beatitudes. In the Appendix I simply duplicate her listings and if or when I invoke any of them I shall explain them and indicate how it is grounded in the first principle of morality in the reasoned formula or as what it becomes in the light of faith. The latter can be expressed: "To will those and only those possibilities which contribute to the integral human fulfillment being realized in the fulfillment of all things in Jesus."

CONCLUSION

The chapter opened with the question, "Why is the Immoral Immoral?" The Catechism's answer was supplemented by Pope John Paul II's profound explanation in the encyclical, *The Splendor of Truth*. Germain Grisez's more explicit reply complements both the above. The criterion of morality and the first principle of morality make clear why the immoral is immoral.

Now with these four chapters the reader is equipped to understand the treatment of the moral issues connected with life and sex.

In order to link what makes any act immoral with the specific issues to be treated, I conclude this chapter with Grisez's directives for approaching moral issues. All terms and insights have been explained above.

HOW TO APPROACH MORAL ISSUES
TWO STEPS

<u>FIRST STEP</u>

CLARIFY THE ACTION BY ANSWERING 2 QUESTIONS.

1. What impact will the action have on various instances of basic human goods either promoting or harming them in oneself and/or others?
   [Must go beyond impact on instrumental goods, such as property, liberty, and natural resources to see what is at stake for

those goods which are aspects of the being and flourishing of persons: life, truth, friendship, etc.]
2. Which elements of the action's impact are included precisely in what I will choose, if I choose to do the action or in the benefits I will anticipate, and which are neither included in the means or the end, but rather are part of what I will accept as side effects? In making a choice, a proposal is adopted to do something for the sake of some benefit. Morally speaking, what is done is the execution of the proposal adopted. Thus in making any choice, one chooses precisely the content of the proposal adopted and intends precisely the anticipated benefit.

But one also foresees effects other than the very carrying out of the choice and the benefits from doing so. These effects, foreseen but neither chosen nor intended, are side effects.

The difference between choosing a means, intending an end, and accepting side effects often is morally significant.

SECOND STEP

EVALUATE THE ACTION BY APPLYING MORAL PRINCIPLES: (the criterion of morality) the first principle of morality, the Modes of Responsibility, and the Modes of Christian Response.

Once the instances of basic goods on which an action bears and the voluntariness with which it bears on them are clearly understood, the action has been grasped precisely insofar as it is a moral act. Knowing clearly what is to be evaluated, one now must evaluate it by applying moral principles. (*Living A Christian Life*, 265)

++++++++

EXAMPLE: SEAN AND RICHARD

FIRST STEP

CLARIFY THE ACTION BY ANSWERING 2 QUESTIONS.
1. Sean's proposal to move his wife, Helen, into hospice care promotes the basic human good of (marital) friendship.

Richard's proposal of euthanasia is a choice to destroy the basic human good of life with the intention of pursuing the basic human good of (filial) friendship.

2. Sean explicitly chooses to pursue the good of (marital) friendship. Hospice care will relieve Helen's pain. Sean's choice expresses and is means to the good of (marital) friendship.

Richard chooses as means to pursue the good of (filial) friendship to destroy the good of life.

SECOND STEP

EVALUATE THE ACTION BY APPLYING MORAL PRINCIPLES.

Sean's choice is compatible with integral human fulfillment. It meets the criterion of morality: it is inclusivistic choosing. It does not violate any of the modes.

Richard's choice of means is exclusivistic choosing, for it goes against the good of life. It is not compatible with IHF for it violates the good of his mother's life. The eighth Mode of Responsibility is violated for he allows love of mother's relief to move him to violate her life. It also violates the eighth Mode of Christian Response.

PART TWO

CONTEMPORARY PROBLEMS: LIFE

CHAPTER 5

SUICIDE, ASSISTED SUICIDE: THE PROBLEM

To think philosophically about ethical issues is uncommon and difficult. But that is what is required when the specific moral principles undergirding accepted custom are called into question. From the distinctions pointed out regarding Ethos (custom), Ethics (specific moral principles), and Metaethics, it is easy to see the progression from the logical to the philosophical.

We dared to lead readers there, to ask what makes the immoral immoral. Choosing exclusivistically, choosing in a way incompatible with integral human fulfillment is what makes an act immoral. Immoral choosing affects personal fulfillment and when imbedded in community custom fulfillment of the society. Hence, it is important for personal and social happiness that we discover the truth about moral issues.

Four chapters of tough reading may not be sufficient for readers to feel assured they really have understood the fundamental ethics treated. As we apply this ethics to contemporary issues the reader may find it helpful, even necessary, to reexamine our opening four chapters.

Our first issue, assisted suicide, clearly resembles the situation of abortion before Roe v. Wade. Organized groups are seriously agitating to change people's attitude toward euthanasia and helping people to die—as well as their attitude toward long-established laws prohibiting assisted suicide.

We shall try to clarify the issue and the present legal status, the reaction of the medical profession as well as that of Congress. Readers should feel well informed on how unsettled the Ethos is on assisted suicide. Only then in Chapter 6 shall we address the moral issue involved.

Many factors are of concern in dealing with people in pain and close to death, but certainly people are conscious of the moral dimension in this issue. Since assisted suicide is the next step in the development of the "culture of death," it may help to let the moral dimension emerge within the legal and political situation.

ASSISTED SUICIDE, PRELUDE TO THE SUPREME COURT DECISION

What is happening in America's rush into the culture of death? Why this swift move to suicide and assisted suicide? With almost a million-and-a-half abortions each year, now a serious poll in April, 1996 found that 75% of Americans favor physician-assisted suicide. This figure is up from 65% in 1990 and 53% in 1973. This mercurial change of attitude toward killing is reflected in the ballot initiatives to permit physicians to assist terminally ill patients wanting to commit suicide. The initiatives failed in Washington and California in 1991 and 1992. But in 1994 Oregon voters passed a similar referendum. Dr. Jack Kevorkian has helped over 100 people to die, and yet has repeatedly been cleared of criminal charges in spite of Michigan's ban on assisted suicide. Finally, having gone one step further, and on television, he has been imprisoned.

A "sea change—overnight—in public policy" took place on this issue in two major court decisions, which, of course, the Supreme Court has reversed. Keep in mind that 32 states have formal, explicit bans on assisted suicide, and virtually all the remaining states prohibit it through court decisions or through implications of criminal statutes. Oregon alone, and just eight years ago, has passed a law permitting assisted suicide. Then in March of 1996 in San Francisco the United States Court of Appeals for the Ninth Circuit struck down Washington's law banning assisted suicide by an 8 to 3 decision.

The majority vote relied on the constitutional "liberty" reasoning articulated in the 1992 Supreme Court's reaffirmation of a woman's right to choose abortion in *Planned Parenthood v Casey*. What is that "liberty"? "At the heart of liberty is the right to define one's own concept of existence, of meaning, of the universe, and of the mystery of human life." (*Casey*, 505 U.S., at 851) That freedom, the Ninth Court of Appeals stated, applies likewise to the terminally ill, mentally competent adult's right to have physicians assist their efforts to kill themselves. Thus the court stresses, "the compelling similarities between right-to-die cases and abortion cases" made Casey "a powerful precedent for physician-assisted suicide."

One month later, April 2, 1996 a three judge panel of the Second Court of Appeals ruled that doctors could legally help terminally ill patients commit suicide, striking down parts of a long-standing New York State ban on assisted suicide. This court found justification for its decision, not in the abortion-rights precedent, but in the Fourteenth Amendment's equal protection clause.

If terminally ill patients on life support systems are allowed to hasten their deaths by directing the removal of such systems, they should be allowed to hasten their deaths by self-administering prescribed drugs. This amazing failure to recognize the difference between choosing to permit death to occur and choosing to cooperate formally in direct killing will be addressed later.

The Supreme Court overturned these two decisions. Still states may indeed ban assisted suicide, if they so wish.

KIND OF LEGAL THINKING IN THE LOWER COURTS

Before developing what is at issue the importance of these two Circuit Court decisions warrants mention. Although the decisions by the two Circuit Courts of Appeal focused very narrowly on competent, terminally ill adults, their extreme importance extends far wider. The Washington state case was "the first right-to-die case…any …federal court of appeals has ever decided." Their importance likewise stands out inasmuch as it is clearly the first step toward approval of euthanasia. As Circuit Judge Beezer in his dissent warns, "If physician-assisted suicide for mentally competent, terminally ill adults is made a constitutional right, voluntary euthanasia for weaker patients, unable to self-terminate, will soon follow. After voluntary euthanasia, it is but a short step to a 'substituted judgment' or 'best interests' analysis for terminally ill patients who have not yet expressed their constitutionally sanctioned desire to be dispatched from this world. This is the sure and inevitable path, as the Dutch experience has amply demonstrated." (*Compassion in Dying* v. State of Washington, Ninth Court of Appeals, 857)

Keenly aware that we are not competent to attempt a critique of legal decisions, we limit ourselves to some obvious intellectual problems these lower court decisions generate and to reaction to some principles invoked by the courts.

"DUE PROCESS CLAUSE" OR "EQUAL PROTECTION CLAUSE"

The Ninth Circuit Court bases its position explicitly on the "Due Process Clause" of the Fourteenth Amendment, declaring that "a liberty interest exists in the choice of how and when one dies." This "liberty interest" is at times referred to as a "right-to-die" and as "the right to physician-assisted suicide."

Acknowledging that others are free to believe "that death must come without physician assistance" the tone of the majority opinion becomes almost angry as it goes on to say, "They are not free… to force their views, their religious convictions, or their philosophies on all the other members of a democratic society." (Ibid. 839)

That these judges find a constitutional "right-to-die" and seem indignant that those who disagree might be substituting religion or philosophy seems strange when a three-judge panel of the same Ninth Circuit Court had earlier overturned the opinion of the Chief District Judge striking down Washington State's law by declaring, "There is no due process liberty interest in physician-assisted suicide." Stranger still when the Second Court of Appeals, a few weeks after the Ninth Court's decision bluntly states, "There is no fundamental right to assisted suicide, even in the very limited cases of mentally competent persons, who in final stages of terminal illness, seek the right to hasten death." (*Federal Reporter*, 3rd Series) Later on we read, "Clearly, no 'right' to assisted suicide has ever been recognized in any state in the United States." "The right to assisted suicide finds no cognizable basis in the Constitution's language or design, even in the very limited cases of those competent persons who, in the final stages of terminal illness, seek the right to hasten death. We therefore decline the plaintiff's invitation to identify a new fundamental right, in the absence of a clear direction from the Court whose precedents we are bound to follow." (Ibid. 724) And as we shall see, the Supreme Court confront and deny the Ninth Circuit Court's position. Why their indignation?

Of interest, yet no surprise, the Ninth Court builds on Roe v Wade which established liberty interest in having or not having an abortion. As there is a right to abortion, so there is a right to die. The conclusion in Roe v Wade and the Ninth Court case is the same—and the reasoning is the same.

In their final point they build the case for patients having the right to make their own decisions about matters so highly "central to personal dignity and autonomy." They link this with the established legal right to hasten one's death by refusing medical treatment. And by implication they assume the arguments equally justify physician assistance for suicide.

This final factor in the decision striking down Washington State's prohibition of assisted suicide opens into the pivotal argument by the New York Second Circuit Court. The majority position of the Ninth Court absolutely denies any difference between assisted suicide and withholding or withdrawing life support systems or/and administering pain relief, well aware this will hasten death.

"More specifically, we see little, if any, difference for constitutional or ethical purposes between providing medication with a double effect and providing medication with a single effect, as long as one of the known effects in each case is to hasten the end of the patient's life. Similarly we see no ethical or constitutionally cognizable difference between a doctor's pulling the plug on a respirator and his prescribing drugs which will permit a terminally ill patient to end his own life." (Ibid. 824)

As reported above, the Second Court explicitly and definitively denied there is any constitutional right to assisted-suicide. However, they appealed to the Equal Protection Clause of the Fourteenth Amendment to strike down New York's statute banning assisted-suicide.

Having shown that suicide ceased to be a crime, though still "a grave public wrong," and later not even a "grave public wrong," the Court reports that New York continued to treat assisted-suicide as a crime. However, even this was chipped away: "After these cases were decided, the New York legislature placed its imprimatur upon the right of competent citizens to hasten death by refusing medical treatment and by directing physicians to remove life-support systems already in place." And in this specific case, Quill v. Vacco, "The New York statutes criminalizing assisted suicide violate the Equal Protection Clause." "New York does not treat similarly circumstanced persons alike in that those in final stages of terminal illness who are on life-support systems are allowed to hasten their deaths by directing the removal of such systems, but those who are similarly situated....are not allowed to hasten death by self-administered prescribed drugs." And indeed, "the state does not have any apparent interest in requiring the prolongation of a life that is all but ended." (*Federal Reporter*, 3rd Series, "Quill v. Vacco," 717)

REACTION OF MEDICAL PROFESSION

In 1996 the American Medical Association confronted the decisions of the Ninth Circuit Court and the Second Circuit Court of Appeals. Despite the courts' ringing support for physician assisted-suicide, the AMA voted overwhelmingly to continue to oppose the practice.

Nancy W. Dickey, M.D., chairperson of the AMA Board of Trustees insisted, "It's important to recognize that there's a difference between law and ethics." Observing that the AMA expects physicians to obey laws, she went on, "But we may require a higher standard than the law." (*A. M. NEWS*. "Association Stands Firm in Opposition to Suicide," 1996)

Among the impassioned testimonies against physician participation was the charge that the decisions were "a breath-taking example of judicial malpractice." "Physicians," Dr. Rex Greene of California declared, "must not allow the legal profession to define our ethical parameters." (Ibid.)

Although those speaking for maintaining the AMA's position against assisted-suicide were 10 to 1, earnest voices were raised to change the policy. Dr. David Carter, past president of the Rhode Island Medical Society, supports assisted-suicide; he urged the AMA to reexamine the issue. The vote at this year's meeting was on a proposal that the AMA take a stand of neutrality on the issue. Carter asked, "What business is it of organized medicine to require the continuation of agony when the result (of death) is imminent and inevitable?"

Incidentally in 1996 Carter's Rhode Island Medical Society became the third state medical group to stand neutral on this issue of assisted-suicide. The other two states are Michigan and Oregon.

Two other reported items hint at serious divisions among physicians. Ulrich Danckers, M.D. challenged the delegates, "It is intellectually dishonest for us to collectively get on our high moral horse by declaring the practice unethical and then look the other way when our members in ever-larger numbers quietly endorse the practice at the bedside."

Warning that he spoke "for many more delegates than meets the eye" he explained he felt more free to speak than most inasmuch as this was his last year as a delegate. Others, he explained were afraid to speak out against the board's position "for fear of being tainted with the same brush the board has used against Dr. Kevorkian."

The second suggestive item was the vote of the Young Physicians Section. Yes, they remained supportive of the present AMA's position on assisted suicide, but asked the AMA Council on Ethical and Judicial Affairs to discuss a number of principles as they reviewed the physician's role in end-of-life treatment. For example, the physician's responsibility to preserve one's "quality of life," and not necessarily just to preserve or sustain life. (Ibid.)

Under the editorial title "Ethicide" *American Medical News*, April 6, 1996 begins with, "Wrong messages about physician assisted suicide were delivered in two courtrooms recently." It was referring to the jury in Pontiac, Michigan that found Jack Kevorkian innocent on charges of assisting in two suicides. The other courtroom was the Ninth Circuit Court of Appeals we have treated.

"We can't recall a time when medical ethics has suffered such a damaging series of blows in rapid succession." In the editor's judgment these decisions undermine medicine's most fundamental principle: First, do no harm.

What was found truly disturbing was the implication of the majority decision of the Ninth Circuit Court that medical ethics rest on judicial interpretation.

Nor did the editor miss what is in many minds. "All of this comes at a time when profits and cost containment are already putting pressure on other ethical standards in medicine." Certainly physicians must be trusted by patients as their advocates—not cooperators with those claiming that some patients are needlessly "taking up space." Judge Reinhart, in his majority opinion, dismissed such "slippery slope" arguments. But the substantial minority report links all this with the Netherlands' experience of euthanasia.

There can be little doubt that physicians have been forced to think hard about assisted-suicide and what is next down the road. Gary Lee, M.D., one of the doctors who challenged the law legalizing assisted-suicide recently passed in Oregon, expressed distress at the Ninth Court's decision. Insisting on the real difference between withdrawing non-beneficial care from dying patients and assisted-suicide, this oncologist and hospice director takes a very strong stand. "If you can't see the ethical distinction between withdrawing futile, non-beneficial treatment and actively engaging in someone's demise, then this clearly indicates to me the court knows too little about the profession of medicine to rule on it." (*A. M. NEWS*, "Support for Assisted Suicide," March 25, 1996)

CONGRESSIONAL REACTIONS

Such questioning of the court's role prompted Charles T. Canady (R, FL), Subcommittee chairman of the House Judiciary to arrange the nation's first congressional hearing on assisted-suicide. Disturbed by the recent California and New York based federal appeals courts striking down laws against assisted-suicide, he explained," With no national debate these courts are attempting to implement a broad public policy that would profoundly affect the way Americans deal with life and death, and drastically alter the role of physicians in our society."(*A. M. NEWS*, 1996, "Bill Prohibits Federal Funding for Suicide Assistance")

Reaction to all this movement toward assisted-suicide evoked another congressional proposal. Rep. Dave Camp (R,Mich.) introduced a bill to ban federal funding for assisting suicide. Both the Ninth Circuit Court of Appeals' decision and the statement by Oregon Medicaid's director motivated Camp. The director stated that if assisted suicide law goes into effect then Medicaid funds would cover it.

Expressing regret that Camp's bill is necessary, Burke Balche of the National Right to Life Committee sounded an alarm. He calls attention to a footnote and a few lines in the text of the decision which have frightening possibilities. Although the decision focuses upon the mentally competent adult terminally ill, the very language indicates that "decisions made by 'surrogates' to kill their incompetent wards are constitutionally protected." (Ibid.)

First, the footnote, #120, relates to the court's recognition that physician-assisted suicide and physician-administered medication are closely related. The court limits its decision to the former, the latter "must be answered directly in future cases, not in this one." To be candid, they look on the critical dividing line in "right-to-die" cases "as the one between the voluntary and involuntary termination of an individual's life."

The footnote distinguishes various meanings of euthanasia and ends, "Finally, we should make it clear that a decision of a duly appointed surrogate decision maker is for all legal purposes the decision of the patient himself."

As for the text, summarizing their positions that there is a "constitutionally recognized 'right-to-die'" the court observes, "Our conclusion is strongly influenced by, but not limited to, the plight of mentally competent, terminally ill adults. We are influenced as well by the plight of others, such as those whose existence is reduced to a vegetative state or a permanent and irreversible state of unconsciousness." (*Compassion in Dying*, 816)

How well grounded Balche's warning is! In fact Chief Justice Rehnquist calls attention to this same problem, referring to it as the Court's "expansive reasoning...(which) provide(s) ample support for the State's concern." He likewise notes the Ninth Circuit Court's statement which worries Balche: "the decision of a duly appointed surrogate decision maker is for all legal purposes the decision of the patient himself." Again, "in some instances the patient may be unable to self administer the drugs and... administration by the physician may be the only way the patient may be able to receive them." Indeed family members and loved ones "will inevitably participate in assisting suicide." ("Washington v. Glucksberg")

The decisions favoring assisted suicide by the Ninth and then the Second Court of Appeals were immediately challenged and brought to the United States Supreme Court which overturned both.

THE UNITED STATES SUPREME COURT

The battle about assisted suicide has really only begun. The Supreme Court decision on assisted suicide by no means settled the issue. The United States Supreme Court heard arguments January 8, 1997 on assisted suicide and on June 26, 1997 decided that the Constitution does not prohibit states from banning assisted suicide.(Washington, et al.. . . . v. Harold Glucksberg et al., 1997. In *The United States Law Week*, June 24, 1997)

Chief Justice Rehnquist "delivered the opinion of the Court." All nine judges concurred, but Justice J. O'Connor and Justice J. Stevens wrote concurring opinions which provide solid constitutional grounds for proposing more refined laws for assisted suicide.

The Court first addressed the Washington state law banning assisted suicide. This law had been declared unconstitutional by the Ninth Circuit Court of Appeals, in violation of the Due Process Clause of the Fourteenth Amendment: "the Constitution encompasses a due process liberty interest in controlling the time and manner of one's death. . .there is, in short, a constitutionally recognized 'right to die.'"

In reply, Chief Justice Rehnquist first points out, "In almost every State—indeed, in almost every western democracy—it is a crime to assist a suicide. . .Our laws have consistently condemned, and continue to prohibit, assisting suicide." (Ibid. 4671)

As for the constitutional claim, Rehnquist identifies "the question before us" as "whether the 'liberty' specially protected by the Due Process Clause includes a right to commit suicide which itself includes a right to assistance in doing so." His answer, concurred in by all nine justices, is, "We are confronted with a consistent and almost universal tradition that has long rejected the asserted right, and continues explicitly to reject it today, even for terminally ill, mentally competent adults."

The attempt by the Ninth Circuit Court to deny any significant difference between refusing unwanted medical treatment which hastens death and the choice "to hasten impending death by consuming lethal medication" is rejected: "the two acts are widely and reasonably regarded as quite distinct," and the latter "has never enjoyed. . .legal protection" similar to "the long legal tradition protecting" the former.

As previously noted, appeal to *Casey* was influential in the reasoning of the Ninth Circuit Court. "Like the decision of whether or not to have an abortion, the decision how and when to die is one of 'the most intimate and personal choices a person may make in a lifetime,' a choice 'central to personal dignity and autonomy.'" Again, and very pertinently, "At the heart of liberty is the right to define one's own concept of existence, of meaning. . .and of the mystery of human life."

Chief Justice Rehnquist counters, "Many of the rights and liberties protected by the Due Process Clause sound in personal autonomy does not warrant the sweeping conclusion that any and all important, intimate, and personal decisions are so protected."(Ibid. 4676) In view of the history of law decisions about assisted suicide, namely rejection, he reasons that the asserted right to assistance in committing suicide is not a fundamental liberty protected by the Due Process Clause. He claims the State has an interest in protecting vulnerable groups like the poor, the elderly, the disabled from abuse, neglect and mistakes. The Supreme Court recognized the genuine risk of subtle coercion and undue influence on such groups. The Court likewise views with concern the opening to euthanasia the Ninth Court formulations provided. The example of the practice of euthanasia in the Netherlands is noted. (Ibid. 4677)

After declaring that the Washington law does not violate the Fourteenth Amendment, the Court suggests "the earnest and profound debate about the morality, legality and practicality of physician assisted suicide. . .continue." Thus the door to assisted suicide is not firmly closed. (Ibid. 4678)

The Court next addresses explicitly the New York law forbidding assisted suicide. The Court of Appeals for the Second Circuit found that this law violated the Equal Protection Clause. New York allows some patients in the final stages of terminal illness "to hasten their deaths" by directing the removal of life-supporting systems. But others likewise in the final stages of fatal illness are not "allowed to hasten death by self-administering prescribed drugs." Incidentally, recall that this Second Circuit Court acknowledges that New York's statutes "do not impinge on any fundamental rights"—contrary to the Ninth Circuit Court's rejection of the Washington law banning assisted suicide. (1997 WL34807, p. 3)

The Supreme Court reversed that decision of the Court of Appeals for the Second Circuit. Acknowledging that the Equal Protection Clause "embodies a general rule that States must treat like cases alike but may treat unlike cases accordingly," the Court denies that removing life-support systems and assisted suicide are alike. Not only do they refer to standard medical acceptance of and insistence on the distinction but they explain how those removing life-support systems "intend, or may so intend" (The qualification is necessary in view of Justice Stevens' claim, to be repeated later) benefit, not harm to the patient but to assist at suicide a doctor "must, necessarily and indubitably, intend primarily that the patient be made dead." ("Primarily" is also important in view of what Justice Stevens holds.) (Ibid. 5)

What about "aggressive palliative care"? Yes, "in some cases, painkilling drugs may hasten a patient's death, but the physician's purpose and intent is, or may be, only to ease his patient's pain." (Ibid.)

In a footnote, reference is made to the principle of double effect. Representatives of the State of New York insist "the concept of sedating psychotherapy is based on informed consent and the principle of double effect." Another important point is made in another footnote, "Thus, the Second Circuit erred in reading New York law as creating a 'right to hasten death.'" It recognized a right to refuse treatment, never equating this with suicide.

Concurring Opinions: Grounds for Assisted Suicide

While all nine justices concurred in the decision, Justice O'Connor refers to the Due Process Clause (appealed to in the Ninth Circuit Court's decision that Washington's law banning suicide violated the Constitution). She agrees that there is no "generalized right to 'commit suicide,'" but anticipates that the democratic process will eventually craft procedures for safeguarding liberty interests, providing for individuals seeking to end their suffering, and "the State's interests in protecting those who might seek to end life mistakenly or under pressure." (Ibid. 9)

Justice Stevens goes much further. Agreeing with the decision that "Washington's statute prohibiting assisted suicide is not invalid. . . in all or most cases. . ." he points out that this position "does not foreclose the possibility that some applications of the statute might well be invalid." In general, assisted suicide will be found a violation of the Washington law, but some instances may not be. (Ibid.)

He, like Justice O'Connor, recognizes that the Due Process Clause has application in this issue. Putting it negatively Stevens states, "I fully agree with the Court that the 'liberty' protected by the Due Process Clause does not include a categorical 'right to commit suicide which itself includes a right to assistance in doing so.'" To him clearly "there are situations in which an interest in hastening death is legitimate." Indeed at times "it is entitled to constitutional protection." (Ibid. 10)

Building on the Court's decision in the Cruzan case, Stevens, as does the Ninth Circuit Court, invokes Casey: "Avoiding intolerable pain and the indignity of living one's final days incapacitated. . .is certainly '(a)t [sic] the heart of [the] liberty. . .to define one's own concept of existence, of meaning, of the universe and of the mystery of human life.'" (Ibid. 12)

After countering any thought that the State's legitimate interests excludes all assisted suicide, Justice Stevens turns to the New York State case, which invoked the Equal Protection Clause. He concurs with the Court decision that this clause "is not violated by the resulting disparate treatment of two classes of terminally ill people." Yes, the distinction between permitting death and causing death "provides a constitutionally sufficient basis for the State's classification." However, he challenges that "in all cases there will be in fact a significant difference between the intent of the physicians, the patients or the families in the two situations." (Ibid. 14)

For Stevens, the intention of the patient directing removal of life-support system and of the patient seeking physician assistance to end his/her life may have little distinction: in both cases "the patient is seeking to hasten a certain and impending death." The same is true of the doctor prescribing "lethal medication" or/and terminating life support. The intent might well be the same, namely to hasten death.

On the other hand, the physician prescribing medication which is lethal "does not necessarily intend the patient's death—rather that doctor may seek simply to ease the patient's suffering." To argue his point, Stevens reminds us that the American Medical Association approves "terminal sedation"— i.e. dosage of painkilling drugs sufficient to alleviate pain even if clearly it will hasten death. What is the purpose? To ease the suffering. What is the actual cause of death? "(T)he administration of heavy doses of lethal sedatives." Stevens claims this "same intent and causation may exist when a doctor complies with a patient's request for lethal medication to hasten her death." (Ibid.)

Accordingly, the majority notes differences in the intent and the causation between withdrawing life-support and assisting the patient to commit suicide. The differences do support the Court's rejection that the State may not ban assisted suicide, but they may not be applicable to individual terminally ill persons.

Stevens's principal point (and what will fuel the assisted suicide movement) is that this decision of the Supreme Court that laws banning suicide are not violations of the Equal Protection Clause or of the Due Process Clause, "does not mean that every possible application of the statute would be valid." An interest in hastening death may not only, in particular situations, be legitimate, "but. . .there are times when it is entitled to constitutional protection." Our decision "does not foreclose the possibility that some applications of the New York statute may impose an intolerable intrusion on the patient's freedom." (Ibid. 15)

Justice Breyer concurs but explains how he differs from the Court. The Court described the liberty claimed as a "right to commit suicide with another's assistance." Another formulation merits consideration, a "right to die with dignity." However worded, "at its core would lie personal control over the manner of death, professional medical assistance, and the avoidance of unnecessary and severe physical suffering—combined." (Ibid.)

Careful attention to the pecisely reasoned positions of Chief justice Rehnquist and Justice Stevens sharpens the issue. (Rehnquist v. Stevens, p. 114)

Rehnquist v. Stevens

Chief Justice Rehnquist brings attention to this profound difference. "A doctor who assists a suicide...'must, necessarily and indubitably, intend primarily that the patient be made dead.' " (In contrast with permitting death)

This necessity is denied by Justice Stevens. But to situate the problem it helps to keep in mind another disputed fact. Rehnquist writes that in refusing life sustaining treatment a patient "dies from an underlying fatal disease or pathology." But when a patient takes lethal medication, "he is killed by that medication." (Ibid. 5)

Stevens counters by bringing up terminal sedation which hastens death. Granted the purpose or intention of the physician may be to ease the suffering, "the actual cause of death is the administration of heavy doses of lethal sedatives." Thus, the distinction Rehnquist appeals to—namely the causation of death—stands challenged. It served Rehnquist's purpose which is to show a real difference between removing life support and assisted suicide. But Stevens uses the alternate comparison and distinction, heavy dosage of relief medication chosen to relieve pain which at the same time hastens death and assisted suicide. In this case the causation is the same—the medication. (Ibid. 14)

To meet the challenge it is essential to insist that action, causation, from a moral view is not identical with physical causation. When a woman shoots a life-threatening intruder, she psychologically "intends" that the bullet hit the intruder. Morally she normally "intends" to protect herself and her children. Once again, the action, what she does, is the execution of the proposal chosen. That this is a real and significant difference can be shown by comparing her reaction and that of a hired assassin. As explained before, if the person shot continues to live, the assassin shoots again, for he/she intended the first time to kill. The woman, confident her goal of self-defense has been achieved, calls 911.

The intruder, perhaps, dies—from the action of the shooting. But killing was not the moral act she chose to perform.

In reply to Stevens, yes, the physical cause of the patient's hastened death is the administration of the "sedating pharmacotherapy." But the moral action is a pain-relieving action.

As stated above, Stevens denies Rehnquist's claim that a doctor assisting the suicide "must, necessarily and indubitably, intend that the patient be made dead." As Stevens sees it, "A doctor who prescribes lethal medication does not necessarily intend the patient's death—rather that doctor may seek simply to ease the patient's suffering." (Ibid. 14)

Subtle but objective intellectual analysis is required. In ambiguous cases (double-effect cases) one must answer two questions: What am I doing? Why am I doing it? No "why" can change what one is doing from an immoral to a morally good act. Keeping this distinction in mind can help distinguish what I do as means to a desired end and what I foresee as a consequence of what I do and permit.

John and Jim, physicians and brothers, discuss what to do to relieve their dying mother's suffering. Why they will do whatever they do clearly is agreed upon, relieve mother's suffering. John suggests a massive overdose of morphine. He wants to kill her as the means to get her out of her suffering. Jim, equally committed to the same "why"—to relieve the mother—says, "No. Let's move her into Hospice Care where relief of suffering can be provided." Same intention, same "why" aimed at, two different "what's" to be done.

Stevens seems to have so focused on the "why" a doctor acts -"to ease the patient's suffering"—that he dismisses the question, "<u>What</u> am I, is he, doing?" Both questions must be answered. As is evident in the example of John and Jim, the same answer to why, the same benefit prompting action, may bring about different actions. And if <u>what</u> I am doing is harming life, no "why" changes that.

Well, how do you know whether what you are doing is harmful itself as a means to achieve the good or is beneficial with consequences harmful to life, foreseen and permitted? Look to the content of the proposal you choose and which you are contemplating executing.

The doctor who prescribes lethal medication has, after deliberation, chosen the proposal to kill—yes as means to relieve suffering, but nonetheless a proposal to kill. So Rehnquist is correct, in such an action the doctor "necessarily and indubitably must intend primarily that the patient be made dead."

The doctor who chooses the proposal to administer a heavy dosage necessary to relieve the pain may well foresee and accept the consequence that death will be hastened. What he or she is doing is easing the suffering. The effect of shortening the patient's life is not part of his or her proposal, not part of what he or she is doing.

Stevens is on target, however, when he "worries" this issue of "intending." He draws attention to the fact that the terminally ill patient asking that the life support be removed may "intend to hasten a certain, impending death." Thus the patient can have the same intention as the one who seeks assisted suicide. The doctor removing the life-support system can similarly be choosing to hasten the patient's death like the doctor assisting the suicide.

Chief Justice Rehnquist provides for such possibility by qualifying what the physician intends. The physician withdrawing life-support "purposely intends, or may so intend, only to respect his patient's wishes..." (Emphasis added) The same when aggressive pain relief is involved, "the physician's purpose and intent is, or may be, only to ease his patient's pain." (Emphasis added)

From a moral point of view, the traditional approach was to scrutinize an action according to 1) the nature of the act, 2) the end and 3) the circumstances. All three must be in accord with moral criteria. So that the immorality of any one aspect rendered the action immoral. The corrupt political leader makes giving alms to the poor immoral by his intention to "buy" their votes. To accept the gift of a kitten because your roommate is allergic to cats is immoral.

Actions which can be objectively, genuinely analyzed as a good kind of action can be made bad by interpreting it differently. A policeman, for example, having injured his assailant in self-defense can say, "I had to injure/kill him in order to protect myself." If it was legitimate use of that amount and kind of force necessary to defend himself, the action, what he did, need not be so analyzed—injuring or killing as means to self-defense. Normally expressing himself that way may simply be inaccurate due to lack of sophistication. For normally a policeman would mean that he did what was necessary to defend himself. Evidence is that, again normally, he would call for an ambulance if he found the assailant no longer a threat but still living.

On the other hand, police policy might have been correctly established and so taught and understood, but a particular policeman might like hurting people and so "follow" policy but intend hurting or killing an assailant.

Dr. Preston, mentioned above, might well have limited himself to prescribing only what is accepted dosage for relieving pain out of fear of the law, but very much intended to hasten the death of his patients.

So Justice Stevens is correct when he claims the dying patient can/may intend to hasten his or her death by having life-support removed and so intend what the suicide seeking assistance intends. But that only reveals how an action good in itself can be made bad. While no why, no good intention can change a bad action into a good one (The end does not justify the means), a bad why, a bad intention can change a good action into a bad one.

If, as seems clear, actions capable of alleviating pain are morally good, they cease to be morally good when a patient or a doctor employs them with the intention of hastening death. Accordingly, Stevens really has it backwards: suicide is a choice to kill oneself. Assisting suicide is a choice to ensure death occurs. To use action capable of doing good, easing pain, in order or as a means to hasten death, makes those actions killing actions. From a moral point of view all of these actions are immoral. From a legal point of view, while suicide is no longer classified as illegal, assisted suicide does violate the law. Hence, to use actions, legally justifiable (easing pain, removing life-support) with the intention to hasten death, to help oneself or another to kill him or herself, may not constitute a violation of the law; it remains immoral.

A very long aside, for we are not addressing the legal issue of assisted suicide, but the moral issue. Coming to grips with pivotal differences among the Justices helps in understanding the distinctions necessary in the moral treatment.

Nothing in the Constitution prevents States from prohibiting assisted suicide. Hence there is no constitutional right to commit suicide or to have medical assistance to do so. Still, statutes forbidding assisted suicide may possibly be found in violation of the rights of some individuals in certain conditions. Hence, as the chapter began, "The battle about assisted suicide has really only begun."

CONCLUSION

Obviously the problem of assisted-suicide is very real as a legal, a practical, a moral issue. In the next chapter we shall offer a reasoned position on each.

Assisted suicide is the first moral issue to which we shall apply the moral approach explained in Chapters 3 and 4. The mounting pressure to allow physicians to help terminally ill patients kill themselves—opening into the Netherlands' quagmire of euthanasia—makes evident the urgency of the task. The United States Supreme Court has ruled that prohibition of assisted suicide by state laws, traditionally taken for granted, is warranted by our Constitution.

There is, then, no constitutional right to commit suicide. At the same time the Court suggests that "the earnest and profound debate about the morality, legality and practicality of physician-assisted suicide. . .continue."

The kind of problems raised and the kind of arguments proposed both in the lower courts and the Supreme Court prepare us for the next chapter. Is it ever morally justifiable to kill oneself or others? What is critical is the difference between choosing to kill and choosing to permit dying.

CHAPTER 6

SUICIDE, ASSISTED SUICIDE—REASONED AND CATHOLIC RESPONSE

It is sobering to realize that the Ninth Circuit Court of Appeals as well as the Second take for granted that our Constitution sees nothing wrong in choosing to kill—oneself or another. The Supreme Court denies that there is any constitutional right to die but urges national debate on "morality, legality and practicality of physician assisted suicide."

KIERKEGAARD, SUICIDE AND NEO-PAGANISM

Our country's swift embrace of the culture of death, startling as it is in one sense, should not have surprised us. When the Supreme Court decided *Roe v Wade* many saw the handwriting on the wall. To kill the unborn will lead to assisted suicide, which will lead to voluntary active euthanasia, which will lead to non-voluntary and involuntary euthanasia. The intermediate step, assisted suicide, is now pushing onto the world's stage.

Although an extraordinarily high percentage of Americans profess belief in God, such belief seems not to inform their morals. Secular Humanism appears to energize their morals—in judgment, if not always in conduct.

Excessive exaltation of freedom (people are to control their lives more and more) joins with secular humanism to fuel the movement to kill at the terminal part of life, following success of the movement to kill as life begins. Secular humanism exalts human beings, denying the existence of God. It is not coincidence that with the ascendancy of secular humanism's influence the thrust to suicide and assisted suicide is growing so strong.

Søren Kierkegaard, the father of existentialism, linked suicide among pagans with their lack of belief in God and in human dependence on God. As we revert to paganism, the right to personal suicide is being demanded. This, Kierkegaard declares, is the most common form of despair, despair which is unconscious that it *is* despair.

"Paganism as it historically was and is, and paganism within Christendom, is precisely this sort of despair." (*Sickness unto Death*, in Bretall, *A Kierkegaard Anthology*, 347) He acknowledges that amazing exploits were performed by pagans, yet asserts, "Every human existence which is not conscious of itself before God as spirit, every human existence which is not thus grounded transparently in God. . .or which takes its faculties merely as active powers, without being conscious whence it has them. . .every such existence is after all despair." (op. cit. 348) Because the pagan was (is) not conscious of himself before God as spirit, "Hence it came about that the pagan judged self-slaughter so lightly, yea, even praised it, notwithstanding that for the spirit it is the most decisive sin, that to break out of existence in this way is rebellion against God." (Ibid.)

The pagan, lacking the God-relationship and sense of the self, looks on suicide as something indifferent, "a thing every man may do if he likes, because it concerns nobody else. . .The point in self-slaughter, that it is a crime against God, entirely escapes the pagan." (Ibid. 349)

At this point Kierkegaard crystallizes the relationship between absence of belief in God, suicide and despair. "One cannot say, therefore, that self-slaughter was despair. . .one must say that the fact that the pagan judged self-slaughter as he did was despair."

The great Danish thinker alarmingly distinguishes paganism before and within Christendom. "[P]aganism, though to be sure it lacks spirit, is definitely oriented in the direction of spirit, whereas paganism within Christendom lacks spirit with a direction away from it or by way of apostasy, and hence in the strictest sense is spiritlessness." (Ibid. 348)

The handwriting has been and still is on the wall. And Americans in this culture of death are in despair. A friend, confined to bed for years with multiple sclerosis, was recently treated for depression by a psychiatrist. As the medicine began to work, he bubbled, "I didn't know I was depressed." Americans need religious medication to rediscover the goodness of life and to break out of the despair they are living in, unaware of their condition.

Life, Love, and Sex

Use of the expression, "handwriting on the wall" relates to the Bible and the message is sobering. The Chaldean King, Belshazzar is reported to have angered God by his pride, ignoring that "the Most High God rules the kingdom of men" and by sacrilegious use of the sacred vessels pillaged from the temple in Jerusalem in worship of false gods. In the midst of the banquet, "the fingers of a human hand appeared, writing on the plaster of the wall. . ." Daniel interpreted the writing for the terrified king. " 'Mene,—God has numbered the days of your kingdom and brought it to an end. Tekel,—you have been weighed in the balance and found wanting. Peres,—your kingdom is divided and given to the Medes and the Persians.' That very night Belshazzar. . .was slain." (Daniel, 5)

How much of the writing on our wall parallels the biblical source? As with abortion, the debate is not directly about suicide and assisted-suicide, but about underlying presuppositions, in our case, belief in God and no belief in God, about our being totally free owners of our lives or our being stewards of our lives, serving the Lord God Almighty.

The moral question has emerged from discussion on laws banning assisted suicide. Present "Ethics" or customary practice, at least technically, excludes assisted suicide.

Undergirding this "Ethics" is the moral principle that assisting in suicide is immoral. Many intelligent, caring persons are pushing to change the law and to establish the custom of helping people to die. These advocates of change obviously assume that it is morally justifiable to kill oneself and to assist others to kill themselves.

We are ready to address directly the questions: Is it morally justifiable to kill oneself? Is it morally justifiable to help someone kill him or herself?

MORALITY OF SUICIDE AND ASSISTED SUICIDE

CATECHISM OF THE CATHOLIC CHURCH

Fifteen state attorneys general filed suit with the United States Supreme Court which prompted review of the Second Circuit Court of Appeals which struck down New York's law banning assisted suicide. Not only was the decision reversed, but as Nancy W. Dickey, MD, Chair of the AMA Board of Trustees stated in reaction to the New York decision, "It's important to recognize that there's a difference between law and ethics."

Laws are, from an ethical point of view, required to be in accord with morality. By no means, however, ought everything morally good or bad be legally prescribed or proscribed. But whatever is legally approved ought to be morally right. So much is this the case that many, many people assume that what is legal is morally justifiable. Law is a most important moral educator. Hence the need to argue the morality of assisted suicide.

The fifth commandment, "You shall not kill" expresses the Church's position on killing. "Human life is sacred because from its beginning it involves the creative action of God and it remains for ever in a special relationship with the Creator, who is its sole end. God alone is the Lord of life from its beginning until its end; no one can under any circumstances claim for himself the right directly to destroy an innocent human being." (*Donum Vitae*," Intro. 5, in *Cat* . #2258)

Just what is forbidden by the fifth commandment? Direct and intentional killing. Not only the murderer but also those who cooperate voluntarily in murder are guilty of grave sin.

Obviously suicide comes under the prohibition of killing an innocent person. "We are stewards, not owners, of the life God has entrusted to us. It is not ours to dispose of." (*Cat.* # 2280) Three reasons are given. It contradicts the human natural inclination to preserve one's own life. Thus it violates just love of self. By unjustly breaking ties of solidarity with family, nation, and other societies to which we have obligations, suicide offends love of neighbor. Need we say that is it contrary to love of God?

Voluntary cooperation in suicide, assisted suicide, is declared immoral.

Church teaching on assisted suicide is stated clearly and neatly. One does not expect the Catechism to indulge in rhetoric or even in theological development.

The Catechism concludes with caution about judging suicides. "Grave psychological disturbances, anguish or grave fear of hardship, suffering or torture can diminish the responsibility of the one committing suicide." (#2282)

GRISEZ ON SUICIDE

We are presupposing the exposition of Grisez's ethics in Chapters 3 and 4. Recall the role of basic human goods which ground all choices and the meaning of morality as that aspect of choices by which they nurture human being or diminish human being. Inclusivistic or exclusivistic choosing constitutes the criterion of morality leading to the first principle—one ought to choose in ways compatible with integral human fulfillment.

Since assisting a person to kill him/herself requires one to embrace the intention of the suicide, Grisez begins with the morality of suicide. (Exposition based on *Living a Christian Life*, Grisez, Chap. 8, A-C)

Foundational to his position is the rejection of dualism. Each of us is a bodily person, not a consciousness that has a body. What one does to a human body, one's own or that of others, one does to the person.

Definitely it makes a difference if one holds a dualistic view of the human person, viewing bodily life as an instrumental good serving conscious satisfaction. For in this view, one is not killing a person if one destroys a body which is no longer providing satisfaction for the conscious subject.

The first substantive basic human good, you will recall, is "life," human life. Even secular humanists usually take for granted that life is good. They do, indeed, deny this theoretically and in particular instances act contrary to this truth. For Jews and Christians, however, human life is sacred as well as good.

As emphasized before, morality is in the will, not in the effect. What is immoral about suicide is <u>not</u> that the person is dead. He might be dead by a heart attack or by lightning. If suicide is immoral it is because the person <u>chooses</u> to kill himself.

Only after detailed development of the immorality of direct killing of innocent persons does Grisez address suicide. "Why Should Human Life Always Be Treated with Reverence?" opens Chapter Eight in *Living a Christian Life*. Nineteen pages later Grisez focuses on deliberate intention to kill the innocent. Not only the distinction between intending and permitting is treated, but also the precise understanding of moral action (See Chapter 4). So the brief treatment of suicide has been well prepared.

To choose to kill myself is seriously immoral. Even if I want to escape from or to avoid pain, even if I want to avoid shame or to avoid burdening loved ones or to make a profound political statement, I am destroying personal, bodily life. It is always wrong to harm a basic human good even to achieve some other good.

Grisez lists four reasons why suicide is wrong. Often it is unjust—leaving unfulfilled one's duties toward others or imposing unreasonable burdens on them. Suicide, apart from the case in which justice is violated, is immoral because it is choosing to kill an innocent person. It is also wrong because it is the rejection of God's sovereignty and God's loving plan. Finally, suicide is incompatible with love—of self, of neighbor, of God. (op. cit. 477)

Suicide is seriously immoral precisely inasmuch as one freely and deliberately chooses to take one's life. But that is so manifestly evil and normally repugnant that many who do the deadly deed are not really responsible. Pressured by a desperate desire to escape severe suffering or the anguish of deep depression a suicide may have no more responsibility than one who suffers a fatal heart attack. (Ibid. 481)

Grisez, after insightfully suggesting the possibility of a non-free act of killing oneself, cautions that the impossibility of judging responsibility in suicide is double edged. Yes, people who have committed suicide ought not be condemned and despised. But people considering killing themselves cannot be certain that such a deed would not be gravely responsible. (Ibid. 481)

Needless to say, a person who calmly and deliberately plans his or her suicide for an anticipated situation is freely choosing to kill him or herself. Conceivably, such a person may erroneously judge suicide is justifiable; if so, the reason he or she may be excused is not that he or she does not freely choose it.

Suicide, of course, is radically different from martyrdom. Thomas More, for example, refused to do what he thought wrong, foreseeing and accepting that he would be killed. He did not choose to kill himself.

On the other hand, setting oneself on fire to demonstrate the horror of war is still suicide, in spite of the heroic intentions. Such people probably are confused or have accepted unreflectively maxims or attitudes from their religion or culture justifying such acts of sacrifice. Objectively this is wrong.

Since the moral evil of assisting someone to do evil seems so obvious, Grisez despatches assisted suicide in a few paragraphs. In *Living a Christian Life* he refers to the growing movement toward assisted suicide and states strongly that intentional killing remains wrong even in the circumstances that are appealed to in justifying such actions, like the terminally ill and those suffering protracted and severe pain. Appreciative of the problem of suffering involved Grisez goes on to urge that "the good purposes it is meant to serve should be pursued by providing better and more appropriate care, including adequate pain relief." (Ibid. 477)

Elsewhere he quotes St. Alphonsus Liguori on "Cooperation." "Thus [cooperation] is formal which concurs in the bad will of the other, and it cannot be without sin." So if suicide is immoral, and "even intentional mercy killing or suicide motivated by feelings of sympathy or sadness is incompatible with volitional love," the person formally helping is choosing to act immorally. ("The cold-blooded hit-man and the sympathetic wife will the same thing in one respect: both choose to kill.") (Ibid. 480)

APPLICATION TO A DIFFICULT CASE

Grisez's thinking becomes clear in his reply to this question. "Will one's spouse's rejection of euthanasia for the other violate the Golden Rule?" (*Difficult Moral Questions*, #45, 209) The question comes from the Netherlands. This woman's husband, Pieter, has suffered severe damage from two strokes. He has been discharged from the hospital and his wife, with the aid of a day nurse, is caring for him. He has developed a persistent cough which the doctor expects to develop into pneumonia. The doctor has suggested euthanasia, assuring her she should have no qualms about it, since it is perfectly legal. In his view, "It is the right time for us to help Pieter be released from his useless body."

The pastoral worker who brings Communion supported the doctor's suggestion. She pointed out that Dr. Klaussen is a good physician and said the wife should "go along with what he thinks best". Quoting St. Paul she also referred to Catholic belief that "Life is changed not ended." She challenged Pieter's wife with the Golden Rule, "Do unto others as you would have them do unto you," for surely the wife would not want to be in her husband's condition.

Grisez first picks up the Golden Rule challenge, clarifying that the pastoral worker's question is misleading. Christ's directive concerns what one does, not people's conditions. What the pastoral worker ought to have asked was, "If you were in your husband's condition, would you want to be killed?" Since the wife judges killing oneself or having oneself killed is wrong, she obviously will not violate the Golden Rule by rejecting Dr. Klaussen's proposal.

Both the doctor and the Catholic pastoral worker assume euthanasia is morally all right. The doctor also presupposes dualism—that Pieter is a consciousness or a spirit that has a body.

Grisez interprets the Scripture appealed to within their context, showing Scripture's respect for life. Likewise he insists that Dr. Klaussen's medical competence does not lend authority to his moral judgments. The legalization of euthanasia, of course, by no means changes its "intrinsic immorality."

Beyond functioning as a theologian Grisez cautions Pieter's wife not to leave Dr. Klaussen alone with her husband and to be equally careful with the pastoral worker. Finally, he suggests she meditate on the fact that Jesus suffered for us as she lives out the burdensome care of her husband.

Does this mean a patient must undergo all available medical procedures? Can one do evil by omissions? Challenges like these complicate our issue and reflect concerns raised by the justices voting to overturn the ban on assisted suicide.

OMISSIONS, KILLING AND LETTING DIE

Near the end of Act Three of Lillian Hellman's *Little Foxes*, Regina learns her husband is tying her hands, thwarting her plans for sharing in the family business expansion. As long as he lives, despite his heart condition, she is helpless. Her bitterly hurtful remarks upset Horace. Putting his hand to his throat he reaches frantically for the medicine bottle. It slips and smashes on the floor. He cries out to Regina, "Please. Tell Addie ... The other bottle is upstairs." Regina doesn't move. Suddenly light dawns on Horace and in a panic he struggles from his wheel chair, desperately tries to climb the stairs—but collapses on the landing. Regina waits,—moves slowly to the foot of the stairs and calls his name. No reply. Only then does she call Addie. Not long afterwards Horace dies.

One might say that Regina did not <u>do</u> anything. Still she killed her husband. Moral action is execution of a proposal. Seizing the unexpected opportunity to save her plans and get rid of a husband she despises, she by omission executed the proposal to have Horace dead.

Omissions of this kind—one realizes a proposed state of affairs by not causing or preventing something—are very important if one is to understand the morality of withholding treatment from dying patients or refusing treatment for oneself and in general letting people die. This is the kind of situation the two appeal courts argued about.

Regina killed Horace by a nonperformance. Similarly, choosing not to perform a simple operation on a newly born child suffering from various defects, which operation would normally be done, so that the child will die is to choose to kill the child. Legally it may not even attract the attention of the police because the death certificate can honestly report death from complications related to the child's defective condition.

Deliberately choosing to hasten death is causing death. Morally, the question is, does one's performance or omission execute a proposal to bring about a state of affairs which includes death?

Note that to adopt a proposal to bring about the death of a person does not mean one considers the person's death desirable in itself or that one will be pleased by his or her death. Deep compassion may be felt for the person and one may adopt the deadly proposal most reluctantly and grieve at the death. Still, to adopt a proposal to hasten death, to overdose a dying patient, is to kill. And by choosing not to cause or prevent something one can also be truly choosing to kill.

Some people misunderstand the meaning of "letting some one die." They fail to distinguish choosing to kill by omission and letting die.

Refusing or Omitting Treatment

Some omissions of treatment can be done without choosing to harm a person. Harm is <u>accepted</u> as the result of the omission of treatment. The most obvious instance is a medical emergency situation in which triage is activated: decisions are made to treat some of the injured and to put off treatment of others, possibly with fatal consequences to those not treated first. Clearly the deliberate non-treatment need in no way involve a proposal that these people die.

As regards our issue of suicide and assisted suicide, there are certain grounds on which a person might reasonably judge treatment undesirable. "…burdens that attach to the care itself can provide adequate reasons to forgo it. These burdens can be grouped in three categories.
    i)   Care imposes economic costs and utilizes facilities and services which usually could be put to other good use.
    ii) Many things which can be done for the sake of health also can have bad side effects for health itself. Surgery always carries some risks of death and/or disability; medications often interfere with various functions. Examinations and treatments often are

painful and pain can interfere with good functioning, especially at the psychic level.

iii) Many things which can be done for the sake of health have bad side effects for other human goods. They may restrict one's inner life and activity, prevent one from moving about freely, isolate one from family and associates, and so on." (*Living a Christian Life*, 527)

Granted, a possible treatment morally wrong in itself ought to be excluded regardless of any likely benefits. But normally at issue is a treatment not wrong in itself, a treatment which it would not be wrong either to accept or to forgo. And so the benefits and burdens of the treatment must be evaluated. But how? Grisez proposes they be evaluated by moral standards, because there is no rational way to commensurate or weigh benefits and burden. (Based on *Living a Christian Life*, Chap. 8, E3)

Consequentialists and proportionalists claim commensurating is possible, indeed that we do so constantly. Both the Ninth and the Second Courts of Appeal attempt to weigh state interests and the individual's interests.

This form of utilitarianism is a bête-noire of Grisez. He has written extensively on this popular approach to ethical problems. Essentially his point is that there is no non-arbitrary standard or scale to weigh diverse values. It is like asking which is more valuable, a copper penny or a dollar bill? Assuming purchasing power is at stake, the answer is obvious. But if making an electric connection? Thus consequentialists tend to adopt the standard proper to one value and so what is opposed to that value seems inconsequential. How, for example can you weigh the pain, the inconvenience, and so forth connected to chemotherapy and life?

Grisez does indeed evaluate the burdens and benefits of treatments, but by applying moral standards.

Having brought to mind the benefits and burdens of a proposed treatment or procedure, the first thing to focus on is one's religious responsibilities or duties toward other people. It may well be that these require one to accept the medical care despite its burdens. A mother, needed by husband and children, may find herself obliged to undergo a serious operation or a painful treatment. A man, the pivotal witness for a person charged with murder, may be obliged to do the same. A playwright or a constitutional lawyer with significant work unfinished likewise may find themselves obliged to undergo treatment. Note, in none of these cases are burdens and benefits weighed one against the other.

Fairness often is the moral principle that allows a decision to be made among the benefits and burdens involved in accepting or refusing medical care. Would it be fair to expect others to bear the burdens if I undergo the treatment? Often, fairness requires one forgo the treatment despite likely benefits. Not infrequently a parent on dialysis confronted with the prospect of further complications listens to his physician propose expensive testing procedures, a serious operation, further incapacitation. Then he chooses to forego them in order to avoid the consumption of what money he has left and which he has promised for the education of his grandchildren as well as to allow his children to get on with their own lives rather than be burdened with caring for him.

Conceivably, mercy may prompt a person to refuse a proposed treatment in order to avoid burdens to others, including cost, even when fairness does not make clear what to decide.

What if the above standards do not lead to a decisive choice and both options, to accept or refuse, remain morally available? One can examine the motives prompting one toward each option. Putting aside merely emotional motives, e.g. anxiety, one focuses on the genuine reasons and one tests the consonance of each with one's personal vocation.

"Moreover, there are persons, especially the dying, who have no special responsibility to try to prolong life, who may see no reason why they must accept the burdens of life-sustaining care. If they neither will death as an end nor choose it as a means, but prefer to accept it rather than accept the burdens of some or all kinds of care, they may forego the burdensome care." (*Living a Christian Life*, 528)

In all these examples, the patient is not choosing death, but choosing to avoid burdens and accepting the consequent death. Furthermore, the evaluation of benefits and burdens is effected not by weighing them, but by allowing moral standards to guide the decision.

APPLICATION OF THE TWO STEP APPROACH

Should a wife consent to removing her husband's respirator "to get it over with"?

This is the kind of case which causes anxiety for the loved ones of a terminally ill patient and which was appealed to in the Second Circuit Court of Appeals to overturn New York's ban on assisted suicide.

Grisez's response to the question puts in sharp focus the necessary insights and distinctions at issue. (*Difficult Moral Questions*, #46, 214) Roger, 71, breathes with a respirator and has a stomach tube. Something went wrong during a multiple bypass surgery. The encephalogram was "very abnormal," the brain scan showed many damaged spots on both sides of Roger's brain. The intensive care physician urged that the respirator be removed "to get it over with."

Grisez first summarizes his advice in these points. The respirator should not be removed unless Roger is weaned from it gradually. Removing him

Life, Love, and Sex

from intensive care should be considered. Other appropriate care should be continued. Grisez then develops each point.

To remove the respirator "to get it over with" would be to choose to kill Roger. This might be psychologically more acceptable to the physician than, let's say, administering a deadly drug. And with the wife's consent there would be no risk of professional or legal sanctions. Grisez states bluntly, "Since consenting would have been consenting to murder, you rightly rejected it."

The wife judges that Roger "would not want to go on with intensive care without hope of recovering" and is quite reasonably concerned about cost and other burdens. Grisez acknowledges that someone could decide to remove the respirator without adopting the proposal to end Roger's life: the choice could be to end all care in order to avoid for the patient the burdens of continuing care. Death would be accepted as a regretted side effect. Nonetheless, Grisez looks on a choice to end all care for someone as morally questionable. He gives two reasons.

Only if nothing that could be done would promise any benefit worth the trouble of pursuing it would ending all care be appropriate. But Roger's life could be sustained at least briefly in a more humane environment. Care in Roger's case can manifest respect and love.

Second, even though the intention in ending all care need not be homicidal, to do so brings about death so surely that others generally will find difficulty seeing how it differs from the choice to kill. Thus others may be encouraged to embrace homicidal choices. So for Grisez, only if ending all care is morally obligatory is it warranted. If, for example, a shortage of respirators meant the continuing care for a patient with very poor prospects would deprive another person with much better prospects of needed care.

So much for his first point. Without ending all care his wife could direct Roger be moved out of intensive care—perhaps to avoid expense and because of the repugnance to such care without likelihood of recovery to both patient and loved ones. "So, intensive care certainly is not morally required for patients unlikely to recover…" Weaning Roger from the respirator is advised as well as directives for no emergency measures to be taken to sustain his life.

Third point. Appropriate care be continued. For example, stomach tube be left in place to supply water, nutrition, and so forth. I omit other details Grisez proposes.

Grisez thus illustrates that choosing to kill is immoral, but choosing to avoid certain burdens such as excessive expense and excessive care can warrant rejection of certain medical procedures.

Readers have just been confronted with what can be called "the ambiguous case." An action being considered will bring about a good effect yet also result in a bad effect. Medicating for pain relief hastens the patient's death. Traditionally the "principle of double effect" is appealed to in such cases.

We have treated this issue in Part One, but it may help to run through the reasoning in our present context of assisted suicide.

THE AMBIGUOUS CASE

"The court's interpretation—or misinterpretation, depending on one's point of view—of the principle (of double effect) has sparked fireworks in the medical community." July 1, 1996 *AMNEWS* reports that the denial of any ethical distinction between providing suicide assistance and providing pain relief resulting in death provoked a number of physicians to cry foul. The author states it is a minority of physicians who judge the "unintended side-effect" business is a facade that needs to be exposed.

That minority, however, have "obfuscated the matter by trying to erase the. . .distinction. . .between killing a patient and allowing the patient to die from an existing lethal pathology for which there is no morally obligatory means of treatment for that patient." (Furton, "Physician Assisted Suicide and Euthanasia," *Catholic Health Care Ethics, 2001*, 13/5) Hence the need to explain and justify the distinction.

Circuit Judge Kleinfeld, joining in dissent to the Ninth Court's decision offers a devastating example (referred to in the Supreme Court's decision on assisted suicide) to refute the claim that the above distinction is a distinction without a difference. General Eisenhower ordered American soldiers onto the beaches of Normandy conscious beyond doubt that he was sending many to certain death. His purpose, his intention in this command was to liberate the beaches and ultimately to liberate Europe from the Nazis. If one applies the majority's theory of ethics one would have to say that his purpose was legally and ethically indistinguishable from a purpose of killing American soldiers.

The distinction between choosing to do something and choosing to permit a consequence of one's action is employed constantly and everywhere without any problem—yet in terminal medical situations and the like many intelligent, sincere people have great difficulty accepting it.

You drive to work, without choosing to wear out your tires or to consume gasoline. Two boys throw a frisbee to one another, without choosing to wear out their shoes. You compete for a position, aware success means someone else does not get the job. You take the last seat on a subway, without choosing to prevent someone else from having a seat.

In criminal law intention, not consequences alone, is essential. A man backs out of his driveway and hits a child unexpectedly riding her bicycle at that place. He will feel miserable, but, unless he was careless no one will judge him culpable for any damage to child or bicycle. Repeatedly we read of a youngster darting onto the street and a car knocking him or her down—and "the driver was not charged with any crime."

Reports from battlefields frequently make note of "collateral damage" of certain bombings. The traditional ethics of war prohibiting deliberate killing of noncombatants allows for reasonable indirect killing in proportion to the significance of the target.

Almost everyone understands choosing to do and merely accepting certain consequences in these familiar situation. But a well known article sums up the thinking of those who deny there is any distinction between killing and letting die. (James Rachels, "Active and Passive Euthanasia," *The New England Journal of Medicine*, vol. 292, no. 2) The author apparently thinks an example reveals the idiocy of such a distinction. Two men, Bob and Jim, let us say, each has custody of a young cousin. The cousins are designated heirs of fortunes which, if they die, pass on to their respective custodians.

Bob drowns his young cousin in the bath tub and reports the death as an accident. Jim plans to do the same, but when he arrives at the bathroom he discovers the boy lying face down in the water, having slipped and hit his head on the side of the tub. "Great," says Jim, "I don't have to do anything. I'll just let him die."

The author concludes that Bob's action and Jim's omission are the same, equally immoral. And thus killing and letting die are the same.

The reply, of course, is that the author is right in finding Bob and Jim equally immoral. Bob and Jim are both guilty of murder. Jim chooses to kill his cousin by omitting an action he ought to have done. But "letting die" is something else altogether.

Omission can be as much a choice, and in this sense the execution of choice, as positive action. If I want a person dead (for whatever reason) and I refuse to fetch the needed medicine and refuse precisely in order to have the person dead, I, from a moral point of view, have chosen to kill. Legally I probably will not be charged with a crime only because the crime will not be detected or proved.

WHAT IS ACTION FROM A MORAL POINT OF VIEW?

This leads us to a few words about "what we do" when we choose to do something. Choice occurs only when we experience a conflict of wantings. Granted such experience we deliberate about what we find "good" in the wantings that are of interest in this case. Much like a deliberative body we make proposals, as it were, for the opposing choices. Choice is the embracing of one of the proposals and execution of the proposal is "doing" that which effects the good which made the proposal seem worthwhile.

For example, I learn that a professorship is available. It is very appealing for various reasons. I propose to pursue that position. It is no secret that many candidates will be vying for it. I know, therefore, that if I succeed, others will not have that job.

As I prepare and present my reasons why I should be given the post, I am executing the choice to obtain it—and for the goods I've seen in it. Outside of my choice is the known consequence that others will not have the position Keeping others from that position is not what I choose, not what I "do."

Voluntarily permitted consequences are outside of what I choose to do, but I may be seriously at fault if I go ahead and do what I propose to do. Take the woman who is bothered by rabbits eating the plants and vegetables in her garden. She considers putting out poison to kill the rabbits. She remembers the neighborhood children run through her yard. If she puts out the poison, harm to the children is outside her choice and intentions. But she has a grave responsibility requiring she not endanger the children. Her guilt would not result from a choice to hurt the children, but because she would not want her children endangered this way.

Let us move closer to assisted suicide. Compare Dr. Jane with Professor John. Dr. Jane performs unnecessary surgery to earn large fees in order to provide for her mother. Professor John plans a dangerous experiment. What Dr. Jane is choosing to do is immoral—it is incompatible with life and health. No good end changes what she is doing and what she is doing is harming human life and health.

The professor's experiment cannot be analyzed so simply. If there is urgent need to carry out the experiment—if he has obtained honestly informed consent and if he does not expose the subjects to dangers he would protect himself and loved ones from, then he would not be doing anything immoral even if some participants are injured. On the other hand, to conceal the risks or to expose subjects to dangers he would not want himself or family exposed to, what he plans is immoral. This is so, not because he would be choosing to harm the subjects, but because he would be violating the golden rule.

Now what about assisted suicide as distinct from administering pain relief which may hasten death? The suicide is, presumably, deliberately choosing to kill him or herself. In assisted suicide the physician is choosing to cooperate formally in the suicide's killing of him or herself. Morally, the physician is doing a gravely immoral act by formal cooperation with the immoral act of the suicide. He or she is choosing to kill. Whatever be the legal judgment, clearly the physician is choosing to cooperate in killing.

The point to be made for our concerns is that assisting a person to kill himself or herself is significantly different from removing life-support systems and administering drugs sufficient to control pain, even though doing so may well hasten death.

Dr. Thomas A Preston, one of the physicians bringing suit in the Ninth Circuit Court case, sees no difference. To him the morphine drip is "undeniably euthanasia, hidden by the cosmetics of professional tradition and language." He highlights his interpretation: "If I administer morphine to a suffering and dying patient to relieve pain, I am legal and ethical; if I say it is to end her life, I am illegal and unethical." (Quoted in "Assisted Suicide or Pain Relief? (*A. M. News*, 1996, p. 28)

He is right—in this sense: if <u>what he intends</u> is to kill, that is what he is doing, even though the action need not be objectively interpreted that way. Consider this example. I injure or kill an assailant. I intend to protect my life, using that amount of force necessary to do so. I foresee and accept injury or death for the attacker. On the other hand I might actually intend to kill him (I've long hated him and am happy to have this excuse to kill him.) Legally, of course, it may be impossible to bring me to trial if I did intend to kill in context of self-defense. Again, I might say, "I had to kill him. I killed him in order to protect my life." If I understand what I am saying and mean it, like Dr. Preston I am choosing to kill—as a means to be sure—but I intend to kill. However, as explained above, killing in self-defense does not objectively need to be so interpreted. Most often such language is merely an inaccurate expression: I choose to defend myself and the amount of force necessary to do so involves the assailant's death.

To lay bare the intention, contrast my acting in self-defense with a hired killer's action. The hired killer shoots his victim and realizes the victim is still alive. He shoots him or her again—he intended to kill in the first shooting.

If in my self-defense I discover that attacker is still alive, but incapacitated, I do not shoot again. I summon aid. This makes clear I did not intend the attacker to die, I intended to protect myself. Once out of danger, I seek help for him.

It is also essential to recognize the difference between the word "intend" in contrast with what is accidental and within a humanly, psychological analysis of moral choosing. My shooting the assailant is "intentional" meaning not accidental. I aim at his body. But as explained above—as a human, moral and legal act the intention is to protect my life, not to kill. Legally, of course, it may be impossible to bring me to trial if I did intend to kill in context of self-defense.

If Dr. Preston intends to hasten the death of his patient by providing the morphine within accepted medical limits for relieving pain, he, from a moral point of view, chooses to kill. Presumably, only fear of the law keeps him from overdosing the patient and killing her more quickly.

MORE REFINED EXPLANATION OF THE AMBIGUOUS CASE

That very intelligent people, physicians, lawyers, justices on the Supreme Court, have difficulty accepting the distinction between choosing to do harm and permitting harm warrants further reflection.

Grisez's 1998 refined explanation of the moral order and of moral action clarifies these distinctions. Ethics, he explains, "studies an order that reason, by its considerations makes in the operations of the will—an order irreducible to the orders of nature, logic, and technique." (*Natural Law and Moral Inquiry*, 213) To identify moral action Grisez reminds us that "a deliberative body chooses by adopting a motion, and the proposal that it adopts defines the community's action. Just so, precisely what an individual intends in choosing to do something defines his or her action, and we call what is intended the content of the proposal adopted by choice." "Thus every moral act is <u>essentially</u> determined both by the <u>intention</u> of its <u>specifying object</u> and of the <u>good</u> or goods <u>hoped for</u> [Emphasis added] in choosing that object." He goes on to mention the modifications of a moral act beyond its essential determinants. (Ibid. 219)

Two examples illustrate this insight. Sam chooses to play tennis for exercise. "...he adopts a proposal to play tennis...the specifying intention of his act of tennis playing." However, this proposal includes as an essential determination the intention of exercise or the good of health. Needless to say there are additional modifications of the moral act.

Sally, on the other hand, is a professional and as such chooses to play tennis to support herself and to help her parents. As in Sam's choice, the object of her act is to play tennis—but with a significantly different second <u>essential</u> determinant. Sam's tennis playing is essentially a health pursuing act. Sally's is essentially a life-supporting act.

An application: If Wallace strikes Alice in the face, what kind of moral act is it? Striking Alice may be an anti-friendship act or a loving act in the case that Wallace cares that Alice not become hysterical (Ibid. 219-20).

Dr. Preston's administration of morphine seems to be a life-ending choice. Most doctors administer morphine in such cases as a pain-relieving action.

The Ninth Court sees "little, if any, difference...between providing medication with a double effect and providing medication with a single effect as long as one of the known effects in each case is to hasten the end of the patient's life."

In our analysis of action or of what we do, we showed what we do is the execution of what we choose. And what we choose is circumscribed by the proposal we embrace. What we <u>foresee</u> as resulting from what <u>we do</u> but is not what we proposed to do, lies outside of what we do.

Helen is suffering great pain. Doctor Alex, after deliberation over his choices, prescribes a heavy dosage of morphine, having learned that less does not bring relief. He judges this dosage may well hasten Helen's death. What he does is execute his proposal chosen. What he proposed was to give the heavy dosage wanting and intending to relieve Helen's pain. Hastening her death lies outside what he chooses to do, just as the deaths of so many allied troops lay outside General Eisenhower's proposal to liberate the beaches of Normandy as a step toward liberating Europe.

The effect of what Dr. Alex does is relieve pain. A secondary effect, lying outside what he chooses to do, is to hasten Helen's death. Assuming he is complying with Helen's wishes and that there is no good reason to avoid hastening her death, Dr. Alex's action is morally good.

One's attitude of will is different toward the object of what a person wills from the attitude toward what he or she permits.

Chief Justice Rehnquist analyzes action in much the same way when he says, "the law distinguishes actions taken 'because of' a given end from actions taken 'in spite of' their unintended but foreseen consequence."

Replying to the Ninth Court's denial of any difference between medication with a double effect and medication with a single effect as above, we point out there is signal difference in the attitude of the will toward the harm involved. Dr. Alex wills relief to Helen, he does not will the harm of hastening her death; he permits it. In the terms employed by Rehnquist, Dr. Alex prescribes the heavy dosage of morphine "because of" the alleviation of pain it will provide; he prescribes the medication "in spite of" the side effect of hastening Helen's death.

Jim, on the other hand, asks Doctor Phyllis to prescribe a lethal dosage; he has resolved to kill himself because of his pain and depression. Dr. Phyllis, after deliberation over her choices, chooses to prescribe a dosage of morphine she judges will kill Jim. What she is doing is to execute the proposal she has chosen. The proposal is to comply with the suicidal intention of her patient. Reluctantly or not she identifies with his intention. If you ask me to provide the matches and kerosene to assist you to take revenge by burning down an enemy's barn, I identify with your decision of setting the barn on fire, if I provide these.

Like Dr. Jane performing unnecessary operations, nothing can change what Dr. Phyllis is doing—identifying with Jim's decision to kill himself. She may disagree with his decision, but she embraces it, perhaps reluctantly.

APPLICATION OF THE TWO-STEP APPROACH TO MORAL ISSUES

ASSISTING SUICIDE IS IMMORAL.

In Chapter 4 we explained Grisez's two-step approach to moral issues. Applying this approach reveals precisely why assisted suicide is immoral.

FIRST STEP

CLARIFY THE ACTION BY ANSWERING 2 QUESTIONS.
1. Assisting suicide destroys life.
2. Destruction of life is included in what one chooses—normally as means to relieve suffering.

SECOND STEP

EVALUATE THE ACTION BY APPLYING MORAL PRINCIPLES.

The criterion of morality identifies assisted suicide as immoral. Choice of assisted suicide is exclusivistic choosing. It violates the first principle of morality: to choose to destroy life, to kill, as means or as end is not compatible with integral human fulfillment.

It violates the 8th Mode of Responsibility: One should not be moved by a stronger desire for one instance of an intelligible good (friendship, relief of suffering) to act for it by choosing to destroy . . .some other instance of an intelligible good (life).

It violates the 8th Mode of Christian Response: Do no evil that good might come of it.

TRANSITION

Inevitably our country will have to confront the issue of assisted suicide. We have seen why reason and faith assure us that both suicide and assisted suicide are immoral.

Two gravely important factors in the popular debate need to be opened up. Essential as a condition for people to be open to reason or to respond to the teaching of faith is rapid improvement of palliative care. Hospice is leading the way. So we shall report on this great resource. In the appendix for this chapter we let Grisez speak to the legal aspect.

CARE FOR THE DYING: HOSPICE

Prompting the popular thrust to embrace assisted suicide, among other influences, is fear of dying alone and in excruciating pain. Dissolving such fear may well facilitate objective confrontation of the moral issue. Morality in a pluralistic society must be argued by reason, as little influenced by emotion as possible.

A most important reaction to Dr. Kevorkian and the two court decisions on physician assisted suicide has been the awakened concern about palliative treatment and care for the dying. At the 1996 AMA House of Delegates' meeting a board report, approved at the meeting, asks the association "to design and implement a comprehensive physician education plan on end-of-life care." Mindful of past failures it urged physicians to redouble their efforts to ensure that dying patients are given optimal pain treatment. In fact the report stated that suicide requests should be recognized as a signal that needs are unmet and further evaluation is necessary.

AMA President, Lonnie R. Bristow, insisted that the push to legalize assisted suicide is not "a victory for personal rights," but a "sign of society's failure to address the complex issues raised at the end of life." (A. M. NEWS, 5/13/96, p. 3)

It is striking that Barbara Coombs Lee, chief petitioner of Oregon's Death with Dignity Act, reported that since the law was passed "palliative care has received greatly increased attention in Oregon's medical community and referrals to hospices have increased 20%."

The quality of palliative care undergirds the issue of assisted suicide. Experience of severe pain and a keen sense of non-integration and meaninglessness motivate a cry for death. Fear of the same in anticipation could prompt a cry for a Dr. Kevorkian! Watching a loved one so suffering makes suicide and euthanasia come to mind.

First a word about what is being done generally.

The medical profession got a wake-up call by the Ninth and Second Courts of Appeal in 1996 when the Courts ruled for assisted suicide. At their annual meeting the delegates recognized the need to improve the teaching of pain management. But institutions move slowly and with difficulty. As early as the 1980's we read, ". . .the treatment of severe pain. . .is regularly and systematically inadequate. . . This is not for want of tools. It is generally agreed that most pain, no matter how severe, can be effectively relieved by narcotic analgesics." (Angell, "The Quality of Mercy," *The New England Journal of Medicine*, [January 14, 1982] quoted in Albert S. Moraczewski, O.P. "The Ethics of Pain Management," *Catholic Health Care Ethics*, 2001).

In the "Editorial Summation" the editors update the effectiveness achieved, reporting, "100% of pain is controllable if intentional sedation is included." (Ibid.)

Theory is one thing, actual practice another. Only a few years ago Father Myles N. Sheehan, S.J., a physician and a medical school professor, reported that he had had zero hours on end-of-life issues and pain management when he attended medical school. He found it sad to have to say that students received only three hours at present where he was teaching.

More sobering was what a nurse working in Sloan Kettering on pain management had to tell us. She was on a team conducting a workshop on the protocols they had developed for diverse kinds of pain so that no one ought to have to suffer pain. Her husband was being treated in a Manhattan hospital. When a doctor tried to comfort her by saying her husband was under heavy pain sedation she almost exploded for he was being given the equivalent of two percocet tablets. If word about present ability to control pain had not reached this Manhattan hospital, what might be the case throughout the country?

I am gratified that intense research is proceeding on pain control and that such success has been achieved. In Divine Providence the Hospice movement may help to halt the surge toward euthanasia. Hospice has been practicing effective pain control. "Hospice," as is well known, is the "program" of care for those who a physician certifies are likely to die within six months. Recognizing the inevitability of death, hospice care seeks to enhance the remaining days of life despite the effects of illness. The philosophy of hospice is 180 degrees opposite from the philosophy of "the Right to Die" because it provides for living to the fullest what is left of one's life .

The experience of severe pain as well as the anticipation (fear) of suffering severe pain, a common burden shared by both the chronically ill and those sick who have six months or less to live, can certainly lead one to express a desire to die. Hospice commits itself only to the latter group. The recent court decisions limited assisted suicide to the proximately terminally ill. Most assisted suicides that we have heard about by Kevorkian were chronically or emotionally ill. No indication reported suggests they would have met the six month criteria of terminal illness which characterizes hospice eligibility.

The hospice movement has developed a unique kind of health care focusing on the person, rather than on the disease. It is concerned with living rather than dying. It offers comfort, not cures. It celebrates the day, instead of mourning the brevity of life. Day and night it addresses the needs of the whole person—and the whole family—physically, emotionally, socially and spiritually.

No one person can provide such care. Once invited in, hospice brings a team of nurses, social workers, home health aides and chaplains, who consult with a physician. Trained volunteers give family caregivers a break by shopping, running errands, perhaps especially by providing understanding companionship. Speech, physical, and occupational therapists are involved as well as a nutritionist.

Since hospice comes into play only when the person has been certified as likely to die within six months, it can and does deal aggressively with pain and discomfort. Ira Byock, M.D., Ethics Chair Academy of Hospice Physicians, sums up the effect of hospice care in light of the current thrust to assisted suicide for the terminally ill. "If hospice could be characterized as having a standard response, it is, first, that suffering can effectively be relieved by appropriate multi-disciplinary care, and second, that once suffering is controlled and people become confident that they will not be abandoned in their dying, requests for assisted suicide and euthanasia commonly dissipate." (*Journal of Palliative Care*, 9:3/1993, p. 25)

Having come here from England, the Hospice movement now has more than 3100 programs in America. It is growing by 12 % a year. In 1995 15 % of the 2.3 million who died in the United States—namely 375,000 American—had entered Hospice programs. In 1998 nearly 540,000 people were cared for by Hospice programs. The vast majority, 77%, of patients die at home. But there are 98 inpatient Hospice facilities and Hospice care is growing in nursing homes and hospitals. Most programs now are covered by Medicare.

Hospice has been remarkably successful in discovering ways to alleviate both the physical and emotional pain of terminal illness. Sophisticated methods of symptom control have been tested and proven effective through Hospice experience. Another cornerstone of a successful Hospice experience is the support of a caring community (family, Church, friends).

Dr. Byock speaks from years of committed caring for the dying. He sees hospice care as longitudinal and open-ended, going beyond the person's death to support for loved ones in their bereavement. In contrast, suicide and euthanasia, he points out, are abrupt and final. A patient's choice for this way out is stating strongly that medical care is rejected, having nothing left to offer. "The focus for hospice is on life and alleviation of suffering." Assisted suicide and euthanasia aim to eliminate suffering by eliminating the sufferer.

What about alleviation of physical suffering? So certain is Byock that among the dying suffering is unnecessary that he blames Hospice for tacitly tolerating needless suffering in many instances. What he has in mind are those situations in which Hospice clinicians make recommendations to the patient's physician who may be unfamiliar with or perhaps does not accept standard palliative medical interventions. Toleration of the failure to use all possible means to alleviate the suffering may be tactical in long term strategy to have Hospice way of care at the end of life accepted, but it means, in his opinion, that "Hospice must share responsibility for tacitly tolerating the continued needless suffering of many dying patients." (Ibid. 26)

How serious is his claim "that physical suffering among the dying is unnecessary?" While for most people involved in hospice programs assisted suicide is anathema, it is known that some, committed to the program, acknowledge that at times physician assisted suicide is in order. Others quietly refer extremely difficult cases to organizations who take care of patients trying to speed up the dying process.

Not Dr. Ira Block. He acknowledges that in some few patients their symptoms fail standard procedures; and that to claim that physical suffering is unnecessary is not to imply it is always easy. At times intensive intervention is required. Aggressive measures are called for, requiring involvement of "a physician well-read and experienced in palliative care and an informed experienced pharmacist." From experience he knows this works. Assisted suicide is not necessary to relieve pain. (Ibid.)

An experienced nurse, long involved with hospice, puts Byock's claim in perspective. Admitting such aggressive methods may well prove successful as Dr. Byock insists, she is keenly aware that not all physicians involved in hospice will be ready to go to the same lengths. She knows from experience how creative and effective hospice has been in alleviating physical and emotional pain. She cautions, however, against assuring every patient there will be no pain.

But Hospice is far more than pain control. The final days can be a time of great growth. Once physical discomfort is controlled, the final days can become a "rich, rewarding part of the life of the person dying and for the family." People not uncommonly achieve a sense of meaning and purpose in life "that seems actually to have been facilitated by their terminal prognosis." In fact this opportunity for growth should, indeed must become an important feature of the debate about dying. For many of those committed to hospice the growth they have witnessed in the dying is one of the strongest arguments against legalizing assisted suicide or/and euthanasia.

Dr. Byock distinguishes suffering as a medical problem, something to be managed, and a broader, more fully human search for the meaning of/in suffering. For the former, medical science, thank God, has developed interventions frequently effective (although medical schools and the practice of medicine in general have neglected the study of pain relief). In the broader view he is convinced there is empirical evidence that opportunity is hidden within suffering. (Ira R. Byock, M.D., "When Suffering Persists. . .," *Journal of Palliative Care*, March 21, 1994)

Continuing, Dr. Byock challenges: Hospice care providers must delve deep when confronted with persistent suffering. Science does not apply at this point. One has to empty oneself and listen. "We must allow ourselves to become a vehicle for a more profound and subtle knowledge. Some would call this God, others intuition." By means of imaginative, compassionate sharing, persons he has known have experienced relief from deep suffering through surrender. They have surrendered "who they were" to a new reality—"who they are." Exhilaration commonly follows. It comes as no surprise that the experience of this transformation is articulated in word or thought within the conceptual framework of one's religion and culture.

Clinical observation, not religious dogma, witnesses to the transcendent realm the dying person can discover. Besides physical suffering there is suffering derived from the loss of critical aspects of the self. "Despite its horror, the suffering associated with dying can serve to stimulate growth as no other human experience."

The successful pairing of pain and symptom control with "community" support, which works in hospice, should, it would seem, also work for the broader community of chronic sufferers. Unfortunately, no one has yet been able to develop such a "program." Chronic illness is a very complicated area of health care provision.

The medical profession, at least in its rhetoric, clearly has been awakened to the need of devoting more study and training in end of life care. It could also reexamine the way health care is delivered in general, but especially for the chronically ill. They may be able to accommodate some of the tools of hospice, its methods of pain control and community support. Perhaps something as simple as training physicians to take time with patients and to treat the whole person will provide the solution.

Advocates of euthanasia and assisted suicide would do well to examine the effectiveness of pain and symptom control at the core of the hospice experience. Relieving physical pain and psychological depression allows time for inner healing and has the potential to bring together patient, friends and family in mutual support and affection.

Since fear of dying in pain and alone motivates many who argue for assisted suicide, learning about Hospice may dissipate the fear and allow serious listening to moral arguments against assisted suicide.

CONCLUSION

Secular humanism as a form of neo-paganism constitutes the mindset structuring the contemporary thrust to assisted suicide and euthanasia. Both faith and reason find assisted suicide immoral. But the battle against this killing will not be won unless people clearly understand that condemning assisted suicide does not mean one may not refuse medical treatment—as has been carefully explained. Likewise they must understand that choosing to allow a person to die need not be the same as choosing to kill.

If the culture of death is not to be advanced palliative care must everywhere be in place and the danger of legalized euthanasia as in the Netherlands must be clearly understood.

We are ready to confront the next contemporary life problem, capital punishment.

CHAPTER 7

CAPITAL PUNISHMENT—PART I

We move to a more difficult challenge, capital punishment. Traditionally it has been almost universally accepted that assisted suicide is immoral and law ought to forbid it. Concern that medicine can prolong life beyond what is desired, fear of dying in pain, growing determination to control one's death seem to undergird attempts to change the law. Capital punishment likewise has been the law for centuries, morally justified by reason and faith. Has the world been in error? Is capital punishment immoral? Should it be banned by law? What lies behind attempts to change this law?

"The Death Penalty on Trial" was the heading of the lead article in Newsweek, June 12, 2000. "Rethinking the Death Penalty" was blazoned on the cover. Surrounding the four sides of the opening (double) page of the article were pictures of 20 inmates, 20 of the 87 death row inmates who have been freed from prison since 1976, when the Supreme Court allowed reinstatement of the death penalty.

What has prompted any rethinking that is going on is not based on moral claims, but on practical ones. Use of DNA has been able to prove the innocence of some. Investigation by crusading groups has freed others.

Officials in a few states, Illinois, Nebraska, Maryland, Oregon, and New Hampshire are reviewing their judicial systems to ensure that the right persons are being executed. The authors of the article recommended the other 45 states consider six factors if they should decide to revisit the issue. None is the morality of capital punishment.

Six letters reacting to the article were printed in the following issue. Two strongly supported the death penalty. One called it barbaric, another Middle Age thinking. A third took a moral stand; it is "authorization of the state to murder someone. . .It is premeditated. It has a motive. It is wrong. And it should be abolished."

Immediately following the original article two opinions are printed side by side. A bitter father writes, "When Richard Allen Davis gets executed for killing my 12-year-old daughter Polly I'll be there to watch him go down." He sees the United States as a violent, brutal society and so "Our response to that violence has to be harsh and include the death penalty." He respects and has compassion for people who have lost family and friends to vicious killers and yet can take a stand against the death penalty. But he scorns the wealthy who live in "gated communities" and the dilettantes who oppose capital punishment.

A practicing lawyer, now a law professor, acknowledges the horror experienced by the family of a murder victim as well as the necessity that the killer pay dearly, "for otherwise we devalue life itself." However, to execute despite clear evidence that our judicial system is broken is to devalue life even more. He advocates we abolish the death penalty.

Capital punishment agitates American consciences. And generates strange bed-fellows. Some fiercely opposed to abortion support capital punishment. Some fiercely committed to the woman's right to abortion oppose capital punishment.

Recent History—A Puzzling Picture

The all-time high for executions in the U.S. was in 1935: 199 convicts were executed. Significant drops in that number occurred as follows: 1940-124 executed, 1945-117, 1950-down to 82, 1955-76, 1960-56, in 1965-only 7 executions, and in 1966-1 execution. By 1966 crime was down, the economy flourishing, and public support for the death penalty fell to 42% in the Gallop poll. A de facto moratorium on executions resulted in 1967 from "class action lawsuits. . .on behalf of death row prisoners in Florida and California." The Supreme Court had a number of appealed cases before them: the death penalty was challenged as a form of "cruel and unusual punishment," in violation of the eighth and fourteenth amendments to the Constitution of the United States.

The first time the Supreme Court heard arguments on the validity of the death penalty as such was in the Furman v. Georgia case, 1972. The 5-4 vote ruled that the death penalty, <u>as it was being administered by many states,</u> was unconstitutional, violating the eighth and fourteenth amendments. The court left open the basic problem of the validity of capital punishment in itself. Still there were no executions for about 10 years.

Two days before the country celebrated our bicentennial, the Supreme Court upheld 7-2 the constitutionality of capital punishment statutes formulated along the line of certain states. It did not take long for the first execution to take place. On January 17, 1977, in Utah Gary Gilmore, at his request, faced a firing squad. The ten year moratorium ended.

In sharp contrast to other parts of the world the United States, one state after another, resumed killing convicts. Florida was the first in 1979 to follow Utah, Nevada in 1980, Indiana electrocuted Steven Judy on March 9, 1981—the same month the Gallup Poll reported that two-thirds of Americans favored capital punishment for murder. By 1994 thirty-eight states had reinstated capital punishment.

The *Encyclopedia of World Crime* was able to state in 1990, "The United States is only one of a handful of nations which continue to regard the death penalty as a natural deterrent to crime. Forty-one countries. . .have now outlawed capital punishment on humanitarian grounds."

Germany keenly experienced the challenge of the right of a state to kill and in 1949 simply declared in Article 102 of the Basic Law of the Federal Republic, "The death penalty is abolished." Portugal, having celebrated in 1967 the centennial of its abolition of the death penalty, in 1976 renewed its commitment to its abolition by writing in Article 25 of its new Constitution, "In no case will there be the penalty of death." Canada abolished capital punishment in that same year, 1976, followed by Spain and Denmark two years later. France abolished it in 1981, Holland in 1982, Australia in 1985 and South Africa in 1995.

Strange contrast when America is so proud of its freedom and respect for individual rights!

Unlike abortion, capital punishment has been legally approved for centuries, in fact from the beginning of history. Furthermore it has been traditionally justified by Christian leaders with confident appeal to Scripture. Theologians and philosophers of repute have addressed the issue and "proved" its moral status.

A SWEEPING VIEW OF CAPITAL PUNISHMENT IN THE WEST

Many were the crimes punished by death in the Roman Empire. The primitive Church was for the most part against killing, taking seriously Jesus's teaching, "Blessed are the meek," and his call to love enemies. But after Constantine and the acceptance of Christians within the political life of the empire, the Church was at first ambivalent.

However, as more and more Christians came to possess civil power, Christianity added to the Roman law view of capital punishment a biblical justification on the basis of the Word of God in the Old Testament.

Three milestones on the journey of Christian accommodation to the routine use of capital punishment can be identified. As just mentioned—when the "new religion" was embraced by the Roman emperor in the 4th century, instead of the Master's meekness and mercy providing a higher ethic, appeal to the Old Testament strengthened Roman law and led in the opposite direction.

The second milestone: in spite of the flowering in the intellectual spring of Scholastic theology, severe practical problems of controlling heresy and conducting crusades led theologians and canonists to justify positions already embraced. Natural law—"force may be repelled by force"—became justification of the death penalty. Killing was thus put in a positive light. It is simply a reasonable part of the natural order, implicitly seen as accepted, intended and approved by the God of nature. Burning of heretics to protect the faith and civil tranquillity was accepted.

Since St. Thomas Aquinas has had such influence on Catholic thinking on the issue of capital punishment (as in most issues) one should keep in mind two facts. The first is the social setting indicated above. The second was not only the appeal to use of force to repel force but especially the insert on the profession of faith required of the Waldenses (1210). ["the secular power can, without mortal sin, exercise judgment of blood, provided that it punishes with justice, not out of hatred, with prudence, not precipitation."] (Denz. 257)

Thomas was addressing the issue first about 1250. His brother had served in Emperor Frederick II's forces when the feud between the Emperor and Pope Gregory IX reached a boiling point in 1239. After Pope Innocent IV deposed Frederick in 1245 brother Rinaldo changed allegiance and fought with the armies of the Pope. A year later Rinaldo was executed with others for involvement in an alleged conspiracy to assassinate Frederick. Would all this impact Thomas's thinking on capital punishment: the socio-political conflicts, the Church profession that the state had the right to kill, his brother's involvement?

Briefly, St. Thomas addresses the question whether it is permitted to kill sinners. Earlier he has taught we should love sinners. But, yes, if a person is a danger to the community and a source of corruption it is laudable to kill him in order to preserve the common good. He thus justifies intentional killing of such a criminal. Challenged by the objection that it is evil in itself to kill human beings and that the end does not justify the means, he argues (fallaciously, as Grisez notes) that killing such dangerous criminals does not violate their human dignity because they have fallen from that dignity by sinning. While it is evil in itself to kill a person who retains his or her dignity, it can be good to kill a sinner, just as it is to kill a beast. He compares cutting off a part of the body to save one's life as the whole, to the right, the goodness of killing a person as a dangerous part of the community as a whole. An unhappy event to report, this reasoning of St. Thomas.

The third milestone was in the 16th century. Society was already profoundly addicted to the use of capital punishment as its principal way to resolve problems. In an era of religious wars and the killing of heretics capital punishment was becoming more deeply entrenched in its use with enthusiastic approval by both Protestants and Catholics, more so than in any other age in Christian history.

Although the Spanish Inquisition was the saddest chapter of Spanish Christianity a recent scholarly study declares it "acted with considerable restraint in inflicting the death penalty, far more restraint than was demonstrated in secular tribunals elsewhere in Europe that dealt with the same kind of offenses. 2000 death sentences. . .between 1550 and 1800," a far smaller number than that in comparable secular courts. If my math is correct that averages out to 8 executions per year—much fewer than present American executions.

Catechisms came to be written within a context of accepted practice of capital punishment. Peter Canisius's Catechism appeals to Scripture, e.g. Genesis 9.6, to justify it. Still the emphasis was on the commandment, "Thou shalt not kill," and Jesus's nonviolent teaching.

The Roman Catechism began its treatment of the fifth commandment by listing the kinds of killing not prohibited—e.g. "the execution of criminals" and "killing in a just war." Keep this in mind when we report on *Catechism of the Catholic Church* (1994).

CHANGE

In popular thinking at the time of the Enlightenment, initial efforts to banish capital punishment came as an unexplained bolt from the blue . As scholarly studies corrected the myth of the scientific revolution of the 17th century being without antecedent work in the Middle Ages, the same has been shown for capital punishment. Individuals and groups were motivated by the Gospel to criticize the death penalty as "an ungodly abomination" considerably before the abolitionist movements began. There had always been a constant undercurrent among earlier Christians opposing capital punishment.

As early as the 12th century, as we have seen in the case of the Waldenses, Christian critics were objecting to the Christian use of the death penalty. They designated it as a violation of the fifth commandment as well as of the "hard sayings" of Jesus Christ: love, forgiveness, rejection of revenge-taking.

However, voices opening the criticism of the death penalty did not come from mainline churches, Protestant or Catholic. And the movement for its abolition is generally dated from the work of Cesare Beccaria (1738-1794). Written from the perspective of the Enlightenment Voltaire (1694-1778) enthusiastically embraced Beccaria's *On Crimes and Punishment* and propagandized its ideas. Beccaria ignores the Bible, being much more interested in the philosophical construct of the social contract. He finds the death penalty neither just nor useful. The state has no right to take the life of any citizen. "Did anyone ever give to others the right of taking away his life?" Capital punishment is a "war of a whole nation against a citizen, whose destruction they consider as necessary or useful to the general good." Consequently it must be resorted to only as a "last resort." He argues that killing can be necessary in only one case: when the criminal's life, even though he is in prison, can endanger the security of the nation. But in ordinary, peace-time conditions, when such a threat to the nation does not exist, there can be no necessity to kill.

Ironically, is this practical position any different from Pope John Paul II's in *The Gospel of Life*? "The nature and extent of the punishment. . .ought not go to the extreme of executing the offender except in cases of absolute necessity. . .Such cases are very rare if not practically nonexistent." (56)

Beccaria and John Paul II, however, confront the issue of capital punishment in radically different perspectives. Beccaria has absorbed the secular humanism which grows out of but is by no means identical with science and technology. The alienation between scientists and Christian authorities during the 17th and 18th centuries encouraged many to reject Christianity—its formal structures and its faith content. Reason was supreme and the success of the natural sciences was mistakenly taken as justification for scientism, a philosophy on its own. Beccaria no doubt was sincere and I believe people who sincerely search for the truth are implicitly seeking God, even when their systems block out assent to God's existence. More pertinent to the issue is that truth is to be esteemed and appreciated, no matter who discovers or proposes it.

All truths, in principle, are ordered to life-styles. Scientific discoveries lead to technology which leads to industry which affects the way a people lives. Maxwell's equations, arrived at in mid nineteenth century and verified in the laboratory a few years later, led to Marconi's telegraphy—and to radio and television - which have developed vast industries and consume substantial amounts of everyone's time and life.

World-views very significantly enter into the structuring of people's ways of thinking and ways of living. It has, for example, been argued that science and technology began in the West precisely because of the mindset generated by Judaeo-Christian beliefs: the intelligibility of creation and human mission to develop the universe.

Lifestyle, not intellectual or faith convictions, is what is most important. And, normally, a person does not question his lifestyle unless it has been challenged—by experiencing unhappiness, or conflict with a different lifestyle, or by denial of an intellectual presupposition of his own lifestyle.

With regard to capital punishment Christian churches had incorporated it into their lifestyles for centuries before challenge emerged especially by Beccaria and the Enlightenment. Since the framework of this challenge involved a world-view which denied Christian faith and the form of intellectual reasoning was based on empiricism and scientism, Christians felt challenged not only to their view of capital punishment, but to their entire world-view and lifestyle.

It took two centuries of discussion and debate for people either to shed their Christianity and so accept the Enlightenment world-view and methods of reasoning or in any event to recognize that conditions had so changed that capital punishment was no longer necessary. In the latter reaction Christians were able to recognize that abolishing the death penalty was genuinely compatible with and expressive of their commitment to Jesus Christ.

Although it seems that at least in the public area secular humanism guides decision making, not all secular humanists want capital punishment abolished. Still the struggle to achieve that abolition was spearheaded by members of the Enlightenment. Protestant thinkers, some defended capital punishment, some worked for its abolition. An historical work about 1870 dedicated to the death penalty concluded with 35 pages of bibliography since Beccaria, listing in parallel columns those opposed to the death penalty and those supporting it. The author observed that for the last five hundred years, "The Christian Church through most of its leading representatives claimed that the death penalty was divinely mandated." He reports that only very recently had Christians on all sides begun to change. At that point he did not find any Catholic representatives to include.

One Catholic moral theologian that could be included was Father Franz X. Linsenmann writing in 1878. Strangely enough, he found reason to justify capital punishment in the New Testament, John 19—Jesus's reply to Pilate and Rom 13—Paul's reference to the sword wielded by civil authority. But he finds no legitimacy or necessity for using the death penalty. As Linsenmann saw it, he was proposing not a departure from but a return to the best of Christian principles.

It was a long stretch of time and development of thought from Beccaria to Linsenmann, but these two thinkers symbolize a "double enlightenment" process, one secular, the other religious. Actually the two intertwined and overlapped.

Life, Love, and Sex

There was, however, a hiatus in Catholic development along such lines. Upheavals in Europe, especially in Germany and Italy did not help. Pius IX's *Syllabus of Errors* in 1864 has been seen as a declaration of war on everything modern and the loss of the papal states in 1870 provoked his decision to "retreat to the citadel and brood on the evils of democracy and modernity."

Thus it is no surprise to have John Whyte trace the phenomena of "closed Catholicism" as the Church's efforts to survive in an increasingly hostile society.

1. The beginnings of closed Catholicism   (c. 1790-1870);
2. The development of closed Catholicism   (c. 1870-1920);
3. The peak period of closed Catholicism   (c. 1920-1960);
4. The decay of closed Catholicism   (since 1960)

(McGivern, *The Death Penalty*, 262)

A number of voices were raised preparing for the transformation of Catholic teaching on capital punishment, but Pope John XXIII and the Second Vatican Council so emphasized the dignity of the human person and the role of the Church to serve humankind as such that Pope John Paul II's teaching on capital punishment in *The Gospel of Life* was inevitable.

THE AMERICAN SCENE

Before we examine this powerful affirmation of life, let us catch up what had been happening in the United States. And, not surprisingly in view of their very small minority status, Catholic voices are not notable in the 18th or 19th centuries. But they certainly heard both secular and religious spokespeople voicing opposition to capital punishment.

Catholic thought on this grave issue can, perhaps, be highlighted by contrasting treatment of capital punishment in the first and second editions of *The Catholic Encyclopedia* and the stand taken by Msgr. Thomas J. Riley (1958) and that by Msgr. Salvatore J. Adamo (1964).

John Willey Willis, a convert to Catholicism at the age of 30, a distinguished teacher, lawyer and judge, authored the five-page article on "punishment, capital" in the 1910 *Catholic Encyclopedia*. Sensitive to the widespread U.S. anti-Catholicism he reveals a "siege mentality." But he gives due respect to Beccaria's arguments. Keeping a balanced view in reporting pro and con adherents he carefully steers clear of taking a definite stand.

Not only developing thinking but significant executions like Sacco and Vanzetti, Richard Hauptman, the Rosenbergs, and Caryl Chessman prepared the way for a modification of a Catholic article on capital punishment.

The Jesuit, Donald Campion, provided the entry on capital punishment in *The New Catholic Encyclopedia* (1967). Pope John XXIII and Vatican II's influence is clear. Reflecting awareness of social science studies and the dismantling of the traditional mythologies, Campion goes beyond Willis and acknowledges Beccaria as "father of modern penal reform." He acknowledges that few Roman Catholics have been active in the debates concerning capital punishment. But he projects that further Catholic thought on the issue will reflect the contributions of Pope John XXIII and the Second Vatican Council. In his opinion the debate will focus not only on the relative effectiveness or social necessity of the death penalty, but "also the basic right of the state to employ it as a matter of normal social policy."

The two American Catholic clergymen whom we are about to treat were both appointed to state commissions deliberating the future of capital punishment for their respective states. Msgr. Riley (later Bishop) was one of a minority of two members opposing the abolition of the death penalty in Massachusetts in 1958. His explanation of the minority stand was a straightforward account of the pre-Vatican II clerical position. No mention of Jesus's teaching is given. Rather it appealed to logic, psychology and philosophy in abstract fashion.

He is right on target when he holds that the death penalty can only be justified if it serves as a deterrent and only if less drastic measures will not be sufficiently effective. However, he has unshakable confidence that both of those crucial conditions were in fact fulfilled. An intelligent man, Riley acknowledges, "Once we can say that it can be dispensed with, our arguments in favor of it lose force." (John Paul II will conclude that such arguments have lost force.)

Six years later, in the middle of Vatican II, Msgr. Adamo served on the New Jersey Commission to Study Capital Punishment: he took the exactly opposite position. Like Riley he too was one of a two-member minority, but a minority in favor of abolition. His approach, however, is empirical: the application of the death penalty was statistically slanted and unfair to certain ethnic groups. Adamo sees it as "basically an act of vengeance."

Monsignor Riley approves of, sees the need of capital punishment. Monsignor Adamo had caught the spirit of Vatican II as well as the empirical approach of contemporary social science.

It is worth noting that by 1958 when Msgr. Riley took his stand against abolition of the death penalty the number of criminals executed in the U.S. had fallen from 199 in 1935 to less than 76. And when Msgr. Adamo took his stand against capital punishment the number had dropped to about 7. Significantly, by 1966 crime was down, the economy was flourishing and public support for the death penalty had dropped to 42%.

If, as is the case, the Church teaches that capital punishment is in our era wrong, she has a real sales problem since something like 73% of the people support the death penalty.

A letter printed in this year's June 20 issue of *The Pilot* shouts aloud what the obstacle is. Referring to an earlier editorial opposing the death penalty, the author speaks disdainfully of the Church "honing its teaching" rather than admitting drastic change. He has this to say about "another major statement from Rome" on the death penalty: "I have to doubt that it will have any more impact on the Catholic majority than did an earlier papal statement, *Humanae Vitae*."

Clearly, he has no respect for Church documents. One senses bitterness as he reveals "where he is coming from." "I write this as the father of eight children, *born within ten years*, [emphasis added] . . .Should any of my family be murdered by a cold blooded killer. . .I would gladly throw the switch myself. However, were I a celibate bishop, I could take a more abstract approach to the loss."

He knows, he is sure, the death penalty is just and as a father and grandfather he has no qualms about his conviction that a killer of his family would deserve execution. Vengeance would be his. Bishops can stay above the dirty concrete living where emotions are felt and spout abstract principles.

His easy disregard for Church teaching on capital punishment has been well prepared for by the general dismissal of papal teaching on contraception. As we shall see this attitude of ignoring Church teaching was generated by the years of waiting for the papal response to the commission set up to advise the pope on contraception, coupled with vigorous dissent by leading theologians and the silence of our bishops. Why should any Catholic take seriously a teaching that flies in the face of popular opinion, especially when it goes counter to what the Church has been teaching for centuries?

HOW THE BISHOPS TURNED AROUND

That the Catholic letter-writer considers it absurd to say the death penalty is wrong is not surprising. For centuries civil and religious leaders have taken it for granted. Although something like 41 countries in the world have abolished capital punishment and popular support for it in the U.S. fluctuates, for some years now politicians get elected by proclaiming the need of the death penalty, counting on the polls that report 70-80% favor it. A sense of vengeance has long been cultivated as respectable, especially by sports. Pitchers take revenge by throwing to hit batters. Hockey and football players "get" the mean opponent. Teams are urged to beat opponents as repayment of losses.

But more significantly it took decades for our American bishops to achieve a majority opposed to capital punishment.

Entering the 20th century marked "the end of the beginning" of the history of the United States Catholic Church. In 1910 it ceased to be designated a missionary church. Changes in church and society would have to occur before the church would see that greater participation in the capital punishment debate was feasible A few non-official voices were raised.

One of those needed changes was the unanimous adoption by the National Council of Churches of Christ of a statement calling for the abolition of the death penalty in 1968. Prompted by the Second Vatican Council to ecumenism, American Catholics found themselves engaged in a livelier conversation about capital punishment than ever before.

Thus in 1971 two Catholic groups joined eleven Protestant and Jewish organizations to file an *amicus* brief with the Supreme Court, urging that the death penalty be ruled unconstitutional. Individual bishops pushed for its abolition. In 1974 the bishops were to confront the issue.

Searching for knowledgeable theological advice, those preparing a preliminary document came up with the name of Germain Grisez. The bishop responsible for presenting a statement proposed for consideration agreed with Grisez that the bishops "cannot come out flatly against a seeming tradition to condemn capital punishment." Grisez submitted a fifty-one page paper, suggesting Russell Shaw, a collaborator in his work, might draft a shorter version.

The document given the bishops recommended the policy of *non-use* of the death penalty without getting into the question whether the state had the right to impose the death penalty. After serious discussion it was rejected 119 to 103 (3 abstentions). Even a modest resolution by way of substitution, simply saying that they went on record as opposed to capital punishment passed 108 in favor, 63 opposed.

Although in 1974 a majority of the Catholic bishops were opposed to reinstating the death penalty (which had not been used in the U.S. for seven years), a vocal minority remained wedded to the Tridentine outlook rather than Vatican II's outlook.

After the controversial meeting in 1974 the bishops consulted the Pontifical Commission for Justice and Peace. The response in 1976 helped to clarify the situation and to solidify opposition to any use of the death penalty—perhaps reassuring those bishops who had hesitated over the question of the orthodoxy of the change. The document challenged the bishops to be consistent (henceforth an important word) in their defense of life—already strong on abortion and euthanasia.

Four points in the response summarize the basic conclusions of the historical scholarship of the past 50 years.
1. "The Church has never directly addressed the question of the state's right to exercise the death penalty."
2. "The Church has never condemned its use by the state."

3. "The Church has condemned the denial of that right."
4. "Recent popes have stressed the rights of the person and the medicinal role of punishment."

Number one answered extremists who held that previous Church support made retention of the death penalty a virtual Catholic dogma that could not be changed. Number two rejected the claim that the early Church taught an absolute pacifist position. Number three referred to the Waldensian problem and the profession of faith required by them. Number four may be the most important statement. Pointing to the recent development which gives priority to personalist thought and the proper role of punishment, the response made defense of the morality of the death penalty extremely problematic.

1976 brought the Response from Rome given above. It also brought, 2 days before the celebration of our nation's bicentennial, the Supreme Court's decision, 7-2, upholding the constitutionality of capital punishment formulated along certain lines. Only six months passed before the ten-year moratorium on the death penalty ceased. Gradually state after state renewed executions—while country after country was abolishing all capital punishment in their lands.

Within the complexity of the national situation the National Catholic Conference of Bishops in 1980 voted in favor of the abolition of the death penalty: 145 in favor, 31 opposed, 41 abstaining.

The statement has three major parts. We refer to two.

Part One: "in the conditions of contemporary American society, the legitimate purposes of punishment do not justify the imposition of the death penalty."

Part Two: —"it would send a message that we can break the cycle of violence."
—(it would manifest) "our belief in the unique worth and dignity of each person. . .made in the image and likeness of God."
—(would testify to our conviction that) "God is indeed the Lord of life."
—(is) "more consonant with the example of Jesus."

This was the most controversial vote the bishops ever took and so it did not bode well for general acceptance or for any effective national reeducation campaign. Still it was a definite improvement inasmuch as instead of 63 opposing only 31 opposed abolition. And the die was cast; more and more bishops publicly voiced opposition to the death penalty and former defenders of capital punishment became converted or remained silent about the issue.

OFFICIAL TEACHING OF THE CHURCH

With *Catechism of the Catholic Church* (1992; English edition, 1994) and Pope John Paul II's encyclical, *The Gospel of Life* (1995), we have the official teaching of the Church on capital punishment. After a brief report on the teaching in each of these documents we shall develop the reasoning supporting it.

There is no section explicitly devoted to capital punishment in the *Catechism*. It is treated under the subsection, "Legitimate Defense," of the first section, "I. Respect for Human Life [under the Fifth Commandment]." After explaining the right to self defense, the *Catechism* states that to preserve the common good of society the state may render an aggressor unable to inflict harm. This is what justifies punishment commensurate with the gravity of the crime, "not excluding, in cases of grave necessity, the death penalty." However, the state should limit itself to bloodless means if these suffice. (2266-7)

A year after the English publication of the *Catechism* John Paul II addressed the issue of capital punishment in his encyclical on life. He notes evidence of growing public opposition to the death penalty.

As in the *Catechism's* development, the pope places his treatment in the context of self defense. He insists that penal justice must be ever more in line with human dignity. Acknowledging the need to redress the violation of personal and social rights by adequate punishment of the offenders, this, he firmly states, must not go to the extreme of executing the criminal "except in cases of absolute necessity." And he declares, "Such cases are very rare, if not practically non-existent." He concludes by repeating what the *Catechism* teaches.(*The Gospel of Life*, 56)

CONCLUSION

Traditionally, assisted suicide has been judged immoral. Traditionally capital punishment has been judged morally justifiable, at times even divinely mandated. Today's challenge with regard to the former is to defend tradition. Today's challenge with regard to capital punishment is to justify a change.

The centuries-long practice and intellectual and religious justification of capital punishment makes understandable people's intellectual and emotional conviction that the death penalty is morally justifiable and needed. Americans, including American bishops, have fluctuated on the issue. The bishops have crystallized their teaching. Fellow citizens are questioning the practice on grounds other than moral, but we are not, it seems, ready to ban executions.

It is clear that both the universal Church communicating to all Catholics by means of the *Catechism of the Catholic Church* and a papal encyclical as

Life, Love, and Sex

well as the hierarchy of the American Church seriously teach that the death penalty in today's world is wrong.

As we have seen, American Catholics strongly disagree. This demands that we set out the reasons and the reasoning which undergird the teaching.

CHAPTER 8

CAPITAL PUNISHMENT—PART II

We mentioned earlier a letter by a Catholic father who defiantly declared he would gladly throw the switch to execute any cold-blooded murderer of one of his family. He doubted that any Church statement against the death penalty would have any more impact on the Catholic majority than *Humanae Vitae* has had.

His attitude is very understandable. The Church has supported capital punishment century after century. The present teaching of the Church must be perceived as a development and the reasons on which the development depends must be understood. We shall identify teaching and reasons in the *Catechism*, Pope John Paul II's *Gospel of Life* and Germain Grisez's *Living a Christian Life*.

Certainly mounting evidence that some prisoners awaiting execution are innocent prompts concern about this institution of capital punishment. Killing mentally retarded or people who were teenagers when they committed the crimes for which they were condemned to die awakens doubts in many minds whether we should retain the death penalty. Criticism of the United States by Amnesty International for our practice warrants reflection and re-examination. They call attention to killing juveniles, the mentally ill, to wide regional disparities, to the arbitrariness of those selected for execution, to the obvious role of race, to the assignment of inexperienced, often incompetent, counsel to many poor offenders, and so forth. In addition the fact that country after country has decided to abolish capital punishment should alert all that the rightness of capital punishment cannot be taken for granted.

Our intention, however, is not to offer practical reasons for abolishing capital punishment. Rather, we limit our efforts to show why imposing the death penalty in the United States has been judged immoral.

CATECHISM OF THE CATHOLIC CHURCH

Killing is killing, so why is not self-defense wrong when it involves killing? The *Catechism* reflects awareness of such a challenge by pointing out "legitimate defense of persons and societies is not an exception to the prohibition against the murder of the innocent."

It appeals to the principle of double effect and quotes St. Thomas, the source of the insight, "The act of self-defense can have a double effect: the preservation of one's life, and the killing of the aggressor. . . The one is intended the other is not." (#2263) And it insists "Love toward oneself remains a fundamental principle of morality." Again it appeals to St. Thomas. Assuming a person does not use more than necessary violence, self defense is lawful. "Nor is it necessary for salvation that a man omit the act of moderate self- defense to avoid killing the other man, since one is bound to take more care of one's own life than of another's."(#2264)

The *Catechism* goes further, claiming legitimate defense can be a "grave duty for someone responsible for another's life, the common good of the family or of the state."(#2265)

The foundation for the Church's position, of old and now, on capital punishment is precisely legitimate defense. And its treatment of this issue is brief (three numbers) and within treatment of "Legitimate Defense," one of six divisions under "Respect for Human Life" ("The Witness of Sacred History," "Legitimate Defense," "Intentional Homicide," "Abortion," "Euthanasia," "Suicide").

These three numbers in the definitive Latin edition in 1997 have rearranged and modified the three numbers of the 1994 English edition.

The defense of the common good requires rendering an unjust aggressor incapable of harm. The state has the right and the duty to curb harmful behavior and to inflict punishment proportionate to the gravity of the offense. Provided the guilty person has been identified and his responsibility for the crime fully determined, traditionally the Church does not exclude the death penalty, "if this is the only way of effectively defending human lives against the unjust aggressor." On the other hand, if non-lethal means can defend and protect people's safety, the state will limit itself to such since these means are more in keeping with the concrete conditions of the common good and conform better with the dignity of the human person.

The *Catechism* goes on to claim that today execution of the criminal rarely, if at all, is absolutely necessary.

What is the theory of punishment in general operating here? The primary aim of punishment is to redress the disorder introduced by the offense. Punishment also aims at defending public order and protecting people's safety. In addition it has a medicinal purpose: rehabilitation or correction of the guilty person. (#2266)

THE GOSPEL OF LIFE

For the authoritative teaching of the Catholic Church on the morality of capital punishment we have turned to the *Catechism*. Pope John Paul II's encyclical, *The Gospel of Life*, will present the same teaching but in a richer context and a challenge to build a "culture of life" to replace the contemporary "culture of death."

What primarily prompted the revision of the *Catechism* concerning capital punishment seems clearly to have been Pope John Paul II's encyclical.

John Paul II links indivisibly "The Gospel of God's love for men, the Gospel of the dignity of the person, and the Gospel of life." They are a single "good news" message.(2) He reminds us all that the Church at the end of the 19th century came courageously to the defense of the working classes which were oppressed in their fundamental rights. Today, he says, another group of persons is being oppressed in the fundamental right to life. So the Church feels obliged to speak out with similar courage on behalf of those who seem to have no voice. She is guided by the Holy Spirit to "hear the cry of the poor." The encyclical is intended to be a precise, vigorous reaffirmation of the value of human life and its inviolability. It urges all to "respect, protect, love and serve life, every human life!" (5)

Chapter I is entitled, "The Voice of Your Brother's Blood Cries to Me from the Ground." Chapter II, "I Came That They May Have Life." Then in Chapter III, ("You Shall Not Kill.") God's Commandment, e.g., "Thou shalt not kill," is linked always with God's love. Again "man" is described as the living image of God and willed by the Creator to be ruler and lord of the universe. He is not absolute master but "minister of God's plan." Human life is declared sacred; from its beginning it involves "the creative action of God" and remains forever in a special relationship with the Creator—God its sole end. And God alone is Lord of life.

"You shall not kill." Strongly negative, it indicates the extreme limit which one must never transgress. This in turn encourages a positive attitude—absolute respect for life. From its beginning the Church has always taught this. (54)

LEGITIMATE DEFENSE, CAPITAL PUNISHMENT, ITS LIMITATIONS

In number 55 the Pope introduces the issue of self-defense. Murder from the beginning of the Church has always been seen as an especially serious sin. After all, "Only God is master of life." At the same time the Church has always recognized that certain situations in which values proposed by God's law involve a genuine paradox—as the situation of legitimate defense." Certainly, the intrinsic value of life and the duty to love oneself no less than others are the basis of a true right to self-defense. . .'You shall love your neighbor as yourself.'" The Pope concludes, "No one can renounce the right to self-defense out of lack of love for life or for self." Only prompted by heroic love of another can one renounce this right—as Jesus did.

At this point the encyclical explains that legitimate self defense provides the context for the problem of the death penalty. The Pope explains that the problem of capital punishment must be viewed within the context of "a system of penal justice ever more in line with human dignity and thus, in the end, with God's plan for man and society."

John Paul II now summarizes the theory of punishment in general schematized in the *Catechism*. The primary purpose of punishment in society is "to redress the disorder caused by the offense." The state has the obligation to redress the violation of personal and social rights by a punishment adequate for the crime "as a condition for the offender to regain the exercise of his or her freedom." At the same time by this process the state fulfills the purpose of defending public order as well as providing for people's safety. Likewise it offers an incentive and help for the offender to reform and be rehabilitated.

All this demands careful evaluation of the nature and extent of the punishment "and ought not go to the extreme of executing the offender except in cases of absolute necessity: . . .when it would not be possible otherwise to defend society." He sees such cases as very rare today, "if not practically non-existent."

Pope John Paul II would teach, it seems, that the state does have the right to impose the death penalty—but only when it is absolutely necessary in order to defend society. However, he teaches the conditions justifying the death penalty today are practically non-existent. (56)

It is hoped that the preliminary focus on the sacredness of human life and on the human person as the image of God as well as on God as master of life may help people grasp the need of change in the Church's teaching on capital punishment.

GERMAIN GRISEZ

For this outstanding theologian the changed teaching of the Church on capital punishment is a matter of development of doctrine just as Catholic teachings on coercion in matters of religion and on slavery have developed.

His work on capital punishment spans over thirty years, dating from the publication of his article, "Toward a Consistent Natural Law—Ethics of Killing" (1970) through the second volume of *The Way of the Lord Jesus* (1993) entitled *Living a Christian Life*, and unpublished current work. It was the original article which led to his fifty-one page draft statement for the National Catholic Conference of Bishops in 1974.

Living a Christian Life preceded both the *Catechism* and *The Gospel of Life*. However, Catholic bishops had taken a stand on the death penalty in 1980. Grisez lists four of the considerations which the bishops offer in support of the abolition of capital punishment. He observes that these are cogent reasons but claims they point beyond abolition of capital punishment. "[T]hey tend to show that Catholic teaching no longer should accept 'the principle that the state has the right to take the life of a person guilty of an extremely serious crime'." (892)

Anticipating Pope John Paul II's position Grisez reasons that although in the past capital punishment may have seemed justified as a defensive measure, "It is hardly possible to see how the use of the death penalty can be reconciled with Christian conceptions of human dignity and the sanctity of every human life." (893)

In sum, Grisez concludes that Christians have no obligation to support the use of capital punishment even if it is considered morally acceptable in principle. But "The considerations which the American bishops articulate seem adequate to show that Catholics should oppose it in practice." (894)

PUNISHMENT

Both the *Catechism* and *The Gospel of Life* schematized the theory of "punishment" undergirding the Church's teaching. Grisez's insights on the meaning and justification of punishment in general makes the theory more intelligible. Fundamental is the distinction between a deliberate criminal act and the immature behavior of the young or the deranged behavior of sick persons.

Often it is difficult to apply this distinction, for those committing crimes may have mitigated responsibility for various reasons. However, we deny the criminal his personal dignity if we treat him/her as if he/she were only sick or only immature. The person guilty of crime has freely chosen to act contrary to the common good.

Four purposes are related to society's recourse to punishment for crimes. We all, I presume, intuitively recognize the validity of each.

Punishments are designed to defend or protect the community from dangerous criminals. We see the need to "get them off the street." Punishments are prescribed to deter potential criminals. Knowing there are fines or imprisonment for certain behavior helps one to restrain oneself. After some centuries we have reached the understanding that criminals should be rehabilitated. "Finally, there is retributive punishment."

RETRIBUTION

Defense and protection of the community as a purpose for punishment hardly needs explanation . The same is true for deterrence as a purpose. Retribution, on the other hand, is very difficult to comprehend. Readers must be prepared for very focused thinking. (Grisez, *Living a Christian Life*, 891-894)

Essential to a proper understanding of punishment is to insist that retribution is not vengeance. Simple and learned people mistake the two. One senses at times that revenge motivates desire for, and satisfaction in, conviction for heinous crimes.

Our culture conditions us to accept revenge as appropriate. We speak of the "sweet revenge" the favorite football team had beating such and such a team—after years of losses. It has been taken as part of the game for the pitcher to hit a batter to make up for the hit his teammate took in the previous inning. Players in hockey and football are encouraged "to get" an opponent who has hurt one of their players or is playing too well!

On the international scene we keep being stunned at the deep-seated, centuries-old hatreds and antagonisms motivating revengeful violence. Well, to deliberately hurt or want to hurt a person is immoral and few moralists would attempt to justify doing evil to repay evil. Custom does not make a wrong right.

Revenge, then, is always immoral and simply is not the same as retribution.

On the other hand we "just know" it is right that if Jill steals $50 from Sue she is morally obliged to give Sue back $50. Indeed, she could be arrested and, if found guilty, either fined or given a prison sentence. We also "just know" that Jack should not only pay Helen back the million dollars he cheated her of, but he deserves a substantial prison term as well.

But how explain why we "just know" this? What is retribution? Note carefully that if we eliminate retribution from the purpose of punishment the protective, deterrent, and rehabilitative purposes are inadequate to justify a clear distinction between punishment of those who freely do wrong and the training of children or the treatment of mentally disturbed people. It can be appropriate with juveniles and with the mentally sick to protect society by restraint or forms of deterrence and methods of rehabilitation.

CAPITAL PUNISHMENT—PART II

In our efforts to reflect on the nature of punishment we recall that society is groups of families and individuals united to achieve a common good: peace and security within and from without, promotion of common interests, all under a fair system of cooperation. In the Preamble to our Constitution we refer to justice, domestic tranquillity, common defense, promotion of general welfare and the blessings of liberty.

There are multiple, genuine benefits connected with living in society. Fairness requires that each person feel what he/she receives and what he/she is required to do is fair. Just laws prescribe what is to be done or not done in order that the common good be pursued. The criminal chooses to do what he or she desires rather than what society rules should be done. For example, everyone must respect the property and life of others. Observing that rule may prove an obstacle to what I want to do. If I take your money the balance of what you can do is upset. There should be a balance of fair cooperation.

It will be chaos and the community will not come close to achieving its purposes if people can do as they please and take the property of others when they want. It is only fair that law-abiding members not lose out by being law-abiding. For the good of society the loss of equilibrium must be restored. The criminal must be punished, must lose some of his freedom to do as he pleases.

The person who commits a crime freely chooses to act in a way which violates the fair system of cooperation which is essential for the well being of society. A criminal implicitly breaks faith with the other members of the society. He or she takes unfair advantage which threatens the peace of society. Granted the criminal by his action does specific damage—a murderer takes another's life, a robber takes another's property, etc. However, the <u>primary</u> wrongfulness of a criminal action is the criminal's voluntary self-indulgence of his/her own desires and interests: a violation of justice. Note that it is still judged a crime when attempts are unsuccessful. The person has broken faith with the community, taking unfair advantage of law-abiding members.

If the harmonious equilibrium of the society has been disturbed this way, it must be restored. Legal procedures must establish guilt and what punishment is to be meted out to rectify the imbalance. The criminal must suffer a disadvantage proportionate to the unfair advantage he took. Basically, his exercising his freedom to do as he pleased must be curtailed. If he recognizes the fairness of the restriction of his freedom to do as he pleases he presumably repents and consents to his punishment. He expiates his crime. Whether he so consents or not, the punishment undergone means that he loses some good to which otherwise he would be entitled and so society's equilibrium has been restored.

The retribution essential to fair punishment is the restoration of the balance of fairness. Fairness makes it reasonable to be law-abiding and so tends to deter from crime.

But is not suffering a punishment a non-moral evil? Yes, but it need not be evil to <u>inflict</u> punishment. Society through its officials need not intend the evil, it can intend re-establishment of equilibrium in the system of fair cooperation. This purpose, it is well to note, is achieved whether the criminal repent or not.

To the extent feasible, of course, the criminal should compensate the damage she caused to the common good. She might be required to work for the common good—without payment.

What about rehabilitation? Clearly it is most desirable that the criminal come to appreciate the evil she has done, the harm she has caused to the other members and recommit herself to respect the laws.

Rehabilitation, therefore, is not the curing of a sick person, not the education of an adolescent. Rehabilitation means repentance. Hence, a punishment is more likely to serve efficaciously to rehabilitate a criminal if it helps her to recognize the unfairness of what she has done, the justice of the punishment, the need of conversion, and the desirability to recommit herself to the fair system of cooperation. Any attempt to treat a criminal as if he were sick or immature means one has omitted the retributive element essential to punishment.

RETRIBUTION AND THE DEATH PENALTY

What about the death penalty? It would serve to protect society from seriously criminal acts. But since most criminals are securely housed for years, could not life-imprisonment serve just as well? It is more than questionable that capital punishment acts better as a deterrent than long-term imprisonment does. Obviously, it does not rehabilitate, at least in the sense that rehabilitated the prisoner becomes a useful member of society.

As for retribution, in general vindication of the injustice inflicted on society need not, ought not be <u>vindictive</u>. Nor does taking of a life (or lives) require that the state take the killer's life.

A few examples may clarify retributive punishment. Tim is 10, Gregory, his brother, is 6. Their mother serves sausages for breakfast. Tim slides 4 of the 6 onto his plate. Greg complains. Mother solves the problem by taking one from Tim and giving it to Greg. Fair distribution, even though Tim does not like giving up a sausage.

Tim disobeys his parents' order by coming home late without a good reason. He is not allowed to watch his favorite TV show that evening. He exercised his freedom to do as he pleased in disobedience. He loses exercise of his freedom to do as he pleases by the penalty.

Amelia, a CNA in the local hospital, uses a patient's credit card number to purchase things for herself. Apprehended, found guilty, she is required to do fifty hours of community service. She exercised her freedom to do as she pleased to steal. Her freedom to do as she pleases is restricted by being required to do service she would not have chosen. Some measure of restitution would no doubt also be in order.

Harold in jealousy kills Helen's new fiancé. At the trial he is sentenced to life imprisonment. He exercised his freedom to do as he pleased, to vent his anger by killing the fiancé. The state restricts his freedom to do as he pleases by imprisoning him.

As a member of society he implicitly commits himself to fair cooperation in pursuing what he wants. He ought to be able to recognize that the community must do what it can to preserve fair cooperation for the common good and that the punishment is fair. But he does not have to acknowledge that the state has the right to take his life. As a member of society he does commit himself to pursue the common good and engage in fair cooperation; he does not commit himself to give up his life if he does wrong, even heinous wrong.

At this point we ask, "Is it ever right to kill a criminal?" Prof. Grisez thinks it never is right to choose to kill. And he does not see how the state can inflict the death penalty without intending to kill.

Logically, then, it seems he would have to disagree with the *Catechism* and Pope John Paul II to the extent they hold that the death penalty can be seen as a subclass of legitimate self-defense. Recall Grisez in summarizing his position on capital punishment pointed out that "no truth of faith or morals requires Christians to support its use."

Personally, I accept the position that the death penalty is morally acceptable in principle, even though there seems to be no justification for its use today. If a person constitutes a serious danger to society and there is no other means available to protect society, those choosing to kill such a person can be intending to defend society using that amount of force necessary to do so, permitting the death. Grisez acknowledges that Prof. John Finnis, a close collaborator, "argues that capital punishment need not be regarded as an attack on human life;. . .only justice, not the criminal's death, need be intended."

CONCLUSION

The Church has come of age, and, perhaps with the help of contemporary secular humanism, come to appreciate her own beliefs in the sacredness of human life and that God alone is master of life. She has developed her understanding of God's revelation and has changed her teaching about capital punishment. Many factors enter into the Church's previous acceptance of capital punishment, but her teaching today is clear.

While acknowledging that the state possesses in principle the right to execute criminals so dangerous to the lives of others that there is absolutely no other way to constrain them, the Church declares that today such a situation is practically nonexistent.

Reflection on four aspects or purposes of punishment can help us understand why retribution is just and yet does not require the death penalty.

In summary, then, choosing to have criminals killed out of revenge is immoral. Choosing that heinous crimes be punished to the extent demanded by fair retribution is morally justified, indeed obligatory. And fair retribution does not demand taking the life of criminals.

But does society have the right to execute criminals? The *Catechism* and *The Gospel of Life* teach it does but only if it is absolutely necessary to protect the lives of its members; in this era the Church judges that it is not absolutely necessary.

Since the adequacy of non-lethal means to protect society's members is not a matter of faith and morals, the claim that the death penalty is not needed is incidental to the Church's teaching.

A recent article by a supervising deputy attorney general engaged in capital case litigation argues that this is a prudential judgment for each society to make. He is convinced that the death penalty is necessary for a limited number of cases in view of the extraordinary degree of freedom in our country and the amount of violence. However, he insists, in 80% of cases of violence the death penalty is not morally justifiable.

Faithful Catholics have an obligation to assent to the teaching of the Church and although the teaching that capital punishment is not necessary today is incidental to what the Church teaches, it warrants serious consideration. When one includes the grave questions about the adequacy of our justice system, the general success in keeping convicts securely imprisoned and the fact that many first-world nations have abolished capital punishment without apparent adverse effects, it would seem eminently reasonable to support the abolition of the death penalty.

Grisez, on the other hand, radically rejects the death penalty and denies the state has the right to execute criminals. It is impossible, he adds, to impose the death penalty without choosing intentionally to kill. He acknowledges, however, that his close collaborator, Prof. John Finnis, differs on this analysis of what must be intended by imposing the death penalty.

If at some point it can be shown definitively that to impose death as a penalty involves intending to kill, we would in principle have agreement on a consistent ethics of killing.

Following the two-step approach as begun in Chapter 4, we shall lay out the argument first that capital punishment is not immoral in itself. I do hold this as do the *Catechism* and John Paul II's *The Gospel of Life* . (Grisez dissenting) Second, the argument that capital punishment in the United States today is immoral.

APPLICATION OF THE TWO-STEP APPROACH TO MORAL ISSUES

CAPITAL PUNISHMENT IS NOT IMMORAL IN ITSELF.

FIRST STEP

CLARIFY THE ACTION BY ANSWERING 2 QUESTIONS.
1. Capital punishment brings about the criminal's death and protects society.
2. The state can in certain cases be choosing to use this means as necessary for defense of society, permitting the death. Thus legitimate self-defense provides the context.

SECOND STEP

EVALUATE THE ACTION BY APPLYING MORAL PRINCIPLES.
Assuming capital punishment is necessary as the way to protect society the decision to execute the criminal is not exclusivistic choosing to kill as end or as means but a choice of the good of society, using that amount of force necessary to do so, permitting harm to life. In such a case neither the seventh nor eighth Mode of Responsibility is violated. And although the fifth, seventh and eighth Modes of Christian Response provoke a sense of challenge, they do not oppose the state's action.

+++

CAPITAL PUNISHMENT IN THE U. S. TODAY IS IMMORAL.

FIRST STEP

CLARIFY THE ACTION BY ANSWERING 2 QUESTIONS.
1. Capital punishment brings about the criminal's death and protects society.
2. Since protection of society can be achieved in the United States by secure imprisonment which serves as a deterrent and more appropriately as retribution and rehabilitation, to resort to capital punishment is a decision to kill.

SECOND STEP
EVALUATE THE ACTION BY APPLYING MORAL PRINCIPLES.

To choose to kill when there is no need to do so is exclusivistic choosing, a violation of the criterion of morality. It violates the first principle of morality since it is not choosing in a way compatible with integral human fulfillment, destroying the person's life.

The call to mercy of the fifth Mode of Christian Response reveals that killing when unnecessary is unchristian. The seventh and eighth Modes of Christian Response likewise reveal capital punishment in the United States context as unchristian.

+ + +

CHAPTER 9

QUESTIONS NOT ASKED ABOUT ABORTION

We reach our most divisive life issue, abortion. Treating the morality of contraception may well surprise readers for whom it has become a non-issue. The centuries-old acceptance of capital punishment is beginning to be challenged. And assisted suicide, proposed with the same reasoning that brought about *Roe v Wade* and *Casey,* is emerging as the next moral and legal challenge to engage us all. Abortion on the other hand is structured into our life style with its opponents as committed as ever to stopping it, well organized and determined. When people's life-style is challenged and when the fundamental value of life is at stake, emotions flare quickly when opponents meet. Fortunately, the legal and political dimensions are not our concern. In fact, we attempt something prior to and propaedeutic to the moral issue itself. Because 28 years of debate seem to have long been in stalemate, our ambition is to uncover the point at which communication breaks down.

Here is why our objective is so limited. So profoundly divisive is the issue of abortion that J. Bottum (*First Things*, Feb. 1996) forecasts a very black future. Yes, partial birth abortions have intensified the division, but something more ominous must be faced. As those favoring abortion more and more consistently concede the facts about abortion, i.e. that "abortion kills babies," they move to a coherent ethic which openly acknowledges

"There are living human beings whose lives may intentionally be terminated." This ethic produces an utter divide between them and pro-life proponents. This divide, Bottum soberly points out, "would mean the end of discourse. . .It may even mean the end of the culture. . .(and possibly). . .war.."

Bernard Nathanson, M.D. echoes that thought, ". . .the shooting has already begun." Not only does he compare the Dred Scott Decision with *Roe v. Wade*, but he fingers the attempt to remove slavery and now abortion from politics as effective radicalization of the debate. *Roe v. Wade* and *Casey* leave pro-lifers two options. One option is illusory—the pro-life amendment: "An America capable of passing a pro-life amendment would not need one; an America that needs one cannot possibly pass it." (*The Hand of God*, 178) The alternate option is education, advocacy, and appeal to conscience. However, the successive steps, legal and extralegal, to stifle pro-life protests, even in the constitutionally protected area of free speech, are bound to increase incidents of violence. Not by the peaceful protesters but by lunatic fringe zealots who have been responsible for the clinic violence.

There are solid grounds for fearing that precariously balanced zealots seeing no legitimate avenues of protest open to them will turn to violence as a last resort. A cultural war is being waged [between the pro-lifers and the pro-choicers] and the escape valves for tension are being blocked. Inevitably explosions will result. "This is precisely what led up to the climactic events of the Civil War—and we appear to be on that identical path now." (180)

The cultural war that centers on abortion has been compounded by the upsurge of cries for assisted suicide. Interestingly, the argument used by the Ninth Circuit Court to strike down Washington's law that banned suicide paralleled the line of reasoning found in *Roe v Wade* to support abortion. And the Ninth Circuit Court appealed to *Casey* to explain why suicide and assisted suicide must be a fundamental right.

The Supreme Court has reversed both the Ninth and the Second Circuit Courts of Appeal, establishing that the states have the right to ban assisted suicide: there is no constitutional right to physician assisted suicide. The Justices, some had felt, would find themselves in a dilemma: either deny critical presuppositions to the abortion decisions or violate the consciences of millions of law abiding citizens, thus destroying credibility in and trust in the state. They escaped the dilemma by finding that there is no constitutional right to assistance in suicide, but left it to the individual states to decide for themselves whether they should allow it.

So the cultural war on abortion feeds into the debate about assisted suicide—and at the same time the perspective and the reasoning on both sides of abortion get reinforced.

Because proponents of both sides of abortion feel so sure of their position we shall attempt an approach different from the treatment of our previous issues, bypassing the history and description of the issue, going directly to what reason can tell us.

Two facts ground my hope that another article about abortion, which will be based on human reason (not the Christian confession of faith) may prove worthwhile toward furthering rational and constructive dialogue between opponents of this controversial issue. I am convinced that everyone does have the natural law within minds structured for truth. I take that as a fact attainable by human reason. My Christian faith provides the second reason: the Holy Spirit is actively present in our world. This truth will not be acknowledged by those who do not share my faith, and it does not enter into the article itself.

Trusting in the appeal of truth to the human mind, we identify the propositions pro-life and pro-choice proponents seldom, if ever, debate, but which actually determine respective positions. Nine questions uncover these propositions. Each question deserves to be discussed reasonably. Failure to agree on the answer to each question explains why intelligent people differ so radically. If, for example, one person thinks that the fetus is a human person and another thinks it is not, these two cannot debate the morality of abortion. They do not agree on what happens in an abortion. Before these two can talk about the morality of abortion, they must address the question: "What is the fetus which is being aborted?"

Dr. Nathanson embraced the truth of the moral principle that abortion is wrong once ultrasound technology revealed the fetus as "one of us."

I have chosen the thought of Christian ethicist, Germain Grisez, to guide our thinking. Grisez published a substantial study of all aspects of abortion three years before *Roe v. Wade*. He has recently completed three of the four projected volumes on moral theology (each over 900 pages), in two of which volumes he treats abortion.

Grisez subsumes abortion under the general principle that killing the innocent as end or as means is always wrong. In other words, to kill an innocent human person is immoral. The zygote, embryo, fetus is an innocent human person; thus, it is immoral to abort/kill any zygote, embryo and fetus. The facts and the reasoning seem so clear and simple. Why, then, is our country so emotionally divided on abortion? In hopes of providing a framework for civil debate or discussion we propose the following series of questions. These questions will identify precisely where and why people think differently about this issue, and aid us in our search for the truth about abortion. At the minimum the propositions argued for lay bare just why people opposed to abortion think the way they do. Those who disagree are invited to address these same questions and explain why they reach different conclusions.

Life, Love, and Sex

****

QUESTION ONE:

Does the conviction that direct abortion is immoral entail the condemnation of either opponents or those that have abortions as evil?

In order to defuse any possible resistance to engage in a civil discussion we emphasize that we intend to judge no one. The primary objective of searching for truth in moral issues is personal guidance for one's own choices, one's own life. Never is the objective to provide weapons for criticizing others. The aim is to advance rational dialogue and responsible action.

Grisez observes that Christian morality is markedly distinctive in the way it links seeming opposites: we are to love our enemies but we are to refuse to compromise with them. We are to suffer for righteousness but not passively regard the world as broken beyond human effort to repair. And in the context of our question, most pertinently, we are to concede nothing to anyone's moral error, yet judge no one evil.

Six women incarnate those directives.

PRO-LIFE AND PRO-CHOICE CONVERSATIONS

As I prepare to revise once again these questions about abortion, what six women discovered in six years of dialogue has opened my eyes. After John Salvi in 1994 shot up two abortion clinics (two dead, five seriously injured) the need was manifest to discover in mind and heart "a way in which people can disagree frankly and passionately . . .[in] their activism, and, at the same time, contribute to a more civil and compassionate society." Six prominent women, three pro-choice, three pro-life,—facilitated by the Public Conversations Project—met for six years. (*The Pilot*, Feb. 2, 2001)

There was tension, there was anger, but they came to accept one another as persons—as sincere persons. They came to understand better the others' way of thinking and the values they were committed to.

Six years and not one person changed her position. Something did change—they came to respect and care for one another. The Rev. Anne Fowler, Rector of St. John's Episcopal Church in Jamaica Plain, found herself truly moved when the pro-life members walked into the Temple to share in the memorial for the abortion clinic staffers who had died. Nicki Nichols Gamble, president and CEO of Planned Parenthood, was astounded that pro-life leaders were concerned enough about her safety to warn her about possible violence.

The honest, forthright reporting of their experience has given me a new perspective which should ensure that the tone of my remarks will not be rancorous or offensive.

I shall simply assume utter sincerity. Those who judge abortion is at times morally justifiable can be as sincere as I am in judging the opposite. These pro-choice women lived with a moral relativism. They seriously faced what is at stake in abortion and held (strangely for moral relativists) that the women's right to choose was absolute.

I can respect the person who is morally responsible and sincere. And to the extent I come to know that person I can come to love him or her. When I love a person with whom I disagree, I will work mightily to discover a modus vivendi with him or her. I will always be respectful; I will be careful not to offend or hurt. I will protect him or her.

Sincerity always thrusts toward authenticity. In my sincerity I really believe I am right, that I am in the truth.

Love must take prominence in all I do with others. But love ought not be expected to lie, to deny what one is convinced is the truth. Those who say abortion in such and such circumstances is morally all right are in contradiction with those who say about the identical action that it is not morally all right. They simply cannot both have the truth. One position has to be false, one has to be true. The principle of contradiction demands that conclusion. It cannot say which is true.

Civilized Discourse

Can people with contradictory beliefs resolve differences? If not, civilized society is impossible. Civilized society, it has been said, is people locked in argument. Argument, not violence.

A most general form of argument involves a claim, appeal to data, a warrant to link the data with the claim. and when necessary, backing to justify the warrant.

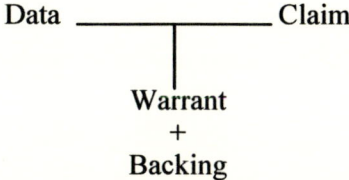

Unless there is agreement on the meaning of the Claim, on the relevance and truth of the Data and the truth of Warrant and Backing, argument is impossible. Without possibility of argument, decisions are made by force or manipulation.

Two World Views

Reflect on the two "world views" which these pro-life and pro-choice women carved out after years of "conversations." Can proponents of these views resolve differences by argument?

PRO-LIFE

The pro-life members of the group describe their views this way:

We believe in one universal truth. We three, as Catholics, believe that each human life has its origin in the heart of God. This divine genesis of the human person calls us to protect and respect every human life from the moment of conception to natural death.

The truth regarding the intrinsic dignity of the human person can also be understood through reason and scientific principles of human reproduction and genetics. Indeed, faith and reason resonate, both affirming the inviolable truth that every human life is inherently sacred.

Abortion kills the most vulnerable member of the human family: the unborn child. The right to be born is the most basic of human rights. If it is not protected then all other rights are threatened.

We understand, all too well, the often desperate and overwhelming circumstances that some pregnant women face. We remain committed to creating an environment in which no pregnant woman feels that she must choose between her own well-being and the life of her child. It is an utter failure of love and community for a pregnant woman to feel that abortion is her only choice.

PRO-CHOICE

The pro-choice members of the group describe their views this way:

We recognize no single, universal truth that determines our moral decisions. On the contrary, we must consider a broad range of values whenever we seek to make wise, ethical, and compassionate choices. We respect a woman's moral capacity to make decisions regarding her health and welfare, including reproductive decisions.

A woman's choices reflect how she weighs her various life circumstances: her important relationships, her economic, social, and emotional resources and obligations, her health, her religious or philosophical beliefs, and the well-being of others for whom she has responsibility.

We live out our destinies in a world of vast and profound complexity, where claims upon our compassion and our judgment compete and often conflict. A woman respects the preciousness of human life by acknowledging and honoring the intricate tapestry of her relationships and commitments; indeed, we believe that the complexity of human life can be a source of moral wisdom and courage.

(*The Pilot*, Feb. 9, 2001)

Worlds apart these two groups felt. Yet the pro-choice women surely would agree with and applaud the last paragraph of the pro-life view. Such an environment must certainly be the desire of both sides. But apart from this obvious agreement, notice that the pro-life have taken the perspective of objective truth, whereas the pro-choice focus on the subjective process of making decisions. Pro-life—objective truth, objective morality; Pro-choice—subjective morality.

The pro-life world-view makes two essential claims:

"Every human life is inherently sacred." (a claim based on faith and on reason) and
"Abortion kills the most vulnerable member of the human family."

The pro-choice members do not address either claim. They are concerned about individual women faced with diverse factors as they strive to make a very solemn decision.

Pro-life proponents could with integrity acknowledge that there is "no single, universal truth that determines our moral decisions"—at least, apart from the first principle of morality—"Good is to be done and promoted; evil is to be avoided," or "One ought always to choose in a way compatible with human goods as involving any human person." Pro-choice proponents seem uninterested in so fundamental an issue. They focus on the multiple values at stake which the individual has to take into account.

Pro-life advocates certainly could acknowledge the need to "consider a broad range of values whenever we seek to make wise, ethical, and compassionate choices." And the Pro-life leaders "respect a woman's moral capacity to make decisions regarding her health and welfare, including reproductive decisions." As Germain Grisez points out, "We must follow our best judgments about what we ought to do. But our best judgments can be mistaken."

From the perspective of the subjective decision making all could agree with the pro-choice's third paragraph. It is a fact that a woman's choices reflect her circumstances, relationships etc. Whether her choices are in accord with truth or not does not deny these factual influences.

Putting aside the implied relativistic morality of the final pro-choice paragraph, pro-life advocates could agree with what actually is said there. Our lives are complex, often with conflict of compassion and judgment. A woman ought to "acknowledge and honor the intricate tapestry of her relationships and commitments." As she agonizes over the issue of taking life a woman must take cognizance of these relationships and commitments. Who can doubt that agonizing moral decisions can be the 'source of moral wisdom and courage'?

But one can grow in moral maturity and wisdom by deliberate but erroneous judgments guiding her choices.

The Mind Is Made for Truth

Jack and Jill catch a brief glance of an elephant, their first encounter with this animal, Jack looking at the front and Jill at the back. As Jack describes the trunk and Jill the tail they become angry with one another and just don't believe the other could be so wrong about an appendage. If one is right the other has to be wrong. Anger and amazement at the obtuseness of the other is based on erroneous assumption of contradiction.

The well educated pro-life women looked on the issue from the perspective of objective morality. The well educated pro-choice women focused on the anguished decision making of a woman with an unwanted pregnancy.

Unfortunately, getting others to take another perspective is far more complicated than looking at an elephant. Whenever anyone acts, including when we think, one wants something. Questions evoke the wanting to know, but one wants other things as well. And knowledge and truth are not ultimate. Living and life-style are ultimate—truth is ordered to living.

We all go through the day guided by our life-style. Embedded in our life-style are moral values or moral principles. Normally we do not question any part of our lifestyle unless we experience challenge: from unhappiness related to the lifestyle, from conflict of lifestyles or from explicit contradiction of an intellectual presupposition of our lifestyle.

Alex, a devout Catholic, falls in love with Harry's wife. He may well start examining his faith which judges that adultery is immoral. Vinnie grew up with abhorrence of drugs. He now shares an apartment with Wally, a dedicated pot-user.

It "feels" right to Wally to indulge; it feels "wrong" to Vinnie. If it is important they not separate, they must disengage the intellectual presupposition undergirding their life-style. "Indulgence in marijuana is (or is not) beneficial." Helen, a straight person, hears a discussion on the morality of gay living and thinks through her beliefs.

God's pedagogy seems long term. The human race for centuries embraced slavery—without qualms. The deep-seated divisions in Christ's church illustrate sincere, God-oriented people holding contradictory beliefs. After long centuries people generally acknowledge that slavery is wrong. The ecumenical movement inches forward, grounding hope that we may some day be one.

And abortion? Raised a Catholic from birth I, and I presume, the three pro-life women, approach the issue of abortion from the perspective of objective truth. If I had, as Dr. Bernard Nathanson reveals of himself, been raised in a non-believing family and community, a community of little moral reflection beyond what is also legal, with multiple significant experiences of the suffering, personal and professional, of botched, illegal abortions, would I see the issue differently? If I had been a woman, breaking free of patriarchal restrictions, aware how contraception and abortion have contributed to feminist career opportunities, perhaps a Protestant with conviction that God deals directly through one's conscience, distrustful of human reason, would I see the issue as I do now?

Nonetheless, the mind is made for truth. (And the Holy Spirit is active.) Since both sides are sincere and since sincerity really does thrust to and presuppose truth, each side must keep searching for truth. Our lifestyles have come into conflict. Hatred, violence do not provide truth. Happiness is based upon truth.

Challenge one another we must. But love one another we also must. Patience, trust that truth will prevail. As time unfolds the consequences of lifestyles, inevitably both sides will discover truths, perhaps different truths. The truths will not be contradictory but will reveal the importance of certain facts.

How long will it take to resolve the differences on abortion? Who knows? We do know God calls us to love, not to hurt one another.

Perhaps the following questions may provoke examination of the presuppositions of the opposing lifestyles. They should alert all to what prevents communication.

Subtleties, Emotional Factors, and Truth

Grisez has no doubt that the deliberate choice to terminate a pregnancy is objectively wrong. However, he remains keenly aware that other factors, subjective factors, also determine personal guilt.

The subtleties of the issues that undergird abortion may leave a person genuinely confused. In the next question, for example, we shall see a Supreme Court judge say neither he nor appropriate experts know when life begins. Some scholars say to be a person is to be a consciousness that has a body. Traditionally it was taken for granted that we are our bodies. Some ethicians who reason that the end justifies the means argue that the woman's needs or wants outweigh the life of the unborn. And so forth. Other subtleties will become evident. As noted earlier, Bernard Nathanson, M.D., one of the aggressive proponents for NARAL (National Association for the Repeal of Abortion Laws) caught the insight while doing research, "This is one of us." This set him in a different direction and gradually he became a strong advocate of life.

Thus even the sophisticated and well educated may be so conditioned as to form a reflective judgment that abortion is morally justified. If they are committed feminists, determined to protect the rights and achievements women have obtained in recent years, they will, of course, be inclined to form that judgment.

Young women, especially young girls, may feel so threatened by an unwanted pregnancy, so pressured by loved ones, they may see no way to protect themselves other than to abort. Is it not possible that they are not truly free in making such a decision? Grisez sees killing as so manifestly evil and naturally repugnant that many who intentionally take life, their own or another's, no doubt are acting with limited responsibility. "Suicide," he states, "often occurs without choice at all! He/she perhaps has no more responsibility for his or her own death than someone who suffers a fatal heart attack." (*Living a Christian Life,* p.48 1,d)

No doubt many people assume that anything legal is moral. After all most laws conform to moral standards; indeed we take for granted that civil laws protect the dignity and value of human life. So many do not even raise a moral question as they face an undesired pregnancy.

In the light of such facts those convinced that abortion is wrong are in no position to judge their opponents or those having abortion. Such conviction does not entail condemnation of anyone. The pro-life participants in those remarkable conversations show us the way; respect and love the opponents, while conceding nothing to what they judge error.

However, this does not mean that it does not matter where truth lies. Actions have consequences and shape persons and through individuals shape the community. And the effect of actions follows objective reality much more than sincere intentions. Hence the need to discover and be in the truth.

Consequently, it is of the utmost importance that the underlying issues which condition judgment about the morality of abortion be crystallized and addressed. So let us open up the questions actually involved in the abortion issue, but which normally are not explicitly discussed.

QUESTION TWO:

Is the zygote, embryo, fetus living or non-living?

Justice Blackmun, in writing the Majority Opinion in Roe v. Wade, makes the startling statement, "We need not resolve the difficult question of when life begins. When those trained in the respective fields of medicine, philosophy, and theology are unable to arrive at any consensus, the judiciary. . .is not in a position to speculate as to the answer."

Bernard N. Nathanson, M.D. refers to Blackmun's statement as "biologically jejune." "Speaking for the 'discipline of medicine,' we know that there is an independent, self-initiating biological entity from the point when the sperm unites with the egg (i.e. the zygote) and we are able to discern its presence and activity beginning with implantation (i.e. embryo). If this is not 'life,' what is? What Justice Harry Blackmun. . .ought to have said is that medicine cannot tell us whether and when alpha (the impartial term Nathanson used for the zygote, embryo, fetus) is a *protectable* life, which medicine cannot say. That is a legal and philosophical matter, one the court evaded by deciding it could not tell 'when life begins.' This is the crucial flaw in the decision. From there, the court quickly determined that alpha is not a 'person' shielded by the language of the Fourteenth Amendment." (*Aborting America*, 207)

Mary Anne Warren, one who argues for abortion, acknowledges Nathanson's point, making a distinction between the genetic sense of "human," i.e. the sense in which any member of the species is a human being—and the moral sense, i.e. a full-fledged member of the moral community. Thus she has no doubt the zygote, embryo, fetus is living. Indeed she recognizes it is human—genetically. What she denies is that the fetus is a person. ("On the Moral and legal Status," *The Monist*, Vol. 57, No. 1, Jan. 1973, II, 2)

Webster's New Collegiate Dictionary defines "living" as a noun as "the condition of being alive." As an adjective it defines "living" as "having life." Under "life" we find "the quality that distinguishes a vital and functional being from a dead body;" "an organismic state characterized by capacity for metabolism, growth, reaction to stimuli, and reproduction." A minimal biological understanding of how the zygote develops into the embryo and then into the fetus until the baby is born banishes all doubt about the answer: "Yes, the zygote, embryo, fetus is living."

It is difficult to understand how anyone could doubt that answer. Mary Ann Glendon, professor of law at Harvard, faults the Supreme Court in *Roe v. Wade* for contributing to confusion on whether the zygote, embryo, fetus is living or not. "In *Roe v. Wade*, the Court again made a fateful semantic choice. By refusing to acknowledge the developing fetus as either human or alive, it entered into complicity with (abortion) advocates' deceptive phrases like 'clump of tissue' and 'product of conception'! Even those who would distinguish between the born and the unborn should be nervous when the state dissembles about the definition of life." ("When Words Cheapen Life," N. Y. Times)

Granted, then, that the zygote, embryo, fetus is living, what else do we know about it?

QUESTION THREE:

Is the zygote, embryo, fetus a distinct individual thing (or part of the mother)?

As with the question above concerning the status of the fetus as living or not living, it is difficult with the third question not to readily acknowledge the individuality of the fetus from the moment of fertilization. By "individual" we do not mean that the zygote, embryo, fetus is an individual person—just that it is an individual something, an entity different from the mother.

The sperm unites with the ovum: each contributes 23 chromosomes to a unique entity of 46 chromosomes. Every cell of the developing fetus will have this same typical set of chromosomes. Every cell of this developing fetus is different from the mother's cells. It is the developing embryo which structures the amniotic sack and the placenta—not the mother. Needless to say the zygote, embryo, fetus is dependent upon the mother, but membranes keep the bloodstream of the fetus and that of the mother apart; nourishment, oxygen, water and other vital factors are exchanged through these membranes.

As a scientific question, the answer seems indisputable: the zygote, embryo, fetus is an individual entity, different from, though obviously dependent upon and growing within the mother. All sides should agree without question that we are concerned about a living individual something within the mother. The next question likewise should easily be agreed upon. The fifth question is where serious difference emerges.

QUESTION FOUR:

If the zygote, embryo, fetus is living and individual, what is it? Is it human?

This is the last of the three scientific questions and one for which reason again demands a resounding, "Yes, the zygote, embryo, fetus is human." Not only can we point to the <u>fact</u> that it is the result of human reproduction, but also to the <u>fact</u> that the chromosomal pattern is proper to the human species. There should be absolutely no dispute about the reply to these first three scientific questions. We are talking about <u>a living human individual</u>.

The conflict about abortion begins only after all this is settled. Question Five moves us off the scientific level, opening us into controversy. Still, common sense reflection should be able to resolve the difference. It is in Question Six that the problems really stand out.

QUESTION FIVE:

Is the zygote, embryo, fetus a potential human being or an actual human being which is potentially an adult?

Here we have, not a scientific question, but a common sense, a philosophic question. The meaning of the question is relatively simple. Is the zygote, embryo, fetus something that will develop into a mature human being—the way a teenager develops into an adult? Is it a developing human being in its early stages?

Some people think the fetus may well be a potential human being, something that later on will be a human being. What is at issue is whether we need to treat it as an actual human being. Babies are actual human beings, most would admit, but is the fetus only potentially such?

Consider this: male sperms and female ova are human, but not actual human beings; they can become actual human beings. They are potential human beings. Once a sperm unites with an ovum, there is a living human individual in the process of developing into an embryo, a fetus, an infant, a mature adult. A human being is an individual, developing being.

We will have to treat this issue of development further when we ask about the personhood of the unborn. Here I will address two objections to this claim that the zygote, embryo, fetus is an actual human being at an early stage of development: the appearance of the fetus and brain development. Clarification on these two points should support our claim.

One of the emotionally charged reasons many consider abortion justifiable is that a zygote, embryo, fetus surely does not look like a human individual. To tell us this one-cell, tiny being is an actual human being strikes many as ridiculous. "I know what a human being looks like," the objector says, "and the zygote and embryo, and early stages of the fetus certainly don't look like any human being I know. Yes, I admit," he continues, "left alone the zygote will develop and become an actual human being."

The challenging reply is—actually, it does look exactly the way a human being looks at that stage of development. If it were to have the features and structure of an easily recognized adult human, it would be a monster.

The objection can seem evident and persuasive because we habitually judge something we see to be a horse, a dog, or cat by past experience of individual horses, dogs, and cats. We do not need, nor do we have recourse to, intelligible criteria, the way we would if we found a very badly decomposed skeleton. Or consider people raised in tropical zones, unfamiliar with snow and ice. Imagine their reaction to our claim that snow and ice are forms of water! Like our objector they could say they know what water looks and feels like—but snow and ice? We would have to explain how water reacts to freezing temperature and yet retains the identical chemical composition.

Well, the zygote and embryo, usually never experienced, clearly are outside the range of sensed standards for recognizing people. According to appearances these strange entities would not be recognized as human beings. In general, for a zygote, embryo and fetus to look like anything other than it does clearly would be monstrous for the developing human individual.

As for the second objection, brain development, some argue by analogy that since brain death marks the death of the person or the human individual, we do not yet have a human individual until the brain begins to function. First of all, only the loss of all brain functions, not just loss of cerebral function, marks the death of the person. More pertinently, the absence of brain functioning does not have the same significance at the beginning of life as at the end. When the entire brain is dead, no life principle is present to integrate the functioning of the organism. The organism has ceased to be. The person is dead. On the other hand, before the brain develops something is integrating the entire embryo's organic functioning: we have a unified human individual in the process of developing. This "something" organizes the development of the brain so that the brain then integrates the functioning of the mature individual. (Grisez, *Living a Christian Life*, 494)

In answer to our question, there is a profound difference between an actual human being which is potentially an adult and a potential human being. The zygote, embryo, fetus is an actual human being which is potentially an adult. Next we will consider if this potential human adult is a person.

Although there is not the same rigor of evidence for agreement on this question as on the previous three, there should be agreement once the meaning of and the difference between an actual and a potential being is explained.

QUESTION SIX:

Is the zygote, embryo, fetus, this living human individual, a person?

Is every living human individual a person? Or is something more required in order to be a person? This is the crux of the issue. For one can formulate the moral issue about abortion by asking: Up to what point of fetal development, if any, and for what reason, if any, is abortion morally acceptable? And this can center precisely upon when the zygote, embryo, fetus becomes a person. Involved also can be the question, "What is it to be a person?" For the person is recognized as possessing inalienable right to life.

This is not a scientific question, but a philosophic and, for some, a religious question. Precisely for this reason agreement is much more difficult to reach, for numerous non-intellectual factors impact on everyone's thinking. We restrict our discussion to philosophic reasoning.

Grisez at this point of discussion about abortion has moved in two different directions. The first approach, found in his early writings, is radical. Since it is impossible to prove that the zygote, embryo, fetus is not a person (and left alone it will, by developing, prove that it is a person), then, morally speaking, it is necessarily immoral to choose to kill what may well be a person. Traditionally, the example of the hunter illustrates this principle. Hearing and seeing movement in the bushes, the hunter wonders whether it is a deer or the farmer in the bushes. He acts immorally to shoot what may well be a person—even if it turns out to be a deer. Grisez's argument is that to abort, to kill a fetus which may well be a person is gravely immoral.(Grisez, *Abortion*, 306)

In a later work, his *Living a Christian Life*, (Chap. 8, D), Grisez takes another approach. He begins by repeating traditional Church teaching, "that human life must be protected and cherished from the beginning, just as at the various stages of its development." Next he addresses a number of current attempts to require something beyond being a living human individual in order to be a person. Since the unborn are judged to lack these additional factors, personhood is denied of the unborn.

To begin with, is personhood a status other people confer? Some people, recognizing that social recognition leads to respect for one's essential dignity as well as for the fundamental rights flowing from it, conclude that personhood is a social status like family membership or citizenship, which parents and society can confer or refuse to confer.

This reasoning is invalid. While certainly there are important social implications to being a person, everything social is not necessarily subject to human determination. Note that human society as a 'society,' as inherently social, presupposes persons, and their equal personal dignity and fundamental rights.

Clearly to be a person does not require that besides being a living human individual one must be granted social status by others.

In Question Five we concluded that the unborn from conception is an actual, not a potential, human being. Mary Ann Warren readily admits that, but insists that the zygote, embryo, fetus is genetically human, a member of the human species. But by no means is the embryo human in the moral sense—as a "full-fledged member of the moral community." And only if the zygote, embryo, fetus is human in the moral sense is it wrong to kill it.

What, then is required beyond being a living human individual? The moral community consists of all and only people, persons. She lists 5 traits central to personhood.
1. Consciousness (of objects and events external and/or internal to the being) and in particular the capacity to feel pain;
2. reasoning (the <u>developed</u> capacity to solve new and relatively complex problems);
3. self-motivated activity—(activity which is relatively independent of either genetic or direct external control);
4. the capacity to communicate by whatever means messages of an indefinite variety of types, that is, not just with an indefinite number of possible contexts, but on indefinitely many possible topics;

5. the presence of self-concepts, and self-awareness, either individual or racial or both." (*The Monist*, vol. 57, No. 1, Jan. 1973)

Beyond being a living human individual some at least of these traits are required to be a person. Warren is willing to admit that not all these traits may be necessary to identify an entity as a person, but insists that any entity lacking all five is certainly not a person.

It is startling to read that genetic humanity is neither necessary nor sufficient for personhood. She does not hesitate to claim that a man or woman whose consciousness is permanently obliterated is no longer a person, that defective human beings are not persons; needless to say, a fetus is not yet a person and so does not have full moral rights. Then, incredibly, she goes on to declare that if technology develops highly advanced, self aware, robots and computers, these must also be acknowledged as persons!

Since the fetus does not possess any of the listed traits identifying persons, no matter how much it resembles a person, even a fully developed fetus has no more right to life than a new-born guppy! Nor does its potential for becoming a person provide any significant right to life. It follows, according to Warren, that a woman's right to protect health, her happiness, her freedom, her life by aborting an unwanted pregnancy always overrides any assumed right attributed to a fetus.

Very consistently, Warren acknowledges that killing an infant is not murder. Of course, killing an infant might be immoral in the way that wanton destruction of natural resources or great works of art is immoral. However, it is "all right" to destroy an unwanted or defective infant.

What is to be said about Warren's position? Grisez quotes *Webster's Dictionary*: a person is "an individual human being." He calls attention to the ordinary usage of the term "person"; it is used to refer to newborn babies, the severely retarded, as well as to normal adults. He suggests we reflect on how people think and talk about themselves. It becomes clear that people do not think of their personhood as an acquired trait; it is seen as an aspect of what they are. "I was born 57 years ago today in Brooklyn." The person saying this intends to refer to "I" as the same being he now is. Person clearly connotes an essential property; this implies that whatever has it has it necessarily and never exists without it. It should be clear that any individual person simultaneously comes to exist and becomes a person. He/she cannot cease to be a person without ceasing to be the individual he or she is.

This explanation is confirmed by reflection on Warren's position. What she has done is take as object for definition mature human beings. It should not seem strange that undeveloped human beings—and, more obviously, developing human beings in the earliest stages of development—fail to fit that definition. What she requires to be a person beyond being a living

Life, Love, and Sex

human individual rules out beings constantly recognized as persons: the comatose, those in permanent vegetative state, defective people, even normal infants! She claims robots and computers may be developed to such a state that the five traits, or at least some of them, are applicable to these non-human things and so will be persons.

Human individuals, Grisez notes, are able to claim their rights as persons only after they become aware of their own interests. Confusing this fact with being a person, some hold that only after birth when a child becomes self conscious, aware of and concerned about his or her future does the child become a person. Before this, they hold, unborn or new born babies are only potential persons.

Grisez proceeds to point out that human individuals can <u>be</u> persons and so can have the right to life before they are or can <u>be aware</u> of such right and are able to <u>claim</u> that right. The unborn and newborn babies are actual persons, not potential persons, although they may be only potentially self conscious and concerned about their futures.

If one moves in cultural circles who focus on "free choice" and embrace abortion as a woman's right, etc. one understandably will welcome and live with Warren's interpretation of "person." Debate in that case becomes confused. What really must be debated is whether or not the fetus is a person as addressed in this section.

PERSON? BODILY PERSON? CONSCIOUSNESS WITH A BODY?

The confusion increases and opponents talk past one another more effectively because of this next understanding of person. Am I my body? or Do I have a body? Undergirding the thought of many supporters of abortion (and euthanasia) is dualism, the assumption that to be a person is to be a consciousness that has a body. "I have my body." To destroy a body, then, is not to destroy a person, especially when consciousness has not yet developed or has ceased. (Grisez, *Living a Christian Life*, Chap. 8, D.1.c)

Persons can be more than their bodies and yet not be realities separate from their bodies; a whole can be more than one of its parts without being a reality other than that part. Experience reveals that a person is not something other than one's living body: one is the subject of not only one's intellectual knowledge, choices and more-than-bodily-use of things to achieve one's purposes, but also subject of one's bodily properties, processes, sensations and one's feelings. Therefore, yes, persons transcend their bodies, but that does not mean that to destroy a living human body is not destroying a person.

Gabriel Marcel long ago clarified the distinction between being and having. I "have" this coat, but I am not this coat. I "have" this hand but I also "am" this hand. My coat is an object outside of my self. My hand is a quasi-object, for "I" as subject also "am" my hand. If you wish to contact "me", you must contact my body—by touch, by sight, by sound, by imagination.

To assume that killing an unconscious fetus (or a comatose being) is not killing a person means that once again the debate swerves off from the morality of abortion to the question, "Is a person a body?"

WERE YOU EVER A ZYGOTE?

Perhaps this is the time to ask, where <u>you</u> ever a zygote? Surely you can remember being 10 or 11 and in the fourth or fifth grade. You have changed considerably, but you have no doubt you are the same person who was that 10 or 11 years old. Your character and personality have developed one way or another, but you are the same person. How far back can you remember? Perhaps you have memories of yourself being at three or four. But <u>you know you</u> existed before that. You have no doubt you were born. The day before you were born, do you have any doubt you existed within your mother as a fully developed fetus ready to be born? (Based on unpublished lecture by Ronald K. Tacelli, S.J.)

<u>Knowing</u> that you existed is different from present <u>awareness</u> of being as well as from <u>remembering</u> yourself being. So you know you were within your mother. It should not be difficult to acknowledge that it was <u>you</u> whom your mother felt kicking inside her about 24 weeks after <u>you</u> were conceived. In fact that expression implies that it was you who were conceived 24 weeks earlier.

We, you, naturally think and speak about the continuity of ourselves from our present being back to infancy, to developing within your mother, to the moment you came into existence as a conceptus, a zygote. The difference between what you are like now and before you were born is great. But all the differences clearly seem accidental, not a change from one kind of being to another. Can size cause an essential change? I am much larger than I was at three years of age. I look very different also. Is the change in my size or my looks as a fetus, embryo or zygote such as to make me a different kind of being? You are a mature human being right now, much more developed in size, strength, knowledge and character than you were as a one year old, more so than you were as an unborn. But does development change the kind of being? Does not development mean it is the same thing before and after development? You live more independently and in a different environment than you did as an infant and as unborn. But not only are you still dependent on many others for your security, even your survival, but especially during your first years as an infant you were very dependent on others.

Twins and Hydatidiform Mole

Can all this be said about everyone? Was everyone once a zygote? No. We have learned that sometimes an early embryo divides and we have identical twins. There is also the rare event. a zygote gives rise to a hydatidiform mole, a growing mass of tissue, genetically different from the woman, but which will never develop into a baby. In view of these facts some deny we can trace ourselves as persons back to the zygote. We only become persons at implantation, perhaps 14 days after fertilization. Taking this position allows for "abortion" during the first 14 days and allows for experimentation on early conceptus.

Grisez rejects the attempt to push personhood forward to implantation. First of all these phenomena are exceptions. Most unborn develop from a single zygote. In most cases we are individuals from the moment of fertilization and we develop as these individuals continuously.

The hydatidiform mole is an organic individual which is genetically human and is a unique being, but it is not a human being. What happens is that there is fertilization of an ovum by a sperm which duplicates and the female nucleus is lost—or sometimes there is fertilization by two sperm and the female nucleus is lost. The essential difference between a normally fertilized ovum and this mole is that the normal has the "epigenetic primordia of a human body normal enough to be the organic basis of an intellectual act." In the case of the hydatidiform mole, the abnormal genetic structure is such that it is intrinsically predetermined never to develop a brain. (*Living a Christian Life*, Chap. 8, D.1.g.)

This can help to understand the continuous development of the normal zygote, embryo, fetus. If the fertilized ovum of what is predetermined to be a hydatidiform mole could be changed so that the brain could be developed, we would have an essential change from one kind of being to another. Normally, changes from zygote to embryo to fetus to born baby are accidental changes to the same, continuously developing human individual, the same person.

What about identical twins? Scientists are not sure what exactly causes twinning. But since it does occur, ought we not assume that the conceptus before implantation and the primitive streak stage (about 14 days after fertilization) is not an individual human being continuously developing into the mature person? Thus only after this point can we say there is a unique human individual.

Grisez replies that, as mentioned earlier, most of the unborn do develop from a single zygote. So we can qualify our claim to say that <u>most</u> people who now exist began as zygotes. Some began not as zygotes but later after twinning occurred.

We can speculate that when a new human divides into identical twins perhaps the fertilized ovum had the genetic primordia for two individuals from the beginning. No one really knows. On the other hand, if that is not the case, the resulting twins can be explained by postulating that we have two generations rather than one.

In this speculation, the first generation came to be by sexual reproduction in the usual way, the second by an unusual process of asexual reproduction. It may be that the first individual reproduced by giving up part of itself (cuttings from a plant can result in a new plant; worms can be cut in two and two worms result) or the first individual died when it split and two new individuals came to be.

Speculation is necessary, since science does not know. "There is no logical or biological reason to reject this explanation." (*Living a Christian Life,* 496)

TO OUR QUESTION

In answer to Question Six: Yes, indeed the zygote, embryo, fetus is a person. Most people can trace their personhood back through the years, to birth, to developing fetus, to zygote. Some few find they began to exist a bit later, after twinning.

People who support abortions prefer not to attend to this permanence of personhood. And they find reassurance in the sophisticated positions we have treated. Hence, serious discussion of abortion requires uncovering these underlying assumptions of different supporters of abortion: that to be a person genetic humanity is neither sufficient nor necessary; that community confers personhood; that to be a person is to be a consciousness that has a body. We have confronted these assumptions and shown why we judge they are false.

For Grisez, the basic moral principle is "to be willing to kill what for all one knows is a person is to be willing to kill a person." Granted, theoretical questions can be raised, but these can be answered with strong factual and theoretical grounds for considering that almost every human person was once a fertilized human ovum. The arguments against this basic moral principle are weak, as we have discovered. Practical doubt cannot be justified. Hence the unborn should be considered persons from the moment of fertilization.

QUESTION SEVEN:

Does a good end justify directly harming a basic human good as means?

Why do discussions or debates on abortion rarely settle anything? Besides the undergirding assumed positions on personhood (all the issues we have already addressed) and which condition one's view on abortion, there is the fundamental, generally unexamined procedure for forming moral judgments. The problem of moral theory is at stake. What <u>makes</u> any act morally good or bad? How do you <u>know</u> whether an act is morally good or bad?

The ethics developed in Chapters 3 and 4 will be summarized as we apply Grisez's ethics to these three questions.

Since morality requires free choice, a good starting point to find an answer to those questions is to investigate objects of choice. Whatever we choose we choose because we perceive it as good, as worthwhile in itself or as means to something else worthwhile in itself.

Certainly everyone considers human life good, worthwhile having, preserving, communicating. Human bodily life is a good intrinsic to human persons, something fulfilling, not something extrinsic and worthwhile only as a means to other human goods. By "good" we mean something worthwhile; and "basic human good" means something worthwhile in itself, not just as a means. Human bodily life is a good intrinsic to human persons, something fulfilling, not something extrinsic and worthwhile only as a means to other human goods. Even dualists, those who look upon human person as a consciousness who has body, some thing other than the person her or himself, usually take life's intrinsic goodness for granted.

Death is looked upon as a great evil. Believers find consolation in face of this evil in belief in an after-life. It would seem that those who lack such hope tend either to let dread of death lead them to despair or, if they resist that tendency, to fail to appreciate how great an evil death is. Since the last years of life can be "unpleasant, death can be looked upon as a potential friend, indeed as the final solution to life's problems." Yet apart from situations where life is burdensome or painful and those in which life is an obstacle to some good desired, everyone treasures life, one's own and, in varying degrees, that of others as precious. We go to extreme and wonderful lengths to provide emergency support for lives threatened in any way. (Ibid. , Chap.8, A. 1. e.)

Human life, then, is a basic human good and perceived as something to be pursued and promoted. Since a human being's life is her or his concrete reality, to intend a person's death either as an end in itself (e.g. out of hatred or revenge) or as a chosen means to some other end is always inconsistent with volitional love for that person. Or so it seems.

Does the End Justify the Means?

It is easy to imagine scenarios in which causing death seems worthwhile and desirable. The frightened teenager who finds herself pregnant and alone, harassed by boyfriend and family to abort her child. The mature woman carrying the child of a man other than her husband, ashamed and aware of scandal to her children and hurt to, perhaps abandonment by, her husband.

In these and other situations, abortion can loom as the solution, as the way to protect love and family.

For so many people, earnest, good people, doing harm to a human good seems justified by a good and a more valuable end. Is not this what our government appeals to in order to justify our Nuclear Deterrence Policy? We are willing, if attacked first, to destroy 50 million Russians and 50% of their industrial capacity. The prevention of nuclear warfare is said to make such a willingness morally justified. It has been suggested that appeal to the end justifying the means on such a devastating scale fuels the tendency to employ it when lesser evil results.

Theoretical justification of the position that a good end justifies doing harm to human goods is proposed by utilitarianism and consequentialist thought. These schools of thought assume that basic human goods can be weighed one against the other. Killing one person to save 1000 others surely is justified—since 1000 lives are worth more than one. It sounds most reasonable. But the same logic ought to justify killing 50 to save the 1000, killing 500, indeed killing 999 to save the 1000. What at first appears most reasonable on reflection does not make sense. Human goods simply cannot be weighed.

The principle that the end justifies any means is precisely what underpinned Hitler's justification for experimenting on political and Jewish prisoners, and Stalin's justification for starving millions of Ukrainians in order to communize agriculture. Certainly it is the principle that underpins abortions chosen as a lesser evil in order to protect a woman's career or friendship or whatever. It is the principle which operates in the decision to kill a person suffering from cancer.

One's entire moral position is called into question by the challenge, Does a good end justify directly harming a basic human good as means? It is essential to recognize that morality is in the heart, primarily in the act of choosing. External effects are obviously of great importance, but morally, only to the extent they are deliberately chosen and thus are related to the heart. Whether I accidentally collapse on you, breaking your nose, or choose to punch you, the effect is the same—a broken nose. It is my choosing to hurt you that makes my act immoral.

In other words morality immediately affects the doer. And what makes any act immoral is the way I choose it: to choose to pursue something worthwhile (and in every choice, morally good or bad, psychologically we must choose something perceived as good) in a way that we respect all other goods is to choose in a morally good way. To choose to pursue something good or worthwhile in such a way that I simultaneously choose to harm another good is to choose in a morally bad way.

This criterion of morality is not saying that "intention" is all we attend to. Both what I am doing and why I am doing it must be examined and both must be in accord with the criterion: Neither what I am doing nor why may involve harming another good.

The woman choosing to abort her child normally is not judging this is good or worthwhile in itself; she chooses to preserve her husband's love or to provide for her career, let us say. To choose to preserve love or to provide for her career is good and in most circumstances would be morally good. In the situation as described she chooses to pursue that good by way of killing a living human being.

You can see how the question about the end justifying the means emerges. The woman in the scenario above judges that love of her husband or a career outweighs the life of the fetus, the unborn child. As argued in this section, human goods simply cannot be weighed one against the other.

Those who focus on women controlling their lives generally presuppose that, bad as killing in general is, when a serious human good is at stake, the end does justify doing evil to achieve good. They thus talk past, without either side hearing what the other says, those who focus on the evil of killing the unborn and presuppose that it is never right to do evil to achieve good. Lives are of literally immeasurable value and so no end, worthwhile as it may be, justifies killing another living human individual.

Question Eight will confront the ambiguous situation when, for example, self-defense involves killing another or doing nothing will result in both mother and unborn will die.

The abortion issue simply cannot be discussed without clear recognition of and agreement about, what makes any act morally good or bad. Unless there is agreement on this, it is difficult to see how abortion can be reasonably and civilly debated. If the reader feels confused on this, recourse to Chapters 3 and 4 will help. Doing so will also help to understand the treatment of Questions Eight and Nine, the ambiguous case.

Things get more difficult in this next question. But just what does make any act morally good or bad will be clarified.

QUESTION EIGHT:

Is It Ever Morally Right to Choose Deliberately to Destroy Human Life?

In Questions Two, Three, and Four we argued that the unborn, from the state of being a zygote to embryo to fetus, is a living human individual. All this based on scientifically verifiable data. Advancing to a philosophical level, in Question Six we likewise argued that the unborn is a person. As Grisez spells out, we say much more when we call a human individual a "person" than when we say that he is a member of the homo sapiens species. The term "person" connotes the dignity, the intrinsic worth, of a human individual and refers to the individual as a subject of rights and responsibilities. Since the question is not a scientific question, the reasoning is philosophic, not scientific. The conclusion, we submit, is still certain.

Life is a basic human good, and everyone is capable of recognizing this. So to will as an end an innocent person's death—out of anger or in a spirit of revenge—or to destroy such a person's life as means to achieve another good clearly is wrong. The first principle of morality is one ought always to choose in a way compatible with integral human fulfillment. The fulfillment of every person is the impartial standard, the criterion of moral acts. Obviously to choose to kill an innocent person is not compatible with the fulfillment of all persons. Expressed in terms of love—to choose to destroy an innocent person's life is no way consistent with love of one's neighbor.

Confusion and difference of opinion can enter here depending on how one understands what "choosing to kill" means. For Grisez, choice is adoption of a proposal. A person experiences a conflict of wantings, deliberates about doing something considered possible and of interest. He/she does this much as members of a deliberative body debate motions. After deliberation, a person adopts a proposal to do something. This is "making a choice," similar to the way adopting a motion by voting is a group's reaching a decision.

What then is an action? An action is "what one does" and "what one does," whether by performance or omission, carries out the choice. The executive carries out the decisions, the enactments of a legislative body. What one does, the carrying out of the proposal adopted, has foreseen consequences which are neither included in the proposal nor sought for their own sake. They are side effects, even though they are accepted.

"Choosing to kill," as just analyzed, is adopting a proposal precisely to kill. Many people, including philosophers, moralists of years ago, as well as consequentialists (even some of my students), understand choice differently. They think of choice as if it were merely the positing of the outward performance or omission. However, the performance or omission is thought of in terms of objective causality in the external world. So "what is chosen" is defined by its immediacy or by its regularity as a result of the objective causality.(Ibid. , Chap. 8, B.1.d.)

"Choosing to kill" in this latter way of thinking means choosing to do/omit something that directly leads to death. For example, Bill chooses to shoot someone in the heart or Jack knowingly takes a lethal dose of opiates. Both posit a cause that immediately leads to death. To proponents of this understanding such performances or omissions are plain instances of intentional killing; choices executed by such performance are always "choices to kill."

We have here two different ways of understanding what "choose to kill" means. People understanding "choice" and corresponding action in these two ways can differ in identifying intentional killing. They can, of course, in some cases agree: a hit-man for the Mafia directly, intentionally kills for his fee; Jesus freely accepted death but did not choose to kill himself; a surgeon does not intend the death of the unborn when she removes a cancerous womb with a twelve-week fetus as means to prevent the death of the mother from cancer.

The two approaches, on the other hand, interpret episodes quite differently and can lead to significant differences in applying the distinction between intending death as a means and accepting it as a side effect. Some people would interpret killing in defense against an unprovoked attacker as intentional killing; of course, they consider the killing justifiable. For example, a woman deliberately shoots a would-be rapist. She views her action as the only way to stop the rapist's attack and so, some insist, she must intend, she must choose, to kill him. Grisez differs. According to his approach the woman could be carrying out a proposal to defend herself against rape. She only accepts his foreseen death as a side effect; she did not choose to kill.

Needless to say her fatal shooting of the rapist is not accidental. In one sense, obviously, she intends to shoot him. From a moral viewpoint, however, Grisez considers she may well be carrying out the proposal of self-defense, accepting death as a side effect. To show this is not double talk, compare this woman's action and the action of a hit-man. In the sense of the shooting not being accidental but "intentional" they are the same. But the difference of the moral "intention" becomes clear if the person shot continues to live. The woman would be likely to call 911, seeking help for the man. Why? Because she has succeeded in protecting herself—which was what she chose to do. Thus it is clear that it was not his death she wanted or chose. The hit man no doubt would shoot his victim again, revealing that his first shooting was a choice to kill.

This subtle, sophisticated explanation of "choice" is a significant contribution by Grisez to ethical theory. Once the distinction is brought to one's attention, one catches further insight into consequentialism and proportionalism. Since the alternative view focuses on the physical act, rather than the interior adoption of a proposal, to do evil to achieve good—in light of the greater good or lesser evil—seems attractive, even reasonable. Since human goods are incommensurable, Grisez rejects consequentialism because it is an unsound process of moral deliberation.

Those who argue for abortion as at times morally justifiable follow a utilitarian or consequentialist form of reasoning. Rarely will the question about the meaning of "choice" or "action" emerge in an abortion discussion. But at some point it ought to.

QUESTION NINE:

Is It Ever Morally Right to Choose Deliberately to Abort the Unborn?

We have shown that the unborn at every stage of development is a living human individual person and that killing the innocent is immoral.

There remain two additional matters of interest: 1) application of the distinction between choosing to kill and accepting death as a side effect in difficult cases and 2) the question of subjective guilt.

Accepting Death As a Side Effect

Grisez addresses the two most troubling situations. First, sometimes the baby's death may be accepted as a side effect to save the mother's life. Sometimes the baby's life should be given priority. Four conditions simultaneously fulfilled identify when the former is morally justifiable. "(i) some pathology threatens the lives of both a pregnant woman and her child, (ii) it is not safe to wait or waiting surely will result in the death of both, (iii) there is no way to save the child, and (iv) an operation that can save the mother's life will result in the child's death." (Ibid. , Chap 8, D.3.d.)

We are facing the most difficult area of moral reasoning, the ambiguous case: a contemplated choice will have two results, achievement of a basic human good and harm to another basic human good. Since Grisez holds that it is never morally justifiable to choose to harm a basic human good, then only when the very act which achieves the good is the act which brings about harm <u>can</u> it be morally justifiable to accept the harm as a side effect. To remove a cancerous womb of a pregnant woman illustrates this condition: the very same act of removing the cancerous womb is the action which results in death of the unborn. The same can be said of removing a fallopian tube containing an ectopic pregnancy.

Grisez pushes the issue. When the four conditions obtain, he even justifies craniotomy which, understood in the alternative way treated in Question Eight, constitutes the direct choice to kill. But if choice is adopting a proposal, in this case the choice can be simply to alter the child's physical dimensions so the child can be removed. Why? Because both mother and child will die if it is not removed. Consider, the baby's death does not contribute anything to the objective sought, that is to save the mother. After all, if the baby has already died, the same procedure will be done.

But more is at stake than ensuring that one is only permitting harm to a good. Grisez concedes a woman raped may well be choosing not to kill the unborn but to free herself of ongoing suffering, permitting the death of the baby as a side effect. However, Grisez judges abortion in this case is still immoral. People, after all, are prepared generally to sacrifice anything except their moral integrity to save their own lives and in general they want others on whom they depend to accept considerable inconvenience or suffering rather than to accept their death. It follows that abortion in the case of rape is unfair. One would expect others to endure such difficulties rather than kill oneself.

Grisez offers a similar analysis for health problems such as a woman suffering from kidney disease who wants to avoid the health problems that are likely to result from carrying the child. She need not be proposing the death of the child, but abortion would still be unfair and so immoral.

Priority of Baby's Life

Justice or mercy can require priority be given to the baby's life. The second serious case differs from the first inasmuch as not both mother and child will die unless something is done. "Sometimes the baby's life should be given priority." He lists three conditions for this second situation. "(i) some pathology threatens the life (or at least seriously impairs the health) of a pregnant woman, (ii) an operation or treatment that is not intentional killing of the baby would benefit her, and (iii) the operation or treatment would lead to the baby's death (or at least risk his or her life)." (Ibid. , e) Many jump to the conclusion that the operation or treatment is morally justifiable. "However, justice or mercy can require that the pregnant woman ... give priority to the baby's life."

As explained above, Grisez's approach rules out an operation which results in the baby's death when it is performed to ameliorate a kidney disease that is not an immediate threat to the woman's life. He likewise declares removal of a cancerous womb immoral if it can safely be delayed, so that the baby may survive. Involved is fairness, not a matter of intentional killing.

What about the situation in which both lives are threatened and both cannot be saved? If an operation can save one or the other, fairness can require that operation be done which is more likely to save at least one of the lives at stake. A procedure surely to result in the baby's death which offers only a limited chance of saving the mother may be unfair discrimination if the alternative would surely bring about the mother's death but there would be a better chance of saving the baby.

Those who support abortions as a woman's right will easily agree with Grisez's conclusion in the first case scenario, when the mother's life is at stake. They probably will not use his reasoning and will insist that moral justifiability is not restricted to such cases. Hence they will not agree with his second case scenario.

More significantly, it becomes clear that the judgment "that deliberate choice to terminate a pregnancy is wrong" is inescapable provided it is understood that the unborn is a living human individual person and that deliberate killing of an innocent person is immoral. There's the rub: the real issues must be made to surface and be directly addressed. Only by addressing the questions above which usually are not confronted can the real issue of abortion be faced and resolved. We leave the question of subjective guilt to our Epilogue.

EPILOGUE

If the answers to these nine questions are true why the claim that the abortion debate is over? Why say, "Anyone who thinks that Roe's open-ended abortion license is still susceptible to further discussion is outside the mainstream of American public life?" Is it that these questions have not been addressed? Why haven't they?

As reported under Question One three eminent pro-life women and three distinguished pro-choice women have been dialoguing about abortion for six years—not one changed her position on the issue. Did they not raise these questions? It seems not. So sensitive are all aspects of the issue that certain "hot button" terms, unacceptable to one or other side, were not allowed to be used and these women had to agree not to argue directly for their cause.

"Understanding" of the others' position, not common ground, was being sought. One pro-life proponent declared she had genuine respect for each of the pro-choice women, but not for their position. Even this was not well received.

Another pro-life participant believes that the dialogue is a "graced opportunity" for the pro-life ethic to be brought forward into the public square in a way never before possible. Many simply immersed in the current life-style, with abortion available as an unquestioned way of life, may find their hearts touched and their minds opened.

This six-year dialogue warrants belief that people supporting choice of abortion may be utterly sincere. And Roe v. Wade may be so non-negotiable that these questions cannot at present be raised—for open and civil discussion.

Conceivably these six women may be ready to raise some substantive questions. I would prefer—for their logical and psychological interrelationship—the order of questions treated in this article. But pro-choice advocates may find the order foreign to their concerns. They may insist on confronting first the terrible suffering of botched illegal abortions—or the necessity that each woman form her own conscience.

That is their privilege and their concerns should be respected. At some point our questions will, I am confident, emerge.

The point being made, however, is that our responses to the questions do not allow or incline us to call abortion proponents "wicked."

Lifestyles condition the questions to be entertained, the perspective to be taken, and the intellectual presuppositions which must be articulated and addressed. Secular humanism shapes or at least affects the lifestyles of vast numbers of Americans. We do not presume that our questions will prove effective—now. We must patiently wait until time brings about the profound changes necessary for the questions to be faced.

Although Bernard Nathanson, M.D. is himself far from typical, his description of his mindset may be an accurate vignette of some pro-choice proponents as well. It should help to understand why sometimes our arguments fall on deaf ears. If we find him sincere in his pro-life stance, we must believe he was utterly sincere in his aggressive efforts for abortion.

Raised by a Jewish father who repudiated the orthodox Judaism of his own youth, Bernard Nathanson became a man of "the ruthless nihilistic pagan attitudes and beliefs that finally drove (him) to unleash—with a handful of co-conspirators—the abortion monster." (Bernard N. Nathanson, *The Hand of God*, 5)

He acknowledges that most of his life he was not seeking anything spiritual. His goals were earthly, concrete, tangible—"readily liquefiable into cash." He refers to himself as a stiff-backed Jewish atheist, contemptuous of religion. Jewish he was but "a perfunctory Jew." (Ibid., 187)

Looking back from his conversion he sees he had been adrift on the seemingly "limitless sea of sensual freedom—no sextant, no compass, no charts." As for many, many Americans morality was limited to and learned from what was legal. Of course, he was absorbed in the manners and mores of his society. Like most people, justice, at least a minimalist concept of justice, and a sense of common decency guided him.(Ibid., 189)

Keep all that in mind as you follow his 75,000 encounters with abortion. In love with Ruth while at medical school he experienced the problem of illegal, back alley abortions. "The night before the abortion we slept together huddled in each other's arms; we both wept, for the baby we were about to lose, and for the love we both knew would be irreparably damaged…" When he helped her out of the taxi after the abortion he was shocked by the spreading pool of blood on the floor of the cab. She sobbed and sobbed as he cleaned her as well as he could. (Ibid., 55-56)

During his residency at Women's Hospital he was at first puzzled by the extraordinary disparity in the spontaneous miscarriages among the private patients of staff physicians (very few) and among the poor patients who came to the clinic. "At least two-thirds of the clinic females ambulanced to our emergency room in the middle of the night, bleeding profusely and in severe pain, were the victims of botched illegal abortions, <u>not</u> spontaneous miscarriages." (Ibid., 80) In the 1940's and 1950's gynecological wards were filled with women with "raging fevers, torn and obstructed intestines, shredded uteri requiring immediate hysterectomy…"(80) victims of illegal abortions.

Understandably, Dr. Nathanson became convinced that abortion laws had to be changed—eliminated. He could take care of well-off pregnant patients by referring them to Puerto Rico and England for abortions. But what about the poor? With Larry Lader and others he organized NARAL (National Association for Repeal of Abortion Laws) which spearheaded the political movement which led to Roe v. Wade and abortion on demand.

Perhaps his description of how he performed the abortion of his own child will crystallize the mindset of abortionists and pro-choice advocates. In the mid-sixties a woman who loved him very much conceived his child. She begged him to let her have their child. Two failed marriages already behind him, he told her he would not marry her and that he could not afford to support a child. He demanded she terminate the pregnancy as a condition of maintaining their relationship. Indeed he professed to being one of the most skilled in aborting and offered his services.

He asks, "What is it like to terminate the life of your own son? It was aseptic and clinical…The procedure went on without incident, and I felt a fleeting gratification that I had done my usual briskly efficient job." Following procedures, he peeled the gauze bag open and made sure all the pregnancy tissue had been evacuated.

"Did you feel sad...because you had destroyed your own child?" "I swear to you that I had no feelings aside from the sense of accomplishment, the pride of expertise." No regret, no remorse. "And that, dear reader, is the mentality of the abortionist: another job well done, another demonstration of the moral neutrality of advanced technology in the hands of the amoral." (Ibid. 59-61)

Keep in mind that until ultrasound was available, physicians doing abortions "knew very little about the fetus and had never seen it except as chopped up, dismembered flesh or as a just-delivered infant." For Nathanson and colleagues "the piteous plight of the unwillingly pregnant woman facing a dangerous, illegal abortion dominated our thinking." They approached abortion uncritically. A moral and spiritual vacuum existed at the core of what they did and yet they experienced unquestioned certainty of the high level of moral rectitude on which they operated.

After leaving his directorship of the abortion clinic Dr. Nathanson became chief of obstetrical services at St. Luke's Hospital. For the first time in years he had some time and space to think. And most significantly, ultrasound technology threw open a window into the womb. Thus began his conversion first to pro-life and then to the point he can close his semi-autobiography with the words of his professor who became a Catholic, "And there was no doubt about it," Stern wrote, "toward Him we had been running, or from Him we had been running away, but all the time He had been in the center of things." (Ibid., 196)

How many pro-lifers have experienced Nathanson's amoral, areligious upbringing or his personal encounters with abortions? Patience and sympathetic respect are in order as we continue to try to discuss the

Life, Love, and Sex

presuppositions undergirding the abortion debate. I still trust that natural law and the Holy Spirit will prove effective in our achieving the truth.

Application of our Two Step Approach to Moral issues won't help for the dialogue, perhaps, but it will crystallize our conviction of the objective morality of abortion.

APPLICATION OF TWO-STEP APPROACH TO MORAL ISSUES

ABORTION IS IMMORAL.

FIRST STEP

CLARIFY THE ACTION BY ANSWERING 2 QUESTIONS.
1. Impact of choice on a basic human good?
   Abortion is choosing to kill a living, human individual person.
2. Attitude of will toward the goods?
   Normally one's choice is to kill as means to some desired end.

SECOND STEP

EVALUATE THE ACTION BY APPLYING MORAL PRINCIPLES.

To choose to kill a human person as means is to violate the criterion of morality. It is exclusivistic choosing as well as the violation of the first principle of morality To choose to destroy life as means is not compatible with integral human fulfillment.

It violates the 8th Mode of Responsibility. One should not be moved by a stronger desire for one instance of an intelligible good (love of self or family) to act for it by choosing to destroy. . . some other instance of an intelligible good (life).

The 8th Mode of Christian Response is likewise violated: Do no evil that good might come of it.

When the mother's life is at stake and other rare situations are spelt out under Question Nine.

CHAPTER 10

CONTRACEPTION - PART I
THE PRESENT SITUATION

Unlike our first two life-issues, there is no legal conflict about our next topic. Furthermore, most people do not even see a moral issue involved. Can you remember the last time you heard a sermon on contraception? Janet Smith, author of *Humanae Vitae, A Generation Later*, began a lecture on contraception some years ago by reporting a niece's reaction. "Aunt Janet, I hear about your lecturing all over the country. I sure hope I can be like you when I'm your age." Janet observed that apart from the embarrassment a woman feels at reference to her age the significance of her lecturing is greatly diminished when you list those willing to talk on the issue. "The list is very short."

Most Catholics, it seems, just like the rest of Americans, take contraception as no more a moral issue than taking aspirin. "Wow! Am I confused. They've been urging us to practice 'safe-sex', to use condoms, etc. And now they're saying contraception is immoral!" Overheard from a young woman during a discussion in a class on contraception. When a family member, a devout Catholic, heard I was writing on contraception she remarked, "That will be a hard sell."

In every drug store one now finds a section dubbed "Family Planning" with display of choices of methods. Physicians of repute, even C Everett Koop, former U.S. General Surgeon, express amazement that Pro-lifers refuse to join forces in advocating contraception in order to cut down the number of abortions.

Representatives of the United States at U.N. world meetings on population and women issues do all they can to get abortion and contraception declared vital means to cope with population and with feminists' objectives.

What will have to change for people to acknowledge that contraception is immoral? First, in my judgment, people will have to recognize how contraception is linked with the human sufferings afflicting society in the sexual revolution. Second, the beauty and value of married love must be recaptured and the denial of love implicit in contraception must be recognized. Perhaps then people will be open to arguments well reasoned although different from natural science reasoning. For Catholics, minds and hearts must be opened to their Catholic faith which appreciates God's gift of the Church as teacher of God's plan for human happiness.

SIGNS OF CHANGE?

Are people ready to acknowledge the connection of so many of our social problems with the practice of contraception? Kim A. Hardey, M.D. writes, "My purpose here is to demonstrate that the acceptance of contraception has contributed in no small way to the moral chaos we now live in. Marriages were supposed to be better. But now the divorce rate, which was 1 in 10 in the early 1960's, approaches 50%. Every child was supposed to be planned and wanted. But now we abort 1.5 million children each year, and child abuse is common. 85% of engaged couples have had premarital sexual relations. The happiness promised to our culture through the use of contraception has not been found."

Convinced that contraception was not part of God's plan Dr. Hardey left his contraceptive practice in Alabama to set up a new practice totally free of any contraception in Lafayette, Louisiana. There he espouses Natural Family Planning. It is encouraging to learn that his conversion as an Ob/Gyn is not unique; he reports that he is aware that some 20 young gynecologists and 150 family practitioners share the same conviction. (*Catholic Dossier*, Sept.-Oct. 1997, pp. 39-41)

Archbishop George Pell of Melbourne, Australia, corroborates the account above in his pastoral letter. He with Archbishop Charles Chaput of Denver, Colorado, were the only 2 bishops in the world who wrote a pastoral letter for the 30th Anniversary of *Humanae Vitae*. "The widespread use of the pill unlocked the sexual revolution - which brought an increase in abortions, marriage breakdowns, the number of single mothers and of homeless children. These dark consequences of casual sex are hidden from view, while sexuality itself is constantly debased in films, magazines, and advertising, and young men and women, their relations often troubled by a lurking mistrust, are more reluctant than ever to commit themselves to each other unconditionally for life. Individuals are asking the Church to legitimize homosexual activity, to bless single-sex unions. We have now the tragic AIDS epidemic. In the area of sexuality the signs of the times have validated Paul VI's pessimism about the future and like the true prophets of the Old Testament he was derided and denounced for his predictions." (*Inside the Vatican*, Jan. 1999, p.16)

Prof. Janet E. Smith, articulate proud defender of Paul VI's encyclical, finds grounds for hope. She first refers to a commentary by evolutionary biologist, Lionel Tiger, in *U.S. News & World Report* (July 1, 1996). He observed

> . . .that tension between the sexes has increased since the pill became available; that males are confused about what it means to be a male and women are now having babies out of wedlock and aborting their children at an incredibly high rate. Tiger states, 'I do not think anyone is to blame here in the sense that they planned a raid on civil society and got away with it. As happens frequently, technology (contraception, in this case) has generated an unexpected result: more abortions, more single-parent families, more men abandoning their role of being good providers and a higher divorce rate.'
>
> The social chaos spawned by the sexual revolution, fueled by the pill, has been well documented though few have made the connections as clearly as has Prof. Tiger. Tiger's ability to see the obvious. . . encourages me, as does much of the experience I have speaking all over the country and even abroad. There is some reason to believe that more and more people. . .are beginning to question the value of contraception and perhaps even the morality of contraception.

Janet Smith finds hope in our Evangelical brethren who seem very responsive to Catholic teaching on sexuality - because of "their efforts to turn their lives over to the Lord."

"Is there," she muses, "hope also in some feminists?" A London newspaper reported, "Feminists were throwing away their contraceptives and practicing natural family planning. All felt healthier than they had in years and . . .rediscovered what it was to have a natural and healthy libido."

Although only 49% of priests and 37% of nuns (as of 1997) accepted the Church's teaching, that number is up from twenty years earlier. Besides, many bishops are providing more workshops to inform and encourage their priests to respect the Church's teaching on contraception. Younger priests and seminarians, she finds, embrace and are even enthusiastic in support of the Church's teaching.

A retired army chaplain, she reports, has undertaken as his mission to spread the word about contraception. He visits parishes, gives a homily against contraception at all the Masses (at some of which he receives a standing ovation). A few weeks later he returns with a team of doctors and married couples for a day-long conference. The team fortifies his presentation of the Church's understanding of sexuality. They provide scientific and personal testimony about natural family planning. (*Catholic Dossier*, Sept.-Oct., 1997, pp. 18-21)

In the Boston Archdiocese notice is regularly given regarding instruction at various places on natural family planning.

Ruth Pakulak, convert, mother, ardent effective spokesperson "for Life," remarked a few years before her death how she felt there was hope when she heard a priest address the issue of contraception in his homily.

And this summer a student, about to graduate from college in the spring of 2000, left me clippings from 2 journals, *Glamour* (February, 2000) and *Self* (May, 2000). One, "So should you join the nearly 900,000 (and growing) women now using it [natural family planning] as their birth control method of choice?" (*Glamour*)

"Q. Is natural family planning a birth-control method worth trying? A. It can be - if you practice it perfectly, natural family planning is 91 percent effective (the Pill rates 99.9 percent). Yet a recent survey found that fewer than half of Ob/Gyn's discuss NFP with their patients. . . Among NFP's advantages: It's virtually free and totally natural.." (*Self*)

As we shall see NFP is at least as effective as the pill, both as a method and as regards use. Apart from such needed correction, who would expect such journals to advertise/promote NFP?

This prompts me to mention the Paul VI Institute for the Study of Human Reproduction. Founded by Thomas W. Hilgers, M.D. in 1985 in response to Pope Paul VI's appeal to the scientific community, this center has had extraordinary success - overcoming severe obstacles, not the least has been financial. The Creighton Model Fertility CareTM System, a system of achieving and avoiding pregnancy, has been developed to the point that its method effectiveness to avoid pregnancy rivals/surpasses that of the pill. The staff there has had a higher success rate for achieving pregnancy than in vitro fertilization has. Details on these successes later. In the process of closely studying the stages women go through during pregnancy they have developed NaPro Technology - a new reproductive and surgical science to monitor women's health. Soon, it is expected, a 35 year research effort will result in a new medical textbook, *The Medical and Surgical Practice of NaPro Technology*TM.

Undergirding this method of natural family planning is solid commitment to Catholic Church teaching. Doctors, nurses, Creighton Model Fertility CareTM System instructors have been trained for all parts of the country.

Paul VI Institute is one of two most valuable scientific projects sponsored by the Catholic Church to confront and provide for pressing contemporary needs. The other is the National Catholic Bio-ethics Center, devoted to medical ethics. Substantial grounds for hope are found here.

NaPro Technology has made significant breakthroughs for women's health problems. It enables the physician to treat ovarian cysts without surgery. It reduces the likelihood of unnecessary hysterectomy, can recognize and treat the cause of infertility, repeated miscarriages, and ectopic pregnancy.

TWO ROADS TO REJECTION OF CHURCH TEACHING

Yes, there are grounds for hope. But those who are providing this hope are definitely in the minority and are counter-cultural.

Numerous factors have been involved in the development of the current contraceptive mentality related to so many social evils. Certainly one significant influence has been the professed intellectual justification and the acceptance of contraception. Can anyone believe that pre/extra marital sex would be so prevalent if it were not taken for granted that contraception is morally all right? The scientific mentality and its philosophical offspring, Secular Humanism, see nothing wrong with contraception. In fact, effective means for contraception are welcomed as social, political blessings.

The Catholic Church is the strongest challenging opponent to this way of thinking. Yet how can we explain that 91 percent of Catholic couples who are fertile contracept? Church credibility has been lost. People obviously are not listening to the Church in forming their moral judgments. Yet God has blessed us with God's Church to teach and guide us to fulfillment in this life and eternity.

This is an historically new phenomenon. I shall limn in two different ways the process by which this phenomenon emerged. Both are related to Paul VI's encyclical, *Humanae Vitae*.

ROAD ONE: FIVE YEARS OF AMBIGUITY

It begins at the Second Vatican Council. Few, if any, bishops went to the Council with birth control on their minds. "But, when the question was raised on the floor, Pope John XXIII removed it from discussion by forming a commission to review the whole subject. Perhaps no other single official action so effectively undermined the authentic renewal which the Council promised." (James Hitchcock, "A Fateful Mistake," *Catholic Dossier*, Sept.-Oct., 1997, p. 51) We shall refine this understanding of the papal commission in view of Paul VI's enlargement of membership and expansion of mandate. But the thrust of Hitchcock's "Fateful Mistake" remains valid.

The Pope's action was interpreted by many or most as a sign that the Church was not certain of its position on contraception. In fact, "the appointment of a study commission signals, in the modern bureaucratic world, an imminent change of direction on the part of an institution, a prestigious committee gathered to give respectability to the change." (Ibid., pp. 51-52)

Pious, non-forceful papal/Vatican statements to the effect that the Church really was not in doubt, failed to convince and for five years this cloud of ambiguity remained over the issue. Theologians, many, seemed to take for granted that the Church's teaching simply was bound to change. Strong confirmation of this interpretation was provided by the leaked reports of the commission (enlarged by Paul VI) in 1966. The "Majority Report" favored changing the position. "Such a change is to be seen rather as a step toward a more mature comprehension of the whole doctrine of the Church. For doubt and reconsideration are quite reasonable when proper reasons for doubt and reconsideration occur with regard to some specific question." (Quoted in Smith, *Humanae Vitae*, p. 18, from "The Birth Control Report")

Thus the notion of "legitimate development". But Charles Curran, radical revisionist dissenter, denied those opposed to *Humanae Vitae* could appeal to "historical development." It was, in his judgment, imperative to declare the teaching is wrong. And, assuming a pastoral posture and authority, declared, "Catholics in good conscience can dissent in theory and in practice from such a teaching." (Loc. cit.)

With or without such explicit assurance many, many Catholic couples had gradually made up their minds that they had no moral obligation to avoid use of contraceptive methods. Perhaps at first they shopped for confessors who explained that the teaching was in doubt and so not binding. Soon many lost any sense of need of Church directives, stopped going to confession, and arrogated to themselves the right to dispense with burdensome religious obligations. (Hitchcock, Ibid.)

Before moving to my second description of the process of this "Fateful Mistake," two points merit mention. People may not attend to the fact that the Papal Commission was from the beginning established as consultative, in no way deliberative. The reports were supposed to be confidential (not to be leaked) and to be delivered to the pope. He would obviously give serious consideration to them, but retained the responsibility to exercise his teaching charism, guided by the Holy Spirit.

On the other hand, it must be faced that after publication of *Humanae Vitae* episcopal conferences issued pastorals which ran from celebration to qualification. Six hundred theologians and other academics signed a statement crafted by Charles Curran "critical of the ecclesiology and methodology" of the encyclical. It explicitly declared that spouses could in good conscience judge artificial contraception morally permissible in certain circumstances. (R. A. McCormick, "*Humanae Vitae* 25 Years Later," *America*, July 12-26, 1993)

Indeed numerous bishops, including some Vatican officials, gave the impression that they personally did not accept *Humanae Vitae*, but felt compelled to affirm it in a purely formal way. (Hitchcock, Ibid.)

Probably no other encyclical has ever occasioned such bitter divisions in the Catholic Church. As we shall see, Curran was perceptive in calling attention both to the "methodology and the ecclesiology" in *Humanae Vitae*. Both were traditional and Curran's criticism of both reveal the radical elements of the aggressive dissent or attempts at revision.

How apt Hitchcock's description is, "Fateful Mistake." Five years of ambiguity obviously suggested that the Church's teaching on contraception would be changed. This suggestion, confirmed by leading theologians, "liberated" Catholic couples so they could respond to the appeal of a contemporary culture undergoing the sexual revolution of the '60's, conditioned by Secular Humanism. Rejecting, or rather ignoring, Catholic teaching, was accepted as consistent with being Catholic. Soon anyone attempting to claim that contraception is immoral was met with the amused superiority formerly experienced by those daring to claim that smoking was harmful.

"Fateful Mistake" indeed and one way of tracing the process by which this historically new phenomenon occurred.

ROAD TWO: THEOLOGIANS BECOME DISSENTERS/REVISIONISTS

That God in God's Providence allowed the Pope and bishops to act as though they were profoundly uncertain about one of its most sensitive moral teachings challenges one to exercise trust in God. Mitigating factors there were. For example, the very atmosphere of an ecumenical council aspired to have the Church equipped to speak to contemporary culture. Concern for world overpopulation had newly surfaced. Liberation of women from stereotype roles and the discovery of the anovulant pill, which allowed the normal physical act of intercourse, and which promised fulfilling marriages and "wanted" children, warranted serious reflection.

And very influential was the bishops' dependence on theologians. Because theologians had for so long been completely in accord with official Church teaching not only did Catholics in general listen to them docilely but busy bishops could devote themselves to being administrators only. If a moral issue arose, they could depend on their theologians. Many bishops seemed to have forgotten they were appointed by Christ to teach God's word - authoritatively. Theologians have their own charism, but not the bishops' charism of teaching authoritatively. I used to joke with Father Francis Lawlor, one of the most learned theologians I ever knew. He was far superior to Cardinal Cushing in his knowledge of theology, but I would remind Frank that I "believed" and looked to the Cardinal to teach me rather than to him. Frank heartily agreed with my attitude.

During the five years of ambiguity and for some years after *Humanae Vitae*, many bishops were hesitant to assume their role of official teachers of Christ's word. Their silence contributed to firming up the practice of contraception, indeed contributed to many priests embracing the position of leading theologians dissenting from Church teaching or at least remaining silent on the issue.

Watching the process by which many theologians moved into dissent and attempted to revise Church teaching should help in understanding this historically new phenomenon by which the teaching Church lost its credibility.

It must be kept in mind that from the earliest centuries the Church has taught actively and firmly that contraception is immoral. Judge John T. Noonan's work is the most extensive history of the Church's condemnation of contraception. His overview of the Church's teaching on this issue is worth quoting.

> Since the first clear mention of contraception by a Christian theologian, when a harsh third-century moralist accused a pope of encouraging it, the articulated judgment has been the same. In the world of the late Empire known to St. Jerome and St. Augustine, in the Ostrogothic Arles of Bishop Caesarius and the Suevian Braga of Bishop Martin, in the Paris of St. Albert and St. Thomas, in the Renaissance Rome of Sixtus V and the Renaissance Milan of St. Charles Borromeo, in the Naples of St. Alphonsus Liguori and the Liège of Charles Billuart, in the Philadelphia of Bishop Kenrick and in the Bombay of Cardinal Gracias, the teachers of the Church have taught without hesitation or variation that certain acts preventing procreation are gravely sinful. No Catholic theologian has ever taught, "Contraception is a good act." The teaching on contraception is clear and apparently fixed forever.
>
> (Quoted in Smith, p. 3)

Such definite finding of the Church's persistent teaching carries considerable weight coming as it does from a man who, as a consultant to the papal commission, reportedly played a role in leading the commission to advise Paul VI that a change was warranted.

But the Catholic Church was not alone in its opposition to contraception. It was a matter of breaking ranks with nearly the entire traditional Christian opposition to contraception when at the Lambeth Conference in 1930 the Anglican Church declared use of contraception by spouses for serious reasons was morally permissible.

Pope Pius XII the next year solemnly reiterated Catholic opposition to contraception in his encyclical *Casti Connubii*. And so with monolithic unity the Church taught that contraception was immoral - until the 60's. The anovulant pill came on the scene. Is it really contraceptive? Concern about over-population was in the forefront. The women's movement burst out, changing women's role in society. Increased financial strains on the family also contributed. Thus scientific discovery together with social signs and pressures, rather than philosophical or theological deliberations, prompted close examination of the morality of the contraceptive pill.

Changing Methodology

Some theologians acknowledging that contraception is immoral, insisted the pill was not contraceptive. But it was soon recognized that from a moral point of view preventing conception by chemical means does not differ from doing so by physical barriers.

However, other theologians began to reason that human beings are to have dominion over nature and science has equipped us to control conception. Provided marriage as a whole is open to children, they reasoned, not every act of intercourse need be open to conception. The marital union would be nurtured by intercourse thus rendering intercourse meaningful and morally justifiable.

It seemed clear from this point of view that every act of contraception need not be immoral - as traditionally taught. But had not contraception been judged intrinsically evil? At this point the traditional approach or the natural law method needed to be changed. Soon theologians, Joseph Fuchs, S.J. for example, were declaring there are no intrinsically evil acts. No moral absolutes. A radical revolution of method emerged, starting with Peter Knauer, S.J. To give a simplified expression of his basic thesis: to cause or permit evils in conduct is morally wrong or right depending on the presence or absence of a commensurate reason. This method of moral reasoning developed as consequentialism or/and proportionalism.

Charles Curran was on target when, as noted above, he criticized the "ecclesiology and methodology of *Humanae Vitae*."

Richard McCormick, S.J. writes about *Humanae Vitae*, "It is quite a different thing to propose a teaching of natural law as certain when, after many years, most theologians can find no persuasive reasoning to support its absoluteness."

Why can not theologians like McCormick find persuasive reasonings for the teaching of *Humanae Vitae*? Is it not because they have abandoned traditional natural law reasoning in favor of proportionalism? Yet McCormick in 1966 was strongly in support of traditional teaching on contraception. Two years later he embraced the position of the "majority report."

Let me schematize the development:

Monolithic agreement that contraception is immoral, indeed intrinsically evil.

Genuine concern for spouses confronted with grave challenges regarding health, finances, emotional needs.

Awakened concern about over-population and the women's movement.

The pill judged not contraceptive.

Then, obviously, the pill is contraceptive but human beings are gifted by God to have dominion over nature and so over fertility. Traditional focus on the unitive and procreative aspects of marriage can be preserved by overall openness to procreation with contraception for planning one's family.

Consequently, contraception is not intrinsically evil, indeed there are no intrinsically evil acts. And now the morality of acts is to be judged by some form of proportionalism - greater good or lesser evil, etc.

Curran perceptively recognized that dissenting from the solemn teaching by Paul VI required a rejection of traditional natural law reasoning. This move led to rejection of traditional understanding of the nature of the Church, the ecclesiology guiding Pope Paul VI.

Changing Ecclesiology

Now to Curran's criticism of the ecclesiology of *Humanae Vitae*. The Church has always held that the Magisterium has power and the right and the responsibility to teach authoritatively specific moral principles. Dissenting (revisionist) theologians found themselves contradicting not ancient but contemporary and reiterated teaching of the Magisterium. Lo, the "discovery" and claim that the Church has no right or power to teach authoritatively any specific moral principles! The Church, they insisted, can teach as binding the most general directives such as "Love one another," but she can only propose specific moral principles as guidelines which the individual remains free to follow or not.

I had never before noticed that McCormick's article, "*Humanae Vitae* - 25 Years Later" appeared in *America*, July 17-24, 1993 and John Paul II's encyclical, *Splendor of Truth* is dated August 6, 1993. The pope declares, "A new situation has come about *within the Christian community itself*, which has experienced the spread of numerous doubts and objectives. . .with regard to the Church's moral teachings. It is no longer a matter of limited and occasional dissent, but of an overall and systematic calling into question of traditional moral doctrine. . .and the Magisterium itself is considered capable of intervening in matter of morality only in order to 'exhort consciences' and to 'propose values' in the light of which each individual will independently make his or her decisions and life choices." (4)

Indeed, McCormick's article describes this "overall and systematic calling into question of traditional moral teaching." He espouses dissent and the suggestion for a special commission to be set up to assess whether or not contraception is intrinsically evil. John Paul II in *Splendor of Truth* teaches authoritatively as the Vicar of Christ that there is no place for dissent on this issue and that there are intrinsically evil acts. He takes for granted what he earlier declared: "The Church's teaching on contraception does not belong to the category of matter open to free discussion among theologians. Teaching the contrary amounts to leading the moral consciences of spouses into error." (*L'Osservatore Romano*, English edition, July 6, 1987)

McCormick describes the deep and grave divisions in the Church and seems to despair that the only way to dissolve the polarization, ("national episcopates . . .hold truly open consultations on birth regulation similar to those that led to the pastorals on peace and the economy") is at all possible. John Paul II acknowledges the deep and grave divisions and lays bare the grounds and causes of the erroneous dissenting/revisionist thinking and exercises his function of unifying the Church by teaching authoritatively - "in obedience to the word of the Lord who entrusted to Peter the task of strengthening his brethren (Cf. Lk. 22:32), in order to clarify and aid our common discernment." (*Splendor of Truth*, 115)

From before Pope Paul VI's *Humanae Vitae* leading theologians were rejecting the traditional Catholic teaching that contraception is always immoral. In the process they came to embrace a method of moral reasoning, proportionalism, which allowed Catholics to adapt to American utilitarian thinking.

Comfortable in being Catholics who definitely share the "American" attitude toward contraception as well as "the end justifies the means" morality which admits no absolutes, Catholics feel free to pick and choose what they will believe and which moral teachings of the Church they will take seriously.

This historically new phenomenon in the Church is no surprise.

Charles Curran was perceptive in picking out both the methodology and the ecclesiology of *Humanae Vitae* in crafting the statement for theologians to sign in criticism of the encyclical. As we have just seen, the theologians moved first to a new methodology and then to a new ecclesiology in their journey to open dissent and to the "new phenomenon" in the Church's life.

Our Pope, John Paul II, has been keenly aware of it and has searched for its roots and causes. His two extraordinary encyclicals on morality identify and address it. Following the division of methodology and ecclesiology we shall summarize his teaching on this new phenomenon.

We actually have covered this quite fully in Chapter Four as we reported John Paul II's teaching in *The Splendor of Truth* and *The Gospel of Life*. So we limit to brief, pointed selection of insights critical of the changed methodology and ecclesiology.

JOHN PAUL II ON METHODOLOGY

First, as regards methodology. "The teleological ethical theories (*proportionalism, consequentialism*), . . .maintain that it is never possible to formulate an absolute prohibition of particular kinds of behavior. . . In this view, deliberate consent to certain kinds of behavior declared illicit by traditional moral theology would not imply an objective moral evil." (Ibid., 75)

"Such theories. . .are not faithful to the Church's teaching... These theories cannot claim to be grounded in the Catholic moral tradition." (76)

Proportionalism as a moral method is found incompatible with Catholic teaching. This incompatibility becomes more evident once denial of moral absolutes and intrinsically evil acts are addressed.

John Paul II declares that there are intrinsically evil acts. "The Church teaches that 'there exist acts which *per se* and in themselves, independently of circumstances, are always seriously wrong by reason of their object.'" (80)

"With regard to intrinsically evil acts, and in reference to contraceptive practices whereby the conjugal act is intentionally rendered infertile, Pope Paul VI teaches: 'Though it is true that sometimes it is lawful to tolerate a lesser moral evil in order to avoid a greater evil or in order to promote a greater good, it is never lawful, even for the gravest reasons, to do evil that good may come of it (cf. Rom 3.8).'" (80)

"Consequently, she must reject the theories set forth above, which contradict this truth." (83)

John Paul II goes beyond these citations - explaining what does make a human act morally good or bad as well as the root cause of error, namely failure to acknowledge that freedom is related to truth. Thus his answer to the deep and grave divisions in the Church as regards methodology is to identify the error of the dissenting/revisionist theologians and to appeal to the faith of all Catholics.

With regard to dissent, first of all he firmly rejects appeal to the practice of Catholics as warranting change in Church teaching. "The fact that some believers act without following the teachings of the Magisterium, or erroneously consider as morally correct a kind of behavior declared by their

Life, Love, and Sex

Pastors as contrary to the law of God cannot be a valid argument for rejecting the truth of the moral norms taught by the Church." (112)

Then John Paul II addresses those teaching moral doctrine. "While exchanges and conflicts of opinion may constitute normal expressions of public life in a representative democracy, moral teaching certainly cannot depend simply upon respect for a process; indeed, it is in no way established by following the rules and deliberative procedures typical of a democracy. *Dissent*, in the form of carefully orchestrated protests and polemics carried on in the media, *is opposed to ecclesial communion and to a correct understanding of the hierarchical constitution of the People of God.* Opposition to the teaching of the Church's Pastors cannot be seen as a legitimate expression either of Christian freedom or of the diversity of the Spirit's gifts." (113)

This explains why the methodology of *Humane Vitae* is valid and makes clear how proportionalism grew out of the conviction that traditional Catholic teaching erred, while fitting well with the utilitarianism of Western culture. Proportionalism fails as a method of moral reasoning and is incompatible with Catholic beliefs.

JOHN PAUL II ON ECCLESIOLOGY

John Paul II insists on teaching in accord with traditional Catholic ecclesiology. Repeatedly he refers to Vatican II's *Dogmatic Constitution on the Church* where the role of the Magisterium to teach authoritatively with the corresponding responsibility of Catholics to accept the teaching is spelled out. Actually, he refers more often to *The Pastoral Constitution on the Church in the Modern World* where the Council fathers teach specific moral principles authoritatively. *The Dogmatic Constitution on Divine Revelation* is appealed to because it articulates how we know God's revelation by the inter-relationship of Scripture and tradition as interpreted by the Magisterium.

THE GOSPEL OF LIFE

The encyclical is written within such an ecclesiology. In the Introduction John Paul II reports the Church's historical role in bringing to bear the message of Jesus Christ on every new historical challenge. To explain the purpose of the encyclical he observes, "It seems necessary to reflect on the whole of the Church's moral teaching." The reason? Fundamental Catholic truths are being distorted or denied. In fact dissent has gone beyond being limited and occasional to "overall and systematic calling into question of traditional moral doctrine." Indeed it is claimed the Magisterium is empowered only to "exhort consciences" and to "propose values."

Actually, of course, the pope recalls for us that the Second Vatican Council reminds us, responsibility for the faith and the life of faith of the People of God is particularly incumbent upon the Church's Pastors. They are authentic teachers endowed with the authority of Christ. (*The Splendor of Truth*, 64)

There can be no doubt of the understanding of the nature of the Church John Paul II works with. It is the same within which Paul VI operated in *Humanae Vitae* and which Curran objects to. However, it is in the next encyclical, *The Gospel of Life* (March 25, 1995) that the Pope forcefully emphasizes the Church's right, the empowerment from Christ, the responsibility to teach specific moral principles authoritatively.

Addressing the criticism that the Church is accused of promoting abortion, "because she obstinately teaches the moral unlawfulness of contraception," John Paul II reiterates that both contraception and abortion are immoral: "the former contradicts the full truth of the sexual act as the proper expression of conjugal love (and "the life which could result. . .becomes an enemy to be avoided at all costs") while the latter destroys the life of a human being." (*The Gospel of Life*, 13)

But in what some might well perceive as "in your face" response to dissenting revisionist theologians Pope John Paul II solemnly denounces contra-life acts.

"Therefore, by the authority which Christ conferred upon Peter and his successors, and in communion with the bishops of the Catholic Church, *I confirm that the direct and voluntary killing of an innocent human being is always gravely immoral*. This doctrine, based upon that unwritten law which man, in the light of reason, finds in his own heart (cf. Rom 2.14-15), is reaffirmed by Sacred Scripture transmitted by the Tradition of the Church and taught by the ordinary and universal Magisterium." (57)

The Pope could make this denouncing of direct killing stronger only by stating that he was solemnly defining it. The next paragraph spells out the condemnation of such acts as end or as means and as pertaining to fetus, embryo, infant, adult, the old or suffering or dying.

Germain Grisez years ago urged that the Church's right to teach authoritatively specific moral principles be made demonstratively clear by having a Synod define that abortion is always immoral. Whether Pope John Paul II ever heard of Grisez's article with this proposal, in *The Gospel of Life* he does just that. And I think he was demonstrating the right and responsibility to so teach.

"Therefore, by the authority which Christ conferred upon Peter and his successors, in communion with the bishops - who on various occasions have condemned abortion and who in the aforementioned consultation, albeit dispersed throughout the world, have shown unanimous agreement concerning this doctrine *declare that direct abortion, that is, abortion willed as an end or as a means, always constitutes a grave moral disorder*, since it is the deliberate killing of an innocent human being. This doctrine is based upon the natural law and upon the written Word of God, is transmitted by the Church's Tradition and taught by the ordinary and universal Magisterium." (62)

How can anyone claim to speak as a Catholic and deny there are intrinsically evil acts condemned as immoral authoritatively by the Church?

Finally, in similarly strong terms John Paul II condemns euthanasia. "Taking into account these distinctions [use of "methods of palliative care"] in harmony with the Magisterium of my Predecessors and in communion with the bishops of the Catholic Church, *I confirm that euthanasia is a grave violation of the law of God,* since it is the deliberate and morally unacceptable killing of a human person. This doctrine is based upon the natural law and upon the written word of God, is transmitted by the Church's Tradition and taught by the ordinary and universal Magisterium." (65)

In the following number, 66, suicide, assisted suicide and especially non-voluntary euthanasia are condemned.

Charles Curran rejected *Humanae Vitae* criticizing the methodology and the ecclesiology of the encyclical. This he wrote shortly after publication of the encyclical. Years of doing theology along the lines of proportionalism and of the claim the Church is limited in what it could teach authoritatively developed a hardened attitude among many theologians and a conviction of validity of their approach because the thinking conformed to the day's utilitarian mindset and American freedom.

John Paul II has consistently and regularly taught traditional doctrines, but only in 1993 did he publish a sweeping analysis and critique of the moral theology dominant after *Humanae Vitae*.

In the light of *The Splendor of Truth* and *The Gospel of Life* it is difficult to see how theologians can continue to teach as Catholic the denial of intrinsically evil acts, proportionalism, or deny the Church's right to teach specific moral principles authoritatively.

CONCLUSION

Catholics in the pews as well as those who no longer or infrequently attend Church contracept like the rest of the world. The morality of contraception is simply not considered. Such a lifestyle arose in part because of the "Fateful Mistake" which generated expectation that the Church would change its teachings and because leading moral theologians taught that spouses were free to contracept when they had serious reasons for doing so.

To reach such a position the theologians had to reject traditional natural law reasoning which held there are intrinsically evil acts, and so they had to develop another methodology, proportionalism, and to deny the Church was given the power to teach specific moral principles authoritatively.

Without doubt these moral theologians were sincere and committed to the Church. They were struggling to "make the Church relevant." They taught the sacredness of marriage, its unitive and procreative aspects. What they rejected was that every conjugal act must be open to procreation.

Needless to say they never intended to teach that contraception was no more a conscience issue than taking aspirin. But their teaching contributed to that belief and hence to the contraceptive society.

There are some signs that the first thing needed to have people acknowledge that contraception is immoral is emerging. Some people are recognizing the link between contraception and so many social evils. John Paul II's approach in presenting the beauty and value of married love will contribute to the discovery that contraception is implicit denial of marital love.

I see few signs that established theologians are becoming docile to the authentic teaching of the Church. But there are reports that younger seminarians and religious do esteem God's word as mediated through the Magisterium.

If the Church can become reunited on the methodology and ecclesiology so that we can gradually reeducate our people to God's plan for human temporal and eternal happiness, then we may be able to become leaven for the world.

Sadly, however, I believe much more human suffering will be needed before hearts may melt and ears be open to sound reasoning and truth.

In the meantime, people can profit by seeing what the Church actually does teach on contraception and the solid reasoning behind it. If this is grasped, the teaching can be attuned for contemporary ears.

CHAPTER 11

CONTRACEPTION - PART II
THE TEACHING AND REASONING ABOUT CONTRACEPTION

I begin this chapter on the feast of Sts. Peter and Paul, renewing my gratitude to God for my faith and for God's gift of the Church to teach and guide me.

Perhaps what I read earlier this morning prompted that reaction. Speaking of John and Robert Kennedy the author observes, "It is their total secularization that is striking. They privatized their faith. . .Fr. Andrew Greeley sometimes seems to suggest we are all Kennedy Catholics now. All those beliefs and practices are negotiable, nothing that should bring us into collision with our fellow Americans."

This may be an exaggeration. Certainly there are signs of great faith. God is still guiding us. So many seem to be growing in prayer. So many are committing themselves to serve the poor and the afflicted. Unfortunately, however, there is much truth in that scathing description of the loss of Catholic faith. What else explains that 91% of Catholic couples who are fertile contracept - or that Catholics have no more moral qualms about contraception than about taking aspirin? The confidence, even belligerence, of some theologians as they insist on proportionalism and the limited authority of the Church to teach could be attributed to assurance that comes from swimming with the tide - by being assimilated into American culture.

What gives me peace and confidence that all will be well is twofold: conviction that everyone has the natural law built within and belief that the Holy Spirit is active.

It seems we shall have to experience greater suffering before society awakens to the connection of these sufferings with the immorality of contraception, premarital sex, abortion, etc. And a new evangelization must occur before Catholics discern the promptings of the Holy Spirit. Jesus must be experienced as real and living and the fact recognized that he guides his people through the pope and bishops.

As we await the unfolding of history and the action of the Holy Spirit we can only do what we can to explain why contraception is wrong. People are not yet ready to hear this. But once society awakens to the need of re-examining our moral standards and the new evangelization occurs, they will have at hand a reasoned position to consider.

HUMANAE VITAE AND THE *CATECHISM*

However valid the interpretation of the "Fateful Mistake" in leaving people in ambiguity for five years, the official Church teaching, objectively at least, gained new credibility for it had examined the question of contraception afresh, full attention paid to the concern of over-population, human dominion of the material universe now capable of being extended effectively to fertility, to the new role of women in society, to the increased sense of freedom and responsibility with regard to planning one's family, not to mention the emotional and financial pressures on spouses.

After thorough consultation on all these issues Pope Paul VI published *Humanae Vitae* as the Vicar of Christ in 1968 reiterating traditional Church teaching and addressing contemporary concerns and challenges to that teaching.

As reported earlier, the encyclical was met with dissent, demonstrations, even qualifications by episcopal conferences. No Church teaching ever caused divisions in the Church as did *Humanae Vitae*. Not even the Synod of Bishops in 1980 on the Christian family managed to affect the divisions, by that time firmly hardened. John Paul II was asked unanimously by the members of the Synod to be their spokesman, leaving him a long list of proposals as the fruit of their reflections. To fulfill that mission the Pope in 1981 published *The Role of the Christian Family in the Modern World*. Reiteration and resounding support of *Humanae Vitae* was its message.

To simplify our treatment of contraception we shall summarize official Church teaching by recourse to the *Catechism of the Catholic Church* and expose in detail Grisez's theological analysis. The *Catechism of the Catholic*

Church, English edition, came to us in 1994 and summarized the work of Paul VI and John Paul II. Treatment of contraception occurs as Section III under the sixth commandment. That the Catechism addresses contraception under the sixth commandment is of interest because Germain Grisez will insist that contraception is not like fornication or masturbation, sins against this commandment. Clarification of this claim later.

"SECTION III - THE LOVE OF HUSBAND AND WIFE"

The opening sentence says it all. "Sexuality is ordered to the conjugal love of man and woman." To understand the morality of sexual conduct and of contraception one must understand conjugal love and marriage.

Sexual intercourse "concerns the innermost being of the human person as such." It is not simply biological. "It is realized in a truly human way only if it is an integral part of the love by which a man and woman commit themselves totally to one another until death." The Catechism is quoting John Paul II's Apostolic exhortation mentioned above. Repeating Paul VI's teaching the Catechism states that the two meanings or values of marriage (the good of the spouses themselves and the transmission of life) cannot be separated. "The conjugal love of man and woman thus stands under the twofold obligation of fidelity and fecundity." (#2360-63)

"Conjugal Fidelity"

In marriage a man and a woman "give themselves definitively and totally to one another." No longer two, they form one flesh. This constitutes the marriage covenant "of life and love established by the Creator and governed by his laws." The pledge of fidelity links spouses with Christ's fidelity for his Church. (#2364-5)

For those who assume the Church has only recently acknowledged the love aspect of marriage it is delightfully surprising to read what St. John Chrysostom says in the 4th century.

> St. John Chrysostom suggests that young husbands should say to their wives: I have taken you in my arms, and I love you, and I prefer you to my life itself. For the present life is nothing, and my most ardent dream is to spend it with you in such a way that we may be assured of not being separated in the life reserved for us. . . .I place your love above all things, and nothing would be more bitter or painful to me than to be of a different mind than you. (#2365)

"The Fecundity of Marriage"

"A child does not come. . . as something added on to the mutual love of the spouses, but springs from the very heart of that mutual giving, as its fruit and fulfillment." Immediately the Catechism quotes the most significant sentence of *Humanae Vitae*: "Each and every marriage act must remain open to the transmission of life." Again from the encyclical: "This particular doctrine, expounded on numerous occasions by the Magisterium, is based on the inseparable connection, established by God, which man on his own initiative may not break, between the unitive significance and the procreative significance which are both inherent to the marriage act." Shortly after this section of *Humanae Vitae*, every action as end or means, which renders procreation impossible is declared "intrinsically evil."

The reasoning for the teaching is the "inseparable connection" between the unitive and procreative significance of the marriage act, sexual intercourse. (*Catechism*, #2366, 2370)

To this is added John Paul II's insight: "the innate language that expresses the total reciprocal self-giving of husband and wife is overlaid, through contraception, by an objectively contradictory language, namely that of not giving oneself totally to the other. This leads not only to a positive refusal to be open to life but also to a falsification of the inner truth of conjugal love, which is called upon to give itself in personal totality." (#2370)

This personalist approach may speak to contemporary minds. Sexual intercourse stimulates and says, one spouse, for example, to the other, "I give myself totally to you." Performed with contraception he or she says, at the same time, "I do not give you my fertility or capacity for communicating life."

The need, sometimes, for responsible regulation of births is addressed. "For just reasons" — not motivated by selfishness — spacing births may be justified. However, only periodic continence is "in conformity with the objective criteria of morality." Natural family planning will be directly addressed later. (#2368)

The Church's teaching is clear - "each and every marriage act must remain open to the transmission of life." The fundamental grounds for this is the morally inseparable connection of the unitive and procreative significance of the marital act.

GRISEZ BECOMES INVOLVED

Two significant events occurred in June of 1964. Pope Paul VI in an *Allocution to the Cardinals* dated June 23, 1964 declared "certain questions requiring further and more careful investigation have been given over to a commission for the study of population and births, in order that the Holy

Father may pass judgment when its task is completed." Pope John XXIII had in 1963 established the commission to advise the Secretariat of State as the Holy See participated in the international discussion on population. Paul VI enlarged the commission and expanded its mandate. Most pertinently, contraception was not to be addressed by the Council.

June 10, 1964 Grisez's *Contraception and the Natural Law* was completed. His distinctively sensitive perception of critical issues was evident. Not only does he find the actual articulation of arguments against contraception deficient, he rejects the prevalent "conventional natural law theory," recovering St. Thomas Aquinas's insights and approach.

Father John C. Ford, S.J., perhaps the most distinguished American moralist at the time, read Grisez's book in manuscript and later in his review remarked, "Grisez's work is the first philosophical attempt I have seen which makes a substantial, constructive contribution to an understanding of the Church's natural-law position." (Robert P. George, Ed., *Natural Law & Moral Inquiry*, 256)

Grisez and Ford became close friends and collaborators, most immediately in work on the expanded commission to which Ford had been named.

In Grisez's opinion Paul VI from the start believed contraception was wrong. Perhaps because the pill was so recent and functioned differently from the condom and other devices and because some few theologians argued the pill was not contraceptive, the Pope was not sure that it was contraceptive in the traditional sense which had long been condemned. Overpopulation was on his mind: might the pill be the solution? (Ibid., 257)

Pope Paul VI's strategy was to have the council in *The Pastoral Constitution of the Church in the Modern World* state clearly that contraception is always wrong. He would, after the commission completed its investigation and reported to him, decide about the pill. His tactic was to have Ford and a bishop draft certain amendments to this effect. They were sent to the council commission around Thanksgiving of 1965. Members of this latter commission were disconcerted. Some, at least, were opposed to such a position. Some argued the Council Commission were to incorporate the amendments under obedience. As Bernhard Häring reports the situation, "(The majority) first of all ensured their essential freedom by inquiring whether it was a question of giving consideration to the *modi* in accordance with conciliar procedure, or of an order from the Pope." A clear answer was given - that freedom and the fundamental rules of the Council were to obtain.

As Grisez remembers the situation, the Council Commission asked, "Can we put these amendments in our own words?" Running with the permission to do so, they so changed the meaning of the amendments that it was not clear they were saying that contraception is always wrong. Certainly the document can be read as saying that contraception is always wrong, especially since a footnote to the statement referring to the "teaching authority of the Church in its interpretation of the divine law" cites Pope Pius XI's *Casti Connubii* on which *Humanae Vitae* builds as well as two allocutions of Pius XII. However, the statement has been used by revisionist theologians to justify contraception.

And, of course, in the same footnote was added that "certain questions requiring further and more careful investigation" had been turned over to a commission. The Pope would announce his decision "in due course." This is what has been called the "Fateful Mistake." Whatever the intention of the Vatican document, speculation was inflamed about the Church changing its teaching on contraception. (Ibid. , 257-8)

Grisez, always able to see the real and ready to live with it, early on recognized that contraception had won the battle for men and women's minds in secular society and would do the same among Catholics. Nonetheless, he would continue to search for ways to argue for the truth.

For years he has been perfecting his theory of natural law. By the late 90's Grisez was able to look back and evaluate his dependence on St. Thomas. (*Natural Law & Moral Inquiry*, 253)

> He wasn't primarily interested in philosophy, he was interested in doing theology, and you didn't have to have a tight ethical theory and tight moral arguments in his day because in general the big arguments weren't going on in the area of ethics. So the theory in Aquinas is no more refined and perfected than it needed to be, and it didn't have to be very refined and perfected for his purposes. It's sound as far as it goes and very suggestive, but it's not honed and not worked out carefully. He's a gold mine of a starting-place, he's got a lot of good ideas, but he doesn't have any coherent overall theory of ethics, and he doesn't equip you to argue the issues and solve the problems as they've been posed in modern times.

Rather than show the development of Grisez's thinking on this issue of contraception we limit ourselves to his treatment in the second volume of *The Way of the Lord Jesus*.

CONTRACEPTION CONTRA-LIFE IN *LIVING A CHRISTIAN LIFE*

At the very beginning of this treatment two reasons are given that Catholics should <u>believe</u> that contraception is always wrong. Keenly aware of the damage to Catholic <u>faith</u> effected by the "fateful mistake" and the virulent dissent following *Humanae Vitae*, Grisez launches his treatment of contraception by linking it with the demands of faith.

In other words, Catholics should know that contraception is immoral because "First, the Church teaches it." As Grisez sees it, "because the Church has proposed this teaching constantly and most firmly, her infallibility in day-to-day teaching on matters of faith and morals appears to guarantee it." The second reason for belief is the teaching of John Paul II who teaches that this "belongs not only to the natural moral law, but also to the <u>moral</u> <u>order</u> <u>revealed</u> <u>by</u> <u>God</u>. . .handed down by Tradition and the Magisterium." (*Living a Christian Life*, 506)

What he intends in this chapter is to offer a particular way of understanding why the teaching is true. And he limits his consideration to the contra-life aspect of contraception. In the next chapter, on "Marriage, Sexual acts and Family Life," contraception as it occurs within marriage will be treated, as well as its relationship to marital love.

Because methods of contraception are many and because some of them can be chosen for reasons other than to prevent conception, contraception must be understood, if one wants to be accurate, by including intention with the outward performance.

In other words, to define contraception one must do so in terms of beliefs (or understandings), intentions, and choices.

1. Beliefs (understandings): To contracept one must think that
   a. some behavior in which someone could engage is likely to cause a new life to begin and
   b. the bringing about of new life might be impeded by some other behavior one could perform
2. Choices: One's choice is to perform that other behavior
3. Intentions: One's relevant immediate intention is that the prospective new life not begin (though this intention may be subordinate to some further purpose).(Ibid. , 508. See *The Teaching of "Humanae Vitae,"* 41-2)

For Grisez choice is contrasted, not with what is chosen, but with outward behavior and technical performances considered in abstraction from any choice these outward performances carry out.

Since we are concerned with contraception inasmuch as it is a moral act it is essential to focus upon the act as intended. The anovulant pill, for example, is in itself something which prevents ovulation.

Jane and Ray find that raising their three children has become a serious financial burden. They discuss and deliberate and judge they ought not have another child, at least not now, and they consider what to do.

Knowing they will be engaging in sexual intercourse regularly they consider various ways to ensure Jane does not conceive. Deciding that Jane is to go on the pill, as a very effective way to prevent conception, they do so precisely to ensure the prospective new life not begin. Obviously, they do this in order to provide better for their three children. What they choose to do fulfills the definition of contraception.

To highlight the essential contralife intention, consider Helen, a nun, a faithful celibate. Her physician prescribes the pill to treat a pathological condition. Her outward performance is exactly the same as Jane's. She takes the pill as prescribed. But since her intention is to remedy the abnormal physical condition, her action as a moral action is not contralife. It is a health providing act.

On the other hand Muriel, a married woman and sexually active, is diagnosed as having the same pathological condition as Helen. Her physician prescribes the pill as a form of needed therapy. Muriel knows that having sexual intercourse is likely to cause a new life to begin and that this result might be prevented by taking the pill. However, her choice to take the pill is not intended as a means to prevent new life, but as a form of therapy. She intends to do what the doctor judges necessary for her health, knowing and accepting - perhaps gladly, perhaps reluctantly - temporary sterility as a side-effect. Muriel is not contracepting. (Ibid. , 507)

It should be noted that contraception is distinct from any sexual act such as heterosexual intercourse, masturbation or sodomy. A person who has sexual intercourse and contracepts does two distinct things. This stands out clearly if one imagines a woman taking the pill regularly or a man who has himself sterilized, each of whom fails to get contact with a partner with whom to engage in sexual intercourse. Or imagine a man and a woman tempted to fornicate: in most instances they face two choices, whether to fornicate and whether to contracept. (Ibid. , 508)

To understand that contraception from a moral perspective is always a contra-life choice it is important to distinguish the moral act from contraception as a technological intervention in the biological process. In the latter understanding, contraception need only prevent the sperm from fertilizing an ovum. No human individual's life is involved; it is not as though a possible baby were waiting to be conceived. And neither the sperm nor the ovum is a human individual. (Ibid. , 509)

However, as a moral act contraception carries out a choice specified by a possible future state of affairs which the person acting intends to effect by his or her act. The couple knows their sexual intercourse is precisely the action which can result in a new person coming to be unless he or she is prevented from beginning to be. They act in order to ensure that new person not begin to exist. Obviously the will to so act is a contra-life will. Every contraceptive act, precisely as a moral act, is necessarily contra-life.

CONTRACEPTION AND CONJUGAL LOVE
LIVING A CHRISTIAN LIFE

Those urging a change in Catholic teaching on contraception insisted that sexual intercourse must be viewed as a personal act, not merely as a biological act, and argued that contraception helps foster conjugal love. *Humanae Vitae* and later Church teaching likewise emphasized the personal dimension of sexual intercourse but insisted, contrary to the above claim, that contraception violates the nature of sexual intercourse precisely as an act of love.

Janet Smith formulates the argument as follows:
1. Acts that destroy the power of human sexual intercourse to represent objectively the mutual, total self-giving of spouses are wrong.
2. Contraception destroys the power of human sexual intercourse to represent objectively the mutual, total self-giving of spouses.
3. Therefore, contraception is wrong. (*Humanae Vitae*, 110)

Although Grisez from the beginning recognized that contraception is "an offense against marital love as well as an offense against procreation." (*Contraception and the Natural Law*, 95) he maintains that contraception is always wrong primarily because it is contra life. Hence, it is within the chapter on "Life, Health and Bodily Inviolability" that we find the fullest treatment of the issue. There he stated only as a contra life act would contraception be considered, promising an explanation of contraception within marriage and its relationship to marital love in the following chapter.

"Chapter 9: Marriage, Sexual Acts, and Family Life" is 184 pages long. In settling down to address these issues Grisez finally came to realize that marriage is a basic human good - to be added to the seven or eight basic human goods listed in previous writings.

It is a beautiful chapter, rich in significant insights. The entire treatment of the morality of sexual conduct is based upon marriage as a basic human good. When a man and a woman marry the common good is the communion of marriage itself. "The *communion of married life* refers to the couple's *being* married, that is, their being united as complementary, bodily persons, so really and so completely that they are two in one flesh." Conjugal love actually is this interpersonal union "when that love takes shape in the couple's acts of mutual marital consent, loving consummation, and their whole life together, not least in the parenthood of couples whose marriages are fruitful." (*Living a Christian Life*, 568)

To explain the relation of this interpersonal communion and parenthood Grisez compares them to the crypt of a church and the upper church. What is originally planned is the entire church. This determines the plan for the crypt. The upper church is not an extrinsic end, the crypt merely instrumental; rather the former will complete the whole structure - the crypt being the first and basic part. Even if the upper church is never built, the crypt is able to serve as, and really be, a church in itself.

When the couple at the wedding say, "I do," (or equivalent) a valid marriage exists and is part of a larger whole. "Always and everywhere, marriage is the relationship recognized as appropriate for begetting and raising children." Conjugal union is intrinsically good, not instrumental to parenthood as the end of marriage. Marital communion is designed to be an intrinsically good part of a large, intrinsically good whole, namely the family.

Parenthood is not the end or purpose, but the perfecting of marital communion. And so it shapes the interpersonal communion. Like the crypt of the unfinished church, marriage in which having children is impossible is still marriage. "For marriage realizes the potentiality of man and woman for unqualified, mutual self-giving, which they undertake and begin by the very act of marital consent." (Ibid. , 569)

It is sexual capacity which enables human persons to participate in the good of marital communion. Consequently, married couples should engage in sexual acts which are reasonable and conducive to marital communion and avoid all other sexual activity. Sexual acts which are not marital violate the good of marriage and so are immoral. Hence, the unmarried should never engage in any sexual act, since all such acts in one way or another violate the good of marriage.

In other words, sexual intercourse between spouses, expresses and stimulates or fosters their marital communion (the common good of their marriage) because their mutual self-giving in the act makes actual their one-flesh unity - provided they willingly and lovingly join in an act suitable to procreating. On the other hand the act of sexual intercourse simply is not a marital act if one or both engage in a sexual act unwillingly/unlovingly or do anything inconsistent with the act's being suited to procreating.

If the sexual act is not a marital act, it is not an act of conjugal love - the reciprocal self-giving which brings about one-flesh unity. Grisez refers to Pope John Paul's insight, "the innate language that expresses the total reciprocal self-giving of husband and wife is overlaid, through contraception, by an objectively contradictory language, namely that of not giving oneself totally to the other. . . falsification of the inner truth of conjugal love. . ." (Ibid. , 635, footnote 162).

Grisez relates his treatment to the traditional formulation - "unitive meaning" and "procreative meaning" of the marital act. "Using this terminology, the point is that the unitive meaning of marital intercourse includes its procreative meaning and is specified by it. . .the two meanings are inseparable, for a whole cannot be without its parts." (Ibid. , 635)

NATURAL FAMILY PLANNING

No treatment of contraception can avoid the problem of family planning. My students immediately rush to argue, "How can contraception be immoral when it is exactly the same as natural family planning (NFP) and the Church says this is not immoral?"

I find their reaction very interesting for two reasons. First, it reveals their suspicions that although in class I am treating all these moral issues philosophically, they really believe I am simply following the Church's teaching. It is true that the positions Grisez arrives at are compatible with Catholic teaching, but I restrict our use of Grisez to his philosophical reasoning.

Secondly, and I hasten to point this out to them: if NFP is the same as contraception it too is immoral. Not the reverse - - as they try to twist the relationship.

I stand on my head to make clear how contraception differs from NFP - with little success. Grisez recently acknowledged that he needs more clarification of what is and what is not intended in NFP since both some people in favor of contraception and some who judge it immoral maintain that the two do not differ the way he and his colleagues say they do.

> Somewhat similarly, identifying the object of a deliberate omission is not always easy, even if one adopts, as one should, the perspective of the acting person. Thus, though Finnis, May, and we are convinced that couples can practice periodic abstinence to regulate births without precisely intending to impede conception, not only Vacek and others who hold that contracepting often is morally acceptable, but some who hold that it never is, maintain that the two do not differ as we think they do. So, additional clarifications of the distinction between what is and is not intended are needed and, we are confident, can be made without affecting the main lines of the action theory, which St. Thomas already proposed and *Veritatis Splendor* confirms.
>
> (*Natural Law and Moral Inquiry*, 224)

Before we attempt to address that challenge, let me briefly remind readers what NFP is.

NFP: BRIEF HISTORY

It has long been known that normally a woman ovulates only once during a menstrual cycle. And we know that the ovum survives at most 24 hours after ovulation. The meeting between the ovum and spermatozoon is possible then, only during this limited 24 hour period. However, the fertile phase lasts longer, because the spermatozoon can be stored in the cervical crypts - possibly for 5 days. Obviously, therefore, the more precisely the time of ovulation can be detected, the more accurately can be discerned the times to conceive or the best time to abstain if a couple wants not to conceive.

The first natural family planning system in history based on scientific study was "rhythm," independently arrived at in 1930 by Dr. K. Ogino in Japan and Dr. H. Knaus in Austria. They discovered that ovulation occurs approximately two weeks prior to menstruation. Each woman had to discover when ovulation occurred. Not only must individual cycles be taken into account, but also whether stress, etc. might change the time of ovulation as well as the rare second ovulation.

Because this system was unable to provide for such irregularities many couples were disillusioned by repeated failures. So the discovery that the hormone progesterone, produced by the ovary after ovulation, brought about an early measured elevation of the basal body temperature contributed immensely to the efficiency of natural family planning. About the same time signs and symptoms of ovulation were detected and so the sympto-thermal method of natural family planning was developed.

The Australian husband and wife team, both physicians, John and Lyn Billings, correlated certain biomarkers such as vaginal bleeding and mucus discharge with the phases of fertility and infertility in the menstrual cycle. Doctor Thomas W. Hilgers has developed this approach systematically and terms his method the Creighton Model Naproeducation Technology.

In the June 1998 issue of *The Journal of Reproductive Medicine* he published the results of five studies. The method effectiveness was 99.5% for avoiding pregnancy and the use effectiveness 96.8%.

In view of this history and especially of the proven effectiveness of NFP it was astonishing to see that a chart of methods of contraception taught in a school of nursing listed natural family planning as a "method of contraception" and only 80% effective. Apparently, little effort was made to distinguish methods of NFP. All were lumped together.

There is need to correct some mistaken conceptions of NFP. Not only is NFP more effective than a number of commonly used methods and as effective as the pill, but it does not depend on having regular menstrual periods. It can be used during breast feeding etc. Moreover anyone taught by a competent teacher and motivated to use NFP can use it effectively. In fact the methods are so simple they have been successfully adapted to suit the needs of cultures all around the world. It can be argued that NFP couples can make love no less frequently than other couples. The times when this is advisable for those wishing to avoid pregnancy obviously will be different from those not practicing NFP. However, NFP couples report how abstinence can motivate use of other ways of expressing love as well as creating a "honeymoon experience" monthly. Furthermore, divorce rate is significantly lower among NFP couples.

BENEFITS OF NFP

The Pope Paul VI Institute for the Study of Human Reproduction under Dr. Thomas W. Hilgers spells out some of the benefits of the Creighton Model Fertility Care System.

First of all, this method enables a woman to understand her fertility cycles, the shifts in moods, etc. and enlightens the husband about his wife's cycles and significant emotional and physical changes. Likewise it empowers a woman with knowledge to enhance her health. For an accurate record of ovulation and ovarian function is very valuable for the evaluation and treatment of most gynecological problems.

Besides being highly effective for avoiding pregnancy without medical side effects, the Creighton Model is also extremely useful for achieving pregnancy. For couples of normal fertility limited tests show 76% effectiveness in the first cycle, 90% in the second and 98% in the third cycle. On the other hand 20-40% of infertile couples achieve pregnancy in one year using only the Creighton Model Fertility Care System. In vitro fertilization, enormously expensive, does not have so high a rate of effectiveness.

Provided both spouses are motivated to embrace, learn and faithfully follow this NFP, their relationship improves, their sexual satisfaction is enhanced and, significantly, divorce rate is low.

NFP AND MORALITY

But is NFP morally justifiable? The *Catechism of the Catholic Church* devotes less than a page to "periodic continence," firmly stating it is "in conformity with the objective criteria of morality." It corroborates this claim by referring both to *Humanae Vitae* and to Pope John Paul II's *The Role of the Christian Family in the Modern World*.

The Catechism approaches NFP with a very positive attitude, noting how it respects the bodies of the married couples, how it encourages tenderness between the spouses and provides for development of authentic freedom.

Grisez, on the other hand, has dealt at length with the challenge to show why NFP is different from contraception. Focusing on the contralife aspect of contraception, he labors to demonstrate how NFP need not be contralife. (See *Living a Christian Life*, 510-12 and *The Teaching of "Humanae Vitae,"* 81-92)

CONTRACEPTION - PART II THE TEACHING AND REASONING ABOUT CONTRACEPTION

The key challenge to NFP is that the couple contracepting and the couple using NFP want exactly the same thing - to avoid having another baby. They both intend the same objective.

Perhaps specific focus on what is intended may clarify the difference between NFP and contraception.

Harriet and Wilfred have three children and Wilfred is no longer able to work. They judge that they ought not have another child in order to provide for their three children. Harriet goes on the pill.

Gwendolyn and Marvin find themselves in identical circumstances. Gwendolyn already has had bad experiences with the pill. So having heard how effective NFP has become and seeing other advantages to it they decide to use NFP as their method of contraception.

From a moral point of view both couples have chosen an immoral means to achieve their good end. Both recognize that a child may well result from their sexual intercourse; they want that child not to come to be and choose the means to ensure that child not come to be.

Phyllis and John find themselves in the same situation. They judge they have an obligation not to have another child. Knowing that contraception is immoral they inquire about NFP and, impressed by the instructions and assured it can be chosen without contraceptive intent, they decide to practice Natural Family Planning.

What convinced them that NFP is different from contraception was the explanation that <u>what</u> they would be doing could be different even while <u>why</u> they would be doing it would or could be the same as couples contracepting.

<u>Why</u> they were considering doing anything, they saw, was identical with the other two couples- they ought to continue to provide for their three children and avoid having another child which would make that very difficult if not impossible.

<u>What</u> Harriet and Wilfred choose as means to provide for their three children was to *prevent a baby coming to be* by using the pill.

What Gwendolyn and Marvin choose as means to provide for their three children was to prevent a baby coming to be by practicing NFP instead of using the pill.

Thus they transform "what" is morally justifiable in itself, NFP, into an immoral act by their intention. Instead of intending to avoid the undesirable consequences of a baby coming to be, they <u>intend</u> to prevent the baby's coming to be. For them, if NFP were not effective, they would use a condom or some other form of contraception.

What about Phyllis and John? They do not choose anything to *prevent a baby coming to be*. They have learned precisely when Phyllis is fertile, when intercourse is likely to result in a baby coming to be and the situation develop which will prevent them from caring properly for their three children. Their intention in abstaining at these times is to avoid the bad consequences of a baby's coming to be - accepting, not intending the baby's not coming to be. In such a choice there is no contralife will; nor is there in accepting the baby's not coming to be.

Speaking in general, one who considers choosing to do something for a certain good but decides *not to do it* in order to avoid bad side effects does not thereby choose to reject the good not pursued. For example, Jennifer plans to open a restaurant in a small town which actually will compete with Joshua's friend's restaurant. Jennifer asks Joshua for a substantial loan to finance her venture. Joshua considers doing Jennifer this favor, but decides not to loan her the money precisely to avoid contributing to making it difficult for his friend. He is not choosing to prevent Jennifer's venture. He is choosing not to produce problems for his friend.

Consider Hazel, on the other hand, who dislikes Jennifer and to keep her from opening a restaurant solicits signatures to prevent town permission to use her chosen location for a restaurant. She intends to prevent Jennifer from opening the restaurant.

NFP AND END OF LIFE ISSUES

Grisez compares the ethics of responsible parenthood with responsible care for the dying and finds them the same. As a prelude it is essential to distinguish "wanting" as an emotional reaction and a "volitional" reaction.

"Do you 'want' some ice cream?"

"I love ice cream. I very much 'want' it, but know I must avoid it because of my severe diabetes. So I thank you but for that reason I do not 'want' any."

That distinction in mind, compare the following. Jim and Bill, both physicians, are anxious about their mother who is dying and in pain. Both want (emotionally) her not to suffer. Jim chooses to give their mother an overdose of morphine, to kill her and eliminate her suffering. He wants volitionally to kill his mother as the way to stop her suffering. Bill chooses to administer pain medication, sufficient to relieve her pain, foreseeing and permitting the hastening of her death. He does not want volitionally to kill his mother. He permits the hastening of her death.

The three couples above all "want" (emotionally) that no baby come to be. Harriet and Wilfred, like Jim, choose (and so want volitionally) to prevent the possible baby from coming to be. (They choose to use the pill, to contracept.) Gwendolyn and Marvin likewise choose (and so want volitionally) that no baby come to be. They choose NFP as their means to contracept.

Phyllis and John, like Bill, although emotionally they do not want a baby to come to be, choose (and so volitionally want) to avoid the undesirable circumstances a new baby would bring about (making difficult or impossible their providing for their three children).

As Bill has no contralife will in choosing to relieve pain, foreseeing and merely accepting the hastening of his mother's life, so Phyllis and John have no contralife will in choosing to practice NFP as means to avoid the undesirable consequences of a new baby, foreseeing and merely accepting that no baby come to be.

Grisez, in *Living a Christian Life*, confirms the reasoning above by appealing to two traditional teachings which illustrate what a couple practicing NFP can be choosing.

First, at the time all Christians judged contraception sinful, they also looked on fornication and adultery as sinful - and this partly because they might lead to a pregnancy. Thus to avoid conception was presumed to be a good reason to abstain from intercourse for an unmarried couple. Second, when a married couple was confronted with a serious problem such as a wife's health or their poverty so that they had a moral responsibility to avoid having a child, they were encouraged by the Church to abstain from marital intercourse. There was not the slightest suggestion that people in such situations were practicing contraception.

The unmarried couple in abstaining from intercourse were carrying out a proposal - not to prevent the beginning of new life, rather the proposal was to refrain from committing fornication or adultery - while at the same time avoiding pregnancy outside of wedlock.

Clearly also, in the situation above, the married couples who abstained did not intend to impede procreation; they were carrying out the proposal not to cause a complex state of affairs which included a prospective child's coming to be. Inseparably in that complex state of affairs were consequences which were judged bad and these consequences made it reasonable to avoid having a child.

Surely it is clear that married couples, choosing to avoid conception by periodic abstinence, can have the intention similar to couples who in the past abstained continuously. They abstain during fertile times in order <u>not to cause</u> a pregnancy. The intention does not preclude having intercourse during infertile times. If they choose to have normal sexual intercourse at those infertile times, they obviously are not intending to prevent or impede the beginning of new life, since the infertility is due, not to their marital intercourse, but to natural conditions.

This should make clear how the willing that relates to the prospective baby's not coming to be need not be the same in (i) the choice of some form of contraception as in (ii) the noncontraceptive choice to avoid conception by abstinence. In (i) the couple intend precisely to prevent a baby from coming to be - even when this is chosen as means to avoid the undesirable consequences, a good ulterior end. In (ii) the couple's choice is to abstain insofar as it might cause a state of affairs which include things they think it reasonable, even obligatory, to avoid. They do not choose the baby's not coming to be as a means to anything. Indeed they don't even want to cause that state of affairs as a whole; they are choosing not to cause the state of affairs which would include the baby's coming to be. They only <u>accept</u> the baby's not coming to be.

CONCLUSION: AT LAST — A SOLUTION: NFP

If it were to become better known how effective Natural Family Planning is and how beneficial it can be to marriage happiness, and how radically different it is from contraception, people would increasingly be open to acknowledge how wrong contraception is.

A caution, however: "NFP as a mere technique will never solve the pastoral problem posed by contraception. Although technique is helpful, the problem is a moral one, and no technique makes the heart good." (*The Teaching of "Humanae Vitae," 113*)

As was remarked earlier, Catholics today have no more moral qualms about contraception than about taking aspirin. A non-issue shared as such with their fellow Americans. Yet it can hardly be denied that the radical change in our culture's sexual mores is closely linked with contraception. Pre/extra-marital indulgence, living together, the increase of venereal diseases all developed with contraception taken for granted.

Furthermore, the Church's entire teaching about sex and marriage is impacted by the claims for contraception. If sexual intercourse can, as a moral act, be separated from marriage, why is homosexual marriage impossible? If procreation need not be the fruit of marital love, what is wrong with in-vitro fertilization?

Rejection of the teaching of *Humanae Vitae* has brought division to the Church by undermining belief in the Magisterium - no longer seen as empowered to teach us what God wants, no longer esteemed as a blessing.

Hearts are hardened, it would seem, by no means open even to listen to reasoned arguments - by no means open to Church authentic teaching.

More physical and social evils and suffering will, I believe, have to be experienced before hearts and minds are opened to acknowledge the significant connection contraception has with such sufferings. Then people may be ready to entertain the possibility that there may be something wrong, morally, with contraception. And once the effectiveness of Natural Family Planning becomes recognized, a very serious concern will have been met and another barrier to truth will fall.

Widespread suffering may also turn people to prayer, softening hearts so they can encounter Jesus and rediscover the need of Church to nurture union with Jesus.

CONTRACEPTION - PART II THE TEACHING AND REASONING ABOUT CONTRACEPTION

Even after increased suffering opens minds and hearts to the question, things will never be as they were before all these changes. People have experienced the joy and empowerment of freedom and are well informed by media and the internet of the diversity of opinions on all subjects.

Individuals will have to form their own judgment about contraception. Many will recognize the validity of the reasoning above - that contraception is both contralife and contralove. Others may be unwilling or even unable to accept such reasoning, their minds limited to scientific thinking, supported by Secular Humanist philosophy.

Individuals will confront freedom of choice to embrace Catholic faith and the blessing of Church guidance. Pope John Paul II's encyclical, *The Splendor of Truth,* may prove enlightening. And if commitment to Christ becomes effective in loving others, making their lives more human, non-Catholics may look on the Church as partner in their human struggle, and finding her more credible be more open to hear her teaching.

Because I am convinced that all people possess "the natural law" (or "innate life-plan for human liberation and fulfillment") and that God is passionately concerned with God's creation and people, the Holy Spirit actively present, I have confidence that society will move to protect life and health, love and family.

Again, as begun in Chapter 4, we conclude with Grisez's directives for approaching moral issues.

APPPLICATION OF TWO-STEP APPROACH TO MORAL ISSUES

(Catholics have the authentic authoritative teaching of the Church, "Each and every marriage act must remain open to the transmission of life." They and everyone should be able to recognize the validity of the reasoned arguments.

See Chapter 4 for meaning of terms.)

CONTRACEPTION IS CONTRA-LIFE.

FIRST STEP

CLARIFY THE ACTION BY ANSWERING 2 QUESTIONS.
1. Communication of life is directly affected.
2. One or both spouses deliberately choose to do something to impede/prevent new life.

SECOND STEP

EVALUATE THE ACTION BY APPLYING MORAL PRINCIPLES.

To choose to impede or prevent new life is exclusivistic choosing, violating the criterion of morality. Such choice clearly violates the eighth Mode of Responsibility. And for the same reason it violates the first principle of morality, not choosing in a way compatible with integral human fulfillment. The eighth Mode of Christian Response and possibly the fourth are violated.

++++++

CONTRACEPTION IS CONTRA-MARRIED LOVE.

FIRST STEP

CLARIFY THE ACTION BY ANSWERING 2 QUESTIONS.
1. The good of marriage, marital communion, is impacted. Sexual intercourse expresses and fosters a couple's marital communion, the reciprocal self-giving which brings about one-flesh unity. In contraception the self-giving inherent in sexual intercourse is not self-giving, for one or both spouses withhold their fertility.
2. One or both spouses deliberately choose to prevent full self-giving, marital communion.

SECOND STEP

EVALUATE THE ACTION BY APPLYING MORAL PRINCIPLES.

To choose to impede the good of married love is exclusivistic choosing, a violation of the good of marriage. It violates the first principle of morality by not choosing in a way compatible with integral human fulfillment. The eighth mode of responsibility is violated, as well as the eighth Mode of Christian Response.

++++++

Life, Love, and Sex

NATURAL FAMILY PLANNING WITH CONTRACEPTIVE INTENT IS IMMORAL.

FIRST STEP

CLARIFY THE ACTION BY ANSWERING 2 QUESTIONS.
1. Basically by systematically omitting intercourse during fertile periods a couple choose to prevent new life.
2. NFP in itself is morally justifiable, but the intent in such a case is to perform the omissions as means to prevent new life.

SECOND STEP

EVALUATE THE ACTION BY APPLYING MORAL PRINCIPLES.
Since the intent is to prevent new life, the couple choose exclusivistically, violating the criterion of morality. They violate the eighth Mode of Responsibility, choosing to impede a good in order to pursue the good, e.g. of providing for the children they have. For the same reason, the couple violate the first principle of morality, choosing in a way not compatible with integral human fulfillment. The 8th (and perhaps the 4th) Mode of Christian Response is likewise violated.

++++++

CONTRACEPTION - PART II THE TEACHING AND REASONING ABOUT CONTRACEPTION

NATURAL FAMILY PLANNING WITHOUT CONTRACEPTIVE INTENT IS MORALLY JUSTIFIABLE.

FIRST STEP

CLARIFY THE ACTION BY ANSWERING 2 QUESTIONS.
1. A couple choose to omit intercourse during known fertile days with intent to avoid the undesirable consequences of having a child, when they have good reason for not having a child.
2. They pursue, for example, the good of providing for the children they have. They do not choose to prevent a child coming to be and have good reason for permitting that a child not come to be.

SECOND STEP

EVALUATE THE ACTION BY APPLYING MORAL PRINCIPLES.
Omission can be an action but avoiding undesirable consequences is reasonable and in accord with the criterion of morality, inclusivistic choosing. By pursuing the good of providing for the children they have by avoiding undesirable consequences of having a child they are choosing in a way compatible with integral human fulfillment. To permit a child not to come to be while pursuing the good of providing for their children by avoiding undesirable consequences for good reason is in accord with all the Modes of Responsibility. This is in accord with the Modes of Christian Response.

++++++

PART THREE

MORALITY OF SEXUAL CONDUCT

CHAPTER 12

REFLECTIONS ON LOVE

LOVE, SEX, MORALITY, HAPPINESS

Life issues certainly are agitating our country. Besides those we have addressed—assisted suicide, capital punishment, abortion, and contraception—the future of the human race may be profoundly impacted by the alternative ways of passing on life, genetic engineering, and cloning.

Since we have limited our focus to the ordinary concerns about life and sexual conduct, we forgo these challenges. We shall address the perennial issue of sex, but within the daunting attitude changes toward sex, love, and marriage.

Perhaps because the audience we primarily envisage are Catholics, we are drawn to the writings of Pope John Paul II. But his profound, personalist analysis of love does not depend on faith and should find people of all faiths or none resonating with his insights into their own experience.

Karol Wojtyla (Pope John Paul II) bids us reflect on sexual morality within the context of love and responsibility. So we begin our discussion of the morality of sexual conduct by reflections on love.

REFLECTIONS ON LOVE

Generally people think sex when they think love but do not always think love when they think sex. Novels, theater, and television regularly present sex as recreational, as release or fun, or at most as "love for the time being."

Everybody yearns for love and very often indulgence in sex is really vain pursuit of love. So vain that not infrequently women cry after premarital intercourse, keenly aware that they wanted much more than this.

"And therefore the most fundamental way of looking at sexual morality is in the context of 'love and responsibility'—which is why the whole book bears that title." (*Love and Responsibility*, Wojtyla, p.16)

Everybody wants to be happy. For this, love is critical. Not everybody makes conjugal love and marriage the dominant desire in their lives, but everybody experiences the need to harmonize the sexual urge within their pursuit of happiness.

Five chapters will be devoted to the morality which should guide us in harmonizing the sexual urge. But it is an illusion to think we begin reflection on the morality of sexual conduct in a neutral state of mind. Psychology informs us that before birth and as infants our most primitive emotional responses are for survival and security. We cannot remember the primitive experiences but our emotional responses to them remain imbedded in the unconscious. Emotional programming for happiness soon took shape with emotional desire for pleasure, affection and esteem in addition to the emotional need and desire for survival and security. No one is surprised to learn how infants reveal the drive for power and control, which factor into our search for happiness

These emotions are first generated by need, then are experienced as demands which grow into "shoulds."

In the process of socialization we identify with the values of our influential "others": parents, those who supervise us, peers, the media. From these cultural sources we learn what provides security, what gives pleasure and assures affection and esteem, the way to get power.

In our teens, perhaps, we travel various avenues which promise some happiness. Since actually we are made for unlimited happiness, each of these roads disappoints. As the song says, "Is that all there is to . . . . ?"

Our emotional program for happiness is significantly impacted at puberty by emergence of sexual desire. The person's development as male or female is more easily observable in the body than in the psyche. So much is this the case that people tend to think that a person is a man because he has male genitals. Actually the reverse is the case: this person has male or female genitals because he or she is a man or a woman. Every cell in the body is distinctively male or female.

Born male or female, people have a sexual urge to seek the other sex. (Homosexuality has a separate chapter.) This urge does not determine what we do, but creates a base for definite actions. Animals' response to sexual instincts are determined actions. Freedom of self-determination allows people to decide for themselves how to respond to these urges and to take responsibility for their actions.

Under their sexual urge men and women are attracted to one another; clearly the attributes of the two sexes are complementary. Not only can a man supplement his own attributes with a woman's, he feels a need to. The attributes of each sex is valued by the other, valued precisely because of the sexual urge.

Since normally this urge is directed toward a particular human being, it provides the base on which the possibility of love arises. "The <u>possibility</u> of love," we say, for love is fundamentally different from mere biological or psycho-physiological experience of the sexual urge. Free choice and commitment must give definite shape to such attraction in order for love to exist.

Under the influence of urges for sexual union with the other sex persons are able to think and to choose, and in the thinking are able to understand the natural purpose and consequence of sexual acts; they can freely commit themselves to pursue those purposes and take responsibility for actions in that pursuit.

In this context it is important to note the principle that persons may not be <u>used</u>—either as means to enjoyment or any other end. People can use <u>things</u> to achieve ends. But other <u>persons</u> have equal capacity and right to pursue their own ends. We all resent "being used."

NATURAL PURPOSES OF SEXUAL INTERCOURSE

What, then, are the natural purposes of sexual intercourse? It probably took generations for the relation between intercourse and births to be recognized. But for centuries people have known that sexual intercourse regularly results in conception and birth of new life. In fact it is clear that the preservation of the human race depends on people having intercourse.

On the other hand, although many look on sexual intercourse simply as intensely pleasurable experience and release, almost everyone realizes it can be a special stimulus to and expression of the love of total self-giving. Trivialization of sex tends to endanger the love of total commitment.

Later we shall consider how conjugal love embraces the natural purpose of sex: responsibility to hand on life.

This relationship of love and life is the basis of traditional morality in sexual conduct. Some hold there is no need to attend to and respect this relation; they see nothing distinctive about sexual acts to generate specific moral principles. Only generic moral principles such as fairness and avoidance of abuse or taking advantage of another person are applicable. Thus so long as two competent persons freely engage in any sexual activity, according to these same people, there is nothing wrong.

The personalistic principle, on the other hand, rules out as immoral any sexual indulgence in which persons use another or use each other. Sexual intercourse, for example, between two freely consenting adults, can involve mere use, perhaps mutual use, when love is absent.

Much more on the morality of sexual conduct later. But people trained to examine issues within the natural sciences and the empirical perspective will have difficulty following the interpretation given above. For them the sexual urge involves functions directed toward enjoyment, love and a biological end, reproduction. Since human beings are masters of nature, it is up to them to mold those functions whatever way they judge expedient and agreeable. As we use and interfere with nature by artificial means to benefit our lives, so it is up to us to decide whether sexual activity should include reproduction and, if not, how to control this result.

SENSUALITY, SENTIMENTALITY, LOVE

How does the sexual urge ordinarily affect men and women? As sensuality, sentimentality, love. The first two can provide the material for genuine love or remain mere sensuality or sentimentality. (See *Love and Responsibility*, pp. 104-118)

When a man responds to a woman's bodily attraction the response is sensual. The woman is seen as an "object of desire" because of the sexual value inherent in the body itself. His "erogenous zones" are stirred.

Our "sensate culture" exploits sensuality. Hugh Hefner's "philosophy" has infected society most successfully. Behind this philosophy lies either the separation of body and sex from the person (the former left alone as "possible object of use")—or the assumption that the person is exclusively "body and sex" and an object to be used.

Sensuality is not love. How well it is known that sensuality may easily become the opposite of love. Still sensual response is the natural reaction to a person of the other sex and can be raw material for true conjugal love. But for love to develop, the yearning for the sexual value connected with the body must be integrated and become part of a fully formed and mature attitude toward the other as person.

Sensuality, of course, in itself is blind to the person, oriented only toward the sexual value connected with the body. It is characteristically fickle, open to any body where it finds that sexual value, wherever a possible object of enjoyment appears.

Still there is nothing wrong with sensual excitability as a natural and congenital characteristic. Indeed a readily aroused, exuberant sensuality can be the stuff from which a rich personal life is made.

Experience shows that a current of love as desire permeates sensuality. However, unless it is supplemented by the nobler elements of love, it remains nothing more than desire, anything but love.

Sentimentality and Love

Sentimentality is clearly different from sensuality. When the emotion evoked in direct contact between a man and a woman has as its object a sexual value connected with the whole person of the opposite sex, femininity or masculinity is involved. And this is sentiment, the source of affection.

Instead of the desire to use the other, there is desire for nearness, for exclusivity and intimacy, a yearning to be alone together. Experience shows that sentimental attachment can easily move into sensuality. The man is quicker to recognize the pull of sensuality in expressions of affection than the woman.

Another problem with sentimentality is the tendency to attribute to the other qualities one desires him or her to have. Sentimentality is subjective. Hence there is ambivalence in sentimental attachment. It seeks to be near the beloved and at the same time remains remote. For it depends not on the person's true value, but on the values the subject desires to be in the other.

Unfortunately disillusionment often lies in the shadows of sentimental love. Not only may the woman discover that what she reads as sentiment and affection in the man masquerades for his concupiscence and readiness to use her. Besides, both persons may find that the values ascribed to the beloved are fictitious.

Sentimentality like sensuality often leads to true love. By itself it is insufficient because, like sensual attraction, it needs to be integrated with more substantial elements of love. "Love" which remains mere sensuality, a matter of "sex-appeal," will be use of another, not love. "Love" which remains just sentiment likewise will not be real love. The two persons are not really united. Subjectivist sentimentality can grow into true love, but it must be developed from other elements of love.

Can one say that "being in love," when the sexual urge launches itself in adolescence generally is limited to sensuality and sentimentality? Teens are dealing with bodily attraction, closeness and intimacy—in this time of identity confusion seeking to form their own ideas and values. They are dealing with hormonal changes, interactions with the opposite sex and growth in a highly sexualized, media-saturated society.

A college student on reading this chapter recounted, "I thought I was 'in love' at eighteen with a guy I believed cared about me too; it took me a long time to see I was being exploited and used in the relationship. I think teenagers are too young, too impulsive, and too confused to be capable of really integrating love. Adolescence does, however, prepare the person to be able to do so in the future."

Integrating Love

In the process of integrating love what matters most are freedom and truth. Psychological truth, yes: Peter, for example, truly does desire Helen. Helen, in turn, is truly emotionally attached to Peter. But love insists on objective truth and a genuinely free commitment of will can be made only on the basis of truth. Integration of love can take place only on the basis of objective truth.

What does objective truth attain? The spiritual nature of a person indicates that human intelligence and will are spiritual, not material capacities. That is, a person is an embodied spirit, not just a body. The gulf between brute animals and human persons cannot be traversed; they are species apart.

The sexual urge to sexual value becomes integrated when sensual attachment and sentimental affection are adjusted to the recognition that the object of such reaction is a human person. Love may be based upon sensual and emotional reaction to someone of the opposite sex but these reactions must be incorporated with response to the value of the person.

When Harry finds Harriet sensually attractive and warms to her as a female person, does he wonder how she feels, what she as a person believes and values, what her goals are? Or is she merely a female he hopes is available for sensual and sentimental relationship? To relate to her as a female can be fun and bring pleasure. To savor the reality that she is a person generates awe and respect, and he asks himself whether he is truly caring for Harriet or eager to use her.

So many "Harry's" could profit from reflection on Erich Fromm's identification of four characteristics of love. First, love is caring: one cares what happens to anyone, anything one loves. Furthermore, if one loves, one feels responsible for the other. But since these two attitudes alone could smother the one loved, they must be balanced with knowledge and respect. Because one truly respects the other, one seeks to know his/her abilities, values and priorities. In light of such knowledge and respect, a person gives free rein to the other's growth through his/her own decisions.

In our emotionally structured program for happiness, once puberty sets in, desire for pleasure, affection and esteem focus us on love—on union with another. With this union, we think, we will be fulfilled and enabled to seek power and control in our careers.

Knowing how blind our emotions are, especially how blind they were when our program initially took shape as infants and how blinding sexual desire can be, we should appreciate how important it is to reflect on what love is.

As a starting point the love we focus on is always a mutual relationship between persons, a man and a woman. No one can doubt that initially there must be attraction. Founded upon the sexual urge, a woman is perceived by a man as a "good"—a man by a woman as "good."

Just which aspects of a person attract another baffles most people. "What does she see in him?" Still we have noted how both sensual appeal, attraction of another's body, and sentimental affection conspire to evoke personal attraction. Without attraction, no relationship will emerge.

Desire follows upon attraction and is based likewise on the sexual urge. Sex reveals limitation. A man needs a woman, and a woman needs a man—to complete the selves. Love as desire originates in a need. It aims at attaining the good it lacks.

Desire, of course, need not be love, though love involves desire. A man can desire a woman the way he desires food when he is hungry. Once satisfied, he no longer wants either. A woman or a man can use the other as an object, in no way relating to the person.

If love transfuses desire the woman longs for the other as a good for its own sake. She sees the man desired as something good for her. "You are so good for me." There is a longing for the person. Yes, desire is present but is overshadowed by longing for the person. The woman in love is conscious of her desire for this man, but works to ensure that desire does not dominate all the rest that love involves.

Love, however, requires that one go beyond longing for a person as something good for oneself to longing for that person's good. To love is to will good for that person. Desire and goodwill are not incompatible; rather they are closely connected. There is self-lessness in love. There is an unconditional dimension in love as goodwill. Yes, I long for you but, more, I long for your good, for what is good for you.

There is attraction and desire in love, but more and more it moves toward goodwill. In the 70's many seemed to define love as "You make me feel good." Attraction was present as well as desire related to sensuality and sentimentality. But willing good for the other and commitment seemed absent.

What was happening during the counterculture movement of the 70's was a breaking out of culturally restricted living to a NOW-LIVING in freedom and enjoyment . In extreme cases oneself was all-important. Love was endangered. For love requires one to catch insight into the uniqueness, beauty, and loveableness of the other person. One wants to join with and grow with that beautiful other person.

Can John experience attraction to and desire for Lisa together with genuine caring for her and her good without Lisa experiencing the same for him? Unfortunately unrequited love does occur and is the cause of keen disappointment—or worse, loss of the ability to love.

So, for love to be a mutual relationship between a man and a woman, two "I's" must become a "we." Mutual relationship requires reciprocity.

Each "I" desires the other "I" as a co-creator of love—not merely as the object of appetite.

It is precisely this profound desire for someone to co-create love that demands trust, a trust which constitutes the challenge of love and the profound reluctance some feel to committing one's self.

Hence the absolute need to know one's own feelings and intentions as well as those of one's partner. If basically one or both are seeking merely the pleasure or the benefit the other can afford, the relationship will not last. Genuine, reciprocal love cannot develop from two egoisms, or even one.

Essential to all forms of love are attraction, desire and goodwill, which manifest themselves in a specific way in the love of a man and a woman. Sensual emotion for the woman's body, sentimental affection for her as person generate attraction and desire for her which become transformed by recognition of her uniqueness and beauty as a person and concern for her well being. When the woman reciprocates in these ways we are in the area of the paradigm of man-woman love, betrothed love.

Betrothed Love

The decisive character of this betrothed love is total self-giving, the surrender of one's "I" to another person. Self-giving takes love in the form so far described a radical step beyond. It profoundly affects the individual subjects who love and the interpersonal union which it creates. (See Ibid., pp. 119-140)

Just what this self-giving involves becomes startlingly clear when one asks, "Can any person give himself or herself to another person?" Neither physically nor morally can a person do so. Certainly the person as such is not a thing and cannot become someone else's property like a thing. Lisa can come to own Paul's car, but not Paul. Strangely though, what is impossible and illegitimate in the natural order can come about in the order of love. Persons possess a dynamism of their own and specific laws are in force in love.

Paradoxically, it is possible in love to step outside of one's own "I" in self-giving. Paradoxically one's "I" is neither destroyed nor impaired by such a step but enlarged and enriched. Ask a young couple who have solemnly declared, "I take you as my wife—I take you as my husband," whether they feel smaller or larger, diminished or empowered.

They can understand what Jesus means when he says, "He who would save his soul [self] shall lose it, and he who would lose his soul [self] for my sake shall find it again." (Mt 10.39)

For such self surrender a mature sense of values is needed. One must clearly grasp one's own self and self worth.

Incidentally, betrothed love is not the same as the relationship of a devoted doctor with his patients or of a teacher dedicated to her students or a pastor given to his parishioners or a governor to her citizen subjects.

Life, Love, and Sex

Betrothed love is found only in the self giving of the individual person to another chosen person. This love is possible between a man and woman as well as between a human person and God.

This is the kind of love which motivates a man and a woman to marry. It is not marriage, but motivates marriage. Reflection on such a love prompted Søren Kierkegaard to break off his engagement to Regina Olsen. He decided his need to write would make marriage an unsuitable choice for him. Prayer over marriage as a vocation might lead a woman to discern she ought not to marry.

The distinction between betrothed love and marriage will generate a serious question about pre-marital sex. Marriage like pregnancy does not admit an "almost."

A man and a woman may differ in the psychological experience they associate with self-surrender and self-giving. But when groom and bride pronounce their vows, their acts of self surrender combine to produce a perfect whole—the interpersonal act of mutual self-surrender.

Clearly, to give oneself one must be very conscious that in our freedom we possess ourselves and indeed be conscious both of the value of the self one is giving and the trustworthiness of the person to whom one surrenders oneself.

It makes no sense for the groom or the bride to say, "I take you to be my lawful wife/husband," unless the other has offered her or himself to belong to him or her. And she/he gives her/himself not just sexually but entirely. Otherwise *use* of the other's self is involved.

Still one does give oneself sexually and this presupposes both people understand that sexual intercourse is related to communication of life, uniting themselves with God in God's plan for the human race. To present themselves in the prospect of becoming parents affects the nature of the relationship they are committing themselves to, marriage.

Conjugal love prompts the commitment of marriage. Not only do Frank and Elena give themselves one to the other, forming a "we," but they do so aware that involves the "we" as co-principles of new life. Elena, the woman, says, "I so love you, my husband, that I want to share all of me—I want to make a baby with you. I trust you completely to stay with me to raise our child."

Frank in turn says, "You are so beautiful and lovable I want you and no one else to mother my child. This child will be the fruit of our love and I promise to be with you to raise our child."

This we will develop later. But for the present we have schematized the relationship of the sexual urge, love, and marriage.

CONCLUSION

Everyone wants to be happy. From birth and infancy, we saw, we are emotionally programmed to identify happiness with survival, security, pleasure, affection, esteem, and finally with power and control.

Not only do we come to identify the way to achieve each of these elements from our culture, but built in sexual urge drives us to include sexual activity and love as a prominent part of our happiness. Most people decide to structure their pursuit of happiness in love and marriage.

With this as our framework we are ready to examine sexual conduct from an ethical or moral point of view. For happiness requires that we be in the truth in our pursuit of happiness. All our conduct has a moral dimension and only morally good choices can lead to happiness.

Not only do we all—at all times - begin reflection on this issue already emotionally programmed for happiness, but we always begin within a temporally distinctive culture, within generally accepted mores, and within specific intellectual presuppositions. How contemporary culture and intellectual climate influence our thinking on sex must first be surveyed.

CHAPTER 13

INTRODUCING THE MORALITY OF SEXUAL CONDUCT

In the depths of their hearts most people know that love and sex go together. Most people provide for love and sex in their pursuit of happiness. Most people acknowledge some moral restrictions in responding to the sexual urge. Most people are very aware of the conflicting claims about these restrictions, about the relation between sex and love.

Yet recently the curtain rose for the opening of a new play—to reveal a fully naked man on a cross, penis prominent. The first act focused basically on a Mapplethorpe type man luring a beautiful modish woman to be photographed "not nude but naked." The playwright clearly was determined to separate sex from love and dismantle all the restrictions on sex developed by civilization and religion for centuries.

He was making clear that today two radically opposed camps are locked in struggle for human lives and human souls: those who insist there are distinctive moral principles proper to sexual acts and those who insist there is nothing about sex which requires distinctive moral principles, that all such principles be banished.

Beyond provoking the obvious outrage that Christians feel over the denigration of the crucified Christ (Robert Brustein, the director of the theater, to be sure, will never allow any one on his stage defecating on the American flag or urinating on the Torah, sacrileges far less offensive), the opening scene also makes clear that Christians stand in the way of this regressive deconstruction of values. They are the enemy; they block acceptance of such a lifestyle.

This play symbolizes where we are with regard to sex. Few would deny that since the days of the counterculture upheaval in the late 60's into the 70's art, media, film, and television, even the commercial sector have progressively and seductively presented sexual indulgence as something taken for granted. "Once repressive and hypocritical barriers were knocked down, the result was less liberation than binge. We have achieved a triumph in excess." (*New York Times*, Oct. 29, 1995) A recent study in Michigan reports that 40-50% of sixth graders have indulged in sex. One of my college students observed that she supposed discussion of sexual morality and abortion had some value, but both issues are out of date because, once a person decides to have sex, the questions people face today are "With whom?" and "How to do it safely?" As for abortion, the only question was, "When is it appropriate?" Have we regressed to the level prevailing when the Church was launched—when "the pagan world considered [fornication] a perfectly legitimate diversion"? (Montague, *The Holy Spirit*, p. 143) Many signs point in that direction.

"THE TROUBLE WITH PREMARITAL SEX"

The feature article in a recent *US News and World Report* challenges the popular concern about teenage pregnancy and births by demonstrating that "the real problem is adults indulging in premarital sex." "Most of the current social ills tied to sexual behavior—not only children born to unwed parents, but sexually transmitted diseases, abortions and the like—stem chiefly from adults who have sex before they marry, not from sexually active teens." (May 19, 1997, p.57)

Focusing on teen pregnancy has allowed us to "wink at and quietly endorse" adult premarital sex. The definite casualty of the sexual revolution has been the attitude that "virginity should be relinquished only in the marriage bed." The notion that sex is to be reserved for marriage certainly seems antiquated, yet as late as 1968 the majority of Americans held that belief. The birth-control pill and the sexual revolution within the counterculture movement changed that. Without question, TV played a central role in eroding any stigma to premarital sex: a classic example of "defining deviancy down." "What was once considered deviant or abnormal is treated as the norm."

Daytime talk-shows parade the deviant (amazing that people are willing to expose their corrupted lives on live TV!) and must appeal to sufficient audience. Not only does the bizarre deviant crowd the airwaves, numerous regular situation-shows trivialize sex. A student remarked that he and his girlfriend took count of how many partners Elaine, a character on Seinfeld, slept with in one half-hour episode. Premarital sex is so common in TV offerings that one hardly gives it a second thought. But these images gradually seep into viewers' minds subtly poisoning them. They, we, never attend to this until too late; we are then taking such lifestyles for granted.

Practice provoked theory. Arguments were proposed in justification of premarital sex: doesn't hurt anyone who uses contraception responsibly; makes it easier to pick a compatible spouse; prevents early marriages and so avoids the burden of substantial loans as well as childrearing duties while at college.

A prominent conservative jurist and intellectual sums it all up for anyone with doubts (*Sex and Reason*): "There is no good reason to defer premarital sex, a generally harmless source of pleasure and for some people an important stage of marital search." (*U.S. News and World Report* p.62)

The same article puts premarital sex at the heart of the decentralization of traditional values: ". . . sex before marriage has proved to be the runaway horse of traditional values. Once it took off, all the other old-time mores became more difficult to keep in their place." (p.60) Consider the changes that have taken place, as reported in this *U.S. News and World Report* article:

1960's—polls found that at the age of 19, 25% of men and 45% of women were virgins.

1980's—fewer than 20% of both men and women were virgins.

Under the title of "Sexual History" the article reports that 30% have had one or no sex partners since they reached 18; 30% had two or four partners; 22% had five; 20% had ten or more partners.

1950's—9 in 10 women came to marriage without living with their partner.

1990's—only one in three did so.

As regards brides being virgins the figures given are for white women: 1960-65, 43%; only 14% from 1980-85. ("Sex in America: The Social Organization of Sexuality," *Journal of Marriage and the Family*)

The deviant became "normal." Need one note that contraception became very widely accepted during this time and abortion on demand entered the culture as customary? Divorce and wife and child abuse were constantly reported.

Do these "facts" deny or confirm what was said in the previous chapter? Clearly the "facts" describe behavior contrary to betrothed love. But a confirmatory reading can be made of contemporary conduct.

Our built-in sexual urge, we said, drives us to include sexual activity and love as prominent elements of happiness. People clearly are responding to this sexual urge and, although traditional guidelines especially concerning premarital sex have been modified, "Most men and women are still sexually conservative in belief and practice."

In search for happiness, it seems, many have to discover for themselves that sensual desires by themselves do not bring happiness. The heart's hunger is really for love, not sex. The counterculture, reacting against the overstructuring of lives based on assumption of science and technology as ultimate truth, broke from cultural customs without substituting solid intellectual or religious principles to undergird the new customs.

To the extent the new lifestyles impacted lives, people set out to discover for themselves how to incorporate sex into their pursuit for happiness. It took centuries for the human race to discover the relation of intercourse and conception, to discover the need of stable union in raising offspring, to discover that freedom was essential to any human exercise of sex, but especially for committed love which is the basis for that stable union.

Christian faith enriched all this, transforming commitment to stable union, known as marriage, into a sacrament—symbol of the loving relationship of Christ to His Church.

Faith has long been under attack by Secular Humanism which led to the Counterculture Revolution of the 60's and 70's. To me, at least, it is understandable that the customs developed under Christian faith would be challenged when people found their desires frustrated, restricted by such customs. Only experience of consequent unhappiness will prompt re-examination of the recently established attitudes.

People of faith find themselves challenged to recommit themselves in faith if they are to embrace traditional values in sexual conduct. But they must re-examine reason's justification of those values if they are to dialogue with those who do not share their faith. And Christian love requires they try to show them what harm to love and happiness comes from abandoning basic hard-won values.

This may be exactly the right time to make that effort. The emotional need for pleasure and affection grew into demand and then to "should" within the infantile program for happiness which simply must be assessed by reason if one believes with Socrates that the unexamined life is not worth living. So much unhappiness has resulted from "the new sexual morality" that people may soon be ready to accept well grounded principles reason can justify.

Before we initiate an effort to reflect reasonably on sexual conduct, here are some grounds for hope.

NOT ALL IS LOST

Pessimism is not warranted. As G. M. Hopkins, S.J., taught us:
And for all this, nature is never spent;

> There lives the dearest freshness deep down things;
> And though the last lights off the black West went
>   Oh, morning, at the brown brink eastward, springs -
> Because the Holy Ghost over the bent
>   World broods with warm breast and with ah! bright wings.

Even the author of the *US News* article sensed this. The feature article challenges—"if converting Americans to free love and loose mores was the goal, the [sexual] revolution was pretty much a dud . . . most men and women are still sexually conservative in belief and practice. Just over 70% . . . say they have had only one sexual partner in the past year and more than 80% report they have never had an extramarital affair" (p. 58).

Lived experience may be teaching people that sex is not enough. Jennifer Grossman, an MSNBC-TV contributor and author on women's issues, claims that "This all-you-can-eat sexual buffet is leaving a lot of men and women feeling very empty. I see a pattern among my girlfriends—when they sleep with men, they cry. Sleeping with a man you've known for a week is such an 'almost.' It's almost what you want—but a chasm away from what you really need." Her mother's explanation of boys' shyness about commitment was " 'Why buy the cow if the milk is free?' We're in the sexual promised land now; the milk is free, people are surfeited with sex—and yet we're starved for love." Grossman is not arguing for chastity, but explaining why she thinks *The Rules*, a guide for women in their efforts to lure the man to the altar, appeals. Its authors recognize that college-educated women are searching "for a middle ground between casual sex and premarital chastity." The guide gives this advice, "Don't kiss on the first date and don't sleep with him for some weeks or months."

A similar "discovery" seems to be what Lisa Schiffer has to offer. Now a "quasi-religious conservative," this speech writer for Vice President Dan Quayle, admits she did not abstain from premarital sex. Feeling unable to claim that premarital sex is immoral, nonetheless, "More often than not . . . (it) is a bad idea." "The experience of my generation suggests people very rarely get what they are looking for from premarital sex unless what they're looking for is purely sexual. When it's too available, sex itself loses its meaning."

Remarks by some of my students offer even more comforting hope that people may be ready to re-examine current attitudes and values in this area. One senior stated, "This discussion regarding sexual conduct has come at just the right time in my life." She found Grisez's description of intercourse as total self-giving and as a way to stimulate and foster conjugal love a beautiful image of the way she could live with her husband once he was found. Having witnessed during her college years "pain and distrust that has resulted from my friends engaging in sexual acts with acquaintances and boyfriends. . .much too soon in the relationship," she found the idea reinforced that sex is a special bond—one that should be saved for marriage. Frequently unable to defend her convictions, she found Grisez's treatment left her feeling comfortable and confident with her own moral principles.

Another senior acknowledged he, like many others in the class, felt agitated reading Grisez's position "because our sexual desires are so strong that we do not want to believe its inherent immorality." He found that many of his peers when confronted by traditional values tend to defend their own inability to control their sexual desires by arguing that in this or that case indulging sexually is justifiable. His honest appraisal was that we simply have to acknowledge we are human and weak, admit our failures and learn from them.

Finally, a third senior was most honest about discovering and abandoning her strategy of rationalization. "Had I written this paper previous to our class discussions. . .it would have been a whole different paper." Grisez, the author of our texts, she was ready to reject as an unreal idealist: "I choose to live in reality," not some "perfect world." Her friend and a Teaching Assistant helped her to see that Grisez could help her choices to be closer to the ideal of a perfect world.

But it was a fellow student who blew her cover. This other young woman "questioned why we can't just accept that what we are doing is immoral. . . and move on with it." She appealed to people's attitude toward lying. "Don't we all admit lying is wrong, but we lie every day." "Is it that people instinctively know what is right and what is wrong in this area of conduct and so are desperately looking for some justification for their actions?"

My student acknowledges her initial reaction was to defend her position and she did so in class. But that night discussing with her friend, the TA, she realized her fellow student was right and "that was just the reason I couldn't let it go. It was my own guilt over my own actions. . .After realizing my true intentions I took the initial movement toward openness and in response took a second movement toward resolution in my own life and ethical code."

People instinctively know what is right and what is wrong in this area of conduct. Granted, customs can confuse people and block out what their hearts say, still the natural law cannot be completely eradicated. Is it not significant that of the Hollywood elite only 38% are concerned with the way TV is parading premarital sex as normal, yet 83% of the public are concerned?

A quote from Christopher Jencks, Harvard sociologist, suggests people may be waking up. Adult premarital sex "may ultimately prove to be a little like smoking dope in the 1960's. In retrospect. maybe it isn't so good for you after all."

David Whitman's article which we have been reporting by no means urges a return to the traditional position that sex and marriage go together. Ambivalence is present even in the flippant cover, cartoon and all, under the title, "The Trouble with Premarital Sex"—with a summary beside it: "Americans don't think it's much of a problem. Maybe they should."

Still it should provoke re-thinking the role of sex in personal life as well as in society's welfare. The author's conclusion remains challenging, by no means urging chastity ("adult premarital sex . . . is here to stay") but ambivalent.

> In theory, more responsible use of contraception might provide another avenue for eliminating the worst complications of sex before marriage. In practice, though, the increased availability of contraception has not halted the rise in out-of-wedlock births or put an end to abortion and STD's. Adult premarital sex, the little-noticed heart of the sexual revolution, is here to stay. There may be little to do about this silent "epidemic"—except to acknowledge that sex before marriage may not always be the simple pleasure that Americans assume it to be.

(*U.S. News and World Report*, May 19, 1997)

"TRUE LOVE WAITS"

Not all Americans are ambivalent. Not all Americans are so deaf to what their hearts are telling them. Catching the insight that indeed "Sex before marriage has proved to be the runaway horse of traditional values," numerous groups profess and propose chastity. The *US News* article takes note of A.C. Green's *Programs for Youth,* which promotes the cause of premarital abstinence. A.C. Green, a basketball star for the Dallas Mavericks, 33 years old, has never married. He professes to being a virgin, acknowledging that abstaining from extramarital sex is most unpopular. But he is committed to the value of chastity, for himself and for the youth of our country. He wryly observes, "The guys who are parents—especially the guys who have daughters—tend to look at sex before marriage a lot more carefully now."

Another encouraging group is Life Athletes, Inc., a coalition of over 200 professional and Olympic athletes. They are "committed to leading lives of virtue, abstinence, and respect for life." Members make a fourfold commitment, the first two addressing sexual conduct.

1. I will try to do what is right, even when it is difficult.
2. I will give myself only to that special person I marry as my life partner.

What is their objective? "We exist in order to survive in a world where the misuse of sex has hurt many of us. We don't want disease, divorce, and death to keep us from what we want in life. We want relationships that are built on honesty and fairness in relationships that last."

They reach out in all directions, encouraging all to make the Life Athletes Commitments. Their plan, they insist, is not another Sex Ed. or condom distribution program. Likewise it is not a "just say no" program. They focus on the whole person—building better relationships and beginning with themselves.

A more widespread movement is the "True Love Waits"—begun by Protestants and embraced by Catholic groups. "Youth 2000," a movement inspired by Pope John Paul II's call to youth to spread Christ's message, urges Catholic youth to center their lives on Jesus in the Eucharist and to follow Him in a wholesome Catholic lifestyle. Obviously, the movement calls youth to chastity.

These are, I submit, the forerunners of the rejection of premarital sex in an effort to save "love" and the family and the welfare of society.

SPECTRUM OF MORAL POSITIONS

Everyone normally developed recognizes the moral dimension in conduct. Two theories common in this area are cultural relativism and individual subjectivism. According to cultural relativism actions are morally good or immoral because a culture so decides: people are to shape their lives on the culture's moral framework. According to individual subjectivism each individual establishes his/her own code of morality: actions are good or bad because "I" decide they are. Speaking of premarital sex, one of my students acutely observed, "Premarital sex has become so prevalent that very few stop to think about [its] morality...If asked, many would probably reply that it is morally acceptable since they do not want to admit that they or their society could be so morally corrupt." And another student, unaware she was adopting individual subjectivism: "If a person decides to engage in premarital sex . . . I do not see how others can decide what is the moral or immoral thing to do. It is in their best interest to be happy or fulfilled."

Relativism may be deemed absurd in matters of justice (unacceptable, for example, if used to justify grading students according to their agreement with the professor's thought) but taken for granted in sexual matters. Besides relativism often being unreflectively assumed, two contradictory theories hold the field. The traditional position claims that sexual acts should be restricted to marriage. The Catholic Church is far from alone in proclaiming this view. Liberals, however, see nothing distinctive about sexual conduct and so consider sexual indulgence limited only by some general moral principle—pertinent to all areas of conduct. Force, deception, manipulation would render a sex act immoral—just as they would be in any other area of conduct. So long as two responsible people freely consent, any form of sexual activity is morally acceptable. Masturbation, fornication, sodo—freely engaged in are all right in the liberal view. A third view, "sex with love," came to the fore as the norm for some people in the 70's—and today many of my students insist that two people in love have no need of a "piece of paper" to make their expression of love morally justifiable. The same students express similar attitudes toward homosexual lovers. On the other hand, the position has become seriously compromised since the love required may be non-exclusive, non-committed "love." Apparently, for many people, free, affectionate consent is all that is required to make sex morally acceptable.

TRADITIONAL NATURAL LAW MORALITY
vs.
SECULAR HUMANIST MORALITY

Many are puzzled as to why intelligent people differ so radically on sexual issues. The explanation requires keeping in mind that moral judgments about any area of conduct do not stand alone. Explicitly or implicitly such judgments are based on ethical theories which generate general moral principles, which theories presuppose a philosophy of what a person is and a world-view. These numerous factors are involved in the present day attitudes toward sexual indulgence.

In the appendix we shall identify these different factors and indicate how they are related to different stances toward sexual acts. Inclusion or exclusion of moral absolutes, for example, will have significant impact on things like adultery.

Still at issue fundamentally are the questions: Are sexual acts so significantly related to marriage that they generate distinctive moral principles? Or are they simply related to individual freedom?

A radical "new morality," in process of being shaped since the 16th century, has become operative in our culture undermining institutions and conventions at least nominally in force, institutions and conventions based on an "old morality" effectively established by Judaic-Christian beliefs, including natural law ethics. One by one these institutions and conventions have succumbed to the "new morality," based upon Secular Humanism (The successive stages shaping this atheistic philosophy and related to the successes of the natural sciences but achieved by options, not proofs, are reported in my *God Is: From Question to Proof to Embracing the Truth.*).

This conquering process of Secular Humanism is exemplified in the following. "Sex takes its meaning from marriage" becomes "Any form of sex freely engaged in is all right." "Prohibition of abortion" becomes "Abortion on request" and "Prohibiting suicide and euthanasia" is well on the way to becoming "Assisted suicide and active euthanasia are morally acceptable."

Because victory by the "new morality" has not yet been clean-cut, people are confused, thinking they can select parts of the old to blend with the new. Dishonesty results. Different ages give birth to different kinds of dishonesty in moral questions: hypocrisy in the Victorian period, self-deception in our own time. The self-deception involved consists in professing to be honest while evading serious reflection on what would demand radical change of lifestyle.

Four fundamental principles are contrasted in the two world views related to the two moralities, that is, the traditional and the liberal of Secular Humanism. Principles can intermediate between the fundamental principles. Specific issues and principles grow out of fundamental truths and these guide judgments about sexual conduct.

The appendix begins with a synopsis of four fundamental truths. In parallel columns these four truths are spelled out. At first a person may not recognize the impact each of the four has on one's moral thinking. So it would be helpful to read parallel numbers slowly and at least wonder what effect each will have on making a judgment about premarital sex, adultery, and so forth. The impact and connection between truths and principles will be clearly pointed out.

To eliminate confusion as well as to test whether self-deception has crept in, I advise careful reflection on the parallel positions of traditional natural law and Secular Humanism moralities found in the appendix. Notice how radically different they are and how interlinked the parts are in each school of thought.

Intelligent people differ radically on sexual issues because they come at issues equipped with different principles and perspectives.

Here in summary are the four fundamental "truths" involved in the two moralities. First and grounding everything is—God exists or does not exist. The second concerns free will or determinism. The third general position contrasts conviction that human acts directly affect the person choosing, indirectly impacting social relationships and the material world; or they immediately affect the conscious experiences of the actor and only that. Finally, the most important difference lies in acceptance or denial of moral absolutes.

WHERE IS THE TRUTH?

Differences on the morality of sexual acts can often be traced to these differences on fundamental truths and moral principles. Today, many people would find themselves agreeing with parts of the Old and parts of the New. The question springs to mind- Can this be done coherently? Actually, the two moralities seem each an organic unity. If this is so, how can one choose among the parts? Read the Church's treatment in the Catechism; it is ennobling and coherent. Read *A New Bill of Sexual Rights and Responsibilities* (representative of the "new morality"), by Lester Kirkendall, endorsed by 37 leading authors and sexologists; it sounds respectable and sensible.

Since the traditional natural law morality is an organic unity, no one can reasonably embrace some of its positions and abandon others. To abandon any of the intermediate norms implies abandoning some or all of its fundamental principles. The secular humanist morality is likewise an organic whole. To adopt some of its intermediate norms involves accepting some or all of its vital principles. On the other hand for the secular humanist to agree with traditional natural law morality on some issues can be consistent. Since for secular humanist morality the goods are measurable ("Fundamental Principles," #4, above and in Appendix) one may weigh the goods differently and agree with traditional natural law morality. Denying the existence of God, these people admit no absolutes in the areas of being or in truth.

"The truth will make you free." Which world-view is true? Which principles are true?

Secular Humanism keeps increasing its influence on our laws and customs. Restricting consideration to this world and from birth to death its proponents rely on experience, common sense, and science. They ignore philosophical knowledge as distinct from science and reject religion and faith as myth based on imagination and wish fulfillment. Christians and other believers consider issues in terms of conception, birth, death, and eternal life. They trust God's revelation and appeal not only to experience, common sense, and science, but also to philosophical insight and faith.

No wonder people judge sexual conduct differently. Truth is in principle attainable and fulfillment for the individual and for society depends on living the truth. Every single individual has the right and the responsibility to form his/her judgment about what is true and good as well as to choose how she/he will live. Our best judgments, of course, can be mistaken.

So truth does not depend on any individual's judgment about what is true. Objective truth, knowledge which gives us what is reality, is in principle attainable and fulfillment for the individual and for society depends on discovering and living this objective truth.

People can judge that diet X is genuinely beneficial, but if they are wrong, the diet simply will not benefit, may even hurt them. Sincere but erroneous belief about adultery, fornication and sodomy likewise will directly or indirectly hurt the individual and society.

A genuinely adequate treatment of our topic would require thorough examination of those fundamental truths and moral principles. No guarantees are available. No one is infallible (in use of reason alone). But either one has confidence in human intelligence or one does not.

No such adequate treatment is possible in a work like this. Our opening four chapters, especially Chapter 4, however, does provide a serious introduction to the issues.

Recognition that the position one takes on these radical issues does impact on one's moral judgment about the exercise of sex should provide comfort when people disagree with one's conclusions. The ethicist Singer, for example, sees no significant difference between a fetus and a snail. I am, then, not surprised when he advocates abortion as well as infanticide.

Later chapters, for example, will argue that marriage is a basic human good achievable because of our sexual capacity and consequently sexual acts ought to be restricted to marriage. We also shall lay out the reasons why tradition has judged adultery, fornication and so forth, immoral.

The framework for this crucial debate on the morality of sexual conduct is the emotional program we all develop beginning at least as infants. Survival and security, pleasure, affection and esteem, power and control: these we need emotionally, we demand, we consider "shoulds" for happiness. Sexual urge and the resulting drives we all share, but at the same time as adults we must submit these to understanding and free choice. Only too often failure to exercise self control of sensual desires destroys families and individual lives.

The task we set ourselves is to discover how best to exercise our sexual urge for personal happiness and society's welfare.

THE STAKES ARE HIGH

To specify why certain sexual acts are immoral requires theoretical treatment. Theoretical treatment of these issues can seem detached and leave one unmoved. For this reason it is essential to keep in mind what is at stake in sexual indulgence, the grave consequences to the individual and society. Grisez urges that we link the human suffering resulting from lifestyles based on error in sexual conduct with reasoned analyses. So the rest of this introductory article will call to mind those human sufferings. (*Living a Christian Life*, Chap. 9, E, 6, d and e)

Our summary of the feature article in *US News and World Report* reveals that all is not well in our culture of premarital sex. Some women "cry after they sleep with men." People find sex is free "but feel starved for love." "People rarely get what they are looking for from premarital sex." "Sex before marriage may not always be the simple pleasure that Americans assume it is."

The human values at stake highlight the importance of discovering the truth about the morality of sexual conduct. First of all, most people recognize that marrying, having and raising children are among the best things in life—prized for their own sake. Again, although it has taken centuries to achieve, civilized people do esteem integration of one's sexuality with other elements of their personality.

Do we appreciate the fact that these two precious values are at stake as we seek the truth about masturbation, fornication and adultery? Our sensate culture fueling the media and entertainment conceals these human values, rationalizing their habitual and even systematic violation.

To achieve the above integration, people must know what constitutes genuine integration, what is humanly appropriate sexual conduct. What is the relation between marriage and sex? Only with integration is pursuit of the value of marriage and parenthood possible.

Even those who reject Catholic teaching on sexual morality can see how much harm results from acts the Church teaches are immoral. Irresponsible intercourse leaves women abandoned, left to care for children by themselves. Statistics on feminization of poverty paint a painful picture of human destitution. And look at the heart of the women who feel betrayed and forced to struggle to survive and provide for their children—at the heart of children unwanted.

Have you known any young women whose entire lives have been restructured by such experience? Many, thank God, cope courageously, but certainly they will never be the same. In spite of the pain of realization they have been used some may repeat the scenario and lessen their sense of self-worth. Others can grow into strong personalities, more committed than ever to moral and spiritual principles. Still, it is at great cost.

Think of other actual cases you know. Put faces on the statistics. Have you ever trusted completely in your spouse and experienced the stabbing wound and heartbreak of betrayal? Do you marvel that she or he can throw away years of nurtured, committed, loyal love—besides afflicting such suffering on the children?

Knowing the truth about the morality of adultery need not insure people will not go that route, but awareness of the suffering resulting from adultery can make meaningful the technical reasons explaining why it is wrong. Such truth sets boundaries for one's own heart and when society finally embraces the truth, fewer people will get hurt.

Clearly much human suffering follows directly from pre/extramarital intercourse. One strong motivating element in such acts is desire for sexual satisfaction. And the dynamism in seeking sexual satisfaction has been affected by ideology. Granted sexual desire is natural and good, its undisciplined intensity is the fruit of the theory that everyone is entitled to regular orgasm. Putting the theory into practice leads to masturbatory sexual activity as a normal part of many people's lives. As we shall explain, fornication and adultery often are actually masturbatory. Needless to say, this encourages looking on women as sex objects.

If there were not the masturbatory component in the motivation for adultery, fornication and sodomy, they would, we submit, be committed far less often. And if couples regularly subordinate marital good to the experience of sexual satisfaction, most likely they will lack the self-mastery needed to pursue intelligible goods in use of drugs, alcohol and so forth.

Our sensate culture, then, both manifests and serves the masturbatory personality. Pornography, prostitution, as well as the media and advertising encourage the masturbatory component of each person. In the resulting polluted society, chastity becomes almost humanly impossible—difficult even for the virtuous.

The promoters of sexual liberation, the ideology referred to, intended to eliminate the pain of sexual frustration, and to make society more joyful. The result, we see, has been different. The pain of sexual frustration is slight in comparison with the sufferings noted.

Trivialization of sex has trivialized love. People are lonely because of lack of true marital intimacy. No sexual frustration, but people dying wretchedly from sexually transmitted diseases, family stability impacted and immense social costs piling up.

Keep all this in mind as we attempt to reason about the morality of masturbation, fornication and adultery. At the same time wonder about why the sexual motivation is so powerful and deeply rooted in the human psyche? Consider human inclinations from an evolutionary perspective. Does not the very survival and development of the human race suggest the reason?

When the investigation of the morality of different forms of sexual content seems abstract and technical, think again of evolution and all the human suffering related to sexual indulgence.

THE CHRISTIAN DIMENSION

There is a more important aspect of this issue, though perhaps less easily acknowledged, the effect of abuse of our sexual capacity on Christian values. God, it might be said, created human sexuality as part of the language needed to reveal himself. How can one understand the faith without appreciating the significance of a father, of being a child of a father, of being brother, sister, a faithful spouse? And at the heart of God's use of human sexuality in revelation is the natural sacramentality of marriage, the foundation for its specifically Christian sacramentality. Foreshadowing the ultimate fulfillment of the body as a capacity for self-giving is the sacramentality of marriage. This capacity for self-giving relates to communion in the one-flesh reality of Jesus' risen life. Union with the risen Jesus is the body's ultimate end and so every abuse of human sexuality violates the natural marital good but infinitely more important, it violates the body of Christ. "The body," St. Paul tells us, "is meant not for fornication but for the Lord, and the Lord for the body. Do you not know that your bodies are members of Christ? Should I therefore take the members of Christ and make them members of a prostitute?" (1 Cor 6) Fornication and other sexual sins like masturbation constitute abuse of the body of Christ. As we shall see, in many sexual sins one damages the body as a capacity for self-giving in genuine interpersonal communion—and so damages the Christian's capacity for sharing in communion with Christ.

Sexual immorality, moreover, can subvert faith in God the creator. This insight could be developed but here it is enough to say that although St. Paul did not articulate just how sexual immorality leads to unbelief, he did describe their relationship; indeed he brought out in the beginning of Romans how unbelief leads to sexual immorality. "Therefore God gave them up in the lusts of their hearts to impiety. . .because they exchanged the truth about God for a lie. . ." (Rom.1:24)

It goes without saying that sexual immorality also weakens the Church. The stability of families on which the Church depends is affected. Unchaste lifestyles not only undercut vocations to priesthood and religious life but likewise vocations to marriage. If people cannot subordinate sexual desire to marital love, they will not be inclined to marriage as a vocation.

Because sexual immorality tends to degrade one's body as well as the bodies of others, the depersonalizing of bodies generates an attitude of dualism of body and consciousness. Is it the case that acceptance of such dualism may well lead one to abandon hope for bodily resurrection? Would that not make it difficult to believe in Jesus' resurrection or regard Jesus' bodily presence in the Eucharist as real? What would be the importance of believing in his virgin birth or the doctrine of original sin transmitted by propagation? How could one believe in an incarnate God? In general, sexual immorality once accepted as a lifestyle subverts the incarnationalism and sacramentalism at the heart of Catholic faith.

If we keep in mind these appalling consequences related to sexual immorality, we will appreciate why it is important to get to the truth about sexual conduct. We will not let the clinical, logical tone of our analyzing block out how much is at stake.

SUMMARY AND CONCLUSION

Although not all is lost, contemporary lifestyles reflect significant abandonment of sexual values. Because Secular Humanism is undermining customs established under the influence of Judaic-Christian values, a profound but subtle struggle is going on between those who insist there are distinctive moral principles proper to sexual acts and those who deny there are any such principles, even demand such principles not be claimed by others.

Besides identifying the spectrum of moral stances toward sexual conduct we have placed the world-views and basic principles in stark confrontation. Only closely reasoned analysis can discover where the truth lies. And since such analysis can seem detached and leave people unmoved, it is important that we keep in mind what is at stake. Considerable human suffering has resulted from lifestyles built on false presupppositions about sexual conduct.

For the welfare of the human race in time and eternity, it is critical that we discover how God intends us to live our sexual lives. Now may be the time, people may be ready to rediscover the truth. We are ready to learn what reason teaches and how the Church can help us.

CHAPTER 14

THE MARRIED

Germain Grisez, a theologian in tune with the Magisterium, sheds new light on timeless issues in Chapter 9, "Marriage, Sexual Acts, and Family Life," in the second of a projected four-volume series entitled *The Way of the Lord Jesus*. This second volume is called *Living a Christian Life*. A married man and champion of the Church's traditional teaching on sexual morality and family life, Grisez offers profound insights that enrich the authoritative teaching of the Magisterium.

Rather than trying to improve on the inspiring, positive focus of the new Catechism, love and self-mastery, Grisez offers intellectual explanation and justification of the truth of the Church's position on the morality of sexual conduct. Pivotal to Church teaching is that sexuality enables men and women to join together in permanent and exclusive union, marriage. Sexual acts are proper and exclusive to marriage.

The Catechism's treatment of sexual conduct is different from Grisez's. The Catechism begins with a quotation from John Paul II's encyclical on marriage and family. "God is love . . . Creating the human race in his own image . . . God inscribed in the humanity of man and woman *the vocation*, and with this the capacity and responsibility, of *love* and communion." Immediately it defines sexuality relating it to the capacity to love and procreate. That opens into a consideration of chastity which enables total self-giving in sexual intercourse.

The Church's position on masturbation, fornication and so forth is that they are offenses against chastity, relating them to marriage.

Only after all this does the Catechism address "The Love of Husband and Wife," specifying sexual acts as "proper and exclusive to spouses."

Grisez, on the other hand, launches his treatment by showing that marriage is among the basic human goods people choose, like life, friendship and religion.

MARRIAGE IS A BASIC HUMAN GOOD

As explained in Part One Grisez begins the development of his ethics by identifying the reasons that motivate people to act. Some reasons are things perceived as good, as worthwhile means to achieve other things. But questioning why one acts enables a person to push back to things perceived as good or worthwhile in themselves. These "goods" are "basic human goods." The criterion of morality is "inclusivistic-exclusivistic" choosing. To choose exclusivistically is to choose to impede, harm or destroy a good as means to pursue another good. Morally good choosing is choosing to pursue a good in such a way that one remains open to all the basic human goods.

Only when he began serious study of the morality of sexual conduct did Grisez recognize marriage as a basic human good. This insight governs his entire treatment of sexual activity. Immorality in sexual conduct involves harm to the basic human good of marriage.

Thomas Aquinas and Basic Human Goods

Grisez's basic human goods can be traced back to St. Thomas' explanation of the natural law. The first principle of practical reason is, "Good is to be done and pursued, evil is to be avoided." It is likewise, according to St. Thomas, the first precept of the natural law. Whatever reason naturally apprehends as good is understood in light of this first precept - as something to be done and pursued, harm to it to be avoided. And reason naturally apprehends as "goods" the objects of our natural inclinations. Among these inclinations are those nature has taught all animals - the inclination to intercourse and to care for offspring. Hence human beings grasp intercourse with the opposite sex as good and to be pursued, harm to this or to offspring to be avoided.

Human persons, because they differ from other animals, understand intercourse as good inasmuch as pursuit of it is reasonable or guided by reason. The same is true about the natural inclination toward food. Reason teaches us to eat moderately and not to violate any other good such as friendship in pursuit of food.

Certainly one of our strongest inclinations or appetites is sexual desire. It probably took centuries to harness sexual desires so that human beings let reason guide response to their desires. For example, primitive, spontaneous response like that of brute animals caused trouble until people recognized that forced intercourse is unreasonable. Freedom is required.

Furthermore, centuries also passed before connection between intercourse and birth was discovered. At some point restrictions on sexual desires were established, so that marriage as a more or less stable, heterosexual relationship was recognized by society as the community in which it is appropriate for a man and a woman to engage regularly in sexual intercourse and to beget and raise children.

In other words, desire for sexual intercourse came to be distinguished as raw appetite, sexual release, expression of friendship, and the expression of conjugal love. This last is complex: emotional and volitional desire for someone of the opposite sex with concern for the well-being of the other, exclusive and permanent commitment prompting free mutual consent to join their lives together, to give themselves totally one to the other especially in sexual intercourse - which intercourse renders them one flesh, organically co-principles of life.

Clearly, all this is consistent with our earlier treatment of the sexual urge within our emotional program for happiness as reason and free choice react to this powerful drive.

How enriching is John Paul II's insistence on the difference between the response of sensuality or sentimentality and love, especially betrothed love - to this sexual drive - described in Chapter Twelve.

GRISEZ ESTABLISHES MARRIAGE AS BASIC HUMAN GOOD

An intelligible good which is intrinsically good, pursued as worthwhile in itself, is a basic human good. One way to discover basic goods is to ask why one chooses to do whatever one does. Some goods motivating actions are worthwhile as means to something else. But by probing one reaches a good considered worthwhile in itself.

Often engaged couples reply to the question, "Why are you planning to marry?" by saying, "We are in love and want to spend our lives together and we are ready to settle down and have a family." Put in abstract terms they are saying: we are attracted to one another by erotic emotion, but also we will to form a lasting marital union, which we expect will result in having children.

Our concern is not about "getting married," a "wedding," but the state of being married. Serious discussion can, I discover with my students, get sidetracked if the ceremony of getting married is not distinguished from the institution of being married.

"Always and everywhere, marriage is the relationship recognized as appropriate for begetting and raising children."

Clearly, marriage is a basic human good. It is an intelligible good. Normally emotion motivates people to mate; but people can be interested in getting married before being romantically involved. They can look on being married as worthwhile in itself. They see marriage as truly fulfilling and choose to do what needs to be done to establish marital communion.

Is parenthood included in the basic good of marriage? Procreating and educating children fulfill the couple, as well as benefitting the children. So having a family, parenthood, is not an extrinsic end to which one-flesh unity is instrumental. It is a realization of its potentiality.

Grisez is touching upon a delicate and debated issue - the ends of marriage. Rather than primary and secondary ends, unitive and procreative aspects of marriage are seen as blended. He suggests a striking comparison: the relationship of the crypt of a church and the upper church. The upper church which eventually gets built is not an extrinsic end and the crypt an instrument for it. The church completes the structure - crypt being the first and basic part.

Note that it is the plans for the upper church which determine the structure of the crypt. Still, supposing, as sometimes happens, the upper church never gets built, the crypt can serve as and be an entirely adequate church for worship.

A valid marriage exists when the essential part of the wedding ceremony ends - and the marriage that now exists is by its very nature part of a larger whole. Parenthood is not the "end" or purpose of marriage - conjugal communion is not the instrument for that end. Conjugal communion, brought into existence by the wedding, is intrinsically good. Yes, conjugal communion is ordered to and normally is an intrinsically good part of a larger whole, also intrinsically good, the family.

As the upper church is the completion, the perfecting of the crypt, so parenthood completes, perfects marital communion. For this reason parenthood fulfills marriage; it shapes the conjugal communion of husband and wife.

Note, as illustrated by the crypt, marital communion can exist and fulfill a man and a woman even if having and raising children (which perfects marital communion) is impossible.

What Grisez is stressing is that although marriage and conjugal love "are by their nature ordained toward" children, marriage, precisely because it is a basic human good itself, is not an instrument to procreating. Marriage is not a means to children as an end. Children are not means to the parents' perfection. Parenthood is the specific, intrinsic perfecting of marriage.

Grisez calls attention to the fact that biologically animals, including human animals, as individuals, male or female, are complete in most functions such as growth, nutrition, emotion, sensation. As for reproduction, however, each individual animal is incomplete. Only the mated pair is the complete organism capable of reproducing in a sexual way. A man and a woman become "one flesh," co-principles of new life.

Back to the church example, furniture and decorations complete or perfect a church - but accidentally. Children do not perfect marriage accidentally, but intrinsically. No individual man or woman can have and adequately care for children. Men and women fulfill their potentiality to do so by joining together - as the community which differs specifically from other communities, cooperating for different common goods.

The common good of the community of marriage, that good which couples pursue in choosing to marry is "being married." They are united as complementary, bodily persons, so really and so completely that they are two-in-one-flesh. This form of interpersonal unity is made actual by conjugal love — when, and provided that, love stimulates mutual consent, loving consummation and their whole lives together "not least in the parenthood of couples whose marriages are fruitful."

A few comments on that explanation are in order. Conjugal love is distinct from mutual consent. A distinctive love is associated with marriage. Respect, esteem, caring, feeling responsible for and knowledge of the other as uniquely beautiful and lovable. This love is normally exclusive and generates commitment to permanent union. This conjugal love is not marriage but <u>prompts</u> a couple to freely, mutually consent to enter into marriage.

A man and a woman may experience such love, but be married to other spouses. They might, on the other hand, experience such love and judge marriage just wouldn't work out. He might be an anthropologist working in Africa, she a script writer in California.

Conjugal love then is not marital consent. A couple might not enjoy conjugal love yet deliberately consent to be married.

In traditional language marriage is a natural society. It has an objective structure and meaning. Accordingly, people are free to enter into marriage; they are not free to decide what marriage is to be. They are free to plan how they will live their marriage concretely.

Of course, each couple is free to structure relationships as they like and call them what they like. But they are not free to make a relationship be different from what it essentially is. "Friendship" is, among other things, willing the good of another person. If one person <u>uses</u> the other regularly, it is <u>not</u> friendship. The other may be deceived and think they are relating as friends. They are not.

Choosing to enter a temporary relationship, even with a wedding ceremony, sharing a home with regular sexual intercourse is not really marriage. The contemporary debate over legalizing "gay marriage" is a dangerous misuse of words. Two caring homosexual persons sharing their lives as a couple in fidelity may be granted legal protection and economic benefits, but they simply cannot be the same as a heterosexual couple committed to one another as complementary bodily persons capable of becoming two-in-one flesh, co-principles of new life. To use the word "marriage" for both relationships is equivocal, much as the word "ball" is used for a round rubber object and a formal dance.

In summary, Grisez claims marriage is a basic human good: the committed union of a man and a woman, permanent and exclusive, unitive and procreative. Since it is a basic human good, every person has a natural inclination to that good and a natural inclination to judge marriage is to be pursued, harm to it to be avoided.

PROOF MARRIAGE IS A BASIC HUMAN GOOD

A basic human good is something desirable as worthwhile in itself that satisfies a basic human inclination. History and sociological data prove people experience an inclination to marriage and choose to satisfy that inclination. The community formed by mutual consent in which it is deemed appropriate for a couple to engage regularly in sexual intercourse and for raising a family is rooted so deeply in human nature that it is found in every age and culture.

Granted married people have always experienced serious difficulties, today marriage has become even more fragile - 50% or more of marriages end in divorce. Yet in spite of the difficulties and the devastating statistics, people pursue the good of marriage and assume they will prove to be successful in preserving their love and union.

Marriage fulfills the definition of a basic human good, for it obviously is perceived as desirable and can be willed or chosen for its own sake, worthwhile in itself. As mentioned above, the truth of this claim is witnessed to throughout the world and throughout history.

Marriage clearly is an intelligible good. Although erotic emotions motivate people to mate, as they do other animals, a person can be interested in marrying before experiencing erotic attraction to any particular person. Furthermore, people can wish to be married for its own sake, in the sense that they judge marriage to be potentially fulfilling and so choose to do what is necessary or useful to establish and maintain marital communion.

Finally, and objections come immediately to mind, a basic human good is one toward which all people have an inclination to pursue and an inclination to form a judgment that it is a good, worthwhile in itself. The

Life, Love, and Sex

experience of sexual desire evidences this inclination to such union and warrants the judgment that marriage is worthwhile.

The claim that "<u>all</u> people" experience these inclinations is obviously not based on empirical study. Yet history and sociology certainly provide evidence that <u>most</u> people experience these inclinations.

While every normally developed person has such inclinations, not every person is drawn to actively pursue this good of marriage - just as not every person is drawn to pursue the good of art or scientific research.

In the appendix I address the challenge of virginity, celibacy and homosexuality to the claim that marriage is a basic human good. As for the former, the celibate can recognize marriage as a basic human good and contribute to its pursuit in many ways without embracing it actively in her own life. Homosexuals and lesbians require a more sensitive reflective explanation, but they too experience the inclination to marriage as a basic human good. Please read the appendix for this chapter.

SEXUAL ACTS EXPRESSIVE OF MARITAL COMMUNION

We are ready to evaluate the morality of sexual acts. What was once taken for granted demands radical justification. The sexual revolution initiated in the '60's and '70's has become imbedded in current lifestyles. Although licentiousness, "free love," has not been accepted, living together has become common, which, of course, presupposes contraception is morally justifiable. It is not that people don't consider the moral aspect of their actions before reaching this decision and other pre-extra marital indulgences. They assume there is nothing wrong with what they are doing.

But personal and social happiness depends on living in the truth. God has so loved us that he has revealed how he plans us to live in pursuit of happiness. Catholics know - or should know - that Christ's Church teaches authentically and authoritatively what God has revealed. We shall invoke the Church's teaching and provide Grisez's theological explanation of the Church's position. Others besides Catholics should find Grisez's explanation eminently reasonable.

We begin with sex in marriage. (See *Living a Christian Life*, 633-648)

By showing that marriage is a basic human good Grisez has provided intellectual undergirding for the Church's position on sexual conduct. Sexual acts are proper and exclusive to married couple. This is based upon God's revealed directives and recognized by reason as grounded on the way God made us - sexual beings. For, since sexuality "especially concerns affectivity, the capacity to love and procreate . . ." the unitive and procreative aspects of marriage must always be respected. (*Catechism* 2332, 2362, 2366)

Sexual intercourse enables a man and a woman to become physically one, to express and stimulate total self-giving, and to make them co-principles of possible new life. Married couples should engage in sexual acts conducive to the above unitive and procreative good of marriage. All other sexual activity should be avoided. In sum, if a sexual act is not marital (thus both unitive and procreative) it violates the good of marriage.

Two general ways of violating the good of marriage are thus identified. To be genuine marital acts, sexual acts must be performed willingly and lovingly. Coercion or mere use of the other for one's selfish satisfaction or manipulation to attain an extrinsic purpose renders acts non-marital and immoral. Clearly, if a drunken husband forces intercourse or if a wife has intercourse with her husband while she deliberately wishes it were with another man, it is not a loving marital act.

On the other hand, marital communion is both unitive and procreative. Hence to do anything inconsistent with their act's being of itself suited to procreating makes the act nonmarital and is immoral.

Grisez explains that contraception is a violation of the unitive aspect of marriage as well as a choice to go against the good of life. He sees contraception as contra-love and contra-life.

Very simply, the unitive meaning of marital intercourse includes its procreative meaning. The marital act is a sign of and stimulus to total self-giving; husband and wife become two-in-one flesh. They are able to form this union because they give what the other lacks. This mutual gift empowers them to be and to do together what they cannot be and do apart. The organic incompleteness and complementarity of man and woman precisely in regard to reproduction thus provides the essential condition for the very possibility of their marital communion. It should be clear then that contraceptive intercourse, by not sharing their reproductive capacities, says that there is not total self-giving. Contraception is contra-love.

But Grisez develops contraception at greater lengths when he deals with the issue of life. To define contraceptive choice one must be thinking that sexual intercourse could cause a new life to begin and that some other behavior could prevent this effect. One chooses to perform this other behavior. So the immediate intention is to ensure that new life not begin. Contraception is always wrong for it is always a choice against the good of life.

We have simply telescoped our intensive treatment of contraception as contra-life and contra-love in Part Two. Natural family planning was explained and distinguished from contraception as well.

MARITAL CHASTITY

The strength of sexual appetite demands that every person develop the virtue of chastity - pope, priests, religious, single laymen and laywomen, married couples. Appetites are blind. Reason intervenes to ensure that response to appetites be truly human.

The conjugal love normally experienced in relation to marriage has many facets. Besides erotic desire and affection, conjugal love essentially is mutual and unselfish willing the good of being married as well as the entire personal good of the spouse. When sexual acts are fully integrated with marital communion they are reasonable and worthy. Conjugal love, when consistent and genuine, leads to this integration - to marital chastity.

It is chastity, this reasonable integration of acts, pleasure and love, which subordinate sexual pleasure to love and communion. The intense sensations of pleasure in sexual intercourse are a private and so an incommunicable experience. To focus attention on and strive to intensify this experience as much as possible tends to make the other a means, a "sex object." But chaste marital love can subordinate this experience - so that erotic pleasure no matter how intense says love and is morally good.

Pope John Paul II's teaching that a man can commit adultery in his heart by looking at his own wife with lust was misunderstood. He had in mind this self-centered making of his wife a sex object, rather than looking on her as the person he gives himself to totally. The pope was not saying that a husband and wife may not look at each other with erotic desire or intending to arouse desire. Whatever contributes to loving mutual total self-giving is morally good.

The self-mastery of marital chastity empowers spouses to say both yes and no to their desires. If a person is unable to say no to his or her sexual desire is she/he able to say yes? Is sexual intercourse truly a loving act or a spontaneous, instinctive selfish indulgence? Of itself the sexual drive does not express love. If reason calls for abstinence, love is expressed by abstinence, not by intercourse.

Concupiscence in this context is the sexual drive insofar as it has been affected by sin and tends toward satisfaction for its own sake unrelated to the intelligible good of marriage. Marriage does not quiet concupiscence simply by providing a legitimate way to have intercourse. Actually, satisfying desire tends to intensify it. So marriage does not lessen one's sexual drive in some automatic way. Neither does it focus sexual desire on one's spouse exclusively. Marriage can help to develop the virtue of chastity by conjugal love - and, for Christians, by sacramental grace. In this way the marital good of loving cooperation in one-flesh predominates, subordinating the erotic to conjugal love.

Ignorance of the way love transforms even the most intense sexual pleasure explains something that has puzzled researchers. The authors of *Sex in America, A Definitive Survey* found that contrary to assumptions, the people "most interested in sex and the most sexually active, not the sexual loners" are the ones who search out erotic materials and who masturbate most often (p. 157). If that is true, it would suggest that many people most sexually active somehow fail to subordinate their sexual drive to love of their partner. This would confirm the claim that "satisfying desire tends to intensify it."

Quoting St. Paul's teaching about conjugal rights Grisez calls attention to Paul's formulation which makes clear that the obligation to respect conjugal rights is mutual: "in this matter husband and wife are entirely equal." On both sides "unreasonable refusal of marital intercourse is a grave matter."

Chastity does not exclude all sexual acts by a married couple short of intercourse. Such acts are morally good when they are necessary or helpful to marital intercourse and/or express and nurture marital love. Of course, they are immoral if they are intended to cause complete sexual satisfaction without intercourse or in some other way they violate the good of marital union. For example, some acts are repugnant to one of the spouses and insisting on such is hardly loving.

Karol Wojtyla (Pope John Paul II) goes so far as to address the fact that "the curve of arousal in woman is different from that in man - it rises more slowly and falls more slowly." He insists that the man has a moral responsibility to learn about this difference and to accommodate to it. He also cautions that failure to do so can jeopardize the marriage.

Needless to say the chaste love of husband and wife insists that the circumstances be suitable. Many situations make abstinence appropriate, privacy being unavailable, for example.

ADULTERY

Christian tradition has always held that adultery is always, without exception, sinful. And because the ordinary universal Magisterium has taught it as a truth God has revealed, it must be held as infallibly true.

Most people have no doubt that adultery is wrong and a serious violation of marriage. Usually a spouse experiences the other's adultery as a grave betrayal. After all, love cannot be total without complete trust, so to discover one's beloved has been unfaithful can be traumatic.

Obviously, adultery goes against the good of marriage and the marital rights of the spouse. Unless the adulterous spouse repents, his or her infidelity deprives his or her sexual acts within marriage of their capacity to express self-giving and to signify marital communion. Until there is genuine repentance and forgiveness the innocent spouse naturally finds attempts at intimacy repugnant. Adultery, unrepented, leads to divorce.

Even secret adultery violates the marriage and often the innocent spouse senses something wrong. The deception, especially if the adulterous relationship continues, is seriously inconsistent with union and openness and mutuality. It goes without saying that the possibility of a child compounds the evil and an actual child suffers from absence of parental raising. Incestuous adultery is particularly grave and may constitute rape.

If one holds that marital union is the sacrament of matrimony, then adultery takes on the dimension of sacrilege. Attempted marriage after divorce is a matter of adultery - as is a bigamous relationship.

CONCLUSION

Catholic teaching about sexual conduct is a committed defense of love. God loved us into being as images of himself as love. And the paradigm of love imitative of God as Love is conjugal love. Every person has a natural inclination to marriage and a natural inclination to judge that marriage is good. Marriage is the union of complementary bodily persons constituting them co-principles of life.

God is love and love prompts Love to love us into existence and to keep us in existence. In imitation of this Love loving, the love of human spouses brings new persons into existence.

The morality of sexual conduct, then, is based precisely on the meaning and reality of marital communion. Married couples are to express their love in sexual intercourse respecting the unitive and procreative aspects of this love. What makes certain acts immoral is violation of either the unitive or procreative aspect of marriage.

Again, as begun in Chapter 4, we conclude with Grisez's directives for approaching moral issues.

APPLICATION OF TWO-STEP APPROACH TO MORAL ISSUES
SEXUAL INTERCOURSE IN MARRIAGE IS MORALLY GOOD.

FIRST STEP

CLARIFY THE ACTION BY ANSWERING 2 QUESTIONS.
1. Impact of choice on a basic human good?
   Sexual intercourse expresses and stimulates total self-giving and is normal way to communicate life. Thus expressive of good of married communion.
2. Attitude of will toward the goods?
   A married couple can intend both - explicitly or implicitly

SECOND STEP

EVALUATE THE ACTION BY APPLYING MORAL PRINCIPLES.
The choosing is inclusivistic, pursuing the good of marital communion, open to all the goods. It obviously is compatible with integral human fulfillment and is in accord with all the Modes of Christian Response.

++++++

NON-LOVING INTERCOURSE IN MARRIAGE

FIRST STEP

CLARIFY THE ACTION BY ANSWERING 2 QUESTIONS.
1. Impact of choice on a basic human good?
   Coerced intercourse or intercourse while imagining being with someone other than one's spouse impacts on good of married communion.
2. Attitude of will toward the goods?
   Deliberate choice in either case involves willing harm to married communion, normally as means to another good.

SECOND STEP

EVALUATE THE ACTION BY APPLYING MORAL PRINCIPLES.
Clearly the choice is exclusivistic and not compatible with integral human fulfillment, for one chooses to harm the good of married communion as means to e.g. play. Coercion violates the 5th Mode of Responsibility as well as the 8th and probably the 3rd. Imagining another violates the 4th Mode of Responsibility, the 5th and the 8th. Both fail the 8th of Christian Response.

++++++

CONTRACEPTIVE INTERCOURSE IN MARRIAGE

FIRST STEP

CLARIFY THE ACTION BY ANSWERING 2 QUESTIONS.
1. Impact of choice on a basic human good?
   Choice is to withhold total self-giving in intercourse and to prevent communication of life.
2. Attitude of will toward the goods?
   The choice is precisely to do both.

SECOND STEP

EVALUATE THE ACTION BY APPLYING MORAL PRINCIPLES.

Such a choice is exclusivistic, choosing to withhold self-giving and to prevent communication of life. It is not compatible with integral human fulfillment for that reason. And it violates the 8th Mode of Responsibility (going against the good of love and of life as means to nurture friendship of family etc.). The 8th Mode of Christian Response is violated as well.

++++++

ADULTERY

FIRST STEP

CLARIFY THE ACTION BY ANSWERING 2 QUESTIONS.
1. Impact of choice on a basic human good?
   The adulterer harms the spouse and the good of marital communion and either "uses" the sexual partner, pursuing emotional satisfaction without affection, or substitutes the appearance of marital communion for genuine marital communion.
2. Attitude of will toward the goods?
   The harm to the spouse and the good of marital communion, perhaps reluctantly, is deliberately chosen. Harm to the sexual partner is usually chosen.

SECOND STEP

EVALUATE THE ACTION BY APPLYING MORAL PRINCIPLES.
Harm to the spouse is exclusivistic choosing, violates the criterion of morality. Certainly the choice is not compatible with integral human fulfillment, deliberately hurting the spouse. Using the sexual partner is not compatible with integral human fulfillment and violates the 3rd Mode of Responsibility and usually the 8th. The 6th mode declares substitution of appearance of marital communion rules this as immoral. Some Modes of Christian Response seem to be violated.

++++++

CHAPTER 15

THE UNMARRIED

What the Catechism says to the unmarried about chastity or self-mastery flies in the face of today's Western culture. It says the unmarried are to be continent, to have no deliberate sex. Even the engaged couple is told that God wants them to refrain from deliberate sexual indulgence. This is a hard teaching; the love that urges to intercourse is the same love that their marital consent will seal and make sexual union the natural and proper expression of their love. However, like pregnancy, there is no such thing as being "almost married." A couple is either married or not married.

With that in mind, can engaged couples really be expected to abstain completely from sexual intercourse? It is possible only if genuine love inspires them to choose what is best for each of them and their future marriage. In order to do that, to say "No!" to the powerful demands of the flesh, which also involves avoiding situations that lead to arousal, the couple must help each other—help each to grow in chastity and self-mastery. Through just such difficulty couples learn and earn true love.

Marriage cannot survive, let alone flourish, without mutual respect and fidelity. The struggle to remain chaste can generate respect and fidelity; it deepens their mutual commitment as they look forward to the day when each will receive the other before God in marriage. This struggle by being shared can bring them closer. Helping one another to be chaste can crystallize their shared values, encouraging one another to live up to their values. Praying together, planning fun times, joy times, love times together which avoid situations which strain self-control, each taking responsibility when the other seems weak, all elements of a strategy to protect their love, can unite a couple deeply. Trust in baptismal grace and the infused virtue of chastity should be developed.

As for single people not engaged, how does the Catechism's teaching affect them? Can teenagers and unmarried adults really be expected today to remain virgins and live celibate lives? Recent studies report that in fact this is not the case. The idea that sex is to be reserved for marriage certainly seems antiquated. The pill and the "sexual revolution" made it so. The percentage of women who were virgins at age of 19, we have seen, dropped from 45% in 1960 to 20 % in 1980. 43% of brides (white) in 1965 were virgins, only 14% in 1985. 30% of those polled said they had had two to four partners since they were eighteen, 22% had five, 20% ten or more partners.

The fact is unmarried people are not remaining virgins or celibate. One reason is the implicit assumption that such conduct is morally all right. Our objective is to address that assumption, not to propose tactics to change contemporary mores.

Unfortunately, the opinion that all have the right to sexual satisfaction has gained widespread acceptance throughout society. Given our current attitudes, emotional impact will be lacking in an academic clinical analysis of what makes masturbation, fornication and sodomy wrong. What really "packs a wallop" is the wreckage that Germain Grisez attributes to such practices: deserted wives and children, broken hearts and homes, ruined careers, epidemic sex-related diseases, to name a few results of sex without restraint. It is imperative to link these results of unlicensed sexual indulgence with the precious human and Christian values that have been so manifestly and seriously eroded by sexually sinful behavior.

Even recent studies on sexual behavior suggests people normally recognize the need of sexual restraint. In spite of the sobering statistics there has been no success in converting Americans to "free love." People, according to polls have indeed taken a broader view on sexual indulgence, but most men and women are still what may be called sexually conservative both in what they believe and what they do.

One wonders whether lived experience is teaching people that sex is not enough. Knowledge of what reason and natural law teach about sexual conduct has been muffled by the change in our culture. Perhaps experience that sex is not enough may help people to see that sexual conduct outside of marriage is wrong. Then the natural law on this matter may be restored.

Grisez's insights may indeed be the catalyst to the change necessary.

You probably never thought about it, but there are only three basic sexual acts, each separate and distinct from the other, that unmarried people can engage in—apart, of course, from adultery. The Catechism teaches that all three—masturbation, fornication and sodomy—are sinful.

THE CATECHISM

As mentioned earlier the focus of the Catechism's treatment is love. Created in the image of God, who is love, human beings have inscribed in their nature the capacity and responsibility of love and communion. Sexuality concerns the capacity to love and to procreate.

To fulfill their vocation they need chastity: the integration of sexuality within the person. Reason is to guide people in the exercise of sex. Only the chaste person can meaningfully express love in sexual acts.

The Church understands people, knowing not only God's word, but individual Christians themselves, their strengths and their weaknesses. The Catholic Catechism presents chastity as a process—"an *apprenticeship in self-mastery* which is a training in human freedom." This process of self-mastery is a "long and exacting work." Renewed effort at different (and all) stages of life is necessary. Obviously some stages are more difficult than others, for example childhood and adolescence. Progress is marked by imperfections and too often by sin.

The tone of realism and compassion is found in every section of the Church teaching. By no means does the Catechism teach dictatorially or by talking down to inferiors.

MASTURBATION

The opposite of chastity is lust, "disordered desire for or inordinate enjoyment of sexual pleasure."(*Catechism*, #2351) Sexual pleasure is natural and good; it is morally disordered when isolated from its procreative and unitive purpose.

Becoming specific, the Catechism first treats masturbation, "the deliberate stimulation of the genital organs in order to derive sexual pleasure." (*Catechism*, #2352)

The contra-culture dimension of Catholic teaching is manifest. Recent sociological researchers find masturbation the most problematic sexual subject. They report that almost 40% of men and almost 60% of women stated they never masturbated. Turned around, these figures suggest that 60% of men between 18 and 59 years of age and 40% of women between the same ages masturbated in the past year. About 25% of men and 10% of women admit they masturbate once a week. (*Sex in America*, p. 158)

Acknowledging that Judaism and Christianity always judged masturbation immoral, they report that only in the 18th century was any campaign against it launched. Physicians proposed bizarre medical reasons why it is harmful and more bizarre techniques to discourage it were advanced. Gradually the medical profession came to realize that masturbation does not cause physical diseases, but "doctors, psychiatrists, psychologists, and counselors continued to believe that masturbation caused mental disorders." (*Sex in America*, 159-161)

People in general, they conclude, are split in judging this practice. Under the influence of various religious groups who teach masturbation is immoral, some are inclined to look on it as bad for themselves or their children or that at issue is will power. On the other hand, there are those who feel masturbation is not immoral. Nonetheless, "even the most liberal tend to see masturbation as an activity that is appropriate only for the young or those without partners. Among adults, masturbation has the taint of sexual failure." (Ibid., 162)

Sifting through the data on frequency of masturbation among different groups, the surprising conclusion reached "is that masturbation is not a substitute for those who are sexually deprived, but . . .an activity that stimulates and is stimulated by other sexual behavior." (Ibid., 165)

Earlier we suggested this may well be related to the failure to subordinate sexual pleasure to genuine love. Grisez will point out that fornication often is basically a matter of masturbation and will speak of the masturbatory aspect of our culture.

A final observation from this recent sociological study of men who admitted masturbating one to five times a year: 25% said they felt guilty about doing so, 18% had no guilt feelings. Of those masturbating once a week or more, 41% acknowledge guilty feelings, 43% said no guilt feelings.

Of women who admitted masturbating one to five times a year 47% said they felt guilty, 32% had no guilt feelings. When those who masturbated once a week or more were asked about guilt, only 14% of women said yes. 21% had no guilt feelings. (Ibid., 167)

However these data are to be explained, it is of definite interest that many experienced a sense of guilt about masturbating.

So much for sociological findings. Still no Catholic should be surprised that the Catechism unequivocally teaches that masturbation is immoral because it results in sexual pleasure isolated from the unitive and procreative purposes of sex. In masturbation sexual pleasure is pursued apart from the relationship "demanded by the moral order and in which the total meaning of mutual self-giving and human procreation in the context of true love is achieved." (*Catechism*, #2352)

Many, especially boys and young men, experience distress over a sense of guilt about apparent masturbation. As most know, involuntary nocturnal emission is not sinful. Anyone having a problem with masturbation should seek wise counsel. The Catechism cautions that, while the act of masturbation is wrong, contributing factors often diminish or even exclude moral guilt. Confessors and counselors should examine the possibilities that "affective immaturity, the force of acquired habit, conditions of anxiety, or other psychological or social factor(s)" may constitute precisely such diminishing or excusing causes. (Ibid.)

A distinction is being made here between objective and subjective morality—with reference to the three elements of grave sin: serious matter, sufficient reflection and full consent of the will. The factors mentioned may render the physical act of masturbation a nonfree and so nonmoral act or at least lessen the gravity of the sin.

FORNICATION

A man and a woman, both unmarried, have intercourse. Most Catholics expect that the Catechism, as the authoritative teaching arm of the Church, will state that this is seriously wrong. Fornication is contrary to the dignity of persons and the dignity of human sexuality which is, by nature, ordered to the good of married partners as well as to the generation and education of children. Needless to say grave scandal is added when corruption of the young is involved. (*Catechism*, #2353)

A word about two other topics. Pornography offends against chastity and immerses people in the illusion of a fantasy world. Likewise prostitution is treated: "it reduces the person to an instrument of sexual pleasure." The realism and compassion are again evident when the Catechism suggests that "destitution, blackmail, or social pressure" may attenuate imputability, even though prostitution is always gravely sinful. (*Catechism*, #2354-5)

Although rape today is treated as an issue of force and power, it definitely is also a sexual act. The Catechism recognizes both aspects, defining rape as "the forcible violation of the sexual intimacy of another person." Both justice and charity are violated. Deep wounds are inflicted on the "respect, freedom, and physical and moral integrity," of the person. As is well recognized grave damage, marking the victim for life, is caused. When it is incest or rape of children by those responsible for them, the evil is graver still. (*Catechism*,#2356)

GRISEZ: *LIVING A CHRISTIAN LIFE*

As I have repeatedly remarked, Grisez helps us to clarify exactly what is at issue and thereby understand the Church teaching better.

In *Living a Christian Life* his conviction that marriage is a basic human good holds central position in the entire morality of sexual conduct. Because it is a basic good all people have a natural inclination, in various ways, toward marital communion and are also inclined to form a right judgment that marital union is to be pursued and anything that might harm such a bond should be avoided. Because of the relationship of sexual intercourse with marital communion, all sexual acts by the unmarried are wrong; they violate the one-flesh communion of marriage. (p. 648)

It is essential to recognize that sexual intercourse has a built-in distinctive meaning—which meaning involves total self-giving which in turn constitutes a couple's being co-principles of new life. Thus sexual intercourse by its very nature is ordered to express or to stimulate total self-giving.

A man and a woman enter into marriage, committed to marital communion, or total union, by mutual consent. Marital communion is consummated by the first act of intercourse. All subsequent acts of intercourse between a couple are ordered by their very nature to express, stimulate and foster conjugal love, the heart of marriage, as it was developed in the previous chapter.(p. 634)

MASTURBATION

As already noted, there are three basic sexual acts the unmarried engage in—masturbation, fornication and homosexual acts. As clear as the Catechism teaching is on masturbation, many may require or at least appreciate the further insight which Grisez provides. He explains how the universal good of marital communion is violated by the act of masturbation. Morality immediately affects choices made by free will So what is being chosen when a person deliberately masturbates? It is a choice, except in cases where addiction robs the will of freedom, to alienate or separate the body from the conscious self and to use that body as an end in itself to achieve deliberate sentient pleasure.

One of the basic human goods is self-integrity—harmony among the parts or aspects of a person. Masturbation, then, is wrong because it is choosing to damage the basic human good of self-integrity. In addition it indirectly violates marital communion. Masturbation is especially disordered because this disintegrity harms the unity of a person as conscious subject and sexually functioning body. But the unity of the self as conscious subject and sexually functioning body is exactly what is necessary for sexual intercourse to be a communion of persons—which marital intercourse is. Masturbation damages the body's capacity for the conjugal act as an act of self-giving, thereby damaging indirectly marital communion. (p. 650)

Pope John Paul II has often championed the "nuptial meaning of the body." Obviously, to damage an intrinsic and absolutely necessary condition for attaining the good of marital communion is to harm the sacred union of marriage itself.

The claim that masturbation "damages the capacity" is not based on empirical studies, but on reflection about what is involved in the choice to violate this self-integrity which is "the capacity . . . for self-giving." For sexual intercourse to be communion of persons the person must be his/her body. By attempting to act as though body and self were separate entities one limits the capacity of the bodily unity to be unity of persons.

An argument can also be developed that masturbation violates both the unitive and procreative aspects of the basic human good of marriage. To masturbate limits the natural capacity of sexual intercourse to express and/or stimulate the total self-giving of conjugal love. Either one focuses on oneself and gives oneself to no one or one imagines someone with whom the sexual activity would be more satisfying and one substitutes the unreal for the real experience. Thus the unitive aspect is violated.

Sexual intercourse unites a couple constituting them co-principles of communicating life. No new life can result from masturbation.

FORNICATION

Grisez unhesitatingly agrees with the Catechism's teaching on fornication, but feels compelled to distinguish different contexts in which fornication takes place and then to explain how in each case it violates the basic human good of marital communion.

Couples sleep together without genuine love or caring and with no intention of making a commitment. Often, what is involved is mutual masturbatory self-gratification through intercourse, each partner using the other to reach orgasm. At other times, one or the other uses sex as a bargaining tool—for money, position, as an enticement to marriage or just to confirm the individual's masculinity or femininity. In these contexts fornication has different motives, but is wrong for the same reason masturbation is wrong: it cripples the capacity for self-giving. (p. 651)

In such cases the person has to withhold, to reject the thrust to self-giving and so goes against the good of conjugal union. If trivialization of sex has deadened the sense of total self-giving related to sexual intercourse, she/he may not understand her/his act of intercourse as a negation of conjugal union.

Often, of course, the motive for choosing to fornicate is different from the above scenarios, real affection is experienced. An engaged couple is the paradigm case for intimate relationships similar to marital friendship. They choose sexual intercourse to achieve the intimate communion that pertains to marriage, but without marital commitment. If sexual intercourse for the engaged is immoral, a fortiori it is wrong for less intimate relationships.

What can be wrong with sexual intercourse when a couple are in love, committed by engagement to marry?

Many of my students express disdain about a "piece of paper" being needed as the official marriage seal; they also have difficulty distinguishing between the "marriage ceremony" and a state of "being married." Because, due to extraordinary circumstances, a couple can be married without a

Life, Love, and Sex

traditional ceremony, the students correctly recognize the primacy of marriage over ceremony as well as the importance of conjugal love which motivates the commitment of marital communion. But what they ignore is the difference between conjugal love and mutual commitment.

People seem to convince themselves that if they love one another, sexual intercourse is morally justified. Grounding this position is the fact that the same beautiful erotic love urging them to intercourse is the same love that will motivate them to make the commitment to the permanent, exclusive love of marriage. And contemporary culture makes it easy to slide into this conviction, saturated as the culture is with assumptions that support and encourage it.

However, to be all but married is to not be married. Like pregnancy, there is no "all but." Certainly, if couples speak seriously of being engaged, they must mean it is different from being married.

Bodily union provides experience of intimacy, but by itself all it realizes is the natural capacity of a male individual and a female to mate. As Thomas explained, nature taught all animals to mate, but human beings approach mating guided by reason. The part of marital communion chosen in fornication, even by engaged couples, bodily union, is not an intelligible good apart from the whole. (p. 651)

It may have taken centuries for humans to recognize, but sexual mating is reasonable, is an intelligible good, only insofar as it is an element of the two-in-one-flesh by which a man and a woman become, as it were, one person. What effects the two-in-one-flesh union is marital consent, a willingness to join together as complementary bodily persons. Marriage, we have explained, involves the unitive aspect which renders a man and a woman co-principles of new life.

To substitute an illusory experience of marital communion for the real thing—an authentic commitment to marital communion—is unreasonable and so wrong and immoral. (p. 652) Once again, it is important to enliven the clinical analysis of the subject by recalling the human as well as Christian values that are at stake. So much unhappiness "all around us" is the result of the belief that fornication is natural and morally justifiable.

Reflection on all this human suffering is especially needed if only complications extrinsic to their love (about which they have no doubt) hold up their wedding. Economic problems, for example, prompt delay. So some couples may really mean that in becoming engaged, they gave marital consent.

One student insisted that this possibility must be kept open "to help maintain unity and morality on a universal level." "I do agree that many people hide behind —'Well, we are going to get married' or 'Yeah, but we are engaged to be married so the commitment has already been made.' Yet—it may be—a healthy thing. I agree with the 'sex with love' approach.

If the love is there for real and people are not hiding behind it as an excuse, then true intimacy between these two can further foster the relationship."

Today black and white thinking about the morality of sex strikes many as impossible. A couple in love, with solid reasons for postponing marriage, can find such reasoning very appealing. But reflecting on weddings at which I officiated over the years, I never could have predicted that Imogene and Jack would grow in love but Adelaide and Jim would have their marriage annulled. Both couples seemed to me to sincerely be in love. How does one know "the love is there for real"?

It should be obvious how open to abuse such thinking is. Marriages break up; what if the engaged couple have a serious fight and break up? Do they consider they need a divorce or a declaration of nullity? What about ownership of car(s), furniture, and so forth?

A can of worms can be opened by pursuing the question of marital consent without a ceremony. Suffice it to say, love, even engagement, is not marital consent. And serious human suffering can result from playing fast and loose with centuries-old distinction between marriage and engagement.

"Trial Marriage" and "Living Together"

Two contemporary situations call for explicit attention, "trial marriages" and "living together." A special edition on "The 21st Century Family" treats "trial marriage" under "extended adolescence" (*Newsweek*, Winter/Spring 1990). Referring to it as "cohabitation" that article defines it as "the commitment not to be committed." Fifty percent of all men and women in their 30's were reported as cohabiting before marriage—"better to look— deeply—before they leap." And yet research demonstrates, the article says, "that couples who cohabit before marriage are more likely to divorce than those who do not." One sociologist observes that cohabitation attracts those—and he says this is true especially of men—"who are looking for an easy out." He questions that it contributes anything to marriage.

The study in *U.S. News and World Report* (May 1997) used earlier confirms the *Newsweek* article. "Cohabitation may seem a good 'trial run' for a solid marriage. But in practice, cohabiting couples who marry . . . are about 33% more likely to divorce than couples who don't live together before their nuptials."

Grisez treats this contemporary lifestyle succinctly. "Trial marriage," he remarks, "is an illuminating example of fornication." (p. 652) It is an oxymoron: marriage is basically a mutual consent to permanent communion; a trial marriage attempts to experience marriage without commitment to permanent union. What results is an <u>illusion</u> of marriage. The Catechism condemns trial marriages and explains why: "Human love does not tolerate 'trial marriages.' It demands a total and definitive gift of persons to one another." Faith and human intelligence find this lifestyle unreasonable and

Life, Love, and Sex

lived experience reveals its failure together with the consequent human heartbreak. (*Catechism*, #3391)

"The clergy, once loquacious on the topic of premarital 'sin,' are (equally) subdued. 'Have you ever heard a sermon on "living together?"'... condemnation of adult premarital sex has virtually vanished from religious preaching, even in the homilies of Catholic priests." (*U.S. News* p.57) 'Living together,' I submit, captures the median point of the sexual revolution: "sex must be reserved for marriage" has been abandoned in practice—yet Americans have not been converted to free love.

Men and women do not move in together lightly. Traditional beliefs and values about sex and marriage subtly but definitively corroded by customs and the media, men and women assume they are "free" to engage in sex—especially when they have affection for and care for one another.

One rarely hears mention of the risks such a move entails. According to the *U.S. News* report (May 19, 1997), "Live-in boyfriends are far more likely to beat their partners than are spouses." An interesting correlation is made: they are more likely to get involved with cocaine and cigarettes "after they start cohabiting than beforehand."

Sometimes the relationship may develop into "trial marriage," but initially it is not the intent. Real, intimate friendship nurtured by sexual intercourse prompts the decision that one move in with the other. Since marriage is explicitly ruled out, sexual intercourse is objectively immoral for the reasons given above. It seems clear that they would have to reject or block the thrust to self-giving naturally linked with sexual intercourse. They choose to go against the good of marital communion—specifically the unitive aspect.

Furthermore, there is a distinctive risk involved. Regular intercourse risks generating deep commitment and, as many young couples learn by sad experience, one partner seeks a deeper commitment, maybe marriage, than the other is prepared to give. Isn't this a violation of friendship—seriously hurting the other? Is it right to risk such hurt, excusing oneself that it has been clearly agreed upon? (p. 652)

Since marriage is explicitly ruled out, most likely contraception is used. We have noted the immorality of this, the limiting of total self-giving in love-making, as well as the contra-life aspect of contraception.

The procreative aspect of sexual intercourse excluded, the likelihood of rationalization is high. Is not the real motive for choosing sexual intercourse as expression of affection to satisfy sexual desire? Hence, mutual masturbation is really the case. Grisez suggests that a sign that masturbation is the case is found in something many learn also by sad experience—nonmarital sexual intimacy can obstruct or dissolve friendship—not nurture it. (p. 653)

Although there is silence in the pulpit about the immorality of living together, the Catechism teaches that those embracing such a lifestyle are prohibited from receiving Holy Communion. (*Catechism*, #2390)

Two general insights on sexual indulgence by those unmarried: the traditional attitude toward premarital sex would hardly have been so abandoned without acceptance of contraception. Only in the 1930's was contraception proposed as morally justifiable, and this tentatively and for serious reasons within marriage—by the Anglican Church, the first of the major religions to do so. Today contraception seems taken for granted, even urged as the reasonable way for family planning and for "safe sex," protection against AIDS.

Secondly, a strong traditional argument against fornication is the injustice of bringing a child into the world without a stable family needed for nurturing and education. The immorality of such injustice is a serious reason to avoid fornication. Although the Catechism invokes this argument implicitly, Grisez does not mention it. (*Catechism*, #2353)

Whenever an unmarried man and woman choose sexual intercourse, they compound the immorality of fornication either by choosing—in addition—to contracept or by risking serious injustice to a possible child.

CONCLUSION

Some, especially the young, may be surprised at the clear strong Catholic teaching on pre-marital and extra-martial sex. Some, brainwashed by cultural mores constantly communicated by television, will find the teaching hard to accept. But much, very much is at stake for human happiness and spiritual growth in the question of the morality of sexual conduct. There can be little hope that radical change is possible in the foreseeable future. Secular Humanism frames people's thinking and offers justification for contemporary lifestyles. And the enticement of immediate sexual gratification keeps people happily satisfied with that lifestyle.

The sense of "moral freedom" rampant in the United States prompts Catholics and others to resist "being told" that masturbation, pre-marital sex, living together, trial marriage are all immoral.

Unfortunately, significantly greater suffering, individual and social, it seems, is needed if people are to open themselves to re-examine their lifestyles and their intellectual moral presuppositions.

Fortunately, on the other hand, Americans have not bought into "free love" and loose morals. This is related, I believe, to the reality of the natural law every normally developed person knows. The multiple movements to chastity reflect this natural law and also, very importantly, the active presence of the Holy Spirit.

At some point people will be ready to take a serious look at the reasons for their position of sexual conduct. Catholics should be helped to have clear knowledge of what their Church teaches. They and others may be able to recognize the validity of Grisez's reasonable justification of his position on these issues.

God is love. As images of God human beings are destined to manifest the beauty and value of love. Called to love, people will ultimately acknowledge the need of chastity to nurture and to preserve love. Without love we cannot be humanly fulfilled. Without the self-mastery of our sexuality we cannot love. Natural discipline can help, but the love of God poured out into our hearts, the Holy Spirit, is necessary to achieve that self-mastery and freedom to love.

As for homosexuality, the third form of sexual sin, it has become so widespread and it is such a sensitive subject that separate treatment will address homosexual acts.

Again, as begun in Chapter 4, we conclude with Grisez's directives for approaching moral issues.

APPLICATION OF TWO-STEP APPROACH TO MORAL ISSUES

MASTURBATION

FIRST STEP

CLARIFY THE ACTION BY ANSWERING 2 QUESTIONS.
1. Impact of Choice on a Basic Human Good?
   Masturbation directly attacks the good of self-integrity, attempting to use the body to satisfy conscious feelings, as though the self and body were separate, as though the person were subject which <u>has</u> a body. And masturbation indirectly violates marital communion by damaging the body's capacity for the conjugal act as an act of <u>self</u>-giving.
2. Attitude of Will toward the Good(s)?
   One wills to violate self-integrity and so to damage the body's capacity for the conjugal act as an act of <u>self</u>-giving.

SECOND STEP

EVALUATE THE ACTION BY APPLYING MORAL PRINCIPLES.

To choose to harm a basic human good is exclusivistic choosing, thus violating the first principle of morality, not choosing in a way compatible with integral human fulfillment. The 8th Mode of Responsibility is violated, as well as the 3rd.

The 6th and 8th Modes of Christian Response are violated.

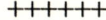

FORNICATION
(WITHOUT AFFECTION)

FIRST STEP

CLARIFY THE ACTION BY ANSWERING 2 QUESTIONS.
1. Impact of Choice on a Basic Human Good?
   Fornication without affection in some cases is mutual masturbation or a bargaining exchange; thus like masturbation a direct violation of self-integrity and an indirect violation of marital communion. Also involved is violation of the good of friendship, using the other person.
2. Attitude of Will toward the Good(s)?
   One wills to pursue self-gratification or achievement of some objective, knowingly violating the above goods.

SECOND STEP

EVALUATE THE ACTION BY APPLYING MORAL PRINCIPLES.
As with masturbation, such fornication is exclusivistic choosing, thus violating the first principle of morality, choosing in a way not compatible with integral human fulfillment. Though the motive may differ from that of masturbation, fornication in such cases bears the same moral character. The 8th and 3rd Modes of Responsibility are violated, as are the 6th and 8th Modes of Christian Response.

(Needless to say, if contraception is used, the good of love and the good of life are violated.)

++++++

FORNICATION
(BETWEEN ENGAGED)

FIRST STEP

CLARIFY THE ACTION BY ANSWERING 2 QUESTIONS.
1. Impact of Choice on a Basic Human Good?
   Sexual intercourse prompted by love without the commitment of marriage violates the good of marital communion.
2. Attitude of Will toward the Good(s)?
   One expresses love without commitment, substituting union of engagement for union of marriage.

SECOND STEP

EVALUATE THE ACTION BY APPLYING MORAL PRINCIPLES.

Most directly the 6th Mode of Responsibility is violated, substituting an illusory union for the real. One is not pursuing integral human fulfillment by pursuit of the illusory. Likewise the 6th Mode of Christian Response is not observed.

(Needless to say, if contraception is used, the good of love and the good of life are violated.)

++++++

FORNICATION
"TRIAL MARRIAGE"

FIRST STEP

CLARIFY THE ACTION BY ANSWERING 2 QUESTIONS.
1. Impact of Choice on a Basic Human Good?
   Marital communion is at stake.
2. Attitude of Will toward the Good(s)?
   Withholding marital consent, one substitutes the appearance of marriage.

SECOND STEP

EVALUATE THE ACTION BY APPLYING MORAL PRINCIPLES.
As in the previous case of an engaged couple the 6th Mode of Responsibility is violated, substituting an illusory union for real consent. One is not pursuing integral human fulfillment by pursuit of the illusory. Likewise the 6th Mode of Christian Response is not being observed.

(Needless to say if, as is likely, contraception is used, the good of love and the good of life are violated.)

+++++++

FORNICATION
(LIVING TOGETHER)

FIRST STEP

CLARIFY THE ACTION BY ANSWERING 2 QUESTIONS.
1. Impact of Choice on a Basic Human Good?
   Marriage explicitly ruled out, sexual intercourse impacts on marital communion and also on the good of friendship, since not infrequently one partner develops the desire for a commitment the other is not prepared to give.
2. Attitude of Will toward the Good(s)?
   This choice involves self-gratification as in masturbation. One blocks out the thrust to self-giving, the unitive aspect of marital communion, and one risks harm to the good of friendship.

SECOND STEP

EVALUATE THE ACTION BY APPLYING MORAL PRINCIPLES.

Marriage ruled out, both the substitution of immediate gratification for genuine marital good and the aspect of illusion mean that the 3rd and 6th modes of responsibility are violated. As in masturbation the damage to the body's capacity for the conjugal act as an act of <u>self</u>-giving involves violation of the 8th Mode of Responsibility. The 8th mode is also violated by risking harm to the good of friendship. Clearly these choices are not compatible with integral human fulfillment. The 3rd, 5th, and 8th Modes of Christian Response are not observed.

(Needless to say if, as is likely, contraception is used the good of love and the good of life are violated.)

CHAPTER 16

HOMOSEXUALITY—PART I
UNDERSTANDING, RESPECT, TRUTH

Homosexuality is such a prominent and sensitive issue that the morality of homosexual acts demands separate and specific examination. The moral issue has not changed, but the socio-political atmosphere begs for a more sensitive and sympathetic expression of the Church's teaching.

"There is no area of sexuality more misunderstood, distorted, maligned, and actually feared than the homosexualities [sic]." (*A Secret World*, Sipe)

Repeatedly we have had recourse to the triptych of Ethos, Ethics, Metaethics. This chapter will be devoted to "Ethos" or custom, the present practice and present way of thinking about homosexual acts. Besides evidence of active "gay" lifestyle we report what is happening in law, the churches, theater, as well as movements claiming effective techniques of changing orientation and even genetic research. In the following chapter we shall apply the metaethics of Part I in order to assess the Ethics or the specific ethical principles that should govern judgment about the morality of homosexual acts.

Since the 1970's men and women have been publicly declaring they are gay; they have "come out of the closet" and they demand respect for themselves and for their lifestyle. As a result medicine, law, and religious institutions have been compelled to re-examine traditions.

Until the '70's psychiatrists defined homosexuality as a psychopathology (mental disorder) and homosexual lifestyle was considered deviant. Often gays have been discriminated against in various ways just because of their sexual orientation; sometimes they have been beaten physically for it. In a recent Broadway play a gay character reacts to police beating participants in a gay demonstration: "What is wrong with this country? They hate us. They —— hate us. They've always hated us. It never ends, the —— hatred."

The emergence of the AIDS epidemic in the early 1980's, with so many gay fatalities, placed them in an unfavorable light, but that has diminished with HIV and AIDS occurring in all groups.

Demonstrations and marches have raised universal consciousness of gay civil rights. Catholic colleges have struggled with the question of recognizing gay organizations.

A distinction to be explained in a later context warrants mention. Homosexuality refers to a person with same sex orientation. "Gay" culture refers more significantly to those who publicly adopt a homosexual lifestyle and are determined to have that lifestyle accepted as legitimate (and more).

HOMOSEXUALITY AND THE LAW

Some laws have been changed to correct unjust discrimination. Although gays suffered a setback when the 1986 Supreme Court decision upheld a Georgia law that prohibits sodomy between adults, even in their homes, homosexuals applauded the recent Supreme Court decision which overturned a Colorado constitutional amendment. (*Romer. . .et al. v Evans et al.*, May 20, 1996) That anti-gay amendment, which was approved by the voters, was judged to be a violation of the American constitutional guarantee of equal protection. Speaking for many, one gay leader was ecstatic over the high court ruling, "I believe it's the capping of our liberation."

It seems both the 6 to 3 majority and Justice Antonio Scalia in his minority opinion focused on the gays as a class. Justice Anthony M. Kennedy, writing for the majority, insisted that a state could not deny a <u>class</u> of people their civil rights. Justice Scalia felt the Colorado constitutional amendment was aimed at denying that a <u>class</u> of people could be granted special benefits.

The salient part of the Colorado Amendment 2 reads, "Neither the State of Colorado, nor any of its agencies. . .shall enact. . .any statute. . . whereby homosexual, lesbian, or bisexual orientation, conduct, practices or relationships shall constitute or otherwise be the basis of or entitle any person or class of persons to have or claim any minority status, quota preferences, protected status or claim of discrimination."

Justice Kennedy wrote: "We cannot accept the view that Amendment 2's prohibition on specific legal protection does no more than deprive homosexuals of special rights." In response to the State's argument that Amendment 2 does no more than that Kennedy replied, "This reading of the Amendment's language is implausible." In fact he judges "the Amendment seems inexplicable by anything but animus toward the class that it affects." Justice Kennedy continued, "We must conclude that Amendment 2 classifies homosexuals. . . to make them unequal to everyone else. . .A state cannot so deem a class of persons a stranger to its laws. . .[It] violates the Equal Protection Clause. . .."

Justice Scalia, on the other hand, claims "the Court has mistaken a Kulturkampf for a fit of spite." (Ibid. —Justice Scalia. . .dissenting) The Amendment is not a "desire to harm" but "a modest attempt by . . .tolerant Coloradians to preserve traditional sexual mores against the effort of a politically powerful minority to revise those mores through use of the laws. . ." Furthermore Scalia stated, "The Amendment prohibits special treatment of homosexuals and nothing more." And noting the Supreme Court decision in 1986 upholding Georgia's law, prohibiting sodomy (*Bowers v Hardwick*), Scalia argued, "If it is constitutionally permissible. . .to make homosexual conduct criminal, surely it is constitutionally permissible to enact other laws merely disfavoring homosexual conduct. . .And *a fortiori* to adopt a provision not even disfavoring homosexual conduct, but merely prohibiting. . .bestowing special protections upon homosexual conduct."

As Scalia views the matter, "The people of Colorado have adopted an entirely reasonable provision which. . .is designed to prevent piecemeal deterioration of the sexual morality favored by the majority of Coloradians, and is not only an appropriate means to that legitimate end, but a means that Americans have employed before."

CHURCHES AND GAYS

It has definitely become politically correct to approve and support the freedom and right of gays to their lifestyle. As for morality, some religious groups support the gay lifestyle. Episcopalian authorities dismissed a charge of heresy against a bishop for ordaining an openly active homosexual as a deacon and for signing a statement supporting the ordination of active gays in 1996.

In 1997 they elected Bishop Frank I. Griswold III, open supporter of the ordination of practicing homosexuals and clearly in favor of same-sex unions, to lead the Episcopalian church into the next century.

Reporting the election of Bishop Griswold, the account observed, "Perhaps at no other time in history have America's mainline Protestant denominations...been so roiled by conflict. At the center of the tumult are questions about homosexuality."

As for the decision in 1996, both the decision itself and especially the way it was reported, caused confusion. According to one local paper, the spokesman for the official body explained that the core of Episcopalian belief included the divinity of Jesus, his death and resurrection, but "had nothing to say about morality"[!] Only a person unacquainted with Christian belief could make such a statement. In a *New York Times* report which seems much more accurate, the spokesman was quoted as saying there was "nothing in the core beliefs about ordination of active gays." Quite a difference between the two reports! Furthermore, he emphasized that they did not intend their findings to bear at all upon the morality of homosexual acts. This was to be addressed by the Church's general assembly in 1997.

Confusion, indeed. Even the Boston Archdiocesan paper, *The Pilot*, wrote in its editorial, "A small group of Episcopal bishops created the distinct impression that the Protestant Episcopal Church in the United States ... was willing to embrace homosexual acts as legitimate and covenantal expressions of love."

The issue of homosexuality is not limited to the Episcopalian church nor is it going away. Introducing a "conversation" on "Homosexual Marriage and the Church" the author identifies the topic as most divisive in churches today. He picks out the variety of issues involved with homosexuality being contested throughout our culture—as well as insightfully specifying the theological bases involved. The former, the cultural issues, are "sexual ethics, the meaning of marriage and the shape of the family." The neuralgic theological issues within the church are "scriptural interpretation, ecclesial authority, and theological understandings of creation and sexuality." ("Homosexuality, Marriage and the Church: A Conversation," *The Christian Century*, July 1-8, 1998)

We shall return to this "conversation" because two discussants are Catholic, one is a member of the United Church of Christ, the last more in accord with official Catholic thinking than the two Catholics. But first we must complete the saga of the Episcopalian Church as it participated in the 13th Lambeth Conference in 1998. Archbishops and bishops of the 40 provinces of the Anglican Communion meet every 10 years. Theoretically the resolutions reached have no binding effect on the autonomous provinces, but the influence of the conference is hardly distinguishable from authoritative statements.

Bishop John Spong of New Jersey, perhaps the most prominent member of the liberal wing of the Communion, insisted on raising the homosexual issue. The liberal wing is strongest in Britain and the United States, the conservative or evangelical wing is found in Africa and Asia. The largest block of participants were African (224 of the 736) with 95 from Asia.

African bishops formulated the motion condemning homosexual practices which passed 526 to 70, with 45 abstentions. The resolution declared homosexual practices were "incompatible with Scripture." Thus were condemned the practices, common in Britain and the United States, "of blessing unions between homosexual couples and of ordaining Anglican priests who are openly homosexual." Another motion recommended homosexual chastity. Since this was seen as opening the door to monogamous homosexual unions it was defeated by replacing "chastity" with "abstinence."

So strong were the feelings on the issue that once the resolution was passed, an African bishop called on Archbishop G. Carey, head of the Anglican Communion, to expel the bishops of the Episcopal Church of the United States "After they signed the pro-homosexual Koinonia statement drawn up by Bishop J. Spong."

Not only does Archbishop Carey lack such authority, but Bishop Spong intends to continue ordaining homosexual men and predicted that openly homosexual bishops will participate in the 14th Lambeth Conference 10 years from now.

So much for the severe divisions in the Episcopalian Church. Official Roman Catholic teaching, as we shall see, is respectful and sympathetic toward persons with a homosexual orientation, but it firmly declares homosexual acts immoral.

John Paul II, in preparing for Jubilee 2000, has attempted to bring all Catholics to unity of belief. Two encyclicals, *The Splendor of Truth* and *The Gospel of Life*, aimed at correcting errors in moral teaching. "It is no longer a matter of limited and occasional dissent, but of an overall and systematic calling into question of traditional moral doctrine on the bases of certain anthropological and ethical presuppositions." The root of these presuppositions is the abuse of freedom, "detaching human freedom from its essential and constitutive relationship to truth." (*The Splendor of Truth* , 4) The pivotal stance of dissent is: there are no absolute moral principles.

Needless to say, dissenting theologians dissent from Catholic teaching about homosexuality. Dissenting Catholic thinkers challenge the official church teaching on theological understanding of sexuality (whether marriage is only between a man and a woman, whether there are moral absolutes)—on the right of the Church to teach authoritatively on specific moral issues such as sexual activity—as well as the authority of the Church to be the authentic interpreter of Scripture. The introduction to the "Conversation" had it right.

All this clearly comes out in the "Conversation." David Heims, the convener and managing editor, asks whether any advance in understanding or clarification has been made in the twenty years of debate on whether homosexuals can be ordained and whether the Church can approve or bless homosexual relationships.

Max Stackhouse (United Church of Christ) reports there is a rough consensus on two points The human rights of homosexuals must be defended and there is need of a policy of tolerance toward people in homosexual relationships. On the other hand, "most churches agree that homosexual relationships are not the ideal, not something the church should praise or celebrate."

Luke Johnson, Catholic professor of New Testament, found that the conversation clarified the importance of where the discussion begins. He believes strongly in God's continuing self-revelation so that we must be obedient to what God may be saying in sanctified unions of homosexuals. Scripture will, then, be important but not definitive. The conversation will go in a very different direction if the starting point is scriptural texts, traditional church teaching and "a sense that the church is primarily the custodian of a body of revelation."

David Matzko, Catholic (I believe) theology professor in a Catholic college, observes that discussion in the 1970's was "from the world of gay politics" and was based on "rights." Recently a theological context is engaged and sanctification is at stake.

Since "orientation" and acts became important, the question of "nature" and "creation" as well as "fall" are discussed. Stackhouse muses, "I'm naturally a polygamist; that's the way God made me. . .and surely I must live it out." Result of creation or of "fall"? Matzko is not satisfied at all with this approach. Homosexually oriented people do not accept the neat distinction between person and what a person does. Orientation affects the way a person comes to be, how the person relates to others and to the world. In marriage it is said the man and woman complete one another. Heterosexuals, whether they engage in sexual intercourse or not, constitute themselves as selves in community differently from the way homosexuals do. These latter do so through an otherness and complementarity of the same sex.

I find this insight of value.

Stackhouse informs the others that in the United Church of Christ the problem is to hear the biblical and classical theological traditions—the voices of homosexuals are loud and clear. To appeal to the former is to present oneself as Neanderthal.

He also explains the changes in his church. They were due to the impact of existential theology in the 1960's and forms of neo-Reformation and liberation theology. Stress was laid on "the freedom of God," which developed into "normlessness." Whatever people found they wanted to do was interpreted as "a calling to live out God's freedom." After hearing a number of sermons on God's freedom, "You had to watch either your spouse or your wallet."

Is God's message normless? Stackhouse raises two most significant issues. The Protestant tradition does not treat marriage as covenant or sacrament, but as contract. So it is up to the individuals to decide what their contract to marriage is. "Covenant," he says, "is an agreement made under terms which are understood to be given by God."

Closely related is whether "generativity"—communication of life is essential to the marriage covenant. "What does it mean that homosexual relations cut off the biophysical dimension of that?"

Johnson reports, "Of all the marriages I know about, it's a lesbian marriage that is the longest lasting, most faithful, most productive, most socially active and most generous." He laments such deeply spiritual persons find no place for themselves in the church.

He rejects rampant individualism and relationships which are solipsistic or self-gratifying. Relationships must be life-giving—but bearing children is not the only way of giving life. Furthermore sacramental actions involve a church consensus. We cannot change the symbolism of the body within the Body of Christ frivolously. But we can be open to what God is revealing of himself in committed homosexual relationships. "I can accept that possibility (committed gay couples who want to be part of the church and want to be sanctified) more readily than I can people who want to use their local Catholic Church as a drive-in service for getting their weekly wafer and who have absolutely no commitment to the church."

For Johnson sexual acts are not a right. Only within a committed relationship is sex appropriate.

Matzko sums up the discussion. ". . .we are all trying to say that faithful heterosexual procreative marriage is a classic model or paradigmatic case." He himself and Johnson add that it is not a limiting case. It does not exclude other cases. He and Johnson differ from Stackhouse, he judges, inasmuch as "Max, you want to make male-female complementarity and the possibility of procreation the limit of possible cases."

Stackhouse says his concern is to protect the idea that there is a norm—but admits a wide range of relative approximations. Still "if we lose or intentionally obscure the ideal, we blur the vision of God's law, purpose and love as governing norms."

Stackhouse is more in accord with the official Catholic teaching than the other two—Catholic thinkers. Such dissenting opinions on homosexuality explain the confusion and divisiveness of *Always Our Children: A Pastoral Message to Parents of Homosexual Children*. This statement was published by the Committee on Marriage and Family of the United States Conference of Bishops. Seemingly it was the position of the bishops of the United States. Instead, it was the opinion of a single committee (by hear-say primarily the composition of one woman on the committee) without any input from the majority of American Catholic bishops.

Significantly, it was very well received by the gay community—but distressed so many of the bishops that a revised version was published later. One bishop reacted: "The document, in a view shared by many, is founded on bad advice, mistaken theology, erroneous science and skewed sociology. It is pastorally helpful in no perceptible way." Cardinal Ratzinger singled out *Always Our Children* as an example of what the papal document on the role of regional conferences of bishops would prevent.

But clearly, homosexuality remains a divisive issue among Catholics.

Some churches, including a small Baptist parish in Framingham, have proclaimed that they welcome active gays and lesbians. Since support of gay lifestyle has become "politically correct" and homosexual morality has been defended or seemingly defended by church groups, it is not surprising that both civil government and churches are facing the issue of gay-marriages. Married or not, gay adoptive parents are attempting to have their lifestyle taught in our schools as simply an alternative lifestyle.

As mentioned, what is new is the socio-political atmosphere. Contributing to the atmosphere are the plays, films, and TV shows which portray homosexual lifestyles either favorably or as grounding that way of life on civil rights.

GAY LIFESTYLE AND THE THEATER

Consider the changing attitudes toward homosexuality in Tennessee Williams' "Cat on a Hot Tin Roof" (1955) and in Lanford Wilson's "Fifth of July" (1978). Tennessee Williams daringly and only tentatively suggests homosexual attraction between Biff, a central character, and a football teammate when they were in college. On the other hand, "Fifth of July" opens with two men kissing—the two most decent and attractive characters in the play.

Since then playwrights and film-makers have not hesitated to base their works on homosexual themes. As of this writing "Rent" and "Victor Victoria" are Broadway plays with homosexual elements. Terence McNally's "Love! Valour! Compassion!" originally produced at the Manhattan Theater Club on November 1, 1994, and transferred to Broadway January 20, 1995, won the 1995 Outer Critics Circle Award for Best Broadway Play. It has recently been released as a film. At Gregory's farmhouse eight gay men hash out their passions, resentments, and fears. Kissing, sleeping together, homosexual acts are taken for granted—and genuine caring and love are sometimes beautifully expressed.

"Angels in America," of course, was the blockbuster play(s) which won the 1993 Pulitzer Prize for Drama and the 1993 Tony Award for Best Play. A powerful work in two parts, "Millennium Approaches" and "Perestroika," this play portrays active homosexuals in all classes of society. Live simulation of anal intercourse on stage tells us how far Tony Kushner, the author, thinks we have come. Incidentally, in both Kushner's and McNally's plays, orgasm is mentioned constantly as I have never before heard in the theater.

Nevertheless, the two full-length plays take on a deeper than usual dimension. Prior, the pivotal character, has a dream of an angel appearing to him, inviting him to become a prophet. To maintain ambivalence whether the experience is real or merely a dream, Prior ordinarily experiences orgasm during the "dream." Summoned to the "Council Room of the Continental Principalities," Prior rejects the anti-migration Book the Angel gave him, because—"We can't just stop —it's what living things do. We desire." At Prior's mention of God, a thunderclap is heard and Prior continues, "He isn't coming back. If he dared to show his face…after all this destruction—how much suffering His Abandonment had created, if He did come back you should sue the bastard."

Oceania, one of the upper order of angels, responds to Prior's repeated rejection of the Book, "He wants to live."

Prior explains he's only thirty years old and wants to be healthy again and asks the angel to make this plague (AIDS) go away. A Principality replies, "Oh, we have tried. We suffer with you. . .but we don't know how."

Europa, another Principality, invites Prior to drink of the bitter water and enter the "Tome of Immobility, of respite, of cessation. . .and never thirst again."

"I. . . can't," answers Prior. "Even sick I want to be alive."

The angel argues, predicting the grim unfolding of these Latter Days. Once again Prior declares, "I want more life. I can't help myself. I do. . . Death usually has to take life away. . .The addiction to being alive. . .If I can find hope anywhere, that's. . . the best I can do. . .I want more life."

In the Epilogue the author links the Soviet Perestroika with gay commitment to live and change the world. Prior compares his situation with the Angel's at Bethesda. In "The Capital M. Millennium. . .The fountain of Bethesda will flow again. . . and there all suffering will be healed, all will be washed clean of pain."

Acknowledging that AIDS will kill "many of us, but not all," Prior defiantly warns, "and the dead will be commemorated and will struggle on with the living, and we are not going away. We won't die secret deaths anymore. . .We will be citizens. The time has come. . .More Life. The Great Work Begins."

In summary, the gay community accepts reality; this AIDS plague will continue to kill many, but not all. If belief in God means to stop trying to change the situation, going back, then they reject God and trust that life will go on, somehow the struggle will make some progress. Hope is not in God but in the human race. And he boldly predicts that gays are here to stay and here as equal- in all aspects of life.

A word about movies and television. *Time* (August 24, 1998) observes, "Gays have come out of the celluloid closet and into the movie mainstream." More gay-theme independent films are showing. In earlier films there were gays, but as side issues. These new films appeal to gay and straight alike. Although some do address heavy sexual issues, most present issues common to all; gays and straights are friends.

Newsweek reports a backlash to gay prominence and freedom, "We're experiencing unprecedented visibility and success," says a spokesman for the Gay, Lesbian, Straight Education Network, "But in periods of social change there's always backlash." In that context the magazine refers to "Ellen." She may have been severely criticized for being too gay, and yet in the '97-'98 season we have had a "record 29 openly homosexual characters on network TV programs."

GENETICS

A changed socio-political atmosphere requires sensitive examination of the morality of homosexual behavior. The issue is certainly complicated. Two men or two women love one another. What can be wrong about love? If there is anything in the research which suggests there is a genetic basis for homosexuality, how can there be anything immoral about the "natural" expression of love in a committed relationship?

Certainly no Christian can fault genuine love wherever it is found. As for the claim that homosexuality has a genetic origin, two points must be made: first, apart from the distinction between genes causing and simply predisposing to homosexuality it must be kept in mind that preconditioning does not change the morality of acting on the inclination. We are as we are and "deal with the cards we are dealt."

We are all born with certain inclinations more dominant than others. Indeed all of us are born with concupiscence, our natural inclinations undisciplined, unordered by reason. All of us are morally responsible for our choices under concupiscence and for our response to our inclinations.

Clearly, contemporary American homosexuals reject the idea that homosexuality is unnatural or pathological. Large numbers of heterosexuals stand with them in their rejection. Perhaps undergirding this stance is refusal to acknowledge "natures." Sartre provided a rationale for such refusal: to consider human nature is possible only on the assumption there is a God who made men and women for a purpose.

The second point that must be made is that all studies so far on this issue of genetics seem to be seriously flawed, at least the popular interpretation of them. Consider two. In 1991, Simon LeVay compared the hypothalami of 41 cadavers (35 male, 6 female). In 19 of the males thought to be homosexuals, the hypothalami were similar in size to those of the females, but only half the size of the hypothalami of the 16 heterosexual males. Apart from the impossibility of drawing a scientific conclusion from such small sampling, even LeVay was uncertain whether the smallness of the hypothalami in the homosexual corpses was caused by the AIDS virus or by sexual orientation alone. In fact, there was some doubt whether all 19 corpses were actually homosexual. Replication of such a study may establish firmer conclusions but certainly is necessary in any case.

To demonstrate the genetic origin of homosexuality, Bailey and Pillard, also in 1991, studied 56 homosexual males with identical twin brothers, 54 homosexual males with fraternal twin brothers and 57 homosexual males with adoptive brothers. 52% of the identical twin brothers were also homosexual, as were 22% of the fraternal twin brothers, and 11% of the adoptive brothers. Arguing that "since identical twins share the same gene pool, and fraternal twins may share only the similar genetic makeup as any two brothers" it has been suggested, "It would appear that the higher concordance among identical twins, and the sizable rate of homosexual fraternal brothers compared with genetically unrelated adoptive brothers, do support the conclusion that there is a genetic contribution to male homosexuality."

Interestingly, Bailey and Pillard themselves proposed a modest conclusion, finding that groups of genes may predispose people to homosexuality. A far cry from concluding that genes cause homosexuality. Critics have asked why, if genetic make-up were the only cause, in 48% of the cases involving identical twins only one brother was homosexual. Once again replication of such a study is needed if there is to be proof of anything.

It seems a fundamental error to assume that human sexuality can be reduced to physical causality only, while ignoring the complexity of the homosexual disposition—ignoring the part that mind, spirit, and family environment play in the development of a homosexual orientation.

Briefly, Dean Hamer's "discovery" of a "gay gene" was repudiated by his peers. Contemporary research into the causes of homosexuality has been categorized as "primitive," given the issue has been so politicized. Evidence of the aptness of such a description can be traced back to the vote taken in the '70's to reject the definition of homosexuality as a mental disorder. One interpretation of the APA vote has been that it was politically motivated. Supporters of the interpretation note that scientists argue and offer proof, they don't vote on scientific issues.

Once again, up to now, serious flaws have marked the studies on this issue.

Surely future studies will be designed to examine all the pertinent factors involved in human development so that it can be scientifically determined if homosexuality is inherited or learned. Unfortunately, the very suggestion of a genetic basis has been taken as fact by many people who also feel that this settles the question of morality in regard to homosexual acts.

Although many assume that homosexual orientation is natural, genetic, one is born that way, others have remained convinced that persons with homosexual orientation can change. One of the better kept secrets in the American Church, Exodus International, a nondenominational Christian fellowship, has blazoned a challenge to the gay community. On July 13, 1998, in association with conservative groups, it took out full-page ads in major newspapers; ex-gays in respectful, caring language invited gays to change. "We changed, so can you." Some questions have arisen about what *changed* means.

As could be expected, advocates for gay life-style responded angrily. Some saw it as a campaign to make homophobia acceptable. Spokespeople for part of the psychological community pronounced that there was no scientific basis for therapy to change sexual orientation. Others linked the ad campaign with election year politics.

Newsweek, August 17, 1998, had "Can Gays 'Convert'?" as its cover story. The magazine's poll found that overall 56% of the general population think orientation can be changed by therapy, will power or religious conviction. Interestingly enough, 11% of gays agree. 33% overall think homosexuality is something one is born with, while 75% of gay respondents judge one is born homosexual.

Exodus International was founded 1976 and has 83 chapters in 35 states. John Paulk, its board chairman, is featured in the ads. Both he and his wife were gay. John was deeply involved in the gay community for 6 years (at least Curt and Candi as lovers, prostitute, drag queen). Anne admits to several fleeting relationships with women in college and one significant relationship after college. Both have met Jesus Christ, ceased to be homosexual, married one another and have a son. John ended homosexual involvement ten years ago. Skeptics can ask, "Were they really gay to begin with?"

Bob Davies, North American Director of Exodus International, declares that thousands of men and women like John and Anne Paulk have left homosexuality. He claims every year their membership is increasing. The problem some raise with this statistic is that it has no longitudinal validity to it. For example, of the thousands who have left homosexuality, what percentage remains separated 5 or 10 years later?

By means of psychology (Some claim a discredited theory of childhood development) and intense scriptural reading, they claim that by recognizing certain deficiencies in their development and through prayer people can change. They reject the "homophobia of censorious conservative churches."

However, Exodus holds that the homosexual lifestyle is a sin, at the same time not a matter of choosing by the sinner.

Change or "recovery" might involve heterosexual marriage or abstinence. Opponents point out that abstinence cannot be used to discount evidence for some genetic causes. They readily acknowledge desires may continue, but temptation is not a sin. The success rate claimed is 30%. Still, long term studies haven't been allowed. Critics call attention to significant failures: Two of Exodus International founders left the organization in 1979, three years after its foundation. They fell in love. In fact because the director returned to homosexual lifestyle, thirteen Exodus ministries have closed.

Besides Exodus with its religious focus there is a secular approach to "reparative therapy." Joseph Nicolosi, a psychologist, is the executive director of NARTH (National Association for Research and Therapy of Homosexuality). In the perspective of this group, homosexuality is a disorder which can and should be treated. NARTH claims a high rate of success, but again they do no long term studies.

It is admitted that the processes of changing utilized in these two organizations are not for everybody. Those gays who are happy probably will not find them useful.

Indeed, critics charge that NARTH preys on vulnerable people—those "broken and ready." One psychologist sternly warns, "Being celibate or trying to have sex with the opposite sex can lead to anxiety and depression." On the other hand, could not guilt associated with a homosexual bond likewise lead to the same problem?

A middle ground has been proposed between the ex-gay claim that anyone can change and the committed gay insistence that no one can change. Those for whom the most significant priority is their faith might find personal happiness by conforming their lifestyle to their faith rather than by pursuing their homosexual orientation. Gay Christians engaged in "reparative therapy" are likened to priests with a vow of chastity.

It goes without saying that many, many people refuse to believe or to accept these movements. The vote in the 1970's by the American Psychiatric and Psychological Association that homosexuality is not a disorder and last year's declaration that "reparative therapy" is scientifically ineffective and possibly harmful are accepted as definitive.

The *Newsweek* article reports on a very significant aspect of the unresolved scientific debate on homosexuality, the matter of genetics. We have already mentioned the three research projects attempting to determine whether sexual orientation is genetic or not. *Newsweek* notes that the studies were small and, as we mentioned, the conclusions were very cautious. It is important to keep in mind that more than 5 years later "the data have never been replicated."

This may have led researchers to insist that the public has not understood "behavioral genetics." It is not like the way eye-color is inherited; behavior is not strictly inherited. What is inherited with regard to behavior has to be brought into play by an enormous complex of environmental factors.

Consequently if there does exist a genetic pattern among homosexuals, this does not necessarily mean that people are born gay. An exceptional comparison is given. Consider the genes for height, which may be considered common in professional basketball players. This does not indicate there is an innate ability to play basketball—even though it does mean that a person will be born with the genetic tendency toward height.

It has escaped researchers how to isolate the environmental factors related to homosexuality: "in blind psychological evaluations, gays are indistinguishable from straight people."

According to *Newsweek* commonly scientists "postulate" that people with homosexual orientation are the result of some combination of genes and environmental factors. Conceivably these factors could be different in each individual case. We haven't developed sophisticated enough measurement techniques to isolate underlying causes.

Tentative conclusion: "We are as much in the dark as ever." As reported earlier, Bailey and Pillard modestly proposed as a conclusion to their study of homosexual males with twin brothers, that groups of genes may predispose people to homosexuality. Obviously, much further research is needed.

REACTION: AMERICAN PUBLIC PHILOSOPHY INSTITUTE

The leap from suggestion of a genetic basis to fact raised concern. To counter what was seen as illogical and harmful, the American Public Philosophy Institute sponsored a conference June 19-21, 1997. At this intellectually and politically conservative conference thirty-five experts on homosexuality (psychiatrists, psychologists, theologians, philosophers and lawyers)told the 450 participants that homosexuality is a disorder—one which can be prevented and treated, one with recovery possible.

Perhaps this conference emboldened Exodus International to take out their full-page ads and claim 30% success in changing one's orientation. A practicing and academic psychiatrist friend of mine observed that it is not clear it can be prevented and that only in some limited cases is recovery possible.

He also reacted to this group's challenging claim that "the homosexual person is...'a fictitious identity'—there are only heterosexual persons who commit homosexual acts." To him that is a "theoretical statement, not that overpowering from clinical evidence."

A former U.S. Army officer warned the conference to view homosexualism with the broader pansexualism: all sex is good and "orgasm is a fundamental right." Grisez, a few years ago, said much the same. Linking human suffering of women abandoned, children unwanted, aborted or abused, and so forth with extra/premarital intercourse, he insists that such acts are motivated, certainly in part, by the elementary desire for sexual satisfaction. "But the devastating power of undisciplined sexual desire is the fruit of the theory that everyone is entitled to regular orgasms and of putting that theory into practice: masturbatory sexual activity is an accepted part of many people's lives."

The speakers urged participants to present a pro-family stance, not an anti-homosexuality stance. The family must be protected and built up, emphasizing that children need both mothers and fathers. They were alerted by Father Richard John Neuhaus that in the struggle for values associated with the family they "must pray for prudence, temperance, fortitude and justice, 'for your task is daunting and opposition formidable.' "

Just how formidable the opposition is can be seen by the establishment of gay and lesbian majors at many universities. Yale rejected an offer by Larry Kramer, an AIDS activist and playwright, and a 1957 graduate, to endow a professorship in gay and lesbian studies. But other universities, like the University of Chicago, expressed willingness to accept it. This suggests that the gay and lesbian movement is rapidly gaining acceptance, respectability, and importance.

Many of my students (and it seems often they are influenced by knowing one or more homosexuals whom they like and respect) evince a conviction that two men or two women who love one another are morally justified in expressing their love sexually. Not only that but they consider any other opinion to be unfair and a violation of the rights of homosexuals.

Newsweek's poll found that those aged 18-29 were significantly more accepting of gay marriages and adoption than those over 30. They suggested the reason: 65% are likely to have a homosexual friend or acquaintance. It may also be that they have not been raised with the same fears of stereotypes of earlier generations.

I am favorably impressed by the caring and loyalty and the sense of fairness the students reveal. And their reaction demands careful scrutiny of the issue. Still, one wonders whether such caring finds its intellectual grounding in ethics of individual subjectivism.

Individualism is so widespread that it is commonplace for a person to slip into thinking that the individual decides what is morally right. Correction: decides what is morally right in certain areas of conduct—like sex, but not in other areas—like justice. They say that when it comes to sex there is no such thing as objective morality. Yet, the same people would cringe if there were not a universal rule to govern the grading of term papers and the granting of bank loans.

CONCLUSION
STRUGGLING TO BE OPEN-MINDED, OPEN-HEARTED

People develop lifestyles which include personal attitudes toward issues like homosexuality. Challenge to one's lifestyle has to occur before that person has any question about what they do or why. One source of challenge is obvious: those who hold traditional attitudes toward the homosexual lifestyle must deal with what we have just reviewed—demonstrations by gays and lesbians, decisions by the courts, divisions in the churches, general acceptance in media and theater. On the other hand, gay lifestyle and agenda meet definite opposition.

Certainly people with homosexual orientation, however acquired, have faced serious problems, emotional problems of adjusting to a heterosexual society that often discriminates and rejects them. Media and theater as well as demonstrations by the gay community have brought recognition of the homosexual situation.

(We understand how Kushner can have Prior say, "If [God] returns, sue the bastard,"—because of his keen sense of the evil of human suffering. Certainly a not unusual reaction to situations involving great pain and apparent evil.) While problems, of any kind or magnitude, do not change morality, it can be extremely difficult to reach conclusions about the morality of issues when they are charged with so much emotion and even more difficult to reach agreement on the conclusions.

The poignancy of the issue recalled to mind a visit to Fruitlands in Harvard, Massachusetts, where stands a beautiful statue of an Indian warrior, "He Who Shoots the Stars." I love that statue so I sat on a nearby bench to gaze at the archer—erect, feet apart, head bent back, searching the sky, right hand at his side, left hand stretched high holding an empty bow, after speeding its arrow to the stars. Moved to prayer, I wondered whether Catholic missionaries had listened to such a warrior to learn how God had come to him and his tribe.

Wondering prompted me to think about gays, lesbians, and Tony Kushner's "Angels in America." If what I write next sounds chauvinistic or patronizing, it is not meant to be. As I prayed before the Indian, sympathy rose in my heart at the thought of people experiencing strong inclinations and being told the actions are wrong, finding themselves or those they care about facing discrimination and violent abuse.

Pope John Paul II's call came to mind, an invitation to unite in celebration of 2,000 years of Christianity, of the Incarnation, God-with-us. He calls Catholics to listen—listen to people of other faiths—and I extended that to as many individuals as possible, for God comes to each person in unique relationship. Catholics have much to learn.

Those missionaries ought to have listened to "He Who Shoots the Stars." On the other hand, they knew that union with Christ was so enriching they had to tell the Gospel story. Catholics today likewise believe God so loves us that God's Son, Jesus Christ, died so we could live as members of the divine family.

To paraphrase St. Paul, "There is neither Jew nor Greek [homosexual nor heterosexual], for you are all one in Christ Jesus." <u>All</u>, homosexual and heterosexual, are equally loved and <u>all</u> are called to let God live through us. Jesus pleads for respect and love for one another. Violence of speech and violence of action are condemned. Homophobia has no place among Catholics. All Catholics have a serious duty to work for elimination of injustice against homosexuals. Acceptance of gay and lesbian orientation should be encouraged; loving, chaste friendships between two people of the same or different sex should be both treasured and respected.

Within the context of such openness and at least the desire to be loving, we search for truth about the morality of homosexual expression of sexuality. Perhaps homosexuals will continue to claim that the heterosexual world doesn't hear them. All we can do is try to be honest and loving as we look into what God has revealed by reason and supernatural revelation, confident that truth puts us in touch with what is real and that whatever God does for us is for our happiness.

CHAPTER 17

HOMOSEXUALITY—PART II
MORAL REFLECTION: FAITH AND REASON

I wish I had been in a position to talk this out with a person of homosexual orientation, one convinced of his position and sincerely seeking to live as God wants. I was impressed that Professor Luke Timothy Johnson found a lesbian couple "the longest lasting, most faithful, most generous" conjugal relationship he had known

In face of that kind of experience and the challenge Professor Johnson issues: "What is God telling us in the many committed homosexual couples in their sincere search for holiness?" I find myself very humble in thinking this issue through.

I do not understand how God is relating to such sincere people. I am responsive to Professor Stackhouse's conviction that God's revelation is not normless. Whatever we may eventually come to understand about God's will in this matter, I remain convinced by reason and by faith that God will not contradict himself.

I must be true to myself and utterly frank about the presuppositions I am committed to. I accept as definitively true what the Catholic Church teaches on this issue as well as the natural law grounding of that teaching.

Believing Catholics will, I trust, find comfort in the compassionate but utterly reasonable treatment by the Church. I must ask those who do not share my Catholic faith and those Catholics who do not share my understanding of what being a Catholic requires to respect my sincerity.

I shall try to explain official Catholic teaching as well as the natural law reasoning which I find solidly convincing. Unless we truly listen to one another the divisiveness will never be resolved and hurt feelings will prevent our loving one another.

If awkwardness, insensitivity, or ignorance occasions expressions which prove offensive, I ask pardon, assuring that I am unaware of offending. If what I hold by reason or by faith offends, I cannot apologize. The reader should be able to recognize "where I am coming from" and, if she or he disagrees, simply reject the presuppositions I embrace as true. I can only tell you what I consider true and risk offense because I do believe "the truth will set you [us] free." Love is never served by denying or obfuscating it.

CATECHISM OF THE CATHOLIC CHURCH

Turning to the *Catechism* we note how it speaks with respect and compassion for homosexuals and strongly condemns unjust discrimination against them. At the same time the *Catechism* repeats the Church's traditional position, firmly declaring that homosexual acts are intrinsically disordered because they close the sexual act to the gift of life and do not proceed from genuine, affective, sexual complementarity.

Of course, the Church emphasizes the distinction between homosexual orientation and homosexual acts. The *Catechism* presents the traditional and certainly reasonable interpretation of what God has revealed about morally good sexual conduct. Recently, as most know, other interpretations of pertinent Scripture texts have surfaced. Thus the Church teaches that while homosexual orientation is a given, homosexual acts are immoral; such behavior causes harm to human beings in this life and the next.

In the *Catechism* we read, " 'Homosexual acts are intrinsically disordered.' They are contrary to the natural law. . .Under no circumstances can they be approved." (#2357) The Church bases her position on her traditional insistence that genital "expression of love is intended by God's plan of creation to find its place exclusively within marriage between a man and a woman . . .[and] second, the. . .[genital] expression of love must be open to the possible transmission of new life." Hence, in teaching that homosexual acts are "intrinsically disordered," the Church means such acts are not consistent with these two principles. The Church declares contraceptive acts also "intrinsically disordered," inconsistent with the nature of marriage. (See #2360-69)

People may not be familiar with the expression "intrinsically disordered." In general, acts intrinsically disordered are always and in themselves immoral. Without exposing a full ethical theory, morally good acts are acts ordered to the fulfillment of the person and thereby to the order God intends and ultimately to God himself.

The Second Vatican Council lists examples of intrinsically disordered or evil acts. "Whatever is hostile to life itself, such as. . .homicide, genocide, abortion, euthanasia; whatever violates the integrity of the human person, such as mutilation, physical and mental torture . . ; whatever is offensive to human dignity, such as. . .arbitrary imprisonment,. . .slavery. . .trafficking in women and children. . ." (*Pastoral Constitution on the Church in the Modern World*, 27) To choose to do any of these acts is intrinsically disordered and evil. No ulterior end justifies them.

To apply this explanation to homosexual acts, consider that the act of sexual intercourse between a married man and woman responds to the natural inclination to unite with another person, which union constitutes them co-principles of new life. This special kind of union as well as the communication of life clearly are human "goods" worthy of pursuit. Choosing such acts is pursuing what is good and ordered to human fulfillment; acts fulfilling for the person order the person toward God, the source of all good and the ultimate good people implicitly seek in pursuing any good. This order is what God had planned in creating.

Anal or oral intercourse simply does not, can not effect the complementary union of persons which makes them co-principles of life. Choosing anal or oral intercourse is a moral act simply incapable of pursuing the good of the marital act. It is not ordered to fulfillment of the person as a person. It is thus disordered—and so unable to order the persons toward God.

Obviously we are focused on the objective nature of moral acts. People can be subjectively in error—and utterly sincere. They can be <u>wanting</u> to express love and commitment. But error or intention does not change "what they are doing" when they choose anal or oral intercourse.

Noting that the number of people with deep-seated homosexual tendencies is not negligible, the Catechism observes, "They do not choose their homosexual condition; for most of them it is a trial. They must be accepted with respect, compassion, and sensitivity. Every sign of unjust discrimination in their regard should be avoided." (#2358)

A further word about homosexual acts as "intrinsically disordered." "Disordered" in English sounds harsh, suggesting a sinful situation or it implies a demeaning of a person. To react to the expression so understood is intellectually, though not psychologically, unwarranted and unfortunate. First of all, the term belongs to the language of traditional Catholic moral theology. It describes an inclination which is not in accord with a norm. In this matter, the norm is an inclination toward a sexual relationship with a person of the opposite sex. It is not the inclination or homosexual orientation the Church declares sinful. It is not "being a homosexual person" that is declared wrong. What are declared intrinsically disordered and immoral are homosexual genital acts. Neither heterosexual orientation nor homosexual orientation inevitably leads to sexual acts.

Secondly, there is no intention to declare the whole personality or the character of the individual to be thereby disordered. <u>The inclination is declared objectively disordered, yes, but not the personality</u>.

These explanations will not, I fear, satisfy homosexuals and their supporters. Sadly, we have a profound impasse. So painful has been (and is) the struggle to come to grips with their sexuality that homosexuals are determined to claim their own identity. Heterosexuals keenly aware of today's need for acceptance of others different in race, religion, gender and sexual orientation commit themselves to support natural, civil and religious rights of homosexuals.

The Catholic Church's expression of sympathy, of condemnation of violence or discrimination against homosexuals is not judged sufficient. Assuming the genetic basis of this orientation, it is taken for granted that God must have designed that people act in accord with their sexual orientation. God cannot have made people this way and intended that a most significant expression of love be denied them.

The Church, on the other hand, feels they have a responsibility to teach God's message, God's revelation of the Good News of salvation and the road to eternal life. As Vatican II made clear, what God has revealed is known from Scripture and Tradition as interpreted by the Magisterium. Furthermore, Church teaching is infallible not only when it is solemnly defined by an ecumenical council or by the Pope exercising his charism of infallibility, but also when "the bishops. . .in communion with each other and with the successor of Peter. . .in authoritatively teaching on a matter of faith and morals . . . agree in one judgment as that to be held definitively." (*Lumen Gentium*, 25)

Faith empowers the Catholic to acknowledge Church teaching as informing us what God wants done. Faith also makes us confident that what God directs us to do leads to human fulfillment—on earth as well as in heaven. So the faithful Catholic knows that insisting on the moral truth that homosexual acts are wrong is founded on love and deep concern for the happiness of homosexuals. "The truth will make you free" and provide peace and fulfillment.

Two or more generations of Catholics seem not to have learned the truths mentioned above. Having been deprived of these facts, many Catholics approach moral issues from a restricted scientific and empirical viewpoint. Since they share this perspective with the cultural milieu it seems obviously correct. So these Catholics embrace the values of the culture they happen to live in. When they learn that official Catholic teaching challenges the conclusions reached, they feel confident in disagreeing; after all, dissenting theologians assure them that the Church simply has no capability to teach authoritatively specific moral principles, such as it teaches about homosexual acts. The Church, they say, can teach authoritatively broad principles such as love of neighbor and can exhort Catholics on specific issues.

All this explains why a good Catholic professor assured me that the Church is simply wrong on this matter and deeper understanding of love and the need of acceptance will bring about change of this teaching. To this I reply that time will provide discovery of the way homosexuals can feel comfortable in their Church, discovery of the way to communicate this teaching so that it makes sense to all. Perhaps only time and human suffering will dispose us to incorporate God's plan of life into our lifestyles.

This sounds coldly clinical, removed from the human emotion and passionate need woven so deeply in the act of homosexual intercourse. It is difficult for homosexuals to agree with the Church's position.

Certainly our intent is not to inflict further hurt. But inevitably those committed to a homosexual relationship will not want to hear that their lifestyle is based on false intellectual presuppositions, supporting actions that are immoral. Because we are so sure of God's instruction and confident in the reasoned explanation, we feel obliged to report what we find to be true; equally because we are convinced that truth alone is the path to fulfillment. Jesus meant it when he said, "The truth will make you free." By pointing out truth in a spirit of compassion, we sincerely hope to help homosexuals be open to receive truth offered with love.

"Angels in America," portraying the physical, mental, and social suffering that afflicts the homosexual community, builds to defiance of the status quo. We join them in defiance of homophobia but we hope neither we nor they defy the truth.

CHURCH TEACHING AND FULFILLMENT

Many, and especially those who have serious questions or doubts about the Catholic Church's teaching on homosexual actions may pose this challenge: the Church makes it impossible for persons with same sex orientation to be fulfilled.

Equating fulfillment with realizable happiness, this is a grave charge and challenge. "The Church makes it impossible for a person to be happy"?! So it is with great concern I try to show this is not so.

Let me attempt to spell out how this challenge arises. First of all, the Church evokes Christ's promise, "The truth will make you free." But when persons with same sex orientation face the truth of their own self-identity as homosexual, rather than finding freedom they are told their orientation is "intrinsically disordered" and that acting in accord with their true identity is immoral. To seek sexual fulfillment according to the way they are, they are told, is sinful, morally forbidden. And to dismiss the claim of the necessity of sexual fulfillment by saying, "Like everybody homosexual persons are called to chastity" is to fail to mention that "chastity" for these persons says "abstinence."

No wonder there is rebellion and gay communities develop—even that Act Out groups spring up. The embarrassment at experiencing one is not like "the others" and the dread to find oneself hurting, or being cut off by family and friends! Then the sense of peace at admitting to oneself one's identity as homosexual—only to discover one's religious community says your orientation is disordered and that acting in accord with your attraction to the same sex is sinful. No wonder there is rebellion.

There is no easy answer to this problem and this suffering. Here is how I see it. Recall that as infants (and earlier) we all experience strong emotional drives for survival and security—then strong inclinations to what gives pleasure, to affection and esteem and early on strong inclinations to power and control. At puberty the sexual urge springs up as a very strong inclination to provide pleasure. For the vast majority the urge is toward a person of the opposite sex. And as socialization corroborates this all people strive to live up to heterosexual interests. The person with same sex orientation may feel, "There is something wrong with me." He or she may also experience that dread mentioned above of disappointing family and friends.

With intellectual maturing and advancing to morality of truth level rather than cultural relativism, all people attempt to assess their emotionally and culturally developed inclinations and desires.

Since these inclinations have been emotionally generated and developed and since we all have been affected by concupiscence as a result of original sin, reason must come in to guide our judgments whether our inclinations are appropriate or not. People of faith are grateful for the help their beliefs afford their reason.

At some point people do—or ought to—ask themselves, "Just what do I want in life? Just how am I going to organize my life? Just what is fulfillment?" Whatever it is, it focuses precisely on the person inasmuch as he or she is a person. What is fundamentally at issue is oneself as a whole person, not as a woman or a man, not as a physician or a banker, not as an artist or an athlete.

Yes, one wants to be fulfilled as a surgeon, but not at the cost of being a good person. One wants to be fulfilled as an artist, but not if it means failing to be good as a person.

Using Grisez's explanation, to be fulfilled involves providing for all aspects of one's person (as body, as mind, as chooser, as culture maker), making commitments which are harmonious and morally good, and living out those commitments. Actions and commitments are morally good or bad according as they are compatible with integral human fulfillment.

The Catholic Church teaches, appealing to reason (natural law) and faith, that homosexual acts are not compatible with integral human fulfillment, are immoral. If so, then persons performing oral and anal intercourse do not fulfill themselves as persons though they may overcome guilt feelings and come to sincerely believe they do.

Let's develop the understanding of what is morally good or bad. Persons attracted to the same sex under their sexual urge are likewise prompted to seek conjugal union. Normally they seek this union with a person of the same sex. They too, as they advance to morality of truth, assess expression of their sexual urge and the whole issue of homosexual acts. Indubitably, it is extremely difficult for them to look on those acts as immoral and to accept this as true. Church teaching and reasoned argument seem weak in view of their desires.

But this experience is not limited to homosexuals. The heterosexual girl who finds herself attracted to her best friend's boyfriend knows she will hurt her friend. She has difficulty acknowledging it is wrong to try to attract the boyfriend.

Anyone strongly desiring to play golf, go fishing, or go to a workshop in art finds it difficult to suppress that desire when a spouse or child needs him or her. Anyone who experiences powerful sexual attraction to another's spouse tends to rationalize that it is all right. He or she must exercise firm self-control, even to admit that to cultivate or physically express this love is immoral.

So the difficulty the homosexual experiences to acknowledge that what they want to do is immoral is shared by all.

On the positive side, the person with same sex orientation can seek fulfillment in deep, genuine love with a partner if they have been fortunate enough to find such a person. The couple can nurture and develop their love—without sexual intercourse. And if occasionally they lose control as everyone does to some extent, they can repent and Catholics have access to Christ's sacrament of reconciliation.

To meet the challenge above, it must be clearly stated that their fulfillment does not require sexual expression. The married man need not lack fulfillment if his wife becomes permanently unable to have intercourse. Difficult, painful, yes, but this situation also can develop deeper love and commitment.

Our intention is not to minimize the limitation and even the suffering entailed. I, every individual, must take myself as I am, my condition and my situation as they are. If there is something about me or the situation which is undesirable, but cannot be changed, I see God's will in it. By prayer and joining my suffering with Christ I can find rich fulfillment. For the Christian fulfillment essentially involves accepting and embracing God's will.

Normally, of course, support from others experiencing what I am experiencing is most helpful and the wise person investigates available possibilities.

Sympathetic as I try to be, I must insist the charge is false that the Catholic Church makes it impossible for homosexual persons to be happy. The Church keenly wants, desires the happiness, the fulfillment of all. Convinced as she is, by faith and by reason, that homosexual acts are immoral, she knows she is responsible and caring when she teaches the truth about homosexual acts. The Church is convinced that the loving thing is to teach the truth. Many no doubt will continue to insist that the Church denies homosexuals can be fulfilled. If, as I am convinced is the case, the Church's teaching is true, to love the homosexual demands she teach what she teaches. I am sorry and sad if some cannot accept this.

L'OSSERVATORE ROMANO

Evidence that the Church is genuinely aware of the seriousness of what is happening on the homosexual scene is shown in the number of documents related to homosexuality the Vatican has published, at least since 1983. Rome is very conscious that conflicts about homosexuality are increasing throughout the West. So it comes as no surprise, but indeed with gratitude, that the Vatican newspaper, *L'Osservatore Romano*, attempted to cover all aspects of the issue in as thorough a way as possible.

The articles, to be published in book form under the title, *Christian Anthropology and Homosexuality,* appeared from March to June of 1997, fourteen articles. They approach homosexuality from the perspectives of anthropology, history, Scripture, psychology, law, sociology, morality, and pastoral concern.

First of all, many may be helped by the distinction and clarification provided by two of the articles. (The distinction reflects interests of European psychologists not necessarily the interest of American psychologists.) Transitory homosexuality the kind which at times marks adolescent ambivalence, is not at issue. Neither is "substitution homosexuality," the kind that can be seen in prisons or other situations where people of the same sex are forced to live together. While there usually is serious sin in these two kinds of homosexual acts, more precisely at issue is "structural homosexuality": predominant, if not exclusive, attraction for others of the same sex. (Ibid., #14)

As for the genesis of "structural homosexuality" there is no compelling evidence warranting general agreement. There is on the one hand the tendency to research that considers homosexuality genetic. On the other hand, many analysts and psychologists treat homosexuality as an "inversion" - a "routine error." (Ibid.)

The author of the last article, a Frenchman, acknowledges the strong politicization of the issue and remarks that the decision of the American Psychiatric Association in 1973 to remove homosexuality from the list of mental disorders was "the first time that an allegedly scientific fact was established by vote." Some may judge this a subjective reading of the facts, an over-simplification of what actually happened.

Another article reports that the six editions of *Comprehensive Textbook of Psychiatry* give six different answers to the question whether homosexuality represents a sexual disturbance. The first edition, 1967, replied clearly in the affirmative. In 1975 the reply in the second edition was less clear. The reply became negative in the third edition in 1980. The fourth (1985) and especially the fifth edition (1989) contained a cautious return to the position that homosexuality is the result of a defective psychological development. Hence, the fifth edition is rather like the first. The author treating the issue in the sixth edition (1995) does everything possible to keep the positions taken in the fifth edition, even though it seems obvious that the editors and others pressured him to modify his position. At the same time, however, one also finds in psychological and psychiatric literature true and proper apologias for homosexual lifestyles. (Ibid., #12)

At present, then, we simply do not know the causes of homosexuality. Two important facts follow: it is not scientifically grounded that being a homosexual person is "natural," genetically determined. Still less is there warrant to assume that acting in accord with one's homosexual inclination is or must be morally justifiable. On the other hand, there is agreement that structural homosexuality appears very early in the formation of the personality, long before the emergence of free choice and personal responsibility.

Incidentally, studies show that the <u>realization</u> that one is a homosexual person - which usually occurs during adolescence, sometimes sooner, rarely afterwards - is generally experienced as a trial or misfortune. Grounding such experience may be the process of socialization and current stereotypes.

The process of discovering that one is attracted to the same sex has a series of stages. To feel that "There must be something wrong with me," to confront the possibility of disappointing and hurting family and friends must be very stressful and painful. One may experience relief when one comes to accept one's true identity as a person with homosexual orientation. But to make that profession and then to experience that society and the Church judge my orientation deviant renews the pain and stress.

As treated above, rebellion is understandable and there is no easy answer to the problem or the suffering involved.

Conflict of Lifestyles

It is sobering to reflect on the recent intense tendency to defend homosexual orientation and active lifestyle. The agitation for legal recognition of homosexual marriages has already succeeded in the European Parliament. In 1994 this body voted in favor of a resolution "that homosexual persons be given equal rights, including right to marry, to adopt children and to political asylum." The fact that it is estimated that only 3 to 5% of the total population in the West are homosexual makes the politicization impressive and a tribute to the courage, conviction, determination, and skill of the homosexual community.

Equally sobering is the realization that the tendency to approve the homosexual life-style does not stem from any scientific basis but from a change in society's moral consensus. Fundamentally the change favors the importance of sexual gratification, making a chaste life almost unthinkable for many people. Linked with the change is exaltation of personal freedom, understood in strongly subjective sense. Since this change in society's moral consensus involves other issues, such as abortion, premarital chastity, divorce and conjugal fidelity - significant traditional doctrines and beliefs - the Church is called to defend time-honored teaching in the whole area of sexual morality. At stake is defense of future families and of individuals who are struggling not to surrender themselves to possible homosexual tendencies.

Grounding the "gay" lifestyle is the presupposition that homosexual acts are morally justifiable. This sometimes leads advocates to try to shock others, challenging them to reexamine the assumption that such acts are immoral. How else explain why a Hunter College professor of religion "described the joys of being serially sodomized in a bathhouse" - speaking before the Academy of Religion?! Traditional lifestyle, to put it mildly, declares the exact opposite. Question, therefore, for intelligence: Are such acts immoral or not?

We have here a crystal-clear example of lifestyles in conflict. Based upon Judaic-Christian principles, customs such as restriction of sex to marriage, acknowledgment of pre/extramarital sex and homosexual acts as immoral are directly in conflict with Secular Humanism's rejection of belief in Jesus Christ and God. Secular humanists see no point to restrictions on sexual indulgence and personal freedom.

Lifestyles generate feelings that what is customary is right, so conflict cannot be resolved by the way people feel. Intellectual presuppositions must be disengaged and the conflicting presuppositions tested for the truth.

HOMOSEXUALITY—PART II MORAL REFLECTION: FAITH AND REASON

Intellectual Examination of the Question

The opening article of the series *Christian Anthropology and Homosexuality* insists "the person was not made for sexuality, but sexuality for the person." In Christ, as there is no male or female, so there is no homosexual or heterosexual, but "all are one in Christ Jesus." Wisely, the Church refuses to consider individuals as "a heterosexual" or "a homosexual," insisting "every person has a fundamental identity: a creature of God. . .his child and heir to eternal life."

Consequently, moral evaluation applies the same principle to heterosexuality and homosexuality. For "the point of reference is the person in his essential defining features, in his basic ends, in his inner drives."

John Paul II's "nuptial meaning of the human body. . .the capacity for expressing love" is incorporated into the author's development. The love in question involves "the total gift of self to the other for the sake of a communion that is interpersonal (unitive meaning) and transpersonal (procreative meaning)."

"Thus the couple, while giving themselves to one another, give not just themselves but also the reality of children, who are a living reflection of their love, a permanent sign of conjugal unity and a living and inseparable synthesis of their being a father and a mother."

The Pope's articulation of the constant teaching of the Church regarding sexual morality in relation to marriage makes clear why the Church judges homosexual acts immoral. "Homosexuality is objectively incapable of achieving the total meaning of mutual self-giving and human procreation."

In heterosexual lovemaking, the bodily persons in becoming "two-in-one-flesh" do so as persons. Such union cannot take place in homosexual behavior. "By lacking complementarity, each one of the partners remains locked in himself and experiences his contact with the other's body merely as an opportunity for selfish enjoyment. . .The other is not really 'other'; he is like the self. . .This pathological 'narcissism' has been identified in the homosexual personality by the studies of many psychologists. . ." Obviously the homosexual act also lacks <u>openness to the procreative meaning of human sexuality</u>.

Another way of stating the Church's position is to note that "every sexual act has, at least potentially, three values: procreative, unitive, and erotic. The first does not exist in the homosexual act. It is not certain that the second is present because union presupposes the difference and complementarity of the sexes (the homosexual structure has a powerful narcissistic element). The homosexual act. . .is limited to the erotic value alone."

Accordingly, reason and faith rigorously judge that homosexual acts are immoral. What about the homosexual orientation itself? Some have accused the Church of unjust discrimination for declaring this orientation "disordered." But the Church in no way was accusing individuals for their orientation. Rather the Church was (is) pointing out that the orientation is a tendency to acts which are intrinsically immoral. Hence, the orientation cannot be described simply as good or neutral.

Subjective Morality of Homosexual Acts

Subjective responsibility and guilt in homosexual acts? The Church maintains an appropriate, respectful balance: "Awareness of the complexity of the conditioning involved in the homosexual tendency requires great caution in evaluating personal responsibility for homosexual acts." (Ibid. , #13) On the other hand, "to believe that the homosexual person is less able than others to control his instincts leads to prolonging in a subtler form the age-old contempt: these human beings are weaker than others." (Ibid. , #14) Like everybody homosexual persons are called to chastity and provided with the means to achieve and preserve chastity in pursuit of holiness.

Called to holiness we all are challenged to cope with the specific conditions and situations in which we find ourselves. God provides us with the commandments, the sacraments, the empowering of the Holy Spirit and the example of Jesus himself. Two problems the homosexual person at times experiences (as do many others) are self-deprecation and loneliness. Christian faith offers grounds for self-esteem as help in the former: loved by God, the indwelling of the Blessed Trinity gradually realized assures us how important and of what dignity each is. The same truth can, should help for the loneliness experience: one is never alone; God is intimately present. In addition, cultivation of "friendship" is needed, something "insufficiently recognized in our culture, which is fixated on love. Many of the values of love can be experienced in friendship, which in ancient thought was one of the highest names of love." (Ibid.)

"Rights" of Homosexual Persons

The Church faces the need of similar balance with regard to "rights." The homosexual person has the right to be accepted as a person and precisely as a homosexual person. Respect is due him/her. Derogatory remarks and, all the more, violence must be condemned. Unjust discrimination is definitely unchristian. The "gay" culture presents a different aspect. A highly politicized term, it does not refer to a homosexually oriented person so much as to one "who publicly adopts a homosexual 'life-style' and is committed to having it accepted by society as fully legitimate. . .a systematic plan for the public justification and glorification of homosexuality is taking shape. . . It aims. . .at a change in legislation so that homosexual unions may enjoy the same rights as marriage, including that of adoption." (Ibid. , #13))

With all due respect, the Church has an obligation to continue to teach and proclaim the truth. Her mission includes the "mission of *safeguarding the purity and specific nature of the sacrament of marriage*; she cannot fail to denounce everything which, by trying to imitate it, is necessarily its caricature." (Ibid. , #14) The Church must strive to encourage the State "to recognize the promotion and defense of families founded on monogamous heterosexual marriage as an essential part of the common good. A State which relinquished its primary *raison d'etre* would ultimately deprive itself of that healthy social fabric, generously open to life and to the proper education of the new generations, which make possible not only a harmonious society but the very continuation of human civilization." (Ibid. , #13)

Those sincerely and earnestly committed to support of the "gay culture" will judge the Church wrong—perhaps looking on her as "the enemy." But certainly Catholics have the civil right to express their understanding of society and society's common good. And, convinced of the truth of the Church's teaching, the Church is motivated not only by concern for society and civilization but also by love for homosexual persons, believing wholeheartedly in Jesus' assurance that "the truth will make you free."

PARADOXES IN THE CHURCH'S TEACHING

Some people may sense paradoxes if not contradictions in what the Church teaches. Are you saying that the Church <u>accepts</u> homosexually oriented persons, but does not accept their actions? The Church teaches that all persons, including those sexually oriented to the same sex, are equally loved by God and invited to love God in return. But she teaches homosexual acts hurt the person, are not in accord with God's loving plan for human fulfillment. God loves the sinner, even while sinning, wanting him/her to repent and return to God's love. But God cannot love sin, for sin hurts the person sinning and breaks off union with God.

Are you saying that God created the person sexually oriented to the same sex, but that person must not act on his or her inclinations, according to his or her created orientation? First of all, this presupposes that homosexuality is genetic. As explained above, there is no scientific evidence this is true. But even if homosexuality is a combination of some genes disposing persons to same sex union and environmental factors, certainly the result is under Divine Providence. Mystery enters at this point. God has not revealed why God permits this. But we are all born and conditioned by situations to have one or other inclinations more dominant so that some people have a harder time with spontaneous anger, others with lying or stealing. And all of us are born with desires not under control of reason. As Max Stackhouse in the *Christian Century* article, "Conversation," asks, "How do we know whether our impulses are result of 'creation or fall' [original sin]? Recall his example: "I'm naturally a polygamist; that's the way God made me, that's my nature, and surely I must live it out."

We simply have to take ourselves as we are. And as we mature and learn God's plan for our fulfillment and salvation, we must acquire the virtues necessary to live God's will. Fundamentally we are not homosexuals or heterosexuals but persons with certain inclinations. Fulfillment is personal fulfillment, fulfillment of the person, not heterosexually or homosexually. Morality is the relation of choices to the person - not to his or her sex or sexual orientation. We have examined why the Church judges anal and oral intercourse intrinsically disordered.

Final paradox: Are you saying that the Church preaches tolerance and respect for all persons, but does not tolerate or respect the homosexual person's choice to act on his or her sexual inclination? The Church calls us to love all people, to tolerate and respect all persons in their differences. Does anyone think we should tolerate all actions? Wife-beating, child-beating, murder, perjury? Some actions are not so evil or harmful to the community that society should outlaw them, punishing violators. But society, in principle, should cultivate belief in the evil of all evil acts. The Church, from Scripture, tradition, and reason, is convinced homosexual acts are immoral and finds herself obliged to teach this. Love prompts such teaching. Not to teach truth, not to help people learn what is good and fulfilling on earth and for heaven - what is humanly harmful and which puts heaven at risk is a non-loving, hateful act. The Church does not advocate punishing people who innocently (subjectively) indulge in homosexual acts.

HOMOSEXUAL ACTS AND REASON

Perhaps theologian Germain Grisez's insights, based on reason, will encourage all to consider seriously the morality of homosexual acts. Grisez places homosexual acts in context and specifies why they are wrong in each context. He consistently bases his findings about conduct on what the will is choosing to do. So he distinguishes between homosexual acts performed with and without love. To indulge in complete sexual acts with a same-sex partner casually, without genuine caring is wrong—just as fornication without love between heterosexuals is wrong and for the same reasons. (This issue was examined in a previous chapter.) Similar scenarios present the same choice: sexual indulgence that is masturbatory or illusionary.

Severe language, but Grisez is presenting a clinical examination of the issue. Like my students, many readers may fail to recognize that Grisez never confuses the act with the person. He can state firmly that homosexual acts are immoral, without saying or implying that he thinks the homosexual is a sinner and is evil. In fact, he expresses the distinctiveness of Christian morality in its linking of seeming opposites, e.g., love your enemies, but refuse to compromise with them; suffer for righteousness, but do not passively regard the world as broken beyond human effort to repair. And most pertinently, concede nothing to anyone's error, yet judge no person wicked. By faith and reason Grisez is certain that homosexuals are in error when they claim that homosexual intercourse is morally justifiable, but he refuses to judge the homosexuals involved. God alone is judge of the human heart.

Many who support the gay lifestyle would agree that casual or manipulative homosexual acts are immoral. However, many such supporters point to "monogamous" long-term relationships and ask why they are wrong. In other words, if marital commitment is the basis for the morality of sexual expression for heterosexuals, why isn't the permanent commitment that homosexuals make to each other equally moral? That is, if it is marriage which makes the sexual activity moral then why can't homosexuals be married?

Homosexual "Marriage"?

Many assume that the situations are parallel and that homosexuals committed in love are morally justified in their forms of sexual expression. Closely linked, of course, is the issue of gay marriages being argued on Capitol Hill. We will not address the marriage issue except to point out that, from a moral perspective, "marriage" applied to homosexual couples is an equivocation, use of the same word for an entirely different reality; like the word "pitch" being used to mean a black sticky substance as well as the delivery of a baseball to a batter—just as "bark" is used to mean the cry of a dog as well as the outside covering of a tree. Marriage, as traditionally understood and as understood for determining the morality of sexual acts, unites a man and a woman exactly as such, as a male and a female of the human species: two persons become one flesh in marriage only because they are a male and female who can join together as a single principle of reproduction. It is their sexual capacity for union which makes reproduction possible. Regardless of how desirable permanent union among homosexuals may be, their union simply cannot be a marital one. Whether permanent unions between homosexuals should be entitled to legal protection, health and retirement benefits, life-insurance, etc., is a separate issue. The morality of sexual acts is the topic at hand and this morality is not fundamentally related to such details.

"MONOGAMOUS" LONG-TERM RELATIONSHIP

Germain Grisez, as carefully explained earlier, bases his reflections about sexual conduct on marriage being a basic human good. On our present issue he devotes most of his treatment to "monogamous" long-term homosexual relationships. He has no doubt that homosexual partners can sincerely love one another committedly. They can express their love in ways appropriate in any friendship. Indeed, couples engaging in homosexual sex can be interested in certain aspects of marital communion, including satisfaction of the inclination to sexual intimacy as well as committing themselves to ongoing partnership in a common life. In other words, there can be genuine caring and commitment. However, acting out those inclinations in homosexual acts for the subjective satisfaction the acts provide, they violate the body's capacity for self-giving just as masturbation violates it, too. Besides, since they know the experience achieved in homosexual acts cannot fulfill the body's natural capacity for self-giving, they act in a self-defeating manner, as do fornicators, in an even more unreasonable way.

Since the reasoned position in the *L'Osservatore* articles—that homosexual acts even between committed homosexuals are immoral—is basically the same as Grisez's, it is important to refine this explanation in both treatments. Sexual intercourse has both a unitive and a reproductive aspect - as marital communion has. The unitive aspect obviously is bodily, but significantly it is also volitional; and, of course, as bodily it includes the reproductive aspect. Heterosexuals normally desire and choose the unitive aspect consciously—with or without also choosing the reproductive element—consciously. Homosexual coupling cannot achieve the bodily aspect of both the unitive and the reproductive. But can it not contribute to the volitional, unitive aspect? Sexual intercourse between heterosexuals expresses and/or stimulates the total self-giving proper to marital communion - going beyond bodily self-giving to internal volitional self-giving. Why then can't homosexual acts stimulate similar internal volitional self-giving?

In light of this qualification I find it more accurate and effective to focus on the inability of homosexuals in anal or oral sexual acts to achieve the marital communion that makes them co-principles of new life. It is from this perspective that the illusory and masturbatory aspects of this choice are clearly immoral. Needless to say, lesbian coupling has the same moral character as homosexual intercourse.

Homosexuals, especially if actively gay and committed in an intimate relationship, will undoubtedly not accept this position and most likely will point out certain misunderstandings about their lifestyle. I honestly admit that if I were in their place I probably would have great difficulty accepting such a conclusion. Perhaps we do have areas of deafness or blindness in our attempt to understand committed homosexual relationships. More significantly, all of us have serious obstacles to overcome when admitting a conclusion that would affect so radical a part of our lives. For example, if I had been born with great wealth acquired through unjust social structures, I would likewise find it difficult to see anything wrong with such structures.

Still, homosexuals must at least acknowledge a challenge to the intellectual presuppositions of their lifestyle.

CATHOLICS AND CATHOLIC TEACHING ON HOMOSEXUALITY

Catholics of an earlier era would not hesitate to acknowledge the immorality of homosexual conduct. The teaching of the Church, hardly new, is certainly clear. Since the very beginning the Church has taught that homosexual acts are immoral.

Unfortunately, if polls are accurate, Catholics seem to think like most Americans on many pivotal moral issues. It seems that Church teaching does not have the impact it should on people's thinking. Such failure can be traced to two facts.

The first cause of failure in this area is our pervasive scientific and empirical mindset. Science and technology have become so advanced that people demand similar warrants for truth in morals - namely, sensible and quantitative verification. However, since what ought to be done can not be argued or verified the way what is done can be, people slip into Consequentialism (what brings about the greater good is morally good; the end justifies the means). It is false that the scientific method is the only or the ultimate standard of truth (Is there scientific proof of love? of beauty? Do fathers know the children are theirs by scientific proof?) Assuming the scientific method is the only standard of truth means reducing faith to a function of imagination and emotion, rather than of intelligence. Yet Catholic faith proposes doctrines as intellectually comprehensible truths about reality.

Secondly, many Catholics have not appreciated what a blessing they possess in God's revelation. We know what God has revealed by our faith exercised in searching Scripture and tradition authoritatively taught by the magisterium, the Pope, and bishops. Faithful Catholics, then, exercise their faith by learning and accepting what the magisterium teaches, grateful to God for clear guidance.

Such understanding of how Catholics can know God's mind on morals has been blocked not only by deficient instruction, especially in the last two generations, but also by the claim of dissenting theologians that the Church through its magisterium is not empowered to teach specific moral principles - such as that homosexual acts are immoral—authoritatively. Pope John Paul II has declared false such dissenting opinions and reaffirmed and exercised the right to teach authoritatively specific moral principles, e.g. that abortion and euthanasia are immoral.

In addition, although dissenting theologians accept infallible teachings of the Church, they limit such teachings to solemn definitions by ecumenical councils and formal definitions issued by the Pope. However, the Church teaches that, besides these two sources, a teaching constantly and universally proposed by the ordinary magisterium is also infallible.

Limiting infallible teaching to what is solemnly defined makes dissenters bold in rejecting the Church's position on homosexual conduct. Clearly this teaching has not been solemnly defined. So, "if it is not infallible, it must be fallible" and hence it can be changed. They not only ignore Pope John Paul II's insistence that the Church does have the right to teach specific moral principles authoritatively, but they block out the third source of infallible teaching. For certainly the Church has taught repeatedly and consistently through the Church's history that homosexual acts are immoral. Thus this teaching is infallible. Contrary to opposite claims and suggestions, this teaching will not change.

Catholics need to re-examine their faith and challenge the world's view. Renewing their faith, rejoicing in possession of truth, they can help enlighten others and show by their lives they have the truth. They can encourage others to step into the light of Jesus Christ by the fulfillment and joy they radiate.

Non-believers find it more difficult to accept our conclusion that homosexual acts are immoral. However, if they accord us the respect they look for, they may experience and acknowledge challenge to the intellectual presuppositions of their lifestyle. Then they may recognize that they cannot reasonably hold their position without assuming that a person decides his/her own morality, a position they do not consistently apply to other areas besides sex. If they do not subscribe to such relativism, they will have to examine whether or not they are assuming that whatever a culture says is morally good is morally good (cultural relativism). Who wants to admit that cannibalism, human sacrifice, Nazi death camps must be morally justifiable? Yet that's what the culture accepted at the time these practices were in effect! Ultimately they will be forced to acknowledge that there is objective truth about morals and will be forced to establish a criterion of morality.

CONCLUSION

In summary, the charged socio-political atmosphere surrounding the homosexual issue does not change the moral question: Are homosexual acts immoral? Church and reason tell us they are. How can this best be taught in a society that is drifting into accepting the homosexual lifestyle, "the homosexualization of American society"?

It was easier to appear openminded and sympathetic about homosexuality in the previous chapter reporting the "ethos" or present attitudes toward homosexual lifestyle. We have been concerned to convey respect and understanding as we addressed the morality of homosexual acts. To report Church teaching that such acts are immoral, to lay out philosophical reasoning to the same effect does not lend itself to suggest respect and understanding.

Two sides of this problem of communication agitate me. I listened to a priest speak at a meeting, profess he was homosexual and lament the hurt he had experienced from his fellow priests' remarks during the preceding discussion. I had not "heard" those remarks about homosexuals as hurtful. We have labored in this chapter not to be offensive to persons of same sex attraction. Maybe we still have failed. If there has been insensitivity in phrasing or perspective, we are sorry. If what is experienced as hurtful is the Church's and reason's teaching, we cannot retract.

That brings us to the second side of the communication problem. To listen we have to quiet ourselves. And to hear? We must want to hear and as in any action some "wants" can conflict. Let us pray that we may grow in assessing which "wants" control our hearing.

This issue will be challenged for a long time. At least we have attempted to make clear the grounds for Catholic belief in revelation and reason. Serious effort to understand the issue and the contemporary situation has been made evident. Some key challenges have been met head-on. Once again I am convinced that people will not at present be able to reach agreement. I remain confident that ultimately we will agree, trusting as I do in the fact that all people know the natural law and trusting in the active presence of the Holy Spirit.

APPLICATION OF TWO STEP APPROACH TO MORAL ISSUES

HOMOSEXUAL ACTS
(WITHOUT LOVE OR IN EXCHANGE)

FIRST STEP

CLARIFY THE ACTION BY ANSWERING TWO QUESTIONS.
1. Impact of Choice on a Basic Human Good?
   As in casual or manipulative fornication, mutual masturbation is involved and so the good of self-integrity is directly violated and indirectly the good of marital communion.
2. Attitude of Will toward the Good(s)?
   One chooses to go against self-integrity in pursuing self-gratification and the good of play. Indirectly one chooses to damage marital communion, since one chooses to damage the body's capacity for the conjugal act to be an act of self-giving.

SECOND STEP

EVALUATE THE ACTION BY APPLYING MORAL PRINCIPLES.
The 8th Mode of Responsibility is violated - choosing to harm the good of self-integrity and indirectly the good of marital communion Obviously, then, the criterion of morality, exclusivistic choosing, rules the actions immoral and so the choosing is not compatible with integral human fulfillment.

The 3rd Mode of Responsibility is violated, choosing to satisfy an emotional desire, unrelated to an intelligible good. Neither the 3rd nor the 8th Mode of Christian Response is observed.

HOMOSEXUAL ACTS ARE IMMORAL.
(WITH GENUINE LOVE AND COMMITMENT)

FIRST STEP
CLARIFY THE ACTION BY ANSWERING 2 QUESTIONS.

1. Impact of Choice on a Basic Human Good?
   Marital communion, primarily as reproductive, is violated. Self-integrity is also violated.
2. Attitude of Will toward the Good(s)?
   Choice is to harm good of marital communion as well as the good of self-integrity.

SECOND STEP

EVALUATE THE ACTION BY APPLYING MORAL PRINCIPLES.
The 6th Mode of Responsibility is violated inasmuch as the partners pursue illusory good of marital communion, unable by anal or oral intercourse to become co-principles of new life. Likewise the 8th Mode of Responsibility is violated, attempting to separate self and body. For these reasons they are not choosing in a way compatible with integral human fulfillment, the first principle of morality.

It is clear that the 3rd, 6th, 8th, and conceivably the 4th Modes of Christian Response are not being observed.

EPILOGUE

Life, love, and sex—issues that touch all of our lives. Sociology and psychology have illuminating insights for us on each of these issues we as a nation are confronting. But they simply cannot tell us what is the morally right thing to do about any of them.

Catholics will want to know what their Church teaches, but today will be slow to accept that teaching unless they understand how the Church reaches its conclusions. We have attempted to satisfy that need. The challenge has been to do that for intelligent, educated people who are unaccustomed to philosophical or theological ways of thinking.

Part I tried to introduce that way of thinking and to equip readers with a specific approach to moral reasoning. After reporting on each particular issue, the ethos so to speak, we exposed official Church teaching and then applied the specific approach to moral reasoning to the issue.

We strove for clarity and for openmindedness—respectful of opposing thought and values.

Our modest effort to help Catholics think through the issues may also interest and help people of other beliefs or no belief.

APPENDIXES

APPENDIX FOR CHAPTER ONE – CONSCIENCE

CONSCIENCE, PERSONAL BUT NOT ARBITRARY

Conscience demands personal assimilation of norms and responsible decisions in light of those norms. "I take my stand on this issue!" And I may be mistaken! So personal a dimension misleads some people to confuse conscience with arbitrariness. Haven't you heard, "My conscience sees nothing wrong with doing X. So nobody can tell me it isn't all right for me to do it." Even more often you may have heard, "I see nothing wrong with doing X. It doesn't hurt anybody. So doing X is morally OK." Sometimes a broader, but still arbitrary stance is taken. "A lot of decent people do X and I wouldn't presume to judge them, so, it would be all right for me to do X also."

This excessive sense of freedom we shall expand on later, but here we shall simply point out that it amounts to moral subjectivism: there is no objective morality; it all depends on the individual and kind of life she/he chooses to live. This may be an attempt at rationalizing one's refusal to submit to moral norms. But it also involves certain confusions.

First of all there is the sense in which conscience <u>is</u> personal – as indeed it is. For conscience is one's own grasp of moral truth. But this does not make it one's wish. <u>Seeing</u> something for oneself is personal. Conscience is personal. What one sees – truly for oneself – is an objective something, which others likewise can see. Conscience grasps moral truth – but this is true apart from, independent of, one's grasping it – perceptible by others as well.

This perspective on conscience as arbitrary can be linked to another confusion: the role of conscience in the face of legal impositions versus moral principle. Because conscience is concerned about moral requirements it provides personal dignity empowering the person to confront and challenge arbitrary, morally unacceptable, legal impositions. What about conscience at odds with certain moral principles? Not the same at all. Here conscience stands before the source of its own authority. Conscience is measured by truth and moral principles expressive of truth! Conscience is not the judge of principles. Persons who find their conscience at odds with true principles need to correct their error. They ought not withstand moral truth claiming personal freedom.

In summary, persons with well-formed consciences can judge legal claims. Moral principles measure whether consciences are well formed or not. The basis of conscientious objection is precisely the dignity of the human person who simply cannot be compelled to do what conscience declares to him or her is wrong. On the other hand the husband who is bored with his wife and family routine and wants to "find happiness" with another woman confronts the moral principle of marital and parental responsibility and simply cannot change by desire those binding responsibilities. His boredom, his desire do not change his promise to be faithful to his wife nor his responsibility as a father. That door closed, he must change his heart and seek help to revitalize his marriage.

This focus on freedom of conscience prompts reflection on Pope John Paul II's insistence that today in many quarters, freedom has been torn from its relation to truth. This "abuse of freedom" will be addressed later, but its impact on conscience warrants reflection here.

"Creative" understanding of moral conscience it has been called. Proponents of this interpretation acknowledge a function for norms. They provide a general perspective which helps a person assess particular situations and put order into his/her personal or social life. Actual choices are very complex, involving the entire sphere of psychology, the emotions, the numerous influences from cultural environment.

And here they introduce the profound, personal, sacred aspect of conscience. Conscience is "the sanctuary of man, where he is alone with God, whose voice echoes within him." The voice of God, they say, leads persons not to some meticulous observance of universal norms but to a creative, responsible acceptance of what is understood as a personal task entrusted to them by God. An erroneous and harmful ploy, subjectivism is the result.

Erroneous Conscience

Reflect on Jean and Lionel, engaged, deciding whether they will or should sleep together. Assuming sincerity on both sides, Jean will have judged, "We can't sleep together until we are married." And she feels she is reporting what God Himself wants them to do. Lionel will have reached the judgment, "We are an exception. It is all right for us to sleep together." And he feels he can honestly say he believes that is what God wants them to do.

It should be clear they both cannot be right. Their judgments are contradictory. One has to be false, one true – just as "Jean is sitting down" contradicts "Jean is not sitting down."

The scenario makes clear that conscience is not what makes judgments true. It discovers truth that already exists. Note first of all, Jean's conscience-judgment that their sleeping together is immoral, leaves her nonetheless, free to sleep with Lionel. Secondly, we confront the sobering fact that the sincere conscience can be in error. Besides, this might be an example of how some interpret the role of norm – namely, they provide a general perspective, reveal what generally is true, but then admit exceptions.

Jean deliberates about sleeping with her fiancé but remembers that sexual intercourse is to be indulged in only when married. The negative norm she recognizes admits no exceptions. Lionel knows the same norm, but judges they are an exception to it.

Later we shall examine the question of whether or not there are intrinsically evil acts, moral absolutes. Two points remain to be made.

(1) A person sincerely seeking the truth can be mistaken. If the mistaken judgment results from sincere, invincible "ignorance" or error, the objective evil of the act is not imputable, i.e. the person does nothing "subjectively" wrong. If both Jean and Lionel were sincerely to reach the judgment that it was all right for them to sleep together, they would err, but if they chose to sleep together, they would do nothing subjectively wrong.

(2) John Paul II insists, however, "It is never acceptable. . .to make the moral value of an act performed with a true and correct conscience equivalent to the moral value of an act performed by following the judgment of an erroneous judgment." The act done in error remains evil, "a disorder in relation to the truth about good."

Speaking of imputability, things are very different, of course, "when man shows little concern for seeking what is true and good, and conscience gradually becomes almost blind from being accustomed to sin." A person can live in a persistent state of grave sin and so find him or herself psychologically unable to uncover the error of conscience because of this bad faith. Such people judge immoral actions justifiable and are responsible for such errors.

After cheating or killing becomes habitual, one may not see anything wrong in making a profit by such means. This is not at all the same thing as a sincerely erroneous conscience judgment.

DEEPER UNDERSTANDING OF THE MORAL DIMENSION

Clearly the process of forming a conscience judgment involves invoking moral norms to judge whether in these particular circumstances it is morally right or wrong to do or to avoid something. "Involves" yes, but it is much more. St. Thomas speaks of a "connaturality" between man and the true good as essential for a mature good conscience. Wanting to be good at being a person, wanting to be holy, wanting to do God's will is fundamental for the connaturality which is rooted in and develops through the individual's virtuous habits: the theological virtues of faith, hope and charity as well as prudence, justice, temperance and fortitude.

Further on we shall deal with moral method. But Cardinal Ratzinger opens up a rich vein of thought about the reality of fundamental moral principles and conscience.

He reports that he first became aware of the question of conscience as the core of the moral process when a senior colleague expressed the opinion, "One should actually be grateful to God that he allows there to be so many unbelievers in good conscience." The Cardinal was shocked at the idea that faith would be a burden, not a blessing, that the erroneous conscience would be the real grace, the normal way to salvation, that untruth would be better than truth, that not having truth would set man free so that man would have to be freed from truth.

Conscience within that perspective appears as subjectivity's shell into which people can escape and hide from reality. Conscience then dispenses from truth. Ratzinger became certain this understanding of conscience is wrong when other colleagues found Hitler and the SS people subjectively innocent, since they followed their mistaken conscience and so no doubt were saved.

Actually, feelings of guilt, the capacity to recognize guilt, is essential to the spiritual human dimension. Feelings of guilt disturb the false calm of conscience, a complaint against one's self-satisfied existence. As physical pain is a necessary warning of trouble in bodily functioning, so this feeling of guilt is a necessary signal of trouble in human wholeness.

We cannot, therefore, identify human conscience with the self-consciousness of the I, with superficial consciousness, with my subjective certainty about moral behavior. Such consciousness may merely reflect social values and the opinions in circulation or it might simply result from a lack of self-criticism, a lack of interiority in listening to the depths of one's soul. Conscience so understood is degraded to a mechanism for rationalization instead of being the transparency of the subject for the divine, constituting the very dignity and greatness of the human person.

How then do we explain the evil acts of Hitler and Stalin? We do not attempt to. God alone can know a man's heart and precisely what he is doing when he acts. But that does not equip us to assume the hearts of those who do evil are innocent. Ratzinger leads to such a conclusion by taking a different perspective from St. Thomas in distinguishing natural knowledge of moral principles and their application to particular situations.

Thomas distinguishes the two levels of the concept of conscience, referring to natural knowledge of moral norms as "synderesis." Ratzinger substitutes a Platonic insight, "anamnesis," for this knowledge. He intends the word and concept to mean what St. Paul expressed in Romans: "When Gentiles who have not the law do by nature what the law requires, they are a law to themselves . . . They show that what the law requires is written on their hearts, while their conscience also bears witness . . ." (Rom 2:14-15)

Ratzinger is talking about something like an original memory of the good and true implanted in us, a tendency toward the divine within all persons, created in the image of God. As a consequence, in our very being we resonate with some things and clash with others. This original memory is not a conceptually articulated knowing. It is an inner sense, so that the one voice echoes from within. Instinctively in proper circumstances the person cries, "That's it! That is what my nature points to and searches for."

This explains why people respond to kerygmatic preaching of the Gospel – people are yearning for that message in the depths of their being. Ratzinger is speaking within the context of Christian faith and living. So proclamation of the Gospel or Magisterial teaching does not impose on hearers, but evokes acknowledgement of what they somehow already know.

I submit another interpretation. In lived experience the appropriate circumstances evoke articulated knowledge of moral norms. So whether people become aware of fundamental moral principles through Church proclamation and moral teaching or from lived experience, all people come to know first principles of morality.

In particular situations "conscience" refers to the human response of utilizing the original, innate memory as well as the articulated norms. Conscience responds in three movements: it recognizes, it bears witness, it judges. But more than mere knowing is operating in the exercise of conscience. The will can block the way to recognizing the norm or it can lead to it. Which occurs depends on an already formed character: this can continue to deform or can submit to being further purified.

Even though one's final, best judgment turns out to be erroneous, it nonetheless binds. One must follow his certain conscience. However, (a significant "however,") it can be wrong to have come to such erroneous convictions – to have stifled the protest of anamnesis of being. For the person acting with an erroneous conscience the guilt can lie much deeper – not in the present act, not in the present conscience judgment, but in neglecting his own being, making him deaf to the internal promptings of truth. "Criminals of conviction like Hitler and Stalin may well be guilty." I may be obligated to follow my erroneous conscience. But at the same time I may be responsible for being in error. All of us must pray with the psalmist, "But who can discern his errors? Clear me of my unknown faults."

APPENDIX FOR CHAPTER TWO

EXALTATION OF FREEDOM OVER TRUTH: ADDITIONAL ERRORS

Other Common Errors

Turning to developments in moral theology Pope John Paul II uncovers serious, harmful errors linked with the exaltation of freedom over truth. First of all, the tension between freedom and nature is resolved by some moralists by treating body and soul as separate (I and my body are treated as two things. Actually, such a dualism is false: I <u>am</u> my body.) In this dualism nature, meaning everything in people and the world – apart from freedom, is raw material for human freedom and power to transform. "This ultimately means making freedom self-defining and a phenomenon creative of itself and its values." "Man," they say, "as a rational being . . . *must freely determine the meaning* of his behavior" e.g. as regards contraception, direct sterilization, auto-eroticism, premarital sexual relations, homosexual relations and artificial insemination. In all these areas the Church by her "morally negative evaluation of such acts" has, they claim, been in error because she failed to recognize that freedom is self-defining. (*Ibid.*,46-47)

Needless to say, the universality and unchanging nature of moral principles are denied. "Situation ethics" is embraced by some: the situation "could legitimately be the basis of certain *exceptions to the general rules* and thus permits one to do in practice and in good conscience what is qualified as intrinsically evil by the moral law." (*Ibid.*,56)

What about the emphasis on "fundamental option?" The Pope acknowledges "the specific importance of a fundamental choice which qualifies the moral life and engages freedom on a radical level before God." But in the traditional understanding, fundamental option "is a question of the decision of faith, of the *obedience of faith* . . . 'by which man makes a total and free self-commitment to God.'" In response to "Jesus' call to 'Come, follow me' we have the greatest possible exaltation of human freedom . . . "Paul proclaims that we are called to freedom but gravely warns, "Only do not use your freedom as an opportunity for the flesh." Freedom is always threatened by slavery. "And this is precisely the case when an act of faith – in the sense of a fundamental option – becomes separated from the choice of particular acts." (*Ibid.*, 66)

Some theologians refer to an obscure notion of fundamental option. "By virtue of a primordial option for charity, that individual could continue to be morally good . . . and attain salvation, even if certain of his specific kinds of behavior were deliberately and gravely contrary to God's commandments as set forth by the Church." Declaring this erroneous, the Pope states, "In point of fact . . . With every freely committed mortal sin, he offends God as the giver of laws and becomes guilty with regard to the entire law . . . and loses eternal happiness." (*Ibid.*, 68)

Perhaps the most serious challenge to what is going on in moral theology – in journals, in university faculties of theology, even in seminaries – is John Paul's criticism of Consequentialism and Proportionalism. He singles out this predominant methodology in moral reasoning and declares it incompatible with Christian teaching. Consequentialism claims that the criterion of morality of our action is derived "solely from a calculation of foreseeable consequences deriving from a given choice." Proportionalism is a refined version of the same. It weighs the various values and goods being sought and "focuses . . . on the proportion acknowledged between the good and bad effects of that choice with a view to the 'greater good' or 'lesser evil actually possible in a particular situation.'" (*Ibid.*, 75) Pope John Paul II finds "consequentialism" and "proportionalism" linked with "a notion of freedom which prescinds from the actual conditions of its exercise, from its objective reference to the truth about the good, and from its determination through choices of concrete kinds of behavior." For theologians following these methods, "free will would... (not) be morally subjected to specific obligations." (*Ibid.*, 75)

A result of these approaches is to deny intrinsically evil acts or moral absolutes, as well as to deny the Church's ability to teach authoritatively specific moral principles. (*Ibid*) In *The Splendor of Truth* and *The Gospel of Life* John Paul II turns to Scripture to insist on moral absolutes and to traditional moral thinking to demonstrate the same, especially by explaining how "the morality of the human act depends primarily and fundamentally on the 'object' rationally chosen by the deliberate will." (Ibid.,78) The Church's response to the exaltation of freedom over truth is found in these two encyclicals.

Pope John Paul II has done what has never been authoritatively done before. He has "reflect[ed] on the whole of the Church's moral teaching with the precise goal of recalling certain fundamental truths which . . . risk being distorted or denied." He relates the problem to "detaching human freedom from its essential and constitutive relationship to truth."

He sees traditional church teaching about natural law, and "the universality and permanent validity of its precepts . . . rejected." Many laymen, laywomen and theologians take the stand that some of the Church's teachings are simply unacceptable. A new ecclesiology has emerged that accommodates their choices by limiting the Magisterium to exhorting consciences and proposing values, "in the light of which each individual will independently make his or her decisions and life choices." The pastoral Magisterium, it is claimed in order to validate their position, has no authority to teach specific moral principles as obligatory. Such an ecclesiology contradicts Vatican II (especially *Dogmatic Constitution on the Church*, 25) and the whole of tradition.

We can now agree heartily with the Pope that these questions are of "*the greatest importance* for the Church and for the life of the faith, as well as for the life of society itself." (*Ibid.*, 4)

GRISEZ ON FUNDAMENTAL OPTION

Germain Grisez's first volume of *The Way of the Lord Jesus, Christian Moral Principles*, examines, issue by issue, the Church's stance on the abuse of freedom. He was one of the first to recognize the radical transformation of traditional Catholic moral theology that consequentialists/proportionalists were attempting.

As for "fundamental option," Grisez appreciates the attempt to modify elements of classical moral theology; in fact, he claims Christians do have a "fundamental option," the basic commitment of faith – the specific act of faith in Jesus Christ. In thorough agreement with John Paul II's rejection of the currently proposed "fundamental option," Grisez pointed out years ago that it is rooted in an incoherent part of Kant's metaphysics and a misunderstanding of the Council of Trent's teaching that we cannot know with the certitude of faith that we are in the state of grace. Since we cannot know that, neither can we know with certitude that we are *not* in the state of grace. It seems to follow that "there must be a fundamental option outside consciousness." To which Grisez replies, "We do know when we commit mortal sins and until such time as we repent, we also know we are not in the state of grace." (*Fulfillment in Christ*, p.195) Analogously, we may not be able to know with certitude that we are healthy, but we certainly know when we are seriously sick.

APPENDIX FOR CHAPTER THREE

Readers desiring fuller treatment of "fulfillment" may consult Grisez and Shaw, *Beyond the New Morality*, Chapters 3 and 4. For the basic human goods, Chapter 7 of the same work should be consulted or better, Grisez, *Difficult Moral Questions* (Vol. 3 of *The Way of the Lord Jesus*), Appendix 1. They may want to examine the process of determining the meaning of moral good and moral bad. *Beyond the New Morality*, Chapter 8, is the source followed.

APPENDIX FOR CHAPTER FOUR

INTERMEDIATE MODES AND THE BEATITUDES

MODE OF RESPONSIBILITY	MODE OF CHN RESPONSE	THE BEATITUDES
1. One should not be deterred by felt inertia from acting for intelligible goods.	Expect and accept all good, including the good fruits of one's own work, as gifts of God.	Blessed are the poor in spirit, for theirs is the kingdom of heaven. (Mt 5:3)
2. One should not be pressed by enthusiasm or impatience to act individualistically for intelligible goods.	Accept one's limited role in the Body of Christ and fulfill it.	Blessed are the meek, for they shall inherit the earth. (Mt 5:5)
3. One should not choose to satisfy an emotional desire except as part of one's pursuit and/or attainment of an intelligible good other than the desire itself.	Put aside or avoid everything which is not necessary or useful in the fulfillment of one's personal vocation.	Blessed are those who mourn, for they shall be comforted. (Mt 5:4)
4. One should not choose to act out of an emotional aversion except as part of one's avoidance of some intelligible harm other than the inner tension experienced in enduring that aversion.	Endure fearlessly whatever is necessary or useful for the fulfillment of one's personal vocation.	Blessed are those who hunger and thirst for righteousness, for they shall be satisfied. (Mt 5:6)
5. One should not, in response to different feelings toward different persons, willingly proceed with a preference for anyone unless the preference is required by intelligible goods themselves.	Be merciful according to the universal and perfect measure of mercy which God has revealed in Jesus.	Blessed are the merciful, for they shall obtain mercy. (Mt 5:7)
6. One should not choose on the basis of emotions which bear upon empirical aspects of intelligible goods (or bads) in a way which interferes with a more perfect sharing in the good or avoidance of the bad.	Strive to conform one's whole self to living faith, and to recognize and purge anything which does not meet this standard.	Blessed are the pure in heart, for they shall see God. (Mt 5:8)
7. One should not be moved by hostility to freely accept or choose the destruction, damaging, or impeding of any intelligible human good.	Respond to evil with good, not with resistance, much less with destructive action.	Blessed are the peacemakers, for they shall be called sons of God. (Mt 5:9)
8. One should not be moved by a stronger desire for one instance of an intelligible good to act for it by choosing to destroy, damage or impede some other instance of an intelligible good.	Do no evil that good might come of it, but suffer evil together with Jesus in cooperation with God's redeeming love.	Blessed are those who are persecuted for righteousness' sake, for theirs is the kingdom of heaven. (Mt 5:10)

APPENDIX FOR CHAPTER SIX

GRISEZ ON LEGALIZING ASSISTED SUICIDE

Neither the *Catechism* nor Grisez's *Living a Christian Life* deals with the legal dimension of this issue. But Grisez, one of the first to read the writing on the wall, anticipated this and cognate issues as early as 1979, when he published *Life and Death with Liberty and Justice*. The subtitle is, "A Contribution to the Euthanasia Debate."

Ten chapters identify the interlocking problem of liberty to refuse medical treatment, suicide, assisted suicide, voluntary and non-voluntary euthanasia, as well as related constitutional problems. All this he treats strictly from the legal perspective. Chapter 11 outlines his ethics which he then applies in Chapter 12 to each of the life issues.

LAWS AGAINST SUICIDE

In Anglo-American law suicide was looked upon as a crime, a form of murder. A sixteenth-century judge's list of objections against suicide explains the attitude of common law toward suicide. "(1) (Suicide) is an unnatural act which violates the natural tendency to self-preservation, (2) … it is a breach of the divine commandment prohibiting killing, (3)…it is a kind of mutilation of the king, since it destroys one of his subjects, and (4) …it also is against the king, since it runs counter to his intention to prevent bad example." (*Life and Death*, 122)

Furthermore, although a successful suicide obviously is beyond the reach of the law, British legal practice found something to say and do: the person was punished after death by a shameful burial and his or her property was forfeited. American legal practice did not go that far. The reasons against suicide required modification but were basically the same.

Over the last century suicide and attempted suicide have gradually lost the legal status of crimes. Two facts affecting this change stand out. Modern conceptions of responsibility tend to support the view that either the typical person committing or attempting suicide is not legally sane or that they are somehow not themselves and do not deserve to be treated as criminals. Perhaps more central to the change in attitude is widespread loss of belief in the sanctity of life which deserves reverence or at least its absolute inherent dignity deserving exceptionless respect. Many people go so far as to claim a right protected by our constitution to die - which position won the day in the Ninth Circuit Court of Appeals.

Our present society, definitely pluralistic in values, cannot base legislation against suicide precisely on the sanctity or inherent absolute dignity of human life. ."(J)ustice and liberty...together provide the standard by which the legitimacy of laws and proposed laws ought to be evaluated." This, Grisez believes, articulates the working consensus undergirding American government and legal practices. He refers to the working consensus as "the American proposition." And realistically confronting the diversity of deeply emotionally held positions on these life issues he insists this standard is the only one which parties to current debates must accept - supposing they intend "to argue as Americans committed to the American proposition."

The decriminalization of suicide reflects a change in the people's consensus. This consensus is what constitutes political society and grounds government's moral basis for using power.

Grisez proceeds to argue that there should be no law against suicide by applying the standard of "the American proposition," justice and liberty. He considers justice is not violated by suicide, even if (as will be argued) morally the right to life is unalienable. Nor does he consider the dangers to society sufficient to warrant restriction of people's liberty on this matter.

I find the case presented quite inadequate. As for justice, what about a person's responsibility to support those dependent upon him or her, children and spouses for example? Is not their right to the person's help being violated? What about other duties left unfulfilled?

And what about the dangers to society? Grisez actually identifies many. First of all, suicide and attempted suicide are socially disturbing and costly. Suicides can influence people who are not well balanced and if suicide becomes accepted, that influence could become even more significant. Juvenile suicide is on the increase: does the growing attitude that suicide is a legitimate way to solve problems encourage this?

This next reason pertains to voluntary euthanasia as well as suicide. If people facing difficult circumstances kill themselves often, this will generate the expectation that people in difficulty have a way out - suicide - and so do not need to be helped.

There is also the burden of costs to the people related to the required investigation of sudden and violent deaths. Which opens up a very serious problem of justice: murder can be made to look like suicide. And if suicide becomes frequent, deceptions will be easier - each case which initially looks like suicide will have to be subjected to less demanding examination.

Grisez notes that if treating suicide and attempted suicide as crimes could do away with this danger, we would have a basis to forbid suicide. But he holds that persons contemplating suicide will not be deterred from doing so regardless of the purpose law against suicide is intended to serve.

Two concerns, I sense, motivate Grisez to support the position that there should be no law against suicide. One is his concern to make clear that liberty to commit suicide does not translate into a right to do so. The other concern seems to be that suicide be in place - legally - to counter the arguments for euthanasia.

Writing in 1979 Grisez perceived the danger of sliding from "liberty to kill oneself" to a "right to die." Already some legal commentaries were suggesting that the "right to privacy" appealed to justify invalidating laws which forbade use of contraceptives and, more importantly, laws forbidding abortions, might well include "right to die." Needless to say, the claim looms more likely each day. In fact the Ninth Court of Appeals reasoned this way.

The right of privacy is treated as a fundamental right and so it can be overridden only by a compelling state interest. If the view that suicide is encompassed by this right were to be accepted, minimum regulation would be dictated. Grisez argues that properly understood the right of privacy is nothing more than certain aspects of the liberty our Ninth Amendment reserves to the people and which is protected by the privileges or immunities clause of our Fourteenth Amendment. If Grisez is correct, such rights entail only immunity from attempts to prevent exercise of them - not empowerment to exercise them.

It seems clear that not every liberty can be given the status of the fundamental rights of freedom of speech and religion. Grisez argues that liberty to commit suicide does not fit any of the various grounds suggested by the Supreme Court on which any liberty could be judged fundamental. Further, he says, the collective conscience of Americans does not commend liberty to commit suicide.

According to him it is not one of the fundamental elements of liberty and justice. At the time he was writing suicide was looked upon as wrong or pitiable. It is not clear that people today feel that way - especially in relation to the old and suffering. Increasingly, people are determined to have control of their lives and of their dying.

Unless palliative care is developed, more pervasively utilized, especially as hospice applies it, people will adopt the attitude that since pain cannot be controlled, people must have the right to terminate their pain and their lives when they decide. Hospice supporters are convinced that pain can be controlled and that the process of dying can provide wondrous growth which assisted suicide and euthanasia prevent.

ASSISTED SUICIDE FROM THE LEGAL PERSPECTIVE

What is the difference between handing another person a gun so he or she can commit suicide and the first person firing the gun at the request of the other? Although ethically it is difficult to see any difference between assisted suicide and homicide upon request, legally they have been, and ought to be, distinguished. For if assisted suicide were legally permissible and homicide upon request were considered assisted suicide, voluntary euthanasia would be legalized.

Legally, if the evidence points to one person having killed another, the case should be tried as homicide. The person accused should have the burden of proving that the dead person had requested and consented to be killed. To put the burden of proof on the prosecution to establish that the person killed did not consent would make things too easy for murderers. If consent is established, this may well be treated as a mitigating factor.

On the other hand, when the evidence points to suicide, it is reasonable to require that the prosecution establish that another has helped. Hence, even if penalties for both crimes be equivalent, homicide with consent and assisted suicide should be treated as technically distinct offenses.

Now why should assisted suicide be a crime? Let us remove a border case: if a person causes another to commit suicide by force, duress or deception this is really homicide.

It seems we face a hazy borderline in the area of assisted suicide. When a competent adult instigates and assists the suicide of a child or a legally non-competent person, does not this involve homicide? What about the possible case: if an expecting heir urges and assists a drunken or weakened relative to commit suicide?

Such examples explain why Grisez argues that since some cases of assisted suicide should be treated as murder, generally assisting suicide ought to be considered murder. In his judgment only such a general rule provides adequate protection for persons who might bring about their own death but without acting in a fully voluntary way. He immediately adds that the general rule could be qualified: if the one assisting can show that the person was competent and acted voluntarily, the general rule could be mitigated.

Granted the reasonableness of taking assisted suicide generally to be murder which can be mitigated we have the reasons why assisted suicide should be treated as a criminal offense.

Note that two excellent reasons for not treating suicide as a crime are that in many instances the person acts with mitigated responsibility plus the obvious fact that the dead person can not be touched by the law. As for a person assisting the suicide, the necessity of facing legal liability normally will restrain the person in this position. And he or she need not be acting with reduced responsibility.

Again, even if one takes the position that people ought to be free to kill themselves, the serious problems listed above related to suicide are reasons we should try to limit suicides by considering assistance as a crime.

Furthermore, consider the situation in which assisting suicide is no longer a crime and homicide with consent is considered equivalent to it, is it difficult to foresee repulsive practices people could be induced to engage in

- and which could be legalized? Historically individuals killed themselves or allowed themselves to be killed for amusement - in order to obtain money for the needs of their dependents. Would not agreeing to fight wild animals or to play Russian roulette for spectator amusement be acceptable if assisted suicide were legalized? Grisez acknowledges that the likelihood at present of such abuse may not be great, but "one can think of cases which differ in degree rather than in kind from such gross instances of exploitation. Certain professional sports verge upon gladiatorial combat." (*Life and Death*, 133)

Finally, and of genuine concern, a person might be subjected to psychological pressure to commit suicide, if instigation to and assistance for suicide are treated as non-criminal. Grisez recounts an episode in Britain which one can easily imagine paralleled in America.

Edith Mott, 87, in a nursing home was badgered by her daughter, Yolande McShane, to escape from her terminal condition. The daughter, in debt, was expecting $70,000 inheritance. Word got to the police who used a hidden camera to film the visit in which Yolande brought her mother fifteen Nembutal tablets and urged her to take them with whiskey. She was arrested, tried, convicted and sentenced to two years in prison.

It seems reasonable to assume that such badgering might well be the experience of many. Would not those in weakened condition probably feel obliged to yield to the badgering?

Recommendations for a Law on Assisted Suicide

Since suicide is no longer treated in law as a crime, Grisez recommends that criminal law should state explicitly that suicide and attempted suicide are not crimes.

However, it should declare that a person supplying or offering aid, a person soliciting or urging another, to commit suicide shall be guilty of manslaughter - whether an attempt is made or not.

The law should treat as a principal in murder a person aiding another in actually committing suicide. The intent is to provide adequate protection for persons who do not bring about their own deaths voluntarily. "Aid" in this case should be narrowly defined so that practical directions and urgent solicitation are excluded.

If the defense can provide evidence that force, duress, or fraud was not used and that the suicide was a competent adult, all this should be seen as mitigating the crime and taken into account in the sentencing.

Such a law would protect the liberty of persons who deliberately and rationally choose to kill themselves. Proponents of suicide would be free to express their position and even publish directions how to proceed efficiently. Anyone who attempts suicide and fails would not be prevented from trying again.

Strict provisions will protect the public at large by discouraging people from murder and trying to make it look like suicide. The right to life of persons who might be led to kill themselves by a non-voluntary or pressured act will be protected.

Such a statute could solve the problem of those whose suffering arouses so much sympathy for legalization of voluntary euthanasia. People would face no criminal obstacle to suicide. Others could help within the law. Those considering suicide could share their condition with friends and perhaps obtain moral support to actually carry out their decision without exposing friends to arrest. Encouragement is not solicitation. If a physician were to provide a patient certain drugs for pain or sleep or tranquilizers while warning to avoid a fatal overdose he or she would not be subject to the law.

REFLECTIONS ON PRESENT STATE

Grisez's insights may be of help as the conflict of the two cultures develops - "the culture of death" and "the culture of life." The United States Supreme Court encourages debate on assisted suicide. Oregon alone has passed a law allowing it. Maine this past election narrowly defeated a referendum that sought to legalize it. The president of the American Medical Association stated that the AMA was pleased "that Maine voters have endorsed physicians' fundamental obligation 'to do no harm,' by defeating a flawed ballot initiative that would have turned healers away from their primary purpose."

Once Oregon legalized assisted suicide some claimed this agenda would sweep the nation. Actually, ten states have passed new laws banning assisted suicide and legalization efforts have been rejected in other places, "most notably by direct votes of the people in Michigan and Maine."

One can argue that when the people who initially are sympathetic to euthanasia in "hard cases" are properly informed about the dangers of its inevitable progression down the slippery slope, they turn against it.

Prudence suggests the war has not been won. Holland has advanced from euthanasia in practice to actual euthanasia legalization. There is clear evidence that euthanasia advocates are committed to having assisted suicide legalized as the stepping stone to voluntary and then non-voluntary euthanasia. The New England Catholic dioceses are well aware of this objective and strategy and have launched a grass roots education program to thwart both euthanasia and assisted suicide as the initial step toward it.

APPENDIX FOR CHAPTER 11

DEVELOPMENT OF GRISEZ'S POSITION

CONTRACEPTION AND THE NATURAL LAW

From his first work on contraception Grisez focused on its anti-life dimension. Things had changed significantly in philosophy. Existentialism and phenomenology had made people in general as well as philosophers more aware of the concrete and of the person. Like many he found the traditional arguments against contraception unsatisfactory - at least in the way they were articulated.

Unlike Paul VI's personalist perspective Grisez in his initial efforts worked within his developing theory of basic human goods. One of these basic human goods, aspects of the person, is life and the communication of life. This theory we schematized in Chapter 4. To choose to impede, harm, or destroy a basic human good is immoral. "Positively to do (anything to prevent the procreative good from being realized) by direct volition will set us absolutely at odds with the essential human good which our very action has made proximately possible of attainment." "But to choose by our very action that the good not be realized is incompatible with fundamentally loving it. . .and man's basic obligation with regard to all the essential goods is that he should be open to them, that he should be willing that they be." (*Contraception and the Natural Law.* p. 91)

It is interesting to see that, in spite of his focus on the anti-life aspect of contraception, Grisez had already caught the insight that contraception is also a violation of the unitive aspect of marriage. "Man and wife cannot express love in any genuine sense if they know they are cooperating in an evil act. Hence, for those who practice contraception while knowing it to be evil such cooperation renders the sexual act an offense against marital love as well as an offense against procreation." (Ibid. p.95. Emphasis added.)

TENTH ANNIVERSARY OF *HUMANAE VITAE* - AND TEN YEARS LATER

As indicated above Grisez collaborated with John C. Ford, S.J. on the latter's role in the Papal Commission for the Study of Problems of Population, Family, and Birthrate. Becoming increasingly aware of the need of a "better moral theology," Grisez discerned he was being "called" to do just that. It did not hurt the launching of his career as "theologian" to have an article published in the prestigious *Theological Studies* co - authored with the distinguished moral theologian, John C. Ford, S.J.

One of the two pivotal arguments of theologians dissenting from *Humanae Vitae* was that the teaching had not been proposed infallibly and was not a matter of faith. Accordingly, the teaching could be mistaken.

For the tenth anniversary of *Humanae Vitae* Ford and Grisez contributed "Contraception and the Infallibility of the Ordinary Magisterium" to the June issue of *Theological Studies*, 1978. As an overall summary, the article begins with the conditions identified by the Second Vatican Council as constituting Church teachings infallible from the ordinary and universal teaching of the Magisterium. Ford and Kelly had already in a 1964 publication addressed the question whether the traditional Catholic teaching on contraception had been proposed infallibly. Their conclusion was that the teaching that contraception is intrinsically immoral was "at least definable doctrine." In this 1978 article Ford and Grisez argued that the conditions listed in *Dogmatic Constitution of the Church* (25) for a teaching to be infallible from the ordinary and universal Magisterium were fulfilled in the teaching on contraception.

Ten years later in 1988, Grisez, together with Joseph Boyle, John Finnis, and William E. May, addressed the second pivotal argument by the dissenting theologians. The latter argued the teaching is incoherent, excluding as it does contraception yet accepting natural family planning. Many of them also insisted on treating contraception in isolation from other moral issues.

The substantial article addressing these issues appeared in *The Thomist*, July 1988, "Every Marital Act Ought to Be Open to New Life, Toward a Clearer Understanding."

They argued, "the most basic, intrinsic reason why it is always wrong to choose to do something to impede procreation" is that this choice is necessarily contra-life. Then they explained why natural family planning is not equivalent to contraception. In the process, they likewise showed how the Church's teaching on contraception is "tightly interwoven with her entire moral teaching concerning sex, marriage, and innocent life." Contraception simply cannot be treated as an isolated issue.

Later in the year, they had these two articles published in a booklet (219 pages). Doing so allowed them to report reactions to the Ford and Grisez article together with their replies to various criticisms.

By 1993 Grisez had crystallized his understanding of the morality of sexual conduct as well as his ethical theory in general, able to apply it to the moral responsibilities of all Christians.

Chapter 8 of his second volume of *The Way of the Lord Jesus* (*Living a Christian Life*) is entitled, "Life, Health and Bodily Inviolability." It is as a life issue that contraception is treated, Section E of this chapter.

CONTRACEPTION IN "'EVERY MARITAL ACT OUGHT TO BE OPEN TO NEW LIFE': TOWARD A CLEARER UNDERSTANDING"

Five years earlier Grisez, Boyle, Finnis, and May addressed contraception with two significant additions to the previous treatment.

Proving that contraception involves a contra-life will establishes that contraception is immoral within marriage or outside marriage. In a sense, this is an incidental point, but it is worth making because although traditionally contraception was condemned as immoral without distinguishing its use in and outside marriage, recent Church teachings on contraception are given within the context of marriage. *Casti Connubii*, for instance, the encyclical by Pope Pius XI, was a reaction to the Anglican Church's teaching in 1930 that married couples for serious reasons could use contraception. In the 1960's the Church was dealing with the context of those claiming that contraception was justifiable within marriage; such proponents weren't at this time trying to replace the whole traditional sex morality. Soon we shall address the reasoning proposed for the immorality of contraception within marriage.

For Grisez et al, then, contraception is always wrong precisely and primarily because it requires a contra-life will. This they establish much as Grisez does in the previous section. But then they confront the type of argument the Majority Opinion (of the papal commission) espoused: proportionalism. According to this approach contraception will, for example, preserve love and contribute to life, and the whole (life and love) outweighs the good of life prevented.

Proportionalism has developed into the most prevalent method of reasoning among Catholic thinkers. Whether things have changed since proportionalism was declared incompatible with Catholic thinking by John Paul II in *The Splendor of Truth* remains to be seen.

Grisez and others summarize their argument developed at length elsewhere that proportionalism is meaningless. To establish the rational preferability of the reason to use contraception over the reason not to contracept, namely life, there must be some standard by which one can compare the two reasons for acting. But there simply is no such standard; there can not be. The goods are incommensurable.

Furthermore, if there were a rational method of establishing that the reason <u>for</u> making a choice were rationally preferable to the reason against making it, then the less rationally preferable would cease to be a reason in respect to that choice; there would be no choice.

Elsewhere this is explained by saying all the good that makes the choice rejected reasonable would be found in the preferable choice and more. So there would be no reason for choosing the other act. (*The Teaching of "Humanae Vitae,"* 52-3)

Long and constantly has Grisez argued against consequentialism and proportionalism. Since Catholic thinkers came to adopt proportionalism step by step in relation to contraception it was most appropriate to show how the objections to Catholic teaching can become very serious and yet remain meaningless at their core. Hence the value of this first additional argument - the rejection of proportionalism.

The second significant addition this article provides concerns the relation of the argument that contraception is essentially contra-life and the argument in *Humanae Vitae* that there is an inseparable connection between the unitive and the procreative meanings of the conjugal act - which connection has been willed by God and man may not break on his own initiative. They argue that the independently established position that contraception is always wrong can help establish the inseparable connection between the unitive and procreative meanings of the conjugal act.

First of all, granted contraception is always wrong, it is wrong to break the connection between lovemaking and life-giving by contraception in marriage.

On the other hand, the connection is broken by conceiving a child apart from marital lovemaking, as by in vitro fertilization. John Finnis was very influential in the Catholic Bishops of Great Britain's Joint Committee on Bio-ethical Issues in relation to in vitro fertilization. Rather than attempting a fully developed argument against this procedure, they rely on this Great Britain study in which Finnis contributed and about which he was in consultation with Grisez. The argument summarized, they explain, articulates one of the arguments in *Donum Vitae*, the document by the Congregation for the Doctrine of the Faith, dealing with in vitro fertilization.

The argument comes down to pointing out that "producing" a baby wills the baby's initial status as a product - something subpersonal. Thus "The choice to produce a baby . . .is a choice to enter into a relationship with the baby as with something subpersonal." This is inconsistent with and so impedes the communion of persons with equal dignity - which is the appropriate condition in any relationship among persons.

The fact that the parents may well intend that the baby be incorporated in an authentic child-parent relationship - with shared personal dignity, does not change the morality of the means employed. The means, we saw, are immoral - violating the personal status of the child so conceived.

The evil becomes pronounced when we reflect on what happens if "the product" proves to be "defective." Normally as unwanted, it is disposed of. They do not mention the large number of aborted embryos or the awesome description of stored embryos with assigned "shelf-life" or the court cases about ownership of the embryos if couples divorce.

Here is the argument for the inseparable connection between the lovemaking and life-giving of sexual intercourse.

> Since contraception is always wrong and since producing babies is always wrong, the only morally acceptable way to engage either in lovemaking or in life giving is by engaging in sexual intercourse that is open to new life. Now, what is universally true of both contraception and producing babies is true of them when done in the context of marriage. And God wills that human persons do nothing wrong. Therefore, there is an inseparable connection established by God, which human persons on their own initiative may not break, between the two meanings of the marital act: the unitive meaning and the procreative meaning.

There is indeed a naturally inseparable connection between the unitive and the procreative meanings of sexual intercourse. After all, by intercourse a man and a woman become a single principle of communication of life. It is a matter of *human* reproduction (procreation of new persons) and *human* sexual intercourse (an interpersonal relationship).

But this naturally inseparable connection can be broken. The claim is that to do so is morally wrong. The natural givenness is not a sufficient reason for the moral wrongness. However, granted contraception is always wrong and producing children is always wrong, the natural structure of sexual functioning grounds the connection that human beings may not break. Technically they can, morally they may not. (Ibid., 98)

Further Explanation

We find Grisez's fuller treatment of this argument that contraception violates the unitive meaning of sexual intercourse in *The Thomist* article reported earlier. The position he and his colleagues take is that contraception is always wrong primarily because it is contralife. The inseparable connection between the unitive and procreative meanings of sexual intercourse they establish by showing that contraception is always wrong and in vitro fertilization is immoral. Consequently, "the only morally acceptable way to engage either in lovemaking or in life-giving is by engaging in sexual intercourse that is open to new life."

An objection: The Church teaches the inseparable connection only in marital acts, not in extra-marital acts such as fornication and adultery without contraception. What makes the connection inseparable is the marital act's specific character in such a way that contraception falsifies the truth of the marital act; not merely that it takes away its life-giving potential.

Grisez and others reply that indeed "the morally inseparable connection between procreation and sexual communion can be fully respected only in marital acts." Yes, in fornication and adultery there can be respect for the act's life-giving meaning by not involving contraception; and the love-making meaning of sexual intercourse need not be violated in "production of babies" without sexual intercourse. So it is only marital acts which can actualize the specific communion of human persons as procreators of new persons.

To explain this point consider how marital intercourse expresses marital love. The mutual commitment made in marrying constitutes the bond that is marital love. This bond makes them one flesh and one person in respect to that part of life that involves genital acts. Marital intercourse actualizes this oneness, enabling them to experience it concretely. Emotions accompany this experience but these are a real, intrinsic part of marital love "only insofar as they belong to intercourse as a realization of the marital oneness."

To obtain sexual satisfaction while contracepting is not to engage in marital intercourse. What a couple does by mutual masturbation, by anal or oral intercourse, or by contracepted intercourse "cannot actualize their marital bond and enable them to experience it."

To rephrase Grisez, when a man and a woman commit themselves in marriage, they create a bond, a union - and precisely because of their organic complementarity that union involves being literally two-in-one flesh. But being two-in-one flesh is achieved in sexual intercourse and sexual intercourse is the act of self-giving and at the same time the act by which the couple becomes a single principle or source of new life.

If the married couple choose to engage in sexual intercourse and to contracept, the self-giving inherent in sexual intercourse is not self-giving - is not uniting them precisely as two-in-one flesh, source of new life. They withhold their fertility.

The emotions experienced in contraceptive intercourse may be the same as those experienced in genuine marital intercourse. There may well be sense of total self-giving. But unless these feelings are integrated with the intelligible good of marital bonding, they are deceptive.

Richard McCormick, S.J., quotes Prof. Lisa Cahill, a married woman, denying what has just been said, "I am confident that most Catholic couples would be incredulous at the proposition that the use of artificial birth control necessarily makes their sexual intimacy selfish, dishonest and unfaithful."

She seems to be confusing emotional response which is no doubt sincere, but emotion at least ambivalent since it is not integrated with genuine marital bond. I compare it to the reaction of slave owners, incredulous at the proposition that their sense of justice toward their slaves is unwarranted. Or the man who told me about his recourse to prostitutes, "Of course I always paid them." He would have been incredulous at the proposition that he had been using those women - or that he had equivalently been masturbating.

Subsumption: Contraception and Natural Family Planning

Dissenting theologians might argue that couples who contracept because they have just reason not to have another child do not differ from couples having intercourse during a sterile period, it being impossible to complete their communion by conceiving new life. So even if contraception is always wrong, couples contracepting do not prevent conception *insofar as conception could complete their communion*, but only insofar as conception would initiate a new life which they ought not initiate. So, they might say, we may have to argue about contraception as contra-life, but contraception in such a case does not falsify the inner truth of their conjugal love.

Grisez and colleagues point out the precise difference in the two cases. During a sterile period it is true the couple cannot actualize and experience marital unity as fully as in fruitful intercourse, but in no way do they falsify their oneness. They are like people who, without lying, tell less than the whole truth.

Contraception necessarily involves a contra-life will. The couple who contracept do not want the baby whose life they might initiate. So because they positively will that a child not come to be, they positively will also that their marital communion not be fulfilled in this act of intercourse. They will their acts of sexual intercourse not be acts of marital communion. They resemble people who tell less than they know by lying.

Non-believers and dissenting theologians at least implicitly deny marriage is as the Church defines it, proposing to define it, for example, as permitting particular contralife acts within marriage to be marital acts. The only effective way to argue against their position is by independently proving the immorality of contraceptive acts. Hence the validity of Grisez's claim that the primary reason contraception is immoral is that it involves a choice against the good of life. (Ibid., 103)

APPENDIX FOR CHAPTER 13

TRADITIONAL NATURAL LAW MORALITY
VS.
SECULAR HUMANIST MORALITY

Natural Law Morality	Secular Humanist Morality
1. God creates and acts in us and in the universe. The world created by God is intelligible and valuable. We discover intellectual meaning of things and the values—including how God is directing creatures to their fulfillment.	1. There is no God. All meaning and value originate in our thoughts and desires. Anything is good which yields a desired state of consciousness.
2. People possess freedom of self-determination and by free choice determine their relationships with God, others, their world and themselves. Choosing in accord with the meaning and value given by God they act in a morally good way. Otherwise they act in a morally evil way. If one's life is evil, one can only blame oneself. Factors beyond one's control may impede happiness.	2. People do not possess freedom of self-determination. Heredity and environment determine one's personality and character, which in turn determine one's choices. If one's life is bad, one is not responsible. To achieve the good life, people must discover techniques to change human nature and the environment.

3. Good human actions immediately affect the person acting but have an impact on objective social relationships and in the material world they carry on God's work of creation. Morally evil actions also immediately affect the person acting and spread <u>real</u> disvalue. Suffering can be valuable.	3. Human actions are good precisely by being conducive to enjoyable experiences: only incidentally do they have effects outside human consciousness. No question of building up a perfect community. Bad actions do not have permanent significance. No importance to them if their impact is felt by no one. To overcome evil, one must alter one's consciousness, e.g. by drugs, psychological techniques, "religious" experience, etc. Avoid all suffering: it alone is intrinsically evil.
4. Human persons and all the goods which contribute to their fullness share in immeasurable dignity. Any act which goes directly against a person and/or the human goods is always wrong. Evil done by such an act cannot be outweighed by any good it achieves. Thus there are moral absolutes.	4. Lived experience alone constitutes human importance. There are no moral absolutes. Actions are only wrong if they cause more pain than enjoyment. Goods are measurable, so evil chosen may be outweighed by the good which results.

Intermediate Principles

1. Human persons are their bodies. Human persons are bodily realities. Th—abortion, infanticide, suicide and euthanasia are immoral attacks on personal goods. Much sexual behavior—e.g. masturbation and bestiality—go against the reality of the person as bodily self, treating sexual powers as mere objects.

2. Sexual capacity and sexual acts are important because personal values are immediately at stake in the very biology of human sex. A man and a woman become "one flesh" as they become a single principle of generation. To exercise such a life-giving act argues for an enduring relationship and argues against the idea that such a relationship is at the disposal of the parties. Contraceptive acts attack the handing on of life and so are immoral.

Intermediate Principles

1. Human persons are conscious subjects who have bodies. Bodily life and sexual conduct are only valuable instrumentally. Thus killing can be justified if there is no self-conscious subject (as in abortion, infanticide, some euthanasia) or if the conscious subject no longer finds bodily life useful (suicide and euthanasia with consent). Masturbation and bestiality are only questions of taste.

2. No personal values are immediately at stake in the very biology of sex. Sexual capacity is at hand for intense and enjoyable satisfaction. People who copulate do each other a valuable service. Nothing follows from the fact that some sexual acts cause pregnancy, unless it occurs. Give and take of enjoyable experience argues for a relationship at disposal of the parties. Contraception is reasonable and human, subjecting infrapersonal biological processes to truly personal value. No personal values are at stake for a merely possible person who never comes to be.

3. What makes a person's life meaningful is one's dedicated work in the service of goods which contribute intrinsically to personal and society's fulfillment. In like measure, persons have community only by joint commitment to each other and to goods to which they are dedicated together. Sexual activity must be limited to a communal relationship suited to serve the relevant basic human goods. Apart from such context sexual activity loses meaning, does not form community, and tends to become masturbatory. Note: a permanent relationship open to all the relevant goods and dedicated to the ministry of serving God in creating new persons is marriage. Thus, adultery, fornication, homosexual activity and other extramarital activities are excluded.	3. A meaningful life consists in a person fulfilling him/herself. Self-fulfillment is gained by achieving one's own projected purposes and enjoying the satisfaction of the "good life." Masturbation is enjoyable, but for normal people sexual relations involving two (or more) persons are more enjoyable than solitary physical satisfaction. Various psychological enjoyments are then opened up and none is inherently wrong. Sex can be enriched for some by experiences of domination and submission; sadomasochistic activity is good for those who enjoy it if no permanent damage is done. Marriage is not a vocation, not a ministry of creating new persons. It is an arrangement, rather, which enriches sexual enjoyment for some people who are not very adventurous, and who prefer a secure source of sexual satisfaction.

4. Human sexual activity is only appropriate within the framework of a mutual commitment in marriage, free consent between spouses is required, and focus primarily on satisfying one's sex drive is wrong. Abstinence, when, indicated, expresses and fosters love just as much as intercourse. Since free choice is fundamental, rape, seduction of children, etc. are immoral.	4. Sexual desire is a basic physiological drive, not unlike hunger. Normal, healthy people have no choice about whether to satisfy this drive, but only about how to do so. One who does not feel need for regular sexual outlets is sick; one who feels the need and cannot satisfy it will become sick. Rape, child seduction are generally wrong because of coercive interferences with the victim's rights, not because of the sexual acts involved. People who refuse to gratify others sexually without a good reason lack decency and consideration; to refuse merely because of a moral scruple is cruel and inhuman. A healthy person will engage in sexual activity of much greater variety, complexity, and frequency than mere physiological need would require.

APPENDIX FOR CHAPTER 14

CHALLENGE TO CLAIM—MARRIAGE IS A BASIC HUMAN GOOD

Virginity, Celibacy, Gays?

What about virginity and celibacy? If marriage is a basic human good, priests and religious or others choosing a celibate life, would be called (or at least choose) to renounce part of integral human fulfillment. Grisez replies that although marriage indeed is a basic human good, not everyone need participate in that good by "being married." The first principle of morality, one ought always choose in a way compatible with integral human fulfillment, does not require that every individual participate in every basic human good in the same mode of participation. Rather, integral human fulfillment means the realization of all the human goods in the entire human community. People called to virginity or celibacy can participate in the good of marriage in several ways: as children of their own parents, as pastors of families, as collaborators with parents in the education of children, and so forth.

After all, I choose the good of aesthetic experience (as well as of friendship) when I give someone tickets to a concert. So I choose the good of marriage when I instruct and counsel couples married or preparing for marriage.

Thomas Aquinas contributes to the issue by an insightful distinction between what is of obligation for each individual and what is of obligation for society in general. He asks, "Is the life of virginity illicit?" The first argument set out for the affirmative is that there is a natural (and revealed) obligation to eat (food is good and to be pursued) but also an obligation to pass on life. To refuse all food violates the first obligation, going against the good of individual life. Similarly to abstain completely from sexual intercourse by which life is communicated violates the second obligation, going against the good of the species.

Thomas accepts the distinction but rejects the conclusion. Obligations binding an individual differ from obligations binding on a group. The obligation to eat binds each individual, eating is necessary if the individual is to survive. However, the obligation of communicating life is binding on the entire human race. But many things are necessary for the entire human race, not only bodily increase. Since at issue is virginity he indicates the human race also needs help in spiritual progress.

Clearly then continuation of the human race is adequately provided for if certain people collaborate for propagation. Others, (in this case those committed to virginity and the contemplative life), abstaining from sexual intercourse may give themselves to contemplation, contributing to the beauty and salvation of humankind.

His example has close bearing on our question. Take the army, some guard the camp, others are responsible for communications, while certain ones actually fight. All these things are necessary, and simply cannot be provided by just any individual.

In claiming that marriage is a basic human good, there is no contradiction in holding that all normally developed persons experience an inclination to marriage, but not all pursue it.

A pressing contemporary objection must be heard. Homosexuals and lesbians do not experience the inclination to marriage as defined.

I have keen sympathy with homosexuals on this marriage issue. the traditional understanding of marriage involves openness to parenthood. Marriage is between a man and woman, who become co-principles of new life. With that understanding it makes sense to claim that homosexual "marriage" is impossible. But if sexual intercourse can be separated morally from conception, as current acceptance of contraception insists, who has the right to demand anything more than personal commitment to share lives for the institution of marriage? Hence the grim importance of revisiting the contraception issue. Since we have done so, we can proceed, but this claim that homosexual unions are essentially different from marriage between a man and a woman presupposes that contraception is immoral.

But as we have already mentioned there is the thrust to legalize homosexual relationships as marriages. Even though the essential factor of being co-principles of communicating life is absent and so any such relationship simply cannot physically (and univocally) be the same as heterosexual marriages, still the thrust to such union seems to be present.

Homosexuals and lesbians do, then, I submit, have the inclination to be with one another, to give themselves totally to the other as well as the inclination and desire to sexual experiences. So often, likewise, one reads of a lesbian couple arranging that one of them find a willing male so she can conceive and bear a child for herself and her lover. Homosexual couples sometimes adopt and raise children.

In view of "gay pride" and the posture of those often referred to as physically challenged in demanding they be taken as they are, proud of the way they are, it is difficult to find non-offensive expressions for examples to illustrate why homosexuals and lesbians can be understood to experience the inclination to marriage. But consider how one born with the need of prosthesis is inclined to want to walk and run rapidly, but cannot. Or one born deaf and mute is inclined to communicate by speech, but cannot. Or how an alcoholic is inclined to drink reasonably, but cannot. Or how all have to contend with concupiscence.

ABOUT THE AUTHOR

The author has taught ethics at the college level for many years so he knows not only the theory behind right choices but also the challenging snags that American culture meets in carrying out these choices. His academics degrees (MA-STL-PhD) and graduate studies at Harvard, NYU, and a fellowship at Yale have blended with his experience in parish and retreat work.

Other books: <u>From Why to Yes</u> and <u>God Is</u>: From Question to Proof to Embracing the Truth.

Printed in the United States
24985LVS00003B/1-30